BIRNBERG, Thomas B. and Stephen A. Resnick.   Colonial development;
an econometric study. Yale, 1975. 347p il tab bibl 74-20077.
20.00. ISBN 0-300-01821-5

An extremely interesting analysis of the process of economic development for ten countries that were either colonies or subject to significant
Western influence: Ceylon, Chile, Cuba, Egypt, India, Jamaica, Nigeria,
Philippines, Taiwan, and Thailand. A structural econometric model is
developed and estimated. Particular attention is given to the role of the
government in promoting the export sector, and to the influence of
political and economic forces external to the colonies in the development process. Cluster and covariance analyses are used to compare the
empirical results among the various countries. Multipliers are derived
and simulations performed to determine the historical accuracy of the
model. Since most of the econometrics is limited to chapter supplements, the book is readable by undergraduates. The emphasis, given
the state in the development process, makes the work novel and an important library acquisition. A limited bibliography is provided.

Colonial Development: An Econometric Study

A Publication of the Economic Growth Center, Yale University

COLONIAL DEVELOPMENT
AN ECONOMETRIC STUDY

THOMAS B. BIRNBERG
and
STEPHEN A. RESNICK

New Haven and London, Yale University Press, 1975

Designed by Sally Sullivan
and set in Times Roman type.
Copy preparation by Jay's Publishers Services, Inc.,
Scituate, Mass.
Printed in the United States of America by
The Colonial Press Inc., Clinton, Massachusetts.

Published in Great Britain, Europe, and Africa by
Yale University Press, Ltd., London.
Distributed in Latin American by Kaiman & Polon,
Inc., New York City; in Australasia by Book & Film Services,
Artarmon, N.S.W., Australia; in India by UBS Publishers'
Distributors Pvt., Ltd., Delhi; in Japan by John Weatherhill,
Inc., Tokyo.

Contents

v

List of Figures and Tables

Foreword

This volume is one in a series of studies supported by the Economic Growth Center, an activity of the Yale Department of Economics since 1961. The Center is a research organization with worldwide activities and interests. Its research interests are defined in terms of both method of approach and subject matter. In terms of method, the Center sponsors studies which are designed to test significant general hypotheses concerning the problem of economic growth and which draw on quantitative information from national economic accounts and other sources. In terms of subject matter, the Center's research interests include theoretical analysis of economic structure and growth, quantitative analysis of a national economy as an integral whole, comparative cross-sectional studies using data from a number of countries, and efforts to improve the techniques of national economic measurement. The research program includes field investigation of recent economic growth in twenty-five developing countries of Asia, Africa, and Latin America.

The Center administers, jointly with the Department of Economics, the Yale training program in International and Foreign Economic Administration. It presents a regular series of seminar and workshop meetings and includes among its publications both book-length studies and journal reprints by staff members, the latter circulated as Center Papers.

Gustav Ranis, Director

Acknowledgments

This book is the product of research at the Economic Growth Center, Yale University. Portions of this research were financed by the National Science Foundation, GS-2804. The views expressed in this book do not necessarily reflect those of the Foundation. Chapters 2 and 4 are partially based upon our article in the *American Economic Review*. Very useful comments were provided by Vernon Ruttan. We especially wish to thank Debra Stinson and Janet Farooq for their research assistance. Ignazio Cocco, Elizabeth Collier, Cheryl Cook, and Robin Kibuka provided valuable research assistance. We want to thank Linda Bell, Louise Galasso, and Peggy Limbacher for typing earlier parts of this book. For the excellent job of typing the final manuscript and numerous tables we would like to thank Cheryl Hunt.

March 1974

Thomas B. Birnberg
Stephen A. Resnick

1

Historical Background

This book examines historically and quantitatively the process of colonial development for selected Asian, African, and Latin American countries with diverse historical characteristics. This process is described and analyzed using a model which is applied to a particular period in the economic history of these countries. This model explains how specific internal and external forces tended to transcend the socioeconomic differences among these countries and transform them in a similar pattern from about the start of the twentieth century until the outbreak of World War II. By taking an aggregate view of the entire process of economic development, we focus on certain critical forces that are crucial to understanding how these qualitative and quantitative relationships worked and changed over time.

It is crucially important to specify the internal force as endogenous government expenditures directed toward the promotion of colonial export supply. We show that to understand the historical process of colonial development one must explicitly consider what the government did (or did not do) to promote export development. This result has important implications for current development theory and policy, for we conclude that if the development process is to be accurately described, then the government's actions must be included as an explanatory factor.

To understand the process of colonial development it is also important to specify the external forces as changes in real income, domestic prices, and trade policies in the developed world, and to measure how these forces affect colonial export demand. We show that colonial export prices are endogenous and determined simultaneously by the expenditures of the colonial government and by the developed countries' demand characteristics and trade policies. To explain the historical development of a colonial export economy requires, then, a structural model of both trade and government sectors.

A common theme in the literature on colonialism is how, at a certain point in history, the growth of industry in the developed world tended to dominate agriculture in the colonial world. This international process brought about dramatic changes in the agrarian societies of the colonial world as imports of manufactures from the developed world replaced rural industry in the colonies and colonial labor was allocated to the production of food and raw materials for a growing export market. An international division of labor tended to emerge as the economic development of the colonies became tied to the development of industry in the developed countries. Thus, an international division of labor and commodity production emerged, which has been characterized as a process of uneven development. In this book we use our model to explain the essential properties of this uneven development by focusing on its supply and demand characteristics. By doing so, we explain not only the development and growth of the colonial export economy, but also the trade-dependent relationship that emerged between the developed countries and their colonies. Our model and analysis show clearly how the supply and demand forces operating upon the colonies were both ultimately determined by economic and political forces in the developed countries.

The role of the government sector and the combination of internal and external forces in determining the development process indicate the importance of a historical perspective in studying development. In fact, the historical process of economic development should not be confused with the more recent models of development based upon import substitution and industrialization or those that focus on the development of the labor surplus economy. Economic development has a long history marked by changes in the international economic and political system, changes in both the agricultural and industrial sectors of all countries as an international division of labor emerged, and changes in the role of the government in all countries, both developed and underdeveloped. Yet the phases of economic change are not independent, since the internal and external forces that transformed the countries studied in this book produced the political and economic environment within which these countries operated after World War II. Thus the initial conditions considered by postwar studies of economic development were determined by the historical developments examined in this study. Too often, however, a change in economic structure seems to give economists the confidence to ignore the usefulness of historical analysis. There is no reason to believe, for example, that the government is no longer important in advancing the economic growth of a country.

Although our model describes a similar development process for the countries in our sample, the results indicate significant differences in the coefficient estimates which explain this common process. In fact, these differences allow the same model to explain accurately the wide range of observed growth rates of colonial exports, the large shifts in endogenous terms of trade and trade balances, and the dramatic increases in colonial government revenue and expenditures. Thus, an understanding of the similar but not identical historical process of colonial development requires analyzing a common circular structure of the countries' trade and government sectors as well as recognizing diversity within that structure.

Although a great deal of historical evidence has been amassed and several hypotheses have been presented to interpret the colonial experience, there have been few systematic attempts to examine empirically the direct and indirect economic linkages between the developed and underdeveloped worlds. In this book, the econometric model specifies these linkages qualitatively and the estimation results provide a quantitative measure of the linkages between each of the variables endogenous to the colonial economy and changes in real income, prices, and trade policies of the developed world. The analysis does not intend nor does it show the actual degree or level of exploitation or which groups within which areas benefited or lost from colonial relationships.

From about the end of the nineteenth century onward, colonial economic development took a new direction. The extensive penetration of Western commodities, organization, and control ushered in the era of the export economy, during which colonialism reached its peak. In order to analyze this period fully, we sought countries for which we could obtain reliable and consistent data from about the start of the twentieth century until the outbreak of World War II. As will be explained, there are specific historical reasons for the starting date for each country. The periods used are as follows: Ceylon, 1897–1938; Chile, 1892–1938; Cuba, 1903–37; Egypt, 1891–1937; India, 1890–1936; Jamaica, 1886–1938; Nigeria, 1901–37; Philippines, 1902–38; Taiwan, 1904–36; and Thailand, 1902–36. These countries are selected as important representatives of this process of colonial development. Their different initial conditions were produced by their diverse histories, types of foreign control and influence, export crops, population levels, and geographic characteristics (such as island economies and large land-based economies). Thus, our selection of countries includes a rather large variety of economic, political, and cultural experiences. The selection is designed to provide an adequate number and range of historical experiences to make sound generalizations about the process of colonial development.

The quantitative results of this study are crucially dependent on the quality of the underlying data set. The data set for each country was collected almost entirely from original country and colonial sources and is included in the appendix. Considerable effort was devoted to compiling the data in order to have consistent and reliable time series, not only to insure accurate estimates but also to make sound intercountry comparisons. Several countries which could have been included in our sample were rejected because of the poor quality of their original data.

Although this book uses econometrics, the analysis of the colonial process and the results derived do not require the reader to be an econometrician; the advanced econometric methods are described in supplements. Nonetheless, our purpose is to use econometrics to show how the economic forces of supply and demand operated to determine the historical process of colonial development.

The first part of this chapter briefly analyzes the initial conditions in each country in order to establish the historical background of this econometric study. Important differences did exist among these countries prior to the period of this study.

The Philippines and Cuba were colonies of Spain for over three hundred years prior to the American period. Jamaica, a British colony since 1655, was an important source of the trade fortunes of English merchants. The economic history of Egypt reveals a pattern of European influence and control since the Napoleonic era. Even before the period of direct control of India and Nigeria by Britain, the British exercised their influence in these countries through the East India Company until 1857 and through the Royal Niger Company until 1899. Ceylon was a major exporter of coffee from 1840 to 1880. In Thailand, the Bowring Treaty of 1885 established British economic and political influence. Chile was a colony of Spain for over two hundred years before it achieved independence in 1818. Taiwan was a province of China for many centuries before it was ceded to Japan following the Sino-Japanese War of 1895. Given the vast differences in initial conditions, it is rather remarkable that a specific econometric model can be applied to describe the process of change in all these countries. Our hypothesis is that common political and economic forces were in operation which tended to transcend historical differences in crops, climate, and culture and which transformed much of the developing world in a similar pattern in a few decades.

The second part of this chapter summarizes how foreign economic and political control was exercised to achieve this common process of historical development. Our particular use of the term colonialism refers to this common process and does not necessarily imply a specific type of foreign political control. Thus, the model explains the development of six countries under direct foreign control—Ceylon, India, Jamaica, Nigeria, the Philippines, and Taiwan—and also of four countries which were not de jure colonies—Chile, Cuba, Egypt, and Thailand. For the latter four countries, this chapter will describe how a more subtle, but no less important, foreign influence was exercised through the international trade mechanism and through financial and trade controls. Common to all ten countries, however, were the internal and external economic forces which determined their pattern of development. From this standpoint, a contribution of this book is that the same econometric model that identifies these forces can describe and measure the process of change in all ten countries. Thus, what we mean by a similar process of colonial development is a specific econometric model that holds for all ten countries and that implies similar economic behavior for a particular period in their history.

There are many countries for which a similar process of development no doubt holds. Other countries, or even regions within countries, may satisfy this model's particular econometric specification for a certain period in their history. Nonetheless, one must closely examine the historical political economy of each country to see if it makes sense to apply this model to that country's history. For instance, a country which successfully established an indigenous manufacturing sector by an import substitution program would not fit our colonial specification. External trade creation and government expenditures directed toward the development of an export economy describe the macroeconomic model in this book, but a different economic process, requiring a different behavioral model, is needed to explain attempts at development through internal trade creation, import substitution, and government expenditures biased toward industrialization. If our model is applied to countries having a different economic process, portions of the model might possibly still be estimated. However, a major misspecification error would occur because of important omitted variables and misspecified behavioral relationships. Obviously, even for a country with different economic behavior, a foreign power may exercise decisive political and economic control over the forces which determine its basic economic activity. This type of control does not mean that a process of colonial development exists equivalent to the one described in this book. Foreign control may be a necessary, but not a sufficient condition for assuring that an economy satisfies the specification of our model. Thus, application of the model to another country requires analysis of both the economic and political history of that country. In this sense, a clear historical perspective in studying the process of colonial development is at the core of this book, and we begin by examining the historical background of each country.

INITIAL CONDITIONS

Jamaica. Jamaica was by no means a newcomer to the colonial system. Under British control since 1655, its sugar and coffee plantations, using slave labor, were an important generator of trade fortunes for British merchants. After slavery ended in 1838, Jamaican real exports fell sharply as increased labor costs combined with bad transport facilities and depleted plantation acreage made many plantations uneconomical.[1] The Jamaican colonial government was changed to strengthen British control after a rebellion in 1865. As the rebellion was caused by poverty and maladministration, the new colonial government used British loans to finance a public works program (1865–79) designed to make up for years of neglect and mismanagement. Our study begins during the period 1880–94 when the colonial government substantially increased its expenditures for railroads, irrigation projects, and roads. These expenditures reflected the government's recognition that increased exports, particularly of bananas, required government assistance in extending transport to new production areas.[2]

India. The defeat of the French in the battle of Plassey (1757)

1. Eisner [49, pp. 236–57] has a detailed analysis of this decline of Jamaican exports.
2. For an analysis of the increased government expenditures on infrastructure after the rebellion, see Eisner [49, pp. 177–78, 217–19, 284–85, 305–9, 368].

established British sovereignty in India. British control was exercised indirectly through the English East India Company, established by Royal Charter. "[This] company, the instrument used in effecting the conquest of India, was a private British trading company with the privilege of monopolizing trade between India and England . . . . The Company became in fact the government of India." [3] The Company was unwilling to invest in more than a few roads and irrigation works, and almost all its expenditures were for military and administrative purposes.[4] Thus, when the Indian Mutiny of 1857 caused the British to end East India Company rule, India was using the same modes of transportation it had for centuries, mostly pack animals, carts, and small water craft.[5] From 1857 until about 1885, the principal transportation improvement was the completion of a basic railroad network of 12,000 miles. However, because of the emphasis on maintaining law and order that followed the mutiny, these routes satisfied military rather than economic needs.[6]

About 1885, the government shifted its policy toward developing an integrated railroad network as it recognized the strong effect of transportation on increasing exports. Of particular importance is the period between 1885 and 1914, when railroad mileage tripled from 12,000 to 35,000 and construction emphasized links and feeders to the principal export producing areas.[7] Our period of study begins when the effects of this construction became noticeable.

Ceylon. Ceylon's export economy started after it became a British colony in 1796. Prior to that time, the Portuguese and after them the Dutch controlled the coast of Ceylon for three centuries. After the British conquest of the Kandyan Kingdom in 1815, the development of Ceylon's export economy started when coffee became the major export product in the 1830s. Transportation of products was very difficult, as vividly described by Vanden Driesen: "The coffee industry was located in the steep, rugged central section of the country. Roads here had many sharp gradients, heavy cuttings and tortuous curves—all of which necessitated a heavy expenditure of both time

3. Lamb [21, p. 465].
4. See Bhattacharyya [38, chs. 2 and 3] and Lamb [21, pp. 465–72] for details about revenues and expenditures of the British East India Company.
5. For a description of the physical condition of Indian transport in 1857, see Lamb [21, pp. 470–71] and Anstey [35, p. 128].
6. For an analysis of the early development of the Indian Railway System, see Anstey [35, pp. 130–33] and Lamb [21, pp. 476–77].
7. Great Britain, Board of Trade [107] and Anstey [35, pp. 132–33].

and money . . . . Heavy rainfall, extreme heat, and the thin rimmed
wheels of the carts which plied between the estates and the shipping
centers, combined to destroy even the newest of road surfaces within
a month or two." [8] The coffee growers in Ceylon realized the need for
improved transportation to reduce the cost of moving imported supplies to their estates and coffee from them. Road improvements in the
1840s and 1850s contributed to the rapid growth of coffee exports.
With revenues increasing from the growth of coffee exports, Ceylon's
government further promoted the export economy by constructing
the Colombo-Kandy Railroad Line, completed in 1867. A substantial
railroad network extending to most of the coffee-growing areas grew
from this line and decreased transport costs by 60 to 75 percent.[9]

Coffee output collapsed in the 1880s due to a fungus disease; a
transition period followed in which tea replaced coffee as the major
export crop. Tea surpassed coffee in acreage in 1886, and tea output
increased tenfold from 1885 to 1900. The roads, railroads, trained
labor, developed land, and capital accumulated during the coffee
period were transferred to other crops—particularly tea at first, then
also rubber—and became the foundation for further expansion of
Ceylon's exports.[10] In the United Kingdom, the largest export market
for tea, a major shift in British taste from Chinese green teas to
Indian-Ceylonese black teas occurred before our period of study.
This shift in demand accelerated the switch from coffee to tea exports
for Ceylon. Ceylonese tea sold at a premium price after about 1900,
when Ceylonese planters adopted finer plucking to produce a higher
quality of tea.[11] The period under analysis for Ceylon begins after this
transition period in which tea replaced coffee.

Nigeria. British influence on the coast of Nigeria in the nineteenth
century was the result of Britain's switch in 1808 from chief participant in the slave trade to leading power in the anti–slave trade movement. Except for the colony of Lagos, which was taken over in 1851,
British control of the Niger Delta was established gradually by the
British Navy's suppression of the slave trade and was administered by
the British consul, Fernando Po. As part of the European scramble
for African territories, the Niger Coast Protectorate was formed in
1884. In 1885, the Berlin Conference recognized British claims to a

8. Vanden Driesen [34, pp. 9–10].
9. Snodgrass [94, pp. 19, 31] and Vanden Driesen [34, p. 11].
10. An analysis of the transition from coffee to tea and rubber is found in
Snodgrass [94, pp. 28–32].
11. Rajaratnam [26, pp. 170–72, 183].

region which approximated modern Nigeria. As the conference required Britain to establish effective control in the Nigerian interior, the British first used as their instrument the Royal Niger Company, a private company granted a Royal Charter with both political and economic control over the Upper Niger. In 1899, the Royal Niger Company's charter was revoked and the company was compensated. Its territory, combined with that of the Niger Coast Protectorate, was established as the Protectorates of Southern and Northern Nigeria. The company was displaced because of British dissatisfaction with its inability to develop Nigeria.[12]

At the turn of the twentieth century, modern infrastructure was almost nonexistent in Nigeria. The principal means of transporting goods was still head portage, and European travelers to the interior moved by either canoe or hammock.

The development of Lagos as a port city was impeded by a shallow bar parallel to its coast that presented much danger to ships and forced all cargo to be transshipped at substantial cost between ocean-going steamers and branch boats.[13] According to Geary, "There were no railways for transport and the Niger could only be navigated by large steamers for the two autumn months of flood. There were no roads, and if there had been, tsetse prevented the use of draught animals, and mechanical transport was in its inception."[14] Our period of study for Nigeria begins when the United Kingdom assumed direct control and began an active policy of encouraging the rapid development of Nigeria's export economy.

The next two countries in our sample, Egypt and Thailand, were not official colonies of the United Kingdom, but the United Kingdom exercised substantial economic and political influence in both countries under the terms of international treaties.

Egypt. Egypt's cotton export economy began in the nineteenth century. Egypt changed from a subsistence economy to an export economy when the government changed the system of land tenure and built irrigation projects, railroads, and harbors. These public works decreased transportation costs and increased cotton and sugar exports.[15]

12. For details on the extension of British economic and political control over Nigeria see Dike [48], Geary [57, chs. 2, 3, and 4], Hancock [60, vol. 2, pt. 2, pp. 154–68], and Kibuka [20].
13. Geary [57, pp. 145–46] and Helleiner [61, p. 4].
14. Geary [57, p. 210].
15. Crouchley [44, pp. 132–33, 139] and Issawi [66, pp. 22–26]. For further

Modern European influence in Egypt began with the successive military occupations of Egypt by the French under Napoleon (1796–1800) and by the British (1801–03). During the nineteenth century, the French and British continued to compete for the control of Egypt, although it was officially ruled by Turkey. French influence in Egypt reached a peak with the completion of the Suez Canal in 1869. British control over Egypt began in the 1870s when Egypt had difficulty paying interest on its foreign debt, part of which was incurred to finance previous infrastructure improvements. The Caisse de la Dette was formed in 1876 to guarantee debt repayment, the Liquidation Law of 1880 extended British influence, and in 1882 the British military occupied Egypt.[16]

Egypt under British control undertook major projects to increase its cotton exports. Of particular importance was the delta barrage, which brought immediate and extensive results: "The successful completion of the Delta barrage in 1890 marks one of the most important stages in the economic development of modern Egypt. It finally established the success of perennial irrigation in the Delta."[17] As a result, cotton output roughly doubled during the 1890s, which marks the beginning of our period.

Thailand. Thailand's export economy experienced its first, slow development in the latter part of the nineteenth century. As will be discussed in the next section, British economic control over Thailand was established under the terms of the Bowring Treaty in 1855. At that time, costly water transportation and the self-sufficiency of each region accounted for the limited movement of goods between villages and regions.[18] Early governmental efforts slowly improved irrigation to increase rice production. By 1850 the Central Plain had an extensive canal system, which was expanded during the period 1850–1900. However, in some years no canal construction occurred and even the existing canals were not always maintained. Limited railroad construction occurred before 1900, but transportation and irrigation facilities remained inadequate. As a result, Thailand's rice exports grew slowly from 1850 to 1900. The first major railroad, from Bangkok

---

discussion of the effects of state investments and international loans on the economy of Egypt, see Luxemburg [75].

16. For a survey of Anglo-Egyptian relations before 1882, see Marlowe [76, chs. 1–5].

17. Crouchley [42, p. 148].

18. These limitations on Thailand's trade are described in Ingram [64, pp. 19–21].

to Korat, was completed in 1900 and this railroad promoted a more rapid growth in rice exports.[19] Our period of study begins in 1902 when this increased growth pattern became established.

Chile. Chile had been a colony of Spain for over two centuries when it achieved independence in 1818. Between 1830 and 1880 Chile was the world's major producer of copper. After 1880, Chile rapidly lost its position as a major copper producer due not only to the development of more efficient, low-cost U.S. mines but also because Chile had exhausted her supply of easily-obtained high-grade ores.[20] However, the decline in copper was offset by the development of nitrate exports in the 1880s. By defeating Bolivia and Peru in the War of the Pacific, 1879–82, Chile obtained a large expanse of northern desert land which contained the world's major deposits of sodium nitrate. By early 1890, Chile had a virtual monopoly in nitrate production, and thus the period of study for Chile begins with the first of several decades of operation of this monopoly.[21] The period starts in 1892 because of the substantial destruction caused by the Revolution of 1891, which established a new parliamentary government.[22]

The period of study of the final three countries in our sample— Cuba, the Philippines, and Taiwan—begins after each country experienced a transfer of colonial control or influence. Cuba and the Philippines were colonies of Spain for over three hundred years before the Spanish relinquished control to the United States after losing the Spanish-American War of 1898. Taiwan had been under successive periods of Chinese control since the sixth century; the last period of direct Chinese control began when the Manchu dynasty reconquered Taiwan in 1683. After China lost the Sino-Japanese War of 1895, control of Taiwan was transferred to Japan. Not only was there a change of economic and political control in all three of these countries, but each country also experienced substantial destruction of property due to both internal rebellion and fighting between the controlling powers.

19. Ingram describes the initial government efforts to improve infrastructure [64, pp. 79–87].

20. Reynolds [89, pp. 211, 216].

21. Chilean control over the nitrate-producing areas was established by a series of international treaties from 1884 to 1896. See Stocking and Watkins [96, p. 120].

22. For details on the destruction caused by the revolution, see Galdames [56, pp. 345–48, 361–64].

Cuba. Under Spanish rule, Cuba had already developed an export economy, with sugar as its principal export. However, Cuban trade was tied more closely to the United States than to Spain. Destruction of property occurred during both the Cuban War of Independence, 1895–98 and the Spanish-American War of 1898. The War of Independence was particularly destructive to Cuba's sugar cane fields and mills.[23] Thus the U.S. military occupation in 1898 was first confronted with the need for massive reconstruction. U.S. military occupation ended in 1902 when Cuba agreed to the conditions of the Platt Amendment which established the foundation for continued United States political and economic control of Cuba.

Philippines. Although the Spanish colonial government spent little to develop the Philippines' export economy, its principal export crops —Manila hemp, sugar, tobacco, and coconut products—were established by 1870.[24] In general, Spanish colonialism in the Philippines did not produce as dramatic an economic change as did American colonialism. In fact, it was not until the early part of the nineteenth century that Spain finally opened the Philippines to world trade. However, the transformation into an export economy had begun by about 1870 as exports of abaca, tobacco, and sugar grew, and the economy became a net importer of rice. Although the colonial government made improvements in transport (many roads and bridges were constructed during the 1830s), in communications (a telegraph system was established in 1873), and in harbor improvement, Spanish colonialism in general did not extensively promote the development of an export economy. Most government expenditures were devoted to the military and police, and extensive official corruption made the government inefficient. Perhaps the two most important developments under Spanish colonialism were the introduction of religious unity to the islands (with the exception of the Muslim south) and the formation of a relatively powerful native elite.[25]

Exports were substantially reduced by the destruction and disturbances accompanying the Philippine Revolution against Spain, 1896–98 and the Philippines' guerilla war against United States rule,

23. For an analysis of economic conditions in Cuba prior to the U.S. military occupation, see Commission on Cuban Affairs (hereafter referred to as CCA) [41, pp. 42–43], Cuban Economic Research Project (hereafter referred to as CERP) [45, chs. 1–11, esp. p. 96], and Jenks [64, chs. 1–4, esp. pp. 18, 36, 128].
24. Sicat et al. [92, ch. 2, pp. 66–67].
25. Resnick [87].

1899–1902. The Spanish-American War of 1898 was not the direct cause of the destruction and disruption.[26] Our period of study begins after peace was restored in 1902. Having established military control, the new American colonial government was faced with the need to increase exports, first to their level under Spanish rule, and then to higher levels.

Taiwan. In the latter part of the nineteenth century, the Chinese made a limited attempt to develop Taiwan's exports by constructing a railroad and improving some ports. But, when the Japanese assumed control in 1895, Taiwan lacked a transportation system sufficient to support a strong export economy.[27] Our period of study does not begin until 1904 for two reasons. First, there was a major rebellion by the Taiwanese against Japanese rule, and police expenses remained especially high until about 1904.[28] Second, until 1904 the Japanese government aided the colonial government by sending it large annual cash subsidies. Early in its control of Taiwan the colonial government used these subsidies for substantial investments in irrigation, railroads, roads, harbors, and agricultural research. In addition, in 1902 it further encouraged export production through subsidies for planting sugar cane, buying fertilizer, constructing modern sugar refineries, and clearing government land for sugar cultivation.[29] By 1904, the first year of our study for Taiwan, the returns on these investments and subsidies were apparent and the colonial government was functioning without large direct cash subsidies from the Japanese government. Thus our period of study begins when there had been established a pattern of colonial expenditures dependent only on revenue raised within the Taiwanese economy.

COLONIAL CONTROLS

In this section we analyze how foreign economic and political control was exercised in each country in our sample. We use the term colonialism when both the trade and government sectors of a country, called the colonial country, are controlled by another country, called the developed country.[30] These controls promote the growth

26. Power and Sicat [85, p. 14] and Corpuz [42, pp. 63–65].
27. Chang [40, pp. 4–8].
28. See Ho [63, ch. 3, p. 24]. For details concerning Taiwanese resistance to Japanese rule, see Davidson [46, chs. 20–22].
29. The early economic development of Taiwan under Japanese colonial rule is described in Ho [63, ch. 3].
30. Other terms that can be used to refer to the developed country are mother country, metropolitan country, and colonizing country

of colonial trade, in which the colony exports food and raw materials to the developed nation and the colony imports intermediate and capital goods from the developed nation. Historically, we find that the colonial government sector was controlled so that most government revenues were derived from the trade sector and so that development expenditures were directed toward promoting export growth. From an economic viewpoint, this historical pattern of foreign control does not depend on de jure political control by the developed country. We examine the exercise of foreign political control over the trade and government sectors in the six de jure colonies in our sample and also in the four other countries in our sample. We find that foreign influence, while more subtle, was no less important in controlling the trade and government sectors of the countries not under de jure control. As a result, all ten countries experienced a common process of historical development that we term colonialism; we conclude that the latter four countries were de facto colonies.

The first six countries to be examined were tied to the United Kingdom: India, Ceylon, Jamaica, and Nigeria were de jure British colonies, while Egypt and Thailand were de facto British colonies. We first discuss some British controls that affected all of the British colonies, and then analyze the specific controls in each colony.

Some examples show how the United Kingdom expected colonies to serve British trade needs. In 1895 Joseph Chamberlain, the British Secretary of State for the colonies, stated that a major British objective was to promote increased colonial exports. Chamberlain regarded many British colonies "as being in the condition of undeveloped estates, and estates which can never be developed without Imperial assistance." [31] Sir Charles Bruce emphasized that British colonies should be developed both to supply the United Kingdom with food and raw materials and to consume British manufactured goods. The justification for this policy was that the United Kingdom depended on the cheap and abundant supply of raw materials and food exported from the British colonies.[32] As a specific example of this policy, during World War I the British Board of Trade asked that "the attention of the Indian government be called to the opportunity offered by India's monopoly in the production of jute to safeguard for the British Empire and its Allies the supplies of the fabric." [33] In

31. Quoted in Geary [57, p. 5].
32. Bruce [39, 2:193–94, 212, 216–17].
33. Hancock [60, vol. 2, pt. 1, pp. 114–15].

Nigeria, British development of the palm oil industry was designed to meet increased demand for vegetable oils for industrial use, soap, and margarine.[34] When the boll weevil reduced supplies of United States cotton, the British textile industry sought to develop a dependable supply of cotton within the British Empire. "As early as 1902 the cotton industry in the United Kingdom had formed a British Cotton Growing Association with the object of stimulating Empire supplies. During the War and in the early years of peace, shortage in the world market convinced the trade that this object was a matter of urgency." [35] As a result, in 1921 a Royal Charter established the Empire Cotton Growing Corporation, which represented both the government and the cotton traders. It concentrated on research, expert guidance, and education, working closely with colonial governments and advising them on transport and irrigation construction. The corporation attempted to increase cotton exports throughout the British Empire, including India, Nigeria, Anglo-Egyptian Sudan, Uganda, the Union of South Africa, and Australia.[36]

In 1919 the British established a system of trade preferences within the British Empire to secure continued supplies of necessary food and raw materials. The cause of this shift of policy toward increased empire trade protection was that World War I weakened Britain's trade position. Trade preferences became much more important during the Great Depression when the 1932 Import Duties Act applied an additional 10 percent ad valorem duty to all imports, exempting those from empire countries.[37]

The United Kingdom used its influence over British private investors as another method of promoting British colonial policies. The Bank of England and the Treasury exercised substantial influence over British private investment. The British government used this influence to forward the official policy of developing colonial trade. This influence extended to decisions by British firms over whether to remit or reinvest their profits from colonial trade. Because private investment strengthened British foreign and colonial policy, the government found it advantageous to assist these investors. Feis concludes that "British capital was soundly placed; the essentials of

34. Hancock [60, vol. 2, pt. 2, p. 159].
35. Hancock [60, vol. 2, pt. 1, p. 123].
36. Hancock [60, vol. 2, pt. 1, pp. 123–25].
37. For a detailed account of developments in the trade preference policy of the British Empire, see Hancock [60, vol. 2, pt. 1, pp. 138–40, 198–230].

British economic and financial policy were well served; the tasks of
the empire were well performed." [38]

The Colonial Stocks Act of 1900 and the Crown Agents system
strengthened British official policy's impact on empire investments.[39]
The Colonial Stocks Act specified that colonial securities registered
in the United Kingdom could qualify as "Trustee Securities," making
them purchasable by British trust bodies and institutions. This act
increased the demand for colonial bonds and made it advantageous to
sell colonial bonds in London. In return, the United Kingdom established the conditions for these loans in order to protect their security.
The government used Crown Agents to formulate colonial investment
plans, to arrange colonial loans and contracts, and to control capital
imports of the colonies. The Crown Agents encouraged the colonies
to contract with British firms and purchase imports from Britain. For
example, in 1923, 95 percent of borrowed funds spent abroad by
India were used for purchases from the United Kingdom.[40]

In summary, the United Kingdom used several methods of economic control applied generally to all its colonies: political power
over colonial decisions, use of trade preferences, and influence over
private British investment. We now examine how British political
control was exercised in each of the six countries tied to the United
Kingdom.

India. After the Indian Mutiny of 1857, the United Kingdom ter-
minated East India Company rule and exercised direct colonial control of India. Britain limited Indian revenues by permitting very few
export duties and by keeping import tariffs at relatively low levels
until 1931.[41] British restrictions on Indian government expenditures
were also a strong factor limiting India's development. The most important constraint on expenditures was the heavy defense burden imposed by the United Kingdom. Expenditures for current defense costs
and for interest on debt (reflecting mostly the cost of past wars) accounted for roughly 50 percent of Indian government expenditures
from 1890 through 1936. These military expenditures were used to
maintain law and order in India and to maintain the British influence
in the Orient. Another important component of Indian expenditures

38. Feis [51, p. 117; see also pp. 86–88] and Levin [72, pp. 170–74].
39. The Colonial Stocks Act could not be applied to the two de facto British
colonies in our sample, Egypt and Thailand.
40. Feis [51, pp. 92–95].
41. Anstey [35, pp. 398–99, 505–8] and United States Tariff Commission
(hereafter referred to as USTC) [113, p. 292].

was the cost of administration. British colonial administrators were paid much higher salaries than were Indian administrators and very few administrative jobs were open to Indians. British conservative influence caused Indian railroads to be poorly administered. While high freight rates discouraged the growth of railroad traffic, the low level of improvements left India's railroads both inefficient and inadequate to meet increasing demand in the twentieth century. Although development expenditures on infrastructure, education, health, and agriculture increased during the period under study, they were still a small share of total expenditure because of the heavy burden of military, debt, and administrative costs.[42]

The United Kingdom discouraged Indian industrial development in order to achieve the British aim of exchanging Indian food and raw materials for British manufactured goods. For many years, Indian tariffs were kept low, and the overall tariff structure afforded minimal protection for Indian industries, thus strengthening the complementary position of the British and the Indian economies.[43] Lamb describes how, as a result, the United Kingdom was quite successful in developing Indian foreign trade into the pattern common to colonial economies: "The coming of unrestricted British enterprise precipitated the development of the Indian economy on colonial lines. In stepping up the supply of raw materials, the British stimulated Indian economic development. In pressing for the conversion of India into a market for British manufactured goods, the British inhibited India's own manufacturing industries and gradually converted India into an agricultural hinterland of Great Britain."[44] For example, under East India Company rule India had been an exporter of textiles, but with the coming of British colonial rule in the mid-nineteenth century it became a net importer of textiles and an exporter of raw cotton. Before World War I, 40 percent of Indian imports were cotton textiles. Pressure from British industries to sell India finished manufactured goods, especially cotton textiles, continued throughout the period of study and obstructed development of Indian industries. Textiles were still the largest category of Indian imports in 1936–37, although it had declined to 18 percent of imports. Besides encouraging exports of raw materials and imports of manufactures, the United

42. Lamb [19, pp. 488–92] provides a detailed analysis of Indian government finance from 1920 to 1940.

43. Lamb [19, pp. 474–88] describes British capital investment and economic controls in India. See also USTC [113, pp. 328–31].

44. Lamb [21, pp. 467–68]; see also Anstey [35, p. 332].

Kingdom also used its controls to tie Indian trade to the British Empire. A majority of Indian imports were from the United Kingdom, and a large part of exports went to the United Kingdom.[45] In particular, Lamb finds that the return to British Imperial Preference in 1919 strengthened "the same old colonial economy relationship." [46] Lamb concludes that the United Kingdom used its colonial controls to meet "the traditional British aim of developing India as a market for British manufactured goods in return for India's food and raw materials." [47]

Ceylon. Ceylon was also subject to direct British political and economic controls. In Ceylon, the pattern of British economic control established during the coffee era, 1830–80, continued: British control of exports and imports, British ownership and management of most estates, and British financial control through banks and "agency houses." British land ownership was established in the coffee era by the land-sales policy. In 1815 the colonial government assumed ownership of all uncultivated land. In 1844, the price on Crown land was raised high enough that buying was effectively limited to Europeans with sufficient capital. Since banking was British controlled, the banks perpetuated British policy by making almost all their loans to European planters and export-import traders and not to Ceylonese peasants.[48] As a result, most export production remained in British hands. Throughout the period under study, the British Empire purchased most of Ceylon's exports and it supplied most of Ceylon's imports.[49] Ceylon was subject to the British "currency board system" which required 100 percent backing for notes and securities, where this backing was financed by Ceylon's trade surplus. Because the British owned most of Ceylon's exporting enterprises, a large amount of the export profits were remitted as dividends to shareholders outside of Ceylon.[50]

Jamaica. During the period covered by our study, the United Kingdom had complete control of Jamaica's government. After the rebellion of 1865, the United Kingdom abolished Jamaica's representa-

45. For details see Lamb [21, pp. 466–67, 476, 494] and USTC [120, p. 328].
46. Lamb [21, p. 487].
47. Lamb [21, p. 465].
48. For further analysis of how the British controlled Ceylonese trade, see Snodgrass [94, pp. 21–23, 69].
49. See tables 2.1 and 2.2 in chapter 2. See also Snodgrass [94, pp. 364–68].
50. Snodgrass [94, pp. 68–70].

tive government, which had existed since 1661, and replaced it with a government appointed entirely by the British. In 1884 the United Kingdom permitted constitutional changes which provided for elected members, and unofficial policy permitted the existence of an elected majority. However, the British-appointed governor retained full veto power. Legislative deadlocks in 1899 resulted in a return to a British-appointed majority.[51]

The Jamaican trade pattern has the characteristics of the colonial model. Jamaica exported mostly raw commodities, the most important being bananas and sugar, and imported mostly manufactured goods. Although much of the banana industry was controlled by an American firm, the United Fruit Company, this company and the owners of Jamaican estates benefited from trade preferences and subsidies from the British government that offset unfavorable demand conditions including U.S. trade restrictions during the 1930s. Despite Jamaica's proximity to the United States, much of its trade was with the British Empire. Except during the 1920s, the majority of Jamaican imports were from the British Empire. After World War I, the U.S. share of Jamaican exports decreased while those of Canada and the United Kingdom increased. This shift was the result of the return to Imperial Preference in 1919. During the 1930s Jamaican exports to the United States dropped to very low levels as a result of U.S. trade restrictions.[52]

Nigeria. With the establishment of the Protectorates of Southern and Northern Nigeria in 1900, Nigeria also became subject to direct British control. Some resistance to the establishment of British control did occur, especially in the North, until 1909.[53] Southern Nigeria had a Legislative Council with an appointed majority, while Northern Nigeria had no Legislative Council.[54] Executive power was exercised by the governor and an Executive Council consisting of senior British officials.

One British restriction on economic development of Nigeria was to limit severely the development of plantation agriculture. Throughout

51. See Bruce [39, 1:226–27, 242] and Eisner [49, pp. 356–58] for details on changes in the Jamaican constitutional government.
52. For distribution of Jamaican trade see tables 2.1 and 2.2 in chapter 2. For an analysis of exports and imports by commodity see Eisner [49, ch. 13].
53. Geary [57, pp. 212–13].
54. In 1914, the two protectorates and the Colony of Lagos were combined to form the Colony and Protectorate of Nigeria. Even then, only Southern Nigeria had a Legislative Council. See *The Statesman's Year-book* [115, 1937, 74:274].

the period of study, the British opposed the general development of palm oil plantations in Nigeria, despite the fact that the collection method of production was wasteful and produced a poor quality of oil. In contrast with policy in the Belgian Congo, which developed large and efficient palm oil plantations, the British government steadily refused to grant concessions of land for plantations in Nigeria to European firms. Thus, in 1936, only twelve plantations totaling 22¼ square miles existed in Nigeria, and almost all palm oil production was in peasant hands. Since investors in palm oil plantations were discouraged in Nigeria, they invested elsewhere. Because of the many advantages of plantation production over peasant production, by 1930 Nigeria had lost to the Belgian Congo its dominant world position as a supplier of palm oil products.[55]

Besides rejecting plantations, the British also adopted a cautious attitude toward technical changes. In the case of palm oil, additions of infrastructure did not change methods of growing or production but only increased the area of production. More far-reaching changes in production techniques were known to be possible, but the conservative attitude of the British colonial government severely limited their application in Nigeria.[56]

Other British controls helped concentrate Nigerian exports in the United Kingdom market. First, when Imperial trade preferences were adopted in 1919, differential export duties on both tin and palm kernels were designed to reserve these Nigerian exports for the United Kingdom alone. The duty on tin succeeded in stopping a U.S. company from establishing a tin-smelting industry. In 1934, an Importation of Textiles (Quotas) Ordinance severely limited Nigerian imports of textiles from Japan. In general, preferential import duties provided major trade advantages for British goods. Nigeria's position as a colonial economy was strengthened in that the United Kingdom purchased the largest share of Nigerian exports and supplied more than half of Nigeria's imports.[57]

55. For a detailed analysis of the question of plantation production in Nigeria, see Hancock [57, vol. 2, pt. 2, pp. 188–200] and Scott [30, pp. 226–27].
56. For a general theoretical analysis see Helleiner [58, pp. 9–13]. For details on specific export commodities see Helleiner [58, ch. 4]. For example: "The tremendous growth of production and exports of Nigerian groundnuts [peanuts] was achieved through a gradual moving out on the extensive margin. . . . Cultivation methods and yield, . . . have in all probability changed very little in the past 50 years." Helleiner [58, pp. 111–12].
57. See tables 2.1 and 2.2 in chapter 2 on Nigeria's international trade ties. For a detailed discussion of British colonial policies influencing Nigerian for-

British controls were strong enough to develop Nigeria's economy into one which resembled the generally accepted image of a colonial economy. Helleiner states that the export and import pattern in Nigeria reflects the "classical colonial pattern." [58] Mars adds that "Nigeria, like other British colonies, has no manufacturing industries worth mentioning." [59]

British economic controls also affected Nigeria's trade balance. For example, in the 1920s and 1930s, only 38 percent to 60 percent of the tin mining industry export value remained in Nigeria. The persistent Nigerian export surplus reflected the fact that interest and dividend payments were being remitted from Nigeria to the United Kingdom. Under the West African Currency Board system there was no way to increase the Nigerian money supply other than through an overall balance of payments surplus. [60]

Both Geary and Hancock found that the basis of economic policy in Nigeria was the policy set forth by Chamberlain: economic development of the Imperial estate of Nigeria was too vast for private enterprise alone; it was a British colonial "responsibility and opportunity" to develop Nigeria. [61] Of the four de jure British colonies in our sample, Chamberlain's policy had the most substantial effect in Nigeria. First, Nigeria was the only British colony during the period of our study to receive grants-in-aid to establish administrative and political control. [62] Second, Nigeria was the only British colony in our sample in which export development expenditures went beyond current needs. Helleiner describes how this policy applied in the case of Nigerian railroads: "Financed by United Kingdom loans, the railway system was built far ahead of development events . . . . In the 1934 report of the Government Railways of Nigeria it was stated: 'The Railway has been constructed and equipped by Government in order to enable the Colony to be developed. The longest possible view ahead has been taken. The trade of the Colony is not yet developed to anything like the transport capacity of its railway route mileage.' " [63]

---

eign trade, see Leubuscher [22, especially pp. 139, 155–59, 166–67] and USTC [120, pp. 341–42, 369].
58. Helleiner [61, p. 23].
59. Mars [23, pp. 67–68].
60. See Bower [4, pp. 10–14], Helleiner [61, p. 21], and Mars [23, pp. 67–70].
61. Geary [57, pp. 1–8, 203–10] emphasizes the influence of Chamberlain on the development of Nigeria. See also Hancock [60, vol. 2, pt. 2, pp. 168–69].
62. Geary [57, pp. 230–33] and Kibuka [19].
63. Helleiner [61, p. 14].

Egypt. The basic motivation behind British policy in Egypt after the completion of the Suez Canal in 1869 is summarized by Feis as "a firm determination that Egypt, as the land of passage to India and the Far East, should not be dominated by any third Power." [64] While French financial interests had dominated the financing of the canal, the United Kingdom established its control by taking advantage of Egyptian financial problems in meeting its foreign debt payments. In 1876 Egypt sold the United Kingdom its shares in the Suez Canal. In order to satisfy bond-holders of the large and growing Egyptian foreign debt, Ismail (1863–79) established the Caisse de la Dette in 1876. It consisted of representatives of six foreign countries who were given virtually complete control of Egyptian revenue and loans. Foreign pressures in 1876 also resulted in an Egyptian constitutional government which included an Englishman serving as Minister of Finance. By the end of 1876 there were a total of five agencies representing international financial control over Egyptian affairs.[65]

When Ismail objected to these foreign controls over the Egyptian government, Britain and France convinced the Sultan of Turkey to remove him in 1879. Anglo-French Dual Control was established over Egyptian finances by two Controllers-General with the power of "inquiry, control, surveillance," and reorganization of Egyptian finances. When Egypt defaulted on her debt payments, the Liquidation Law of 1880 further increased foreign financial control, which was used to cut army and public works expenditures. These actions increased anti-European sentiment, particularly in the Egyptian Army. Egyptian unrest led to the murder of fifty Europeans in Alexandria and the fortification of that town, resulting in the British military occupation of Egypt in 1882.[66]

This military occupation ended Anglo-French dual control and established the United Kingdom as the foreign country controlling Egypt. The Egyptian constitution of 1883 made the British Consul-General the real executive of Egypt through his control over government expenditures; the Egyptian legislature could not oppose him. The British Financial Advisor also had substantial power because of the rule that "no financial decision should be taken without his

64. Feis [51, p. 382].
65. For details see Crouchley [44, p. 122], Feis [51, pp. 382–87], and Marlowe [76, ch. 4].
66. Feis [51, pp. 382–97] has an excellent and detailed analysis of the establishment of British economic and political control over Egypt. For another account, see Marlowe [76, ch. 5].

consent." [67] While the Caisse de la Dette continued to exist after 1882, the British in actuality assumed political and financial control of Egypt. During the next forty years, the British Consul-General and later the High Commissioner was "the de facto ruler of Egypt." [68] In the Anglo-French Agreement of 1904, France recognized Britain's complete control in Egypt in return for the United Kingdom's assent to French control in Morocco. This agreement made it possible to end international control over Egyptian railroads, telegraphs, and ports, and to weaken the power of the Caisse so that its only function was to distribute Egyptian debt payments. The agreement replaced international financial control with British control.[69]

Settling this debt and making tribute payments were major limits on Egyptian expenditures. In 1882, Egypt's public debt was about one hundred million pounds, and by the 1930s it had only been reduced to ninety million pounds. Interest payments on this debt accounted for a large portion of government expenditures during the period under study. Egypt also made tribute payments to Constantinople until 1914. From 1886 to 1914 tribute and debt payments absorbed from one-third to one-half of the Egyptian government's expenditures, making it quite difficult to find funds to invest in economic development.[70]

Besides these restraints on expenditures, a treaty with the United Kingdom until 1930 limited Egyptian tariff rates on imports to 8 percent and on exports to 1 percent. Although Egypt taxed articles to the maximum allowed, the revenue was not sufficient to overcome the drain on expenditures created by debt and tribute payments. This treaty prevented Egypt from employing protectionist policies to encourage industrial development.[71]

The United Kingdom made every effort to make Egypt into a supplier of raw materials needed in the United Kingdom and a consumer of British manufactured goods. The British encouraged cultivation of cotton for export and discouraged other traditional exports, including wheat and beans.[72] Further, Lord Cromer, as British Consul-General, stated that "it would be detrimental to both English and Egyptian interests to afford any encouragement to the growth of a

67. Feis [51, pp. 390–91].
68. Mead [77, p. 6].
69. Feis [51, pp. 394–95] and Marlowe [76, pp. 166–67].
70. Crouchley [44, pp. 124, 236–37] and Issawi [67, p. 27].
71. Crouchley [44, p. 227], Issawi [66, pp. 35–37], and USTC [120, p. 292].
72. Issawi [66, pp. 34–35].

protected cotton [textile] industry in Egypt" and that it was "not desirable to impair the considerable revenue derived from customs duties
on cotton goods." [73] Further, local cotton goods paid an 8 percent
excise tax so they would not be any cheaper than imported goods. The
tobacco industry was stopped by British restrictions: "Cultivation of
tobacco, which supplied the raw materials of one of Egypt's main
industries, was first taxed exorbitantly, then forbidden outright. It is
clear that the British administration did not desire the industrialization of Egypt." [74]

As intended by the United Kingdom, Egypt became an exporter of
raw materials, primarily cotton, and an importer of British manufactured goods, thus functioning as a de facto British colony. Throughout
the period under study, United Kingdom purchases of Egyptian cotton linked Egypt to price and income trends in the United Kingdom.[75]
Until the treaty limiting tariffs expired in 1930, the United Kingdom
was assured that Egypt would be an importer of manufactures, especially British manufactures.

Thailand. The basis of British control in Thailand was the Bowring
Treaty of 1855. This treaty removed Thai legal control over British
subjects and trade in Thailand, legalized the opium trade, gave British
ships free entry into Bangkok, and froze a large part of Thailand's
tax system. Further, the treaty established the pattern for similar Thai
treaties with fourteen other countries.[76] Through these treaties, Thailand lost control over its revenues:

> Strictly speaking, the treaties did not forbid the imposition of *all*
> new taxes, but they accomplished this result in practice by: (1) for-
> bidding any levy on imported articles except for a 3-percent duty,
> (2) fixing the export duties and inland-transit duties on nearly
> every important article of domestic production, and (3) forbidding
> any other levies on these articles. Considering the structure of the
> economy and the nature of the administration machinery, these
> provisions blocked any new taxes except *direct* taxes, and the
> government thought the capitation tax was already high enough.
> An income tax was obviously out of the question.[77]

73. Issawi [66, p. 37].
74. Issawi [66, p. 37].
75. Crouchley [44, pp. 138, 174], Issawi [67, p. 269], and Mead [77, p. 247].
76. For further details on the establishment of the Bowring Treaty, see
Ingram [64, pp. 31–35].
77. Ingram [64, pp. 177–78].

Ingram concludes that "the Treaty represented a substantial surrender of sovereignty by Siam [Thailand]." [78]

The British Financial Advisor functioned as another part of British control over Thailand's economy. Since expenditures could not be made without his approval, the United Kingdom controlled Thailand's government expenditures as well as its revenues. The Financial Advisors were so influential that "the government could scarcely have carried out any financial measures to which he had strong objections. On the whole, the entire line of Financial Advisors (1896–1950) favored conservative monetary and fiscal policies." [79] One example of the British control of Thailand's tax structure occurred when gambling was abolished in 1917. The tax on gambling had been an important source of revenue. Before abolishing gambling, Thailand sought to offset the anticipated tax loss with an increase in import duties, but the United Kingdom blocked this increase. The termination of the Bowring Treaty in 1926 gave Thailand some control over its own tax structure. Thailand raised tariff rates so that import duties as a percentage of total government revenue increased from 7 percent in 1926 to 25 percent in 1935. [80] However, the Financial Advisors and trade and diplomatic ties permitted the United Kingdom to retain considerable influence in Thailand until World War II.

The Thai government followed a cautious and conservative approach to economic development because of the controls and because it sought to avoid foreign intervention. The result was an emphasis on maintaining financial stability rather than on development. International stability was so important that, by running a large trade surplus, the government maintained a currency reserve in London which exceeded the value of baht notes outstanding. Ingram concludes that "the chief aim of monetary policy has been to safeguard the international position of the baht, and the government seems to have put this aim above such national interests as economic development and stability of prices and incomes . . . . Because it tied up national reserves of liquid funds and necessitated the postponement of productive investments, this policy entailed a certain cost to the nation." [81]

78. Ingram [64, p. 31].
79. Ingram [64, p. 196]. For further discussion of the influence of British Financial Advisors in Thailand, see Ingram [64, pp. 151–52, 196].
80. For details on the effects of these tax changes before and after termination of the Bowring Treaty, see Ingram [64, pp. 177–84].
81. Ingram [64, p. 170]. Ingram also analyzes the detrimental effects of these conservative monetary policies [64, pp. 170–74].

British control over Thailand's trade was extensive. The British
Empire purchased most of Thailand's exports and supplied most of
its imports.[82] British policies encouraged Thailand to specialize in the
export of rice[83] and caused it to import foods which it formerly
produced. For example, Thailand became an importer of sugar in
the late nineteenth century because, under the terms of the Bowring
Treaty, it could not use increased import duties to protect its own
sugar producers against the lower prices of subsidized European beet
sugar. The Bowring Treaty also made it difficult for Thailand to
protect domestic industries as it could not change import duties without British approval.[84] This lack of protection combined with the
small domestic market resulted in Thailand importing most of its
manufactured goods.

The principal reason why Britain did not make Thailand a de jure
colony was that Thailand was a convenient British sphere of influence
between British and French possessions in Southeast Asia.[85] From an
economic standpoint, however, Britain exercised de facto colonial control of Thailand's trade and government sectors under the terms of
the Bowring Treaty, through the influence of the British Financial
Advisors, and through its position as the principal trading partner of
Thailand.

Chile. It was primarily through private American investment in
Chilean export enterprises that the United States established its control over Chile's economy. Because of the lack of readily available
capital and technical knowledge, the Chilean government encouraged
foreign capital to develop Chilean resources. In the nineteenth century
the British were the principal investors in Chile, and they controlled
Chile's foreign trade. The United Kingdom made sure Chile functioned
as an exporter of raw materials and as an importer of British manufactured consumer goods, making Chile a British dependency.[86]

This de facto colonial relationship with the United Kingdom was
replaced by a similar relationship with the United States when U.S.

82. See tables 2.1 and 2.2 in chapter 2 for the concentration of Thailand's
trade with the United Kingdom and its colonies.
83. Thailand's secondary exports—tin and teak—were not specifically encouraged by the Thai government, although the government received royalties
on their production. See Ingram [64, ch. 5].
84. See Ingram [64, pp. 112–27] for details on the decline of domestic industries.
85. Ingram [64, p. 173].
86. For an analysis of the period of British control, see Frank [53, pp. 64–71]
and Reynolds [89, pp. 218–21].

capital began replacing British capital in the late nineteenth century. Wilson's "Mobile Address" in 1913 stressed U.S. intentions of displacing European (British) capital in Latin America with U.S. capital. In Chile, this change from British to U.S. investment was already taking place, for the expansion of copper exports in the early twentieth century paralleled increasing U.S. investment and therefore U.S. economic control. By 1924, U.S. capital owned more than 90 percent of the copper industry in Chile, having gained ownership of the Gran Mineria. Large U.S. copper mines became dominant as the industry developed and economies of scale became increasingly important. Chile's nitrate industry also shifted from British to U.S. ownership.[87]

The United States not only obtained control of Chile's export industries, but also became Chile's principal trading partner. After World War I Chile's trade with Germany was cut off and its trade with the United States greatly surpassed its trade with Britain.[88] Chile's strong trading tie to the United States was most obvious during the 1930s. The U.S. fertilizer industry had been a major buyer of Chilean nitrates, but decreased U.S. fertilizer consumption during the Great Depression caused a sharp fall in Chile's nitrate exports to the United States. In addition, the U.S. Tariff Act of 1934 imposed a tariff of four cents per pound on Chilean copper. As a result, Chile's copper exports to the United States fell sharply, from 87,000 tons in 1931 to 5,000 tons in 1933. This drastic reduction in Chilean copper exports resulted in a similar reduction in Chilean imports, besides discouraging foreign investors and reducing government revenues. We conclude that Chile's major exports, copper and nitrates, were both highly dependent on the U.S. market. This dependency helps explain why Chile's trade was one of those most strongly adversely affected by the Great Depression centered in the United States.[89]

87. For a detailed analysis of U.S. control of Chile during the period of our study, see Pike [82, chs. 5 and 7, esp. pp. 144, 233–35]. For another interpretation of this control see Frank [53, pp. 99–105]. Reynolds [89, pp. 214–21] analyzes the development of the modern Chilean copper industry up to World War II and the U.S. dominance of that industry.

88. See tables 2.1 and 2.2 on Chilean trade ties. Pike analyzes the U.S. penetration of the Chilean economy [82, pp. 159–67].

89. For summaries of U.S. influence in the nitrate industry see particularly Stocking and Watkins [96, pp. 147–48] and USTC [119, pp. 206, 220]. The effects of the Great Depression on Chile will be analyzed in chapter 9, and U.S. restrictive policies will be analyzed in chapter 10. See also Ellsworth [50, p. 7] and Reynolds [89, pp. 232–36].

U.S. capital investment gave the United States indirect control over Chile's government revenues and expenditures. Frank describes this control: "The large share of the government's income which depends on revenues from copper exports renders the government budget, and therewith the government's ability to finance capital and current expenditures, highly vulnerable to the metropolitan-controlled production of copper in Chile, the sale of copper abroad, and metropolitan monopolistic manipulation of both." [90] Chileans even feared the United States would establish an official colonial relationship. Ellsworth concludes that Chile had "a fairly typical colonial economy," one which exported raw materials, imported manufactures, and traded mainly with one developed country. [91]

Cuba. The Platt Amendment of 1901 established the basic conditions for continued U.S. economic and political control over Cuba. This amendment was first enacted by the U.S. Congress. As a condition for ending U.S. military occupation in 1902, Cuba had to write the amendment into its constitution in 1901. The amendment was also made part of the United States–Cuba Permanent Treaty of 1903. The amendment specified conditions allowing U.S. intervention in Cuban affairs: to maintain Cuban independence; to insure the existence of an "adequate" government to protect life, liberty, and property; and to maintain U.S. naval stations in Cuba. For Cuba, the Platt Amendment represented a serious loss of sovereignty. The amendment was also very significant in its encouragement of U.S. investment in the Cuban sugar industry. Because of previous damage to Cuban sugar plantations, U.S. entrepreneurs were extremely reluctant to invest in Cuban sugar production until they received the guarantee of U.S. protection embodied in the Platt Amendment. [92] The amendment was used to justify a second period of U.S. military occupation, 1906 to 1909, after the Cuban government resigned due to an armed rebellion. [93]

After 1909, the Platt Amendment acquired a new interpretation called the "preventive policy" which was used to justify U.S. inter-

90. Frank [53, p. 103].
91. Ellsworth [50, pp. vii–viii]. See also Pike [82, pp. 161–62, 233–34].
92. For the history surrounding the Platt Amendment see CERP [45, pp. 150–52], Jenks [68, pp. 72–84], and Thomas [99, pp. 450–56]. The encouragement of U.S. private investment by this amendment is clearly explained by Wright [101, pp. 44, 61–63].
93. The second U.S. military intervention is analyzed in Jenks [68, ch. 6] and Thomas [99, ch. 40].

ference in Cuban affairs in order to prevent the need to intervene. The United States used this "preventive policy" interpretation to interfere several times in order to protect U.S. investments and thus guarantee continued sugar exports. In response to the 1912 Negro Rebellion, U.S. troops and battleships arrived to protect U.S. sugar and mining interests. U.S. pressure in 1912 caused the Cuban government to annul a timber concession, reject attempts by British private investors to build a railroad, accept U.S. conditions for obtaining a foreign loan, and agree to the establishment of a U.S. naval base at Guantánamo. The United States continued the "preventive policy" by advising election settlements in 1916–17 and by placing U.S. troops in Cuba from 1917 until 1922 to protect U.S. properties. During World War I, the United States controlled the export price of Cuban sugar. It withheld shipments of desperately needed flour until Cuba agreed to U.S. sugar control policy, from which the United States gained a 10 percent profit on Cuban sugar. During the depression of 1921, the United States sent financial advisers to protect U.S. investment interests.[94] Thus the Platt Amendment not only encouraged U.S. private investment, which increased Cuban sugar exports, but also provided the U.S. rationale for controlling the Cuban government to protect these investments.

Besides controls contained in the Platt Amendment, the United States increased its influence through the 1902 Reciprocity Treaty which also encouraged U.S. capital investment in Cuba. At the turn of the twentieth century, the United States feared it might lose its dominant trade position in the Cuban market to the United Kingdom. With the purpose of obtaining the most favorable trade preferences from Cuba with the least concessions of its own, the United States negotiated the 1902 Reciprocity Treaty. Through dominance of Cuban trade, and especially through a monopoly of Cuban imports, the United States hoped to maintain close political ties with Cuba and thus keep other powers out.[95]

Throughout the period under study, Cuba's trade functioned as if Cuba were a U.S. colony, supplying the United States with needed

94. For details of U.S. interference prior to World War I, see Jenks [68, ch. 7, esp. pp. 105–7, 114–19] and Thomas [99, pp. 509–24]. For U.S. interference during World War I, see Jenks [68, ch. 10, esp. pp. 196, 203] and Thomas [99, pp. 529–35]. For post–World War I interference, see Jenks [68, pp. 237–64] and Thomas [99, pp. 547–56].

95. Jenks [68, pp. 132–40, 175] and Wright [101, pp. 63–70, 165–76] analyze the influence of the Reciprocity Treaty on the Cuban economy.

raw materials in exchange for U.S. manufactured goods. Beginning with the first U.S. military intervention, Cuban exports centered more and more on the U.S. market. By the late 1920s, the United States purchased 75 percent to 80 percent of Cuban sugar exports, and any decline in these purchases was harmful to the entire Cuban economy. The United States also became the major source of Cuban imports, supplying 87.7 percent in 1909. Trade during World War I strengthened the U.S. monopoly of Cuban imports. Although in the final years covered by our study the U.S. share of Cuban imports decreased, it never dropped below 71 percent.[96]

Another important reason why the United States controlled Cuban trade was that U.S. private investments dominated Cuban export production. U.S. investors acquired ownership of most of the Cuban sugar industry, and its iron and copper industries as well. After the 1920 crisis, much of the Cuban banking system was taken over by U.S. firms, leading to even greater U.S. control over Cuban trade and commerce. By the late 1920s U.S. investors had gained outright ownership of 22 percent of the area of Cuba. These commercial interests did much to maintain Cuba as an exporter of raw materials and an importer of manufactures. Since the sugar industry absorbed most capital investments, development of other industries was quite difficult, making it necessary for Cuba to import manufactured consumer goods. Through these investments many Americans hoped to "Americanize" Cuba and thus tie it closely with the United States.[97]

Although the United States never declared Cuba an official colony, the economic relationship between Cuba and the United States has been called colonial. According to Barnes, "Cuba provides the example of a theoretically independent state which has become in fact an economic protectorate, and also occupies a peculiar political status, owing to the Platt Amendment and the consequent ability of the U.S. to protect economic investments by periodic political interventions." [98] Similarly, the Cuban Economic Research Project concluded that the 1902 Reciprocity Treaty simply displaced Spanish colonial economic controls with those of the United States.[99] Leland Jenks titled his book on the United States–Cuba economic relationship *Our Cuban*

96. For further details see CERP [45, pp. 184, 285–87], Jenks [68, p. 184], and Stocking and Watkins [96, pp. 20, 30].
97. For two analyses of U.S. private investment in Cuba, see CERP [45, pp. 171, 173, 230–32, 262–68] and Jenks [68, pp. 141–50, 155–60, ch. 15].
98. H. E. Barnes, "Editor's Introduction," in Jenks [68, p. xiii].
99. CERP [45, pp. 142, 218].

Colony. Jenks explains that after establishing control of Cuba through the Platt Amendment and the Reciprocity Treaty, U.S. commercial interests entered and functioned in Cuba in a colonizing manner, with the purpose of bringing Cuba under the control of American capitalism. According to Jenks, Cuba's trade made it function as a U.S. protectorate.[100] Although it was not officially an American colony, the combined influence of the Platt Amendment, the Reciprocity Treaty, the close trade ties of Cuba with the United States, and the extensive U.S. private investments caused Cuba to be controlled as a de facto economic colony of the United States.

Philippines. The United States established the Philippine Commission as the highest Philippine authority. Its membership was entirely American until 1901, and it had an American majority until 1913. The commission had sole legislative power until the 1907 establishment of the Filipino Assembly as a lower legislative house; even then the American-dominated commission retained control. The American Governor-General was chief executive, and high executive officers were appointed by the U.S. President and approved by the U.S. Senate. There was also an extensive lower-level staff of Americans working in the Philippines. This preponderance of Americans in the Philippines prompted Theodore Roosevelt to term it "a government of Americans, assisted by Filipinos." While there was a Filipino majority in the Philippine Commission after 1913, the United States retained ultimate control until 1935 when the Philippines became a self-governing commonwealth.[101]

The main objective of U.S. economic policy in the Philippines was to expand its trade with the Philippines. To meet this end, the Philippine Commission emphasized public works directed toward expanding Philippine exports. Liberalized U.S. trade preferences for Philippine exports also encouraged exports. The Philippine Tariff Act of 1902 provided 25 percent preference in the United States for Philippine goods; the Payne-Aldrich Tariff Act of 1909 abolished the import tariff on almost all Philippine items except sugar, rice, and tobacco; the Underwood Tariff of 1913 established free trade between the United States and the Philippines. Because of the increase in free trade with the United States, export duties were dropped entirely in 1916 and customs duties on imports became a less important source of revenue. In later years, the Hawley-Smoot Tariff of

100. Jenks [68, pp. 84, 176].
101. See Corpuz [41, chs. 8 and 9, esp. pp. 162–63, 175, 176, 195–208].

1931 protected sugar exports from the Philippines to the United States, primarily at the expense of Cuban sugar. The Jones-Costigan Act of 1934, while imposing a quota on the Philippines, had much more impact on Cuba.[102]

These U.S. economic policies made the Philippines increasingly dependent on the United States. In contrast, U.S. political policies had the stated goal of Philippine self-government. The increased trade which resulted from U.S. economic policies was almost entirely with the United States. Because of its dependence on U.S. markets, "Philippine foreign trade was highly vulnerable to economic movements or to Congressional legislation in the United States, as became increasingly clear in the depression of the thirties." [103] Thus, despite the U.S. political goal of Philippine self-government, Sicat concludes that the foreign trade of the Philippines was "colonial in character, that is, the exchange of raw materials for finished goods. As in other colonial plantation economies . . . the Philippines was becoming but an extension of the markets of the home country. This economic dependence was felt to be a bar to the attainment of complete Philippine political independence, even after the inauguration of the self-governing Commonwealth in 1935." [104]

Taiwan. Japan's colonial policy in Taiwan was based upon "the development of an economy in Taiwan to complement that of Japan. Indeed, the economic objective of the government, until the mid-1930's, was to develop Taiwan as an agricultural appendage of Japan. In this capacity, the colony supplied Japan with sugar and rice, and to a much lesser extent it served also as an outlet for Japan's manufactured goods." [105] Japanese colonial policy, combined with favorable market conditions for Taiwanese rice and sugar, caused a rapid expansion of Taiwanese agricultural output and exports. Since Japan

102. For details on public works in the Philippines and their effects, see the section on the Philippines in chapter 3. U.S. trade policy for the Philippines is analyzed in CERP [45, pp. 330–33], Power and Sicat [85, p. 14], Salamanca [91, ch. 7, esp. pp. 121–39], Sicat et al. [92, ch. 7, pp. 8–9], and USTC [120, pp. 586–600].

103. Sicat et al. [92, ch. 7, p. 11; see also pp. 8–10]. For data by commodity on increased concentration of Philippine exports to the U.S. market, see tables 6–9 in Salamanca [91, pp. 135–39].

104. Sicat et al. [92, ch. 7, pp. 11–13].

105. Ho [63, ch. 3, p. 2]. Chang makes a similar description of Japanese policy: "The Japanese managed and developed Taiwan in accordance with their traditions of colonial policy: that is, to feed the development of industry in Japan with the agricultural effort of Taiwan. Thus, they did work hard for the improvement of Taiwan's agriculture." Chang [38, p. 11].

wanted Taiwan as a market for its manufactured goods, industry did not develop in Taiwan until late in the period of study. A few industries in Taiwan—ceramic, chemical, and wood and wood products—were allowed to function because Japan did not choose to supply these goods. All other manufactures were of necessity imported.[106]

Taiwan's foreign trade was tied almost entirely to the Japanese market. The Taiwanese sugar industry, which supplied 86 percent of Japan's sugar needs by 1931–35, was thus limited by the size of the Japanese sugar market. Japan was so successful in restricting Taiwanese trade that Taiwan became dependent on Japan for both its imports and exports. This trade relationship between Taiwan and Japan was greatly to Japan's advantage because, after 1909, Taiwan had a large commodity trade surplus. Also, rice exports from Taiwan kept Japan's average consumption high, while Taiwanese consumption actually decreased.[107]

The colonial government administered and policed the native population through the traditional pao-chia system. This system supplied a method for mobilizing a substantial supply of cheap labor which the government used in its public works program. In addition, it provided a structure through which the government could communicate information, especially new developments in agricultural techniques.[108]

Japanese expenditures on infrastructure were used to extend Japanese control. Until 1920 the colonial government financed all irrigation investment. After 1920 it directly financed 30 to 50 percent of irrigation investment and indirectly controlled other investment through the Irrigation Association. Through these investments, the colonial government controlled about 75 percent of all the irrigated land and was therefore in a position to directly control rice and sugar production. The government also invested directly in transportation development and assumed part of the operating costs of private transport and communication enterprises. These expenditures assured the continued functioning of transportation facilities needed to move exports to Japan.[109]

106. Barclay [36, p. 70] and Ho [63, ch. 3, pp. 43–66; ch. 4, pp. 14–24; ch. 5, pp. 1–22].
107. See tables 2.1 and 2.2 and table A.41, column 5. For an analysis of Taiwan's colonial trade relationship, see Barclay [36, pp. 19–22] and Ho [63, ch. 5, pp. 7–12; ch. 6, pp. 9–11, 24].
108. Barclay [36, pp. 50–52] and Ho [63, ch. 3, pp. 24–30].
109. For detailed analysis of the relationship between government expendi-

Other government expenditures which served Japanese ends were those for education and wages. Government policy emphasized educating Japanese children, with Taiwanese education limited to training for a few technical jobs. Since the Taiwanese remained uneducated, the colonial government had no choice but to place Japanese in all positions of importance in Taiwan's economic structure, and the government encouraged Japanese migration to Taiwan to fill these positions. One enticement to Japanese migrants was the policy of paying Japanese almost twice the wage of the Taiwanese for equal work. This expenditure resulted in a large influx of Japanese to run export enterprises and soon created an export sector owned, managed, and operated by Japanese.[110]

The government also had substantial control over the export sector through taxes, subsidies, and regulations. Through taxation, the colonial government diverted resources from the private sector into government-favored development such as the sugar industry. By shifting the excise tax forward to Japanese consumers, the sugar industry maintained large profits which, with government encouragement, were reinvested in sugar production. The government also encouraged increased production by establishing a consistent and dependable land tax requiring a set amount of produce from land owners. Through subsidies to Japanese shipping companies, Japan maintained its monopoly of Taiwanese trade. These subsidies guaranteed transportation between Japan and Taiwan, overcame competition from foreign markets for both Taiwanese exports and its import buying power, and kept Taiwan closely dependent on Japan.[111]

Because of its controls, Japanese capitalists usually consulted the government and supported its goals by investing in increased Taiwanese export production. Government influence in sugar production resulted in those large profits being reinvested in increased sugar production.[112] The government also worked through the Japan Sugar Association (a cartel organized to stabilize sugar production) to persuade some rice farmers to start cultivating sugar for export. Its tools of persuasion were conditional cash subsidies and the withholding of irrigation water needed in rice cultivation. Thus, through direct government ownership and control and through unofficial influence, the

tures and exports, see chapter 3. See also Ho [63, ch. 3, pp. 46, 52–53; ch. 4, p. 35].

110. Ho [63, ch. 3, pp. 38–43; ch. 5, pp. 36–41, 67; ch. 6, pp. 13–17].
111. Ho [63, ch. 3, pp. 14, 46–47, 64; ch. 4, p. 12].
112. Ho [63, ch. 3, p. 63; ch. 5, p. 60].

colonial government in Taiwan strongly shaped Taiwan's economy into the form desired by Japan.[113]

In summary, the colonial government used a variety of controls to develop Taiwan into a supplier of foodstuffs and a consumer of Japanese manufactured goods. It "(1) allocated its expenditures and used its authority to license and to regulate in favor of what it wished to promote, (2) used tax incentives and subsidies to influence the behavior of producers, (3) manipulated indigenous institutions to serve as disseminators of innovations, and (4) claimed a limited but important segment of the economy for government ownership and control." [114]

113. Barclay [36, p. 30] and Ho [63, ch. 3, pp. 7, 44; ch. 4, p. 35; ch. 5, p. 60].
114. Ho [63, ch. 3, pp. 44–45].

2

A Model of Colonial Development

The model describing the basic circular structure of the colonial development process is presented and discussed in this chapter. This aggregate annual model consists of a simultaneous system of five behavioral equations and seven definitional equations which together describe the trade and government sectors of a colonial economy. The model describes how forces, both internal and external to the colony, determine simultaneously the process of colonial development. The key internal force is specified as endogenous government expenditures directed toward promoting the growth of colonial export supply. The external forces are specified as exogenously determined within the developed world and are measured as changes in real incomes, domestic prices, and trade policies in the developed world that shift colonial export demand. Colonial export price is assumed endogenous and determined by the intersection of the colonial export supply and demand schedules. Export earnings are then used to pay for imports. However, since colonial commodity trade is not balanced, the model specifies that import demand is a function of real exports, export prices, and import prices. Both the direct and indirect taxation of real exports and nominal imports generate government revenues. These revenues finance further government expenditures which continue the export growth process and thus complete the circular structure of the model.

The behavioral equations of the model are specified in double logarithmic form to provide a linear linkage between the model's real and nominal variables. The estimated coefficients can then be interpreted as elasticities. A linear specification was tried but was found to yield highly inferior estimates with high standard errors and incorrect signs. Furthermore, plots of the residuals from these linear estimates indicated that the errors were multiplicative rather than additive.

THE TRADE SECTOR

Supply and demand equations for real exports along with a market-clearing equation act together to describe the economic relationship between colony and colonizer. The trade sector is completed by a colonial demand equation for real imports and by definitional equations for nominal exports, nominal imports, the terms of trade, and the nominal trade balance.

Equation 2.1 determines the supply of real exports,[1] the principal commercial activity of the colonial economy. Real export supply is a function of export price, import price, accumulated real government expenditures, lagged real exports, and appropriate dummy variables.

$$\ln X_{S_t}^R = a_0 + a_1 \ln Px_t + a_2 \ln Pm_t + a_3 \ln \sum_{i=1}^{\infty} G_{t-i}^R$$
$$+ a_4 \ln X_{S_{t-1}}^R + a_5 D_{S_t} \quad (2.1)$$

where: X_S^R is the supply of total real commodity exports from the colony,

Px is the colony's Paasche export price index (1913 = 1),

Pm is the colony's Paasche import price index (1913 = 1),

$\sum_{i=1}^{\infty} G_{t-i}^R$ is the lagged value of accumulated real government expenditures in the colony,[2] and

D_S is a dummy variable reflecting the impact of exogenous events upon the colony's supply function.

The Paasche export and import price indexes for each country were specially calculated for this study using the largest bundles of goods for which consistent and reliable quantity and value data were available (see the appendix). Paasche indexes rather than Laspeyres or Fisher Ideal indexes were used because the composition of the commodity bundles changed more rapidly than did prices.[3] The indexes were linked using backward bases because exporters respond to current prices relative to past prices, not current prices relative to

---

1. For ease of exposition, the error terms in all the behaviorial equations in this section have been omitted.

2. The method of calculating this variable is found in the description of the government sector.

3. See Lipsey [74, ch. 3]. For ease of exposition the Paasche and Laspeyres indexes are reported in the data appendix using the base 1913 = 100. In the text we use the base 1913 = 1 so that we can specify that import equation 2.4 has no constant term.

future prices. The base years for the linkages of the indexes were
selected after detailed examination of each country's import and export data so as to account for the principal changes in the composition
of the commodity bundles. The selection avoided years in which tem-
porary shifts in the composition of exports occurred. These shifts,
often quite substantial, occurred as the result of such factors as the
need to satisfy the demand for war materials and food during World
War I; the impact of trade and tariff restrictions; and the result of
droughts, floods, earthquakes, and hurricanes.

This aggregate supply equation assumes that a composite commodity, real exports, depends upon a corresponding export price
index. A priori the sign of the export price coefficient a_1 is expected
to be positive, indicating an upward sloping export supply curve. a_1
is not only the export price elasticity, but also the terms of trade elasticity, since the supply equation can be rewritten as follows:

$$\ln X_{S_t}^R = a_0 + a_1 \ln P_{T_t} + (a_2 - a_1) \ln Pm_t$$

$$+ a_3 \ln \sum_{i=1}^{\infty} G_{t-i}^R + a_4 \ln X_{S_{t-1}}^R + a_5 D_{S_t} \quad (2.1')$$

where $P_T = Px/Pm$ = colony's terms of trade. Comparing equations
2.1 and 2.1', the import price coefficient has changed, but coefficients
for the other variables are the same.

An alternative approach would be to disaggregate exports by major
commodities and their respective prices and use a more complicated
substitution model to obtain supply response to price. For the macroeconomic questions analyzed in this book, however, this method was
not used. Because each country exported more than one crop or raw
material, the whole colonial system of ten countries would have inevi-
tably become quite large if a disaggregated approach had been followed. Furthermore, the determination of an aggregate export function provides the necessary analytical framework for making intercountry comparisons of the international colonial system.

Import prices enter into the determination of real export supply in
several ways. First, these colonial economies were dependent on imports for many intermediate goods such as fuel and fertilizer. Thus,
historically, only India had a small petroleum industry and only India
and Nigeria had coal industries.[4] Fertilizers were major imports in

4. See Anstey [35, ch. 10] and Bower [4, pp. 27–30].

Ceylon, Egypt, and Taiwan.[5] Second, all ten countries imported almost all of their capital goods, including agricultural tools, machinery for mining and agricultural processing, and construction materials. Even though steel production started in India in 1913, India continued to be dependent on substantial imports of iron and steel products.[6] Since the colonial countries were dependent on imports of both intermediate and capital goods, the nonwage costs of export production are assumed to be measured by the import price index.[7] Third, the domestic price of incentive or wage goods is also assumed to be reflected by this index.[8] These imported goods often led to the displacement of inferior rural manufacturers by superior foreign commodities.[9] Increased export production in some countries created a labor force in the export sector that was dependent on imported foods. In Ceylon, for example, the immigrant estate labor from India consumed imported rice and other foods.[10] Further, expatriate managers and traders were dependent on imported foods and manufactures to maintain their standard of living. Thus, in the case of Taiwan, "the large import of food, which for a food surplus country may at first be baffling, was largely to accommodate the needs of the Japanese" living in Taiwan.[11] For these reasons the sign of the import price coefficient in equation 2.1 is expected to be negative.[12] Taken to-

5. On the importance of fertilizer imports in Taiwan, see Barclay [36, p. 37] and Ho [63, ch. 4, pp. 33–34]. See Mead [77, p. 8] on Egypt, and Snodgrass [94, p. 61] on Ceylon.

6. Anstey [35, pp. 242–54, 337].

7. For details for each country see Anstey [35, pp. 29, 218, 337] on India; Barclay [36, p. 37] and Ho [63, ch. 6, pp. 9–12] on Taiwan; CERP [45, p. 287] on Cuba; Eisner [49, pp. 263–67] on Jamaica; Helleiner [61, p. 23] on Nigeria; Ingram [64, pp. 129–31] on Thailand; Mead [77, p. 8] on Egypt; Reynolds [89, pp. 219, 225] on Chile; Resnick [28, p. 63] on the Philippines; and Snodgrass [94, pp. 61–62] on Ceylon.

8. One might further assume that domestic labor was available in unlimited supply for export production—not an unreasonable assumption to make in these countries.

9. See Resnick [28] for a model describing this process in Burma, the Philippines, and Thailand. For other examples, see Bower [4] on Nigeria, and Anstey [35, pp. 207–9] on India.

10. Snodgrass [94, pp. 24–25, 61]. For details on other countries, see CERP [45, pp. 287, 291] on Cuba; Eisner [49, pp. 263–64] on Jamaica; and Reynolds [89, p. 225] on Chile.

11. Ho [63, ch. 6, p. 9]. For further details see Ho [63, ch. 5, p. 40] and Barclay [36, p. 22] on Taiwan; Snodgrass [94, p. 61] on Ceylon; and Ingram [64, p. 130] on Thailand.

12. In equation 2.1′, the sign of the new coefficient of the import price, $a_2 - a_1$, is indeterminate both a priori and empirically (see estimation results in chapter 4).

gether, the export and import prices should reflect the macro profitability of an export economy.

Accumulated real government expenditures enters as a variable because the government is assumed to have been the crucial provider of the necessary infrastructure and social intermediate products associated with the development of an export economy. The growth of trade experienced by these economies would hardly have been possible without expenditures on harbors, wharves, culverts, road systems, railroads, and other public works as well as investments in administrative infrastructure, in health facilities such as malaria and yellow fever control, in the establishment of order through an organized police and army, and in various directly productive agrarian activities such as irrigation, artesian wells, disease research for crops, and communication facilities. Thus, accumulated real government expenditures provided the necessary colonial environment in which producers were able to respond to changing market incentives reflected by export and import prices. It was as if colonial technical progress was embodied within government expenditures, thereby providing a favorable "atmosphere" for the historic development of the export economy.

A major contribution of this study is the specification of government expenditures on the right-hand side of the export supply equation. Although previous studies have attested to the importance of government expenditures in opening up and sustaining the growth and development of the colonial economy, this study provides for the first time an econometric specification to measure quantitatively the linkage between the government and trade sectors of this economy. A priori, the expected sign of the coefficient of accumulated real government expenditures, a_3, is positive, indicating that these expenditures shifted the export supply schedule to the right.[13] The actual value of the coefficient provides a quantitative measure of the marginal productivity of colonial government expenditures in promoting real exports.

Government expenditures are not disaggregated by category basically because such a breakdown is available for only a few countries and then not always on an annual basis.[14] Even if a consistent break-

13. We explored the specific question of the time pattern of governmental expenditures impact by estimating equation 2.1 using alternative distributed lag structures. These estimates yielded results inferior to those derived using accumulated real government expenditures. The estimates in addition often violated the restrictions on the lag parameters or had coefficients with incorrect signs.

14. Some country data are available. See Anstey [35, pp. 628–36] on India;

down were available for all the colonies, there is no theory suggesting what is an export development expenditure and what is not. Therefore, for the questions and the macro approach involved in this study of colonial development, such a breakdown, even when available, is not used. For a particular country, however, depending upon the questions asked, there may be good reasons for separating, for example, expenditures for transport systems from those for administrative bureaucracy. The only adjustment taken with the aggregate view of government behavior in this study is to subtract expenditures neither directly nor indirectly connected with the development of an export economy, such as the royal household expenditures in Thailand.[15]

Private investment was omitted from the model not only because time series data were not available, but also because colonial government expenditures necessarily preceded or complemented private investment. Government expenditures built up the social infrastructure required to provide the proper colonial environment for profitable investment. In this sense, government expenditures provided the "big push" for private capital to invest profitably in the development of the export economy. Even where there exists qualitative historical information about private investment—as there does for bananas in Jamaica, sugar in Cuba and Taiwan, tea and rubber in Ceylon, nitrates and copper in Chile, and tin in Nigeria—government-built infrastructure, especially railroads, roads, and harbors, provided the required low-cost transportation for these profitable foreign investments.[16]

We tested whether or not lagged accumulated real government expenditures, $\sum_{i=1}^{\infty} G_{t-i}^R$, was a time variate in the supply equation. First, we replaced $\sum_{i=1}^{\infty} G_{t-i}^R$ with time and the results contained incorrect signs and high standard errors. Then, we included both $\sum_{i=1}^{\infty} G_{t-i}^R$ and time, and the time variate was insignificant while $\sum_{i=1}^{\infty} G_{t-i}^R$ remained

---

Eisner [49, pp. 360–65] on Jamaica; Ho [62, statistical appendix 9, Government] on Taiwan; Pina and Abed [83, pp. 195–211] on Cuba; Resnick [87, p. 28] on the Philippines; Siam, Ministry of Finance [114] on Thailand. See also League of Nations [113] for data on Chile, Cuba, Egypt, India, and Thailand from about 1928 to 1935.

15. Ingram [64, pp. 192–93].

16. See Bower [4, pp. 16–23] on Nigeria; CERP [45, pp. 165–66, 256] on Cuba; Eisner [49, pp. 284–85, 368] on Jamaica; Ho [63, ch. 4, pp. 20–57; ch. 5] on Taiwan; Reynolds [89, pp. 210–27] on Chile; and Snodgrass [94, p. 28] on Ceylon. See also chapter 3 of this book.

significant. The reason that the stock variable, accumulated real government expenditures, $\sum_{i=1}^{\infty} G_{t-i}^R$, is not a proxy variable for time is that it does not grow linearly over time. This nonlinearity results from major cyclical fluctuations as well as long-term growth rate changes in the flow variable, real government expenditures, G_t^R, used to calculate this stock variable.[17] For these reasons we rejected time as a variable in our model.

Lagged real exports are introduced into equation 2.1 to test for the possibility that there is a difference between short- and long-run supply response. Equation 2.1 is specified to allow for the possibility of a partial adjustment process.[18] The adjustment process could be caused by a lag between planting an export crop and its first production, or by a technical need to maintain production levels.[19] The supply equation 2.1 will be estimated with and without X_{t-1}^R and we leave the choice of whether or not to specify a partial adjustment process as an empirical question.

If producers base their export supply decisions on what they expect the export price to be, then an adaptive expectations process should be specified instead. The estimation equation for adaptive price expectations is nonlinear.[20] Estimation of this nonlinear equation yielded solutions which either violated the usual restriction on the coefficient of lagged real exports[21] or yielded coefficient estimates

17. See the appendix tables for both G^R and $\sum_{i=1}^{\infty} G_{t-1}^R$.

18. Johnston [69, pp. 300–301].

19. Snodgrass [94, pp. 36–39]. For example, Ceylon's major exports, tea and rubber, are tree crops with about a five-year lag between planting and first production. The premium quality of Ceylon's tea was maintained by continual picking.

20. To derive this conclusion, let P_{xt}^* be the expected export price and specify the long-run export supply equation as

$$\ln X_{S_t}^R = \tilde{a}_0 + \tilde{a}_1 \ln P_{xt}^* + \tilde{a}_2 \ln P_{mt} + \tilde{a}_3 \ln \sum_{i=1}^{\infty} G_{t-i}^R + \tilde{a}_5 DS_t$$

where $\tilde{a}_0$, $\tilde{a}_1$, $\tilde{a}_2$, $\tilde{a}_3$, and $\tilde{a}_5$ are long-run coefficients. Assume that price expectations are updated each year according to a linear function

$$P_{xt}^* - P_{xt-1}^* = (1 - a_4)(P_{xt} - P_{xt-1}^*) \qquad 0 \le a_4 < 1.$$

By eliminating expected prices from these two equations, the following nonlinear estimation equation is obtained

$$\ln X_{S_t}^R = \tilde{a}_0(1 - a_4) + a_1(1 - a_4) \ln P_{xt} + a_2(\ln P_{mt} - (1 - a_4) \ln P_{mt-1})$$

$$+ a_3 \left(\ln \sum_{i=1}^{\infty} G_{t-i}^R - (1 - a_4) \sum_{i=2}^{\infty} \ln G_{t-i}^R \right) + a_4 \ln X_{S_{t-1}}^R + a_5(DS_t - (1 - a_4)DS_{t-1}).$$

21. The restriction is $0 \le a_4 < 1$.

which made little economic sense. For those reasons, an adaptive price expectations process was rejected.

Equation 2.2 specifies that the demand for real exports is a function of the export price, the developed country's real income and its domestic prices, lagged real exports, and appropriate dummy variables:

$$\ln X_{D_t}^R = b_0 + b_1 \ln Px_t + b_2 \ln Y_t^R + b_3 \ln Pd_t$$
$$+ b_4 \ln X_{D_{t-1}}^R + b_5 D_{D_t} \quad (2.2)$$

where: X_D^R is the demand for total real commodity exports,

Y^R is real income in the developed country; for some countries industrial production, Q, is used,

Pd is the domestic price level in the developed country; when Y^R appears as a variable, Pd is the implicit GNP price deflator; when Q is used, a Pd was appropriately selected to reflect the commodities traded as either an import price index or a price index of raw materials, and

D_D is a dummy variable reflecting the effect of exogenous events on the demand function for colonial exports.

For countries with a variable exchange rate, the demand price is a new variable Px' defined by the additional equation,

$$\ln Px' = \ln Px + \ln \pi$$

where π is the exchange rate of the colony's currency relative to that of the developed country to which it is tied. As with the supply equation, the demand equation will be estimated with and without X_{t-1}^R in order to determine empirically whether a partial adjustment process is occurring. As we did with the supply equation, we investigated and rejected the possibility of adaptive price expectations in the demand equation.

The colony is not assumed to be a price taker. Instead a market clearing equation holds:

$$\ln X_{S_t}^R = \ln X_{D_t}^R \quad (2.3)$$

Export prices are then endogenous to the colonial development process. The terms of trade must also be endogenous to the colony because they are defined as the ratio of an endogenous export price to an exogenous import price.[22] This assumption is in contrast to much of the development literature, where export prices and the terms of

22. See Theil [97].

trade are assumed implicitly or explicitly to be exogenous to the developing world.

The alternative assumption of an exogenous export price was empirically tested by estimating each country's reduced form equation for the export price. Exogenous variables in the supply and demand equations for each country were significant and were therefore required to explain the export price. Thus the assumption of an exogenous export price was rejected,[23] and the use of simultaneous equations methods is necessary to estimate the demand equation as well as the supply equation.

The political and economic relationship between a developed country and its colony often led to a fairly high percentage of the colony's commodity export and import trade being carried on with the developed country and its other colonies (see tables 2.1 and 2.2). Exports to these other colonies were either for transshipment (e.g., entrepôt trade with Hong Kong and Singapore) or for direct consumption. The model assumes that the economic activity of these other colonies is reflected by and can be measured by that of the developed country. Therefore, the specification of equation 2.2 is based upon the empirical observation that colonial trade was primarily bilateral in nature; this, in turn, reflected the colonial political ties that we have already discussed. For this reason, competitive prices for alternative sources of export supply do not appear in the developed country's aggregate demand schedule, but a domestic price level is included to reflect substitution between domestic and imported goods.

The real incomes and domestic prices of the United Kingdom, the United States, and Japan are thus assumed to be the main driving forces or instruments affecting the economic activity of their colonies (see table 2.2). While the model focuses upon the principal trading relationships that emerged historically, adjustments to this approach are made when the export trade pattern showed an obvious change in direction.[24] For Ceylon, the variable *CAR* reflects the demand for rubber by the United States after about 1905.[25] The United States

23. The importance of specifying the export price as endogenous was originally motivated by estimates of the supply equation with the export price assumed exogenous. These estimates yielded negative, rather than positive, export price coefficients for most countries. This contradicts the econometric evidence in many development studies of supply responsiveness which have found positive supply coefficients.

24. The incomes and prices of other countries are assumed to have negligible effects, given the observed trading patterns (table 2.2).

25. Snodgrass [94, p. 39].

Table 2.1. Distribution of Exports for Selected Years

	Developed country	Percentage of Export Trade with Developed Country				Instruments corresponding to developed country[c]
		1900[a]	1913	1925	1938[b]	
Ceylon	United Kingdom and colonies	78.3	58.0	52.2	72.1	Y^R_{UK}, LIMIT
	United States	7.0	16.5	29.9	12.6	CAR
Chile	United States	3.9	21.0	39.2	30.0	Q_{US}, P^{mm}_{US}, RESTR
	United Kingdom	73.5	39.5	34.6	26.0	
Cuba	United States	76.8	79.9	74.6	80.7	Q_{US}, P^m_{US}, QUOTA
Egypt	United Kingdom	54.5	42.6	43.5	30.9	Y^R_{UK}, P_{UK}, WWI
India	United Kingdom and colonies	59.1	39.4	34.1	45.7	Q_{UK}, P^R_{UK}
Jamaica	United Kingdom and colonies	23.2	24.8	48.6	85.0	Q_{UK}, P_{UK}
	United States	63.8	57.4	40.7	3.7	RESTR
Nigeria	United Kingdom	31.4	50.9	54.7	50.0	Y^R_{UK}, P_{UK}
	Germany	55.8	41.8	21.3	17.7	WWI
Philippines	United States	40.0	34.4	73.0	77.0	Y^R_{US}, P_{US}, QUOTA
Taiwan	Japan	60.0	75.7	82.0	89.6	Y^R_{JP}, P_{JP}, WWI
Thailand	United Kingdom and colonies	85.5	83.2	74.6	79.0	Y^R_{UK}, P_{UK}

[a]The initial year used for Cuba is 1903; for Nigeria, 1901; for the Philippines, 1904; and for Thailand, 1901.
[b]The final year used for Chile, Cuba, and Egypt is 1937; for India, 1936; and for Taiwan, 1935.
[c]For definitions see table 2.5.
Sources: See the first page of the appendix.

Table 2.2. Distribution of Imports for Selected Years

		Percentage of import trade with developed country			
	Developed country	*1900*[a]	*1913*	*1925*	*1938*[b]
Ceylon	United Kingdom and colonies	93.5	86.0	79.3	67.1
Chile	United States	9.4	16.7	27.8	27.7
	United Kingdom	33.1	30.0	20.9	10.5
	Germany	26.7	24.6	11.1	25.8
Cuba	United States	40.5	53.7	63.0	68.6
Egypt	United Kingdom and colonies	43.5	36.6	31.9	26.6
	France[c]	9.3	9.2	9.5	5.2
India	United Kingdom and colonies	79.0	72.2	59.5	49.9
Jamaica	United Kingdom and colonies	56.4	49.2	36.2	47.6
	United States	41.6	46.8	38.1	21.2
Nigeria	United Kingdom	82.5	75.3	79.1	63.2
Philippines	United States	17.0	50.0	58.0	68.0
Taiwan	Japan	33.2	70.5	69.9	83.0
Thailand	United Kingdom and colonies	78.0	86.5	65.6	50.4

[a]The initial year for Cuba is 1903; for Nigeria, 1901; for the Philippines, 1904; and for Thailand, 1901.

[b]The final year for Chile, Cuba, and Egypt is 1937; for India, 1936; and for Taiwan, 1935.

[c]Includes Algeria.

Sources: See the first page of the appendix.

displaced the United Kingdom as Chile's principal trading partner at the start of the twentieth century, when copper exports were developed by three U.S. companies and when control of nitrate production shifted from United Kingdom to U.S. companies.[26] U.S. income and price variables are taken, then, as the main determinants of the demand function for Chile. The dummy *RESTR* accounts for the dramatic decline of Jamaica's trade with the United States after the imposition of the Hawley-Smoot Tariff in 1930.[27] The dummy *WWI*

26. See chapter 1, and also Pike [82, pp. 233–35] and Reynolds [89, ch. 1].
27. See table 2.1.

measures the impact of the complete cut off of Nigeria's trade with Germany during World War I. Before the war, almost half of Nigeria's total exports had been to Germany and about three quarters of her major export, palm products, went to Germany.[28]

The growth in real exports had as its dual the growth of real imports. The increased specialization of the colonial economy was reflected by a shift of resources from traditional activities into commercial ones. Correspondingly, the demand for foreign consumer, intermediate, and capital commodities expanded. Here, the opposite of an import-substitution policy was being pursued. Colonial policy was clearly biased toward the promotion of exports rather than indigenous manufacturing. As a result, the traditional industry associated with the previously agrarian society declined, and was replaced by the expansion of and reliance on imported manufactures.[29] From this process emerged the colonial trade pattern of exporting foods and raw materials in exchange for manufactures from the developed countries. Table 2.3 indicates that the previously discussed export trade ties of the colonies with the developed countries were reflected in the sources of colonial imports.

Equation 2.4 specifies that the demand function for real imports is a function of real exports, the import price, the export price, and appropriate dummy variables:

$$\ln M_t^R = c_1 \ln X_t^R + c_2 \ln Pm_t + c_3 \ln Px_t + c_4 D_{M_t} \qquad (2.4)$$

where: M^R is total real commodity imports by the colony, and

D_M is a dummy variable reflecting the impact of exogenous events on the colony's import function.

The dependence of the growth of real imports upon that of real exports is measured by the coefficient c_1. The appendix tables show that except for Jamaica the colonies had commodity trade surpluses in most years. Thus we cannot specify the identity that the countries balanced their commodity trade.[30] The coefficient provides a measure of the surplus or deficit in the colony's commodity trade balance. To derive this conclusion, we rewrite equation 2.4 in terms of nominal imports and nominal exports as

28. See USTC [120, pp. 340–43] and table 2.1.
29. See Resnick [28] and Ingram [64, pp. 112–19].
30. The unusable identity would be, in the model's notation,

$$\ln P_{x_t} + \ln X_t^R \equiv \ln Pm_t + \ln M_t^R$$

$$\ln M_t = c_1 \ln X_t + (c_2 + 1) \ln Pm_t$$
$$+ (c_3 - c_1) \ln Px_t + c_4 D_{M_t} \quad (2.4')$$

If $c_1 < 1$, then the colony ran a nominal trade surplus, while if $c_1 > 1$, it ran a nominal trade deficit. Equation 2.4 also explains how the commodity trade balance shifts over time. The coefficient c_2 is the import price elasticity of demand by the colony for developed countries' goods. The coefficient c_3 measures the shift of the demand schedule for real imports as export prices change. A priori, we expect the sign of c_2 to be negative and the sign of c_3 to be positive. With both the import and export prices scaled equal to one in 1913, the coefficients c_2 and c_3 describe how these prices change the nominal commodity trade balance of the colony relative to that in 1913.

We complete the trade sector with definitional equations for nominal commodity exports X_t, nominal commodity imports M_t, the terms of trade P_{T_t}, and the nominal trade balance B_{T_t}.[31]

$$\ln X_t = \ln X_t^R + \ln Px_t \quad (2.5)$$

$$\ln M_t = \ln M_t^R + \ln Pm_t \quad (2.6)$$

$$\ln P_{T_t} = \ln Px_t - \ln Pm_t \quad (2.7)$$

$$\ln B_{T_t} = \ln X_t - \ln M_t \quad (2.8)$$

Equation 2.8 defines a nominal trade surplus or deficit when $\ln B_T$ is respectively positive or negative.[32]

The Government Sector

The government sector has two behavioral equations describing first the generation of nominal government revenues from the direct and indirect taxation of real exports and nominal imports (equation 2.9), and second government expenditures, with some lag process from that revenue (equation 2.10).

$$\ln R_t = d_0 + d_1 \ln X_t^R + d_2 \ln M_t + d_3 D_{R_t} \quad (2.9)$$

$$\ln G_t = e_1 \ln R_t + e_2 \ln G_{t-1} + e_3 D_{G_t} \quad (2.10)$$

where: R is total nominal revenues generated in the colony,

31. The endogenous trade variables defined by equations 2.7 and 2.8 were not included in the paper by Birnberg and Resnick [3]. These additional variables are analyzed in this book and do not change the specification of the remaining ten equations which still form the complete behavioral model.

32. In the appendix, the nonlogarithmic nominal trade balance, $X - M$, is reported as the difference between nominal exports and nominal imports.

M is the colony's total nominal commodity imports,

G is the colony's nominal government expenditures, and

D_R and D_G are dummy variables reflecting the impact of exogenous events upon the colony's government revenue and expenditure functions respectively.

The expansion of real exports is assumed to generate revenues either directly from specific export taxes or indirectly, given that taxable real economic activity in the colony was in one way or another tied to real export activity. Revenues from nominal imports were derived directly from import duties and indirectly from taxes on commercial import activity.

A wide variety of taxes were imposed in these countries, but the revenues collected were mainly derived directly or indirectly from their main taxable economic activity, import and export trade. The obvious taxes relating to trade were import duties, export taxes, royalty payments on export products, capital export taxes, and profit taxes imposed on export and import trade. Less obvious, but also important in generating revenue, were land and property taxes on export producers, commodity trade taxes falling on imports (including sales and excise taxes), and government monopoly trade profits from imports such as tobacco, liquor, opium, and salt. Also of great importance were revenues from government enterprises serving the trade sector, including railroads, harbors, irrigation, and electric utilities. Overall, the historical evidence for all ten countries indicates that the revenue derived either directly or indirectly from the trade sector was quite high.[33] For research on a particular country, a disaggregate revenue approach may be possible, but since we are interested in making comparisons between countries, the aggregate revenue equation 2.9 is specified.

The appendix tables show that short-run surpluses and deficits occurred in each country's government budgets, but that in the long run they balanced their budgets. Equation 2.10 was specified to explain this behavior. Equation 2.10 can be derived from a revenue expectation model, where government spending in the current period depends

33. See Anstey [35, pp. 370–79, 628, 630] on India; CCA [41, pp. 354–62] on Cuba; Eisner [49, pp. 369–70] on Jamaica; Helleiner [61, pp. 209, 551] on Nigeria; Ho [63, ch. 3, pp. 9–11] on Taiwan; Ingram [64, pp. 181–85] on Thailand; Mead [77, p. 380] and Issawi [65, pp. 139–40] on Egypt; Resnick [87] on the Philippines; Snodgrass [94, p. 62] on Ceylon; and League of Nations [113] on Chile, Cuba, Egypt, India, and Thailand.

on expected revenue. An alternative derivation of equation 2.10 is that government expenditures are divided between recurrent expenditures, $e_2 \ln G_{t-1}$, and current expenditures, $e_1 \ln R$. This equation provides an empirical test of the hypothesis that the colonial government balanced its budget in the long run. Assuming that $G_t = G_{t-1}$ in the long-run, the government was running a surplus, balanced, or deficit budget according to whether $e_1 + e_2 \lessgtr 1$.

Real government expenditures in a given year are defined by[34]

$$\ln G_t^R = \ln G_t - \ln Pm_t \tag{2.11}$$

The price of imported goods is assumed to reflect the cost of government expenditures directed toward the promotion of the export economy for several reasons. First, almost all government capital goods had to be imported, as they were not produced by the countries. These imports were used to construct and equip transport systems such as railroads and road networks; port and harbor facilities; agrarian infrastructure such as irrigation and drainage works; communication facilities, initially telegraph lines, and then telephones; and electric power investments. These expenditures were to finance the export drive. Second, almost all intermediate goods were, of necessity, imported. These import requirements included fuels to run the government's capital projects and parts to maintain them.[35] This type of dependency of the government on imports is summarized in Ingram's work on Thailand: "As the country has come to rely on railway transportation, trucks, buses, electricity and irrigation works, the import of material and supplies to operate, maintain and replace this equipment has become more and more necessary." [36] Third, government employees, particularly colonial officers, spent a large share of their salaries on imported products. For example, Helleiner states that in Nigeria "government expenditures consisted largely of wages and salaries which were themselves spent in large part on imported consumer goods, especially to the extent that they were paid to expatriate civil servants; increases in wages of Nigeria labor, whether in the form of higher rates of pay or of greater employment, were also, however,

34. For some countries, we added to government expenditures in equation 2.11 the relatively small value of public works expenditures financed by borrowing abroad.

35. For further details on these two points, see the references cited in note 7 in this chapter.

36. Ingram [64, p. 131].

like increases in farm incomes, likely to produce increased imports of consumer goods." [37]

Lagged accumulated real government expenditures are calculated using the inventory formula

$$\sum_{i=1}^{\infty} G_{t-i}^R = \sum_{i=1}^{\infty} G_{T_0-i}^R + \sum_{i=T_0}^{t-1} G_i^R \qquad (2.12)$$

where T_0 is the earliest available year of data for G_t^R. Unlike equations 2.1 through 2.11, equation 2.12 is not log-linear. However, equation 2.12 can also be written in terms of the logarithms of the real government variables as

$$\ln \sum_{i=1}^{\infty} G_{t-i}^R = \ln \left(e^{\ln G_{t-1}^R} + e^{\ln \sum_{i=2}^{\infty} G_{t-i}^R} G_{t-i}^R \right) \qquad (2.12')$$

The initial stock of accumulated real government expenditures, $\sum_{i=1}^{\infty} G_{T_0-i}^R$, was calculated by first estimating the regression equation for the growth rate of G^R,

$$\ln G_t^R = a_0 + a_1 t \qquad t = T_0, T_0 + 1, \ldots, \tau$$

where τ is selected as the year with the longest consistent pattern of growth of G^R. For the base period used in this calculation for each country, see table 2.3, column 3. Let $\hat{a}_0$ and $\hat{a}_1$ be the estimated values of a_0 and a_1 from this regression. Then the estimated initial stock of accumulated real government expenditures can be calculated using the following inventory equation:

$$\sum_{i=1}^{\infty} G_{T_0-i}^R = \sum_{i=1}^{\infty} e^{\hat{a}_0} e^{(T_0-i)\hat{a}_1} = e^{\hat{a}_0 + T_0\hat{a}_1} \sum_{i=1}^{\infty} e^{-\hat{a}_1 i} = \frac{e^{\hat{a}_0 + T_0\hat{a}_1}}{e^{\hat{a}_1} - 1}$$

This base period calculation is necessary because there exist many substantial differences between the growth rate of real government expenditures for the country's estimation period (column 2 of table 2.3) and for its base period (column 4 of table 2.3). With the exception of Ceylon and Chile, the growth rate of real government expenditures was higher during the earlier years of development of these export economies.

Accumulated real government expenditures are not depreciated for several reasons. There exists no a priori information on the actual depreciation of these expenditures. If they are a measure of colonial

37. Helleiner [61, p. 23]. For further examples, see note 7 in this chapter.

Table 2.3. Estimation Periods and Growth Rates of Real Government Expenditures

	Equation estimation period		Initial base period	
	Years	Growth rate of real govt. Exp., G_t^R	Years	Growth rate of real govt. Exp., G_t^R
	(1)	(2)	(3)	(4)
Ceylon	1899–1918, 1920–1938	4.323	1891–1904	4.260
Chile	1892–1938	5.611	1888–1914	5.174
Cuba	1905–1937	2.733	1902–1910	6.182
Egypt	1893–1919, 1921–1937	1.988	1889–1897	4.035
India	1892–1936	1.599	1880–1898	2.452
Jamaica	1888–1938	2.184	1884–1896	4.820
Nigeria	1903–1937	2.157	1900–1914	9.032
Philippines	1904–1938	5.737	1902–1915	7.087
Taiwan	1906–1911, 1915–1919, 1922–1936	4.657	1900–1914	5.883
Thailand	1904–1910, 1913–1917, 1921–1936	3.674	1896–1905	15.329

technical progress, then no depreciation rate should be used. Nevertheless, we carefully checked the sensitivity of our supply equation estimates against those with assumed rates of depreciation. For a range of possible rates of 1 percent to 4 percent, we found small changes in the estimates. As the depreciation rate rose above 4 percent, the estimates became increasingly inferior.

SUMMARY OF THE MODEL

This system of twelve behavioral and definitional equations, 2.1 through 2.12, constitutes for each country an econometric representation of the circular flow of colonial development. To assist the reader, table 2.4 restates these equations in one location, and table 2.5 defines the variables in the model, the variables for specific developed countries, and the dummy variables. A graphic representation of this process is given in the arrow diagram, figure 2.1. This diagram shows how

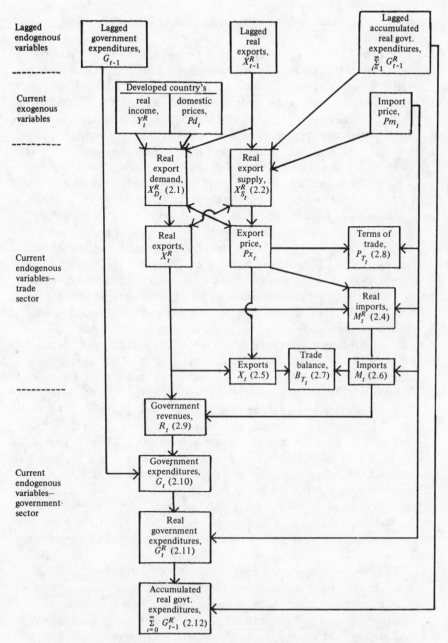

Figure 2.1. Arrow Diagram of Colonial Development. (Equation numbers are in parentheses; dummy variables and the exchange rate are omitted.)

each endogenous variable in the trade and government sectors is determined.

Arrows indicate where the lagged endogenous and current exogenous variables enter into the determination of the current endogenous variable and how the direction of causality is first through the endogenous variables in the trade sector and then through the endogenous variables in the government sector. The behavioral and definitional equations are indicated in parentheses. In outline, equation 2.1 indicates that shifts in the supply schedule for colonial real exports, X_S^R, are measured by increases in accumulated real government expenditures directed toward promoting the growth of real exports and by changes in import prices reflecting the costs of export production. In equation 2.2 shifts in the demand schedule for colonial real exports, X_D^R, are measured by changes in the real income, domestic prices, and trade policies of the developed country to which the colony is tied. The market clearing equation 2.3 specifies that the export price is endogenous to the colonial development process and is determined by the intersection of the colonial export supply and demand schedules. Thus equations 2.1 through 2.3 simultaneously determine the colony's real exports and export price. As the colonies did not balance their commodity trade, the colonial import demand equation 2.4 specifies that real imports shift with changes in real exports and export price. The trade sector is completed by equations 2.5 through 2.8 which define, respectively, nominal exports, nominal imports, the terms of trade, and the trade balance. Equation 2.9 specifies that nominal government revenues are generated from the direct and indirect taxation of real exports and nominal imports. The behavioral part of the model is completed by equation 2.10, which specifies that nominal government expenditures are a function of the government's current revenues and lagged expenditures. Equation 2.11 defines real government expenditures as nominal government expenditures deflated by the import price. The inventory formula for accumulating real government expenditures is given by equation 2.12.

The model provides for possible short-run distributed lag adjustments in the export supply, export demand, and government expenditures equations. However, the long-run circular structure of the colonial development process arises through the increase in accumulated real government expenditures, which promotes export development, which in turn generates further government revenues and expenditures.

Table 2.4. Econometric Model of Colonial Development

$$(2.1) \quad \ln S_{S_t}^R = a_0 + a_1 \ln Px_t + a_2 \ln Pm_t + a_3 \ln \sum_{i=1}^{\infty} G_{t-i}^R + a_4 \ln X_{S_{t-1}}^R + a_5 D_{S_t}$$

$$(2.2) \quad \ln X_{D_t}^R = b_0 + b_1 \ln Px_t + b_2 \ln Y_t^R + b_3 \ln Pd_t + b_4 \ln X_{D_{t-1}}^R + b_5 D_{D_t}$$

$$(2.3) \quad \ln X_{S_t}^R = \ln X_{D_t}^R$$

$$(2.4) \quad \ln M_t^R = c_1 \ln X_t^R + c_2 \ln Pm_t + c_3 \ln Px_t + c_4 D_{M_t}$$

$$(2.5) \quad \ln M_t = \ln M_t^R + \ln Pm_t$$

$$(2.6) \quad \ln X_t = \ln X_t^R + \ln Px_t$$

$$(2.7) \quad \ln P_{T_t} = \ln Px_t - \ln P_{m_t}$$

$$(2.8) \quad \ln B_{T_t} = \ln X_t - \ln M_t$$

$$(2.9) \quad \ln R_t = d_0 + d_1 \ln X_t^R + d_2 \ln M_t + d_3 D_{R_t}$$

$$(2.10) \quad \ln G_t = e_1 \ln R_t + e_2 \ln G_{t-1} + e_3 D_{G_t}$$

$$(2.11) \quad \ln G_t^R = \ln G_t - \ln P_{m_t}$$

$$(2.12) \quad \sum_{i=1}^{\infty} G_{t-i}^R = \sum_{i=1}^{\infty} G_{T_0-i}^R + \sum_{i=T_0}^{t-1} G_i^R$$

Table 2.5. Definition of Variables

Variables Specified in the Econometric Model

B_t	Nominal commodity trade balance
$D_{S_t}, D_{D_t}, D_{M_t},$ D_{R_t}, D_{G_t}	Dummy variables measuring the impact of exogenous events on the colony's export supply, export demand, import demand, revenue, and government expenditure functions, respectively[a]
G_t	Government expenditures
$\sum_{i=1}^{\infty} G_{t-i}^R$	Lagged sum of real government expenditures using 1913 prices

(Continued)

Table 2.5–*Continued*

Variables Specified in the Econometric Model (Continued)

$\sum\limits_{i=1}^{\infty} G^R_{T_0-i}$	Estimated value of accumulated real government expenditure using 1913 prices for base year T_0-1
M_t	Commodity imports
M^R_t	Real commodity imports in 1913 prices
Pd_t	Domestic price level in the developed country[a]
Pm_t	Paasche import price index with 1913 = 1
Px_t	Paasche export price index with 1913 = 1
P_{T_t}	Terms of trade with 1913 = 1
R_t	Government revenue
X_t	Commodity exports
X^R_t	Real commodity exports in 1913 prices
Y^R_t	Real GNP in the developed country[a]

[a]Detailed definitions for specific countries are listed later in this table.

Developed Country Variables

CAR	Motor vehicle factory sales, United States
P_{JP}	GNP price deflator with 1934–36 = 100, Japan
P_{UK}	National income price deflator with 1913–14 = 100, United Kingdom
P_{US}	GNP price deflator with 1929 = 100, United States
P^m_{US}	Fisher import price index with 1913 = 100, United States
P^{mm}_{US}	Import price index of crude materials with 1913 = 100, United States
P^R_{UK}	Saverback Statist price index of raw materials with 1913 = 100, United Kingdom
Q_{UK}	Index of industrial production excluding building with 1913 = 100, United Kingdom
Q_{US}	Index of manufacturing output with 1929 = 100, United States
Y^R_{JP}	Real GNP in millions of 1934–36 yen, Japan
Y^R_{UK}	Real net national income in millions of 1913–14 pounds, United Kingdom
Y^R_{US}	Real GNP in millions of 1929 dollars, United States

Table 2.5–*Continued*

Dummy Variables

FIXED	Thailand, tariffs fixed by the Bowring Treaty until 1926, and thereafter increasing tariffs, 1927–37
INCOME	Chile, increasing income taxes on copper producers, 1926–38
INFRA	Nigeria, completion of infrastructure projects—railroads to Northern Nigeria and port of Lagos—1917–38
LIMIT	Ceylon, international restriction scheme on rubber exports, 1935–38
NET	Change from gross to net railway revenues in Ceylon, 1929–38; India, 1906–36; Nigeria, 1927–38
QUOTA	Cuba, U.S. import sugar quotas and tariffs, 1930–37; Philippines, U.S. import sugar quotas, 1935–38
RAIL	Jamaica, government takeover of railroads, 1900–38
RESTR	U.S. import tariffs and restrictions in Chile, 1932–38; in Jamaica, 1932–38
TARIFF	New tariff schedules in Egypt, 1930–38; India, 1931–37
WORKS	Ceylon, expenditures include public works expenses, 1916–24
WWI	Effects of World War I in Ceylon, 1915–18; Egypt, 1915–18; Nigeria, 1915–21; Taiwan, 1915–19

3

Government Promotion of Exports

A major contribution of this study is specifying and measuring how government expenditures promote exports by shifting the export supply equation to the right over time. In this chapter we examine the qualitative evidence about these expenditures for each country in our sample. We find that there were a variety of government expenditures that did indeed increase exports in each country. However, the importance of specific expenditures varied. For example, irrigation was very important in Thailand, Taiwan, and Egypt, but not in the other seven countries. For some expenditures, such as for transportation, the direct relationship between government expenditures and increased exports can be readily explained. The qualitative information on the relationship between government expenditures and increased exports is most extensive for transportation expenditures on railroads, roads, and harbors and, in some countries, for irrigation and for agricultural research and extension. However, limited information exists about the effect on exports of government expenditures on social intermediate products such as education and health. We do not wish to imply that these expenditures were less important in the process of export development. Instead, our expenditures specification of the aggregate variable, accumulated real government expenditures, in the export supply equation 2.1 is designed to measure the export productivity of expenditures for social intermediate products as well as those expenditures for which there is greater qualitative evidence.

Cuba (1903–37). The two periods of U.S. military occupation, 1898–1902 and 1906–09, established the pattern of Cuban government expenditures directed toward the expansion of the export sector, with an emphasis on increasing sugar exports. The first military government emphasized expenditures for improved sanitation, expanded educational facilities, and the reconstruction of Cuba's infrastructure, particularly roads, railways, and harbors destroyed during the Cuban

War of Independence and the Spanish-American War. These expenditures on Cuba's social and physical capital accelerated the subsequent development of its export economy. Although the Foraker Amendment of 1899 specified that no commercial franchise could be given by the U.S. military government, one exception was made: the Cuban Central Railway was built with private American and British capital. It received the tacit approval of McKinley and was built using "revocable permits" from the military governor.[1]

U.S. political actions taken during the first military government also promoted increased sugar exports. As explained in chapter 1, the Platt Amendment was largely responsible for increased U.S. private investment in the Cuban sugar industry and was used to justify the second U.S. military government, 1906–09. This government emphasized construction of highways, railroads, and harbors. In response to a rapidly expanding transportation network and political stability, American capital flowed to Cuba, increasing sugar acreage, building new sugar mills and enlarging old ones. These capital expenditures caused a substantial increase in sugar production.[2]

The Cuban government continued to spend a substantial part of its revenues on the development of its export economy. From 1909–1925, Cuban government expenditures emphasized construction of the railroads, roads, harbors, sewers, telephones, and aqueducts used to promote the development of sugar exports. The development of Cuba's railroads was of particular importance to the expansion of the sugar export industry, with the construction of more than 2,000 kilometers of railroads. However, prior to 1925, transportation and communications in some areas were still limited. Despite the existence of numerous railroad lines, the cost of transport in these areas was still prohibitive. Construction of infrastructure as authorized under the 1925 Law of Public Works was designed to overcome this deficiency and increase exports. This law provided for aqueducts, roads, sewerage systems, bridges, hospitals, and, most important, the Central Highway. The Central Highway, built at a cost of over $100 million, lowered transportation costs for many products and greatly facilitated the movement of export products to market. During the

1. See p. 12 for initial conditions in Cuba. For details of public works expenditures during the first military government, see CERP [45, pp. 154–67, 190–91], Jenks [68, pp. 150–52], and Thomas [99, p. 438]. While the first military government allowed private capital to build the Central Railway, our period of analysis begins after the end of the first military government.
2. CERP [45, pp. 233–36].

1930s Cuban government expenditures continued to emphasize public works. Despite increasing emphasis on military expenditures, Cuba maintained an expensive public works program financed by special public works taxes and foreign loans.[3]

After the rapid increase of sugar exports in the first decade of the twentieth century, Cuba's whole economy became dependent on the level of sugar exports. The frequent fluctuations in sugar prices and quantities were reflected in the Cuban government sector. The volume of Cuban imports was closely related to its exports of sugar, which meant that customs revenues were directly and indirectly determined by sugar export volume and prices.[4] Customs revenues accounted for 70 to 80 percent of the total revenues of the government until the 1930s, when the sharp drop in Cuba's exports caused this share to decline to about 50 percent.[5] Thus, throughout the period under study, Cuba's revenues and therefore its expenditures were heavily dependent on sugar export volume and price. The sugar industry expanded rapidly until the mid-1920s, and therefore so did government revenues and expenditures. When the sugar industry contracted in the 1930s, government revenues and expenditures fell, too.[6] Thus from the history of Cuba we find that its expenditures heavily favored public works, which encouraged the expansion of export production, which led to the further growth of Cuban government revenues and expenditures due to the dependency of revenues on exports. It is this circular development process that is at the core of our model.

Chile (1892–1938). After taking the nitrate-producing areas from Bolivia and Peru in 1882,[7] the Chilean government set out to encourage the growth of nitrate exports and thereby to increase tax revenues collected from nitrates. The government levied an export tax on nitrate of about $12 per ton, which for many years averaged about half the selling value of nitrates. This tax provided as much as two-thirds of government revenues and remained, until the 1920s, the most important source of government revenues.[8]

3. For analysis and data on public works expenditures before 1925, see CERP [45, pp. 269–74, 377–82] and Thomas [99, pp. 504–7, 555]. CERP [45, pp. 193, 215, 233–36] and CCA [41, pp. 9, 49, 368–72] analyze expenditures authorized by the Law of Public Works.
4. For an analysis of Cuban dependence on sugar exports, see CERP [45, pp. 233–39] and Wright [101, pp. 149–53].
5. CERP [45, p. 218] and League of Nations [113, ch. 41, p. 4].
6. See tables A.11 and A.13.
7. See p. 11.
8. For details on the taxation of nitrates see Stocking and Watkins [96, pp. 118–20].

The Chilean government used a portion of its increased revenues from nitrates to build infrastructure in the nitrate-producing areas in order to promote nitrate exports. Nitrate production was expanded by Chilean government expenditures and foreign capital. The government in particular used revenues from nitrate exports to build roads, railroads, aqueducts, harbors, schools, and other forms of overhead capital.[9] Public railroads rapidly became more important than private railways; from 1893 to 1913, government-owned railroads increased from 1,106 to 5,207 kilometers, while private railroads increased from 1,765 to 2,872 kilometers.[10]

Besides encouraging exports through the construction of infrastructure, the government also used its expenditures to maintain law and order so that nitrate production could continue undisturbed. Throughout the 1890s the government maintained high military expenditures because of the threat of a war with Peru or Argentina over control of the nitrate areas. In the early years of the twentieth century, for fear of losing foreign capital in the northern nitrate mines, the military was also used to break strikes in the nitrate mines.[11]

Both because it was a monopoly product in strong worldwide demand and because of government expenditures on infrastructure and domestic order, nitrate exports increased greatly. Until the close of World War I, the demand for Chilean sodium nitrate helped expand its exports and therefore increased government expenditures financed by the nitrate tax. However, in the 1920s copper displaced nitrates as Chile's principal export. After World War I, nitrate exports began declining due to increased competition from synthetic and by-product nitrate production. At the same time, due to improvements in copper refining technology, Chilean copper production was rapidly expanding. U.S. firms quickly increased their investments in Chilean copper because of Chile's political stability, low tax on copper profits, established copper industry, and existing government-built infrastructure. Three mines owned by U.S. companies dominated the Chilean copper industry.[12]

9. See USTC [119, pp. 107–22] for a history of the Chilean nitrate industry and the government's role in promoting nitrate production.

10. Chile [104].

11. On the control of labor unrest in Chile, see Pike [82, pp. 101–11]. The Chilean boundary disputes with Peru and Argentina are described in Pike [82, pp. 123–26].

12. For a history of the decline of nitrates and the rise of the U.S. copper industry in Chile, see Reynolds [89, pp. 210–21].

Although Chilean capital did not develop most of Chile's copper industry, the Chilean government raised taxes as copper exports increased. In 1926 an increased tax on copper profits resulted in an immediate increase in revenues from direct taxation. Direct and indirect taxes on copper acted to offset decreased revenues from the declining nitrate industry.[13]

With these increased revenues from copper, the Chilean government increased expenditures directed toward an expanded export economy. In 1927 the Ibañez government adopted an expanded public works program. These expenditures on public works later had to be decreased due to the sharp fall in copper exports caused by U.S. trade restrictions. While Chile during the Great Depression did not immediately realize the gains from its expenditures on public works, the foundation was laid for further copper export expansion after the Great Depression ended.[14]

Philippines (1902–38). U.S. policy in the Philippines emphasized public works and other export-promoting expenditures, since a major U.S. objective was to expand its trade with the Philippines. This initial policy established a basic pattern: the Philippines used government expenditures to expand exports with an emphasis on education, communications, and transportation (especially highway construction). In fact, one of the first acts of the Philippine Commission was to allocate two million pesos for the construction of roads and bridges. A few years later, Governor Cameron Forbes became known as "the American road-building governor-general" because of his administration's extensive construction of roads, bridges, and ports.[15] Between 1916 and 1938, the government allocated on average about 54 percent of its budget to development expenditures; actual development expenditures rose from about 20 million pesos in 1916 to 60 million pesos in 1938.[16] Interestingly enough, only about 2 percent of total government expenditures went for national defense (although the proportion rose to about 10 percent from 1936 on), while about 27 percent of expenditures were allocated for education. Government investment expenditures averaged about 18 percent of the total

13. See Reynolds [89, pp. 227–32] for an analysis of the Chilean income tax on copper.
14. For details on the Law of Public Works, see Ellsworth [50, pp. 9, 16–17, 19–21] and Pike [82, pp. 196–200]. For details of Chile during the Great Depression, see chapter 9 and Reynolds [89, pp. 232–39].
15. Zaide [102, p. 264].
16. Resnick [88].

budget during American rule, rising from about 5 million pesos in 1906 to 37 million pesos in 1938. Most of this money was allocated to public works directly related to the growing export economy such as, in order of importance, public highways and bridges; docks, wharves, and harbor improvements; and water control and irrigation systems. Rail facilities improved from about 200 kilometers of railway lines in 1903 to almost 1,400 kilometers in 1934.[17] Total kilometers of roads increased from about 400 in 1908 to 19,000 in 1938. Manila also became known for its modern piers serving ocean transport. In communications, the telegraph lines established by the Spanish in 1873 were increased threefold under U.S. rule, and a telephone system was established in 1905 that by 1935 made Manila one of the major cities in Asia in terms of telephone use.

As a result of these expenditures on infrastructure, agricultural output, particularly for export, increased rapidly.[18] From 1902 to 1914 the quantity of exports of sugar and coconut products more than doubled, with an increasing portion being exported to the United States.[19] Not only government expenditures but also U.S. trade policies facilitated an increase in Philippine exports. Until the 1930s these policies eliminated tariff and quota barriers, which increased U.S. demand for Philippine products, especially sugar. They also facilitated an increase of imports from the United States which acted as an incentive to further exports.[20] In later years, the Hawley-Smoot Tariff of 1931 protected Philippine exports to the United States. Although the Jones-Costigan Act of 1934 imposed a quota on U.S. imports of Philippine sugar, the restrictions on the Philippines were much less severe than those on Cuba.[21]

Increased trade with the United States combined with bilateral trade preferences with the United States caused customs revenues as a percentage of total revenue to decrease. However, customs always

17. In 1916, the Manila-Dagupan Railway was purchased by the government from British interests and became known as the Manila Railroad Company. A smaller railway in the south (the Cebu and Panay) was owned by private U.S. interests.

18. For details on American colonial policy and bureaucracy in the Philippines, see Corpuz [43, ch. 8, esp. pp. 161–64].

19. This conclusion was based on the data used to calculate the export price index for the Philippines. See also Salamanca [91, pp. 121, 135–39].

20. For further details see Resnick [28], Sicat [92, ch. 7, pp. 8–9], and USTC [120, pp. 580–600].

21. For an analysis of U.S. trade policies with the Philippines, see CERP [45, pp. 330–33], Power and Sicat [85, p. 14], Snodgrass [94, p. 44], and USTC [120, pp. 580–600]. For further analysis, see chapter 10.

remained significant to Philippine total revenue, and total revenue continued to grow during the period under study.[22] The government used this increasing revenue to finance its expenditures for schools, health facilities, transportation systems, and other aids to the export economy during the later years under study. Furthermore, Americans allowed the profits generated from the expansion of external trade to remain within the Philippines for reinvestment, especially in sugar centrals.[23]

Taiwan (1904–36). Taiwan lacked a modern transport system when the Japanese took over colonial control in 1895.[24] As this deficiency hindered the development of Taiwan's export economy, Japan in the early years of its rule allocated about 50 percent of colonial government expenditures in Taiwan for development projects. However, strong Taiwanese opposition to Japanese control hindered these early efforts. Further, between 1905 and 1914 the colonial government allotted an average of 17 percent of current expenditures for police to establish control. Once control was established, the adoption of the traditional pao-chia system of community organization allowed the colonial government to maintain order and political stability at very little expense.[25]

The colonial government spent much on transportation development designed to encourage exports, including the construction of railways, roads, harbors, and communication networks. By the 1920s all major railroad trunk lines were completed, making inexpensive transportation for export produce available to most parts of the island. Government expenditures were also used to build roads to encourage trade in outlying areas of Taiwan. Taiwan's harbors were improved by the government to handle a tremendous increase in trade activity. In order to insure that lack of shipping did not limit Taiwan's exports, the colonial government directly subsidized Japanese shipping companies. This caused almost all exports to be shipped to Japan. The colonial government also increased exports by constructing irrigation and drainage projects.[26]

Besides expenditures on transportation and irrigation, the government also promoted agricultural exports by allocating about 10 per-

22. USTC [120, p. 586] and table A.38, column 1.
23. Resnick [28, p. 71].
24. Ho [63, ch. 3, p. 45]. Also, see p. 13 of this study.
25. Ho [63, ch. 3, pp. 20–30].
26. For details on these infrastructure improvements see Barclay [36, pp. 26–27] and Ho [63, ch. 3, pp. 43–53; ch. 4, pp. 35–36].

cent of its expenditures to agricultural research, extension, and sub-sidies. The main agricultural concern of the Japanese in Taiwan was to increase Taiwanese production and export of the foods most in de-mand by Japan, rice and sugar. The government sought to aid rice production through direct investment, grants, and loans to build irri-gation facilities. Because of twenty years of sustained research, the government in the 1920s developed the Ponlai varieties of rice seed, which are particularly suited to Taiwan. Government research also resulted in improved cultivation techniques which, along with a supply of seeds, were disseminated at government expense through an island-wide agricultural extension system.[27]

The government's primary emphasis was on creating increased ex-ports of sugar. Beginning in 1902 it encouraged sugar export pro-duction through subsidies for planting sugar cane, for buying fer-tilizers, for constructing modern sugar refineries, and for clearing government land for sugar cultivation. The colonial government also aided sugar export expansion through land tax incentives, research and extension expenditures, regulations, and partial government owner-ship. Government experimental stations encouraged sugar cultiva-tion for export through the free distribution of cane shoots. In some cases, the government encouraged expansion of sugar produc-tion at the expense of rice production through its control of irriga-tion and subsidies.[28] Thus Japanese colonial government expenditures and policies were instrumental in determining not only the expansion of export crops but also the level of production of each crop. Govern-ment controls and monopolies[29] resulted in large sugar profits, which caused further Japanese private investment in the sugar industry. Ho concludes that "it is not surprising that the sugar companies seem to have had a high propensity to reinvest their profits considering that this is a characteristic that was much encouraged by the colonial gov-ernment, a very influential force among sugar producers." [30] The co-lonial government provided the "environment" for profitable foreign investment and used its controls, both formal and informal, to encour-age large reinvestment in sugar export enterprises.

The expenditures made by the colonial government on infrastruc-ture and agricultural subsidies proved to be extremely effective in in-

27. Ho [63, ch. 4].
28. For details on government promotion of sugar exports see Ho [63, ch. 3, pp. 43–44, 53–66; ch. 6, pp. 13–17] and Barclay [36, pp. 25–30].
29. See pp. 33–35.
30. Ho [63, ch. 5, pp. 64–65].

creasing export production. Throughout the period the government encouraged exports by building, maintaining, and subsidizing an infrastructure larger than the current needs of the island. This action provided the forward linkages necessary to increase agricultural export production. The completion of the rail network and feeder roads resulted in increased crop production. Better seeds, improved cultivation techniques, better knowledge, and an island-wide agricultural extension system accounted for a large increase in productivity for agricultural export crops. Improved strains of rice seeds and their increased availability led to a tremendous and immediate increase in rice yield per acre. Following the introduction in 1922 of the *horai* variety of Ponlai rice and new techniques of cultivation, average rice yield per acre increased substantially—a direct result of government expenditures on agricultural research. Especially after the mid-1920s, the colonial government's application of new agricultural technology strongly influenced the expansion of production for export. Ho finds that the government's successful efforts to increase fertilizer usage accounted for more than half of the increase in agricultural output between 1910 and 1935–39. Irrigation increased the yield per acre, brought more land under cultivation, and even made it possible to harvest more than one crop per year on over a third of the paddy land. Despite the dominance of rice, government efforts to increase sugar export production resulted in a more than sixfold increase in sugar exports from 1902 to 1910, with 75 percent of the 1910 production coming from newly improved mills favored by government subsidies.[31] In summary, "The colonial government can be considered the main catalytic agent accelerating Taiwan's agricultural growth." [32]

Before 1905, Taiwan received direct cash subsidies from Japan to develop infrastructure and increase exports. However, after 1905 payment of a sugar tax by Japan on imported Taiwanese sugar yielded Taiwan 56 million yen between 1905 and 1914. Increased exports, a result of government-built infrastructure, led directly to increased government revenues. The principal sources of increased revenues were the profits from government trade monopolies, surpluses of government enterprises including railroads, harbors, and sugar mills, and excise taxes on sugar and liquor. The growth in receipts of all these taxes was directly and indirectly tied to export growth.[33]

31. Barclay [36, pp. 26, 32–39] and Ho [63, ch. 3, pp. 57–60; ch. 4] analyze the causes of increased agricultural production in Taiwan.
    32. Ho [63, ch. 3, p. 47].
    33. Ho [63, ch. 3, pp. 3–14].

With greater revenues from increased export production, expenditures continued to increase and to be used to encourage agricultural export production. After absorbing about 50 percent of total government expenditures in the early years, development expenditures in later years were maintained at about 40 percent of total governmental expenditures. Because Taiwan had no defense expenditures until the late 1930s, the colonial government directed its entire efforts to internal affairs, especially promoting export production.[34] Thus throughout the period under study, Taiwan's colonial government used an extremely large portion of its resources to realize its goal of increased exports of the food crops most needed by Japan. The dynamic relationship of increased exports, increased revenues, and increased expenditures shows that the colonial government met this goal.

Ceylon (1897–1938). We described the export shift from coffee to tea in Ceylon from 1885 to 1900 in chapter 1. Rubber production expanded rapidly after the start of the twentieth century in response to strong worldwide demand for rubber.[35] Although government expenditures did much to encourage exports, government policy was to avoid interference with or restriction of the export sector.

Throughout the period being analyzed, Ceylonese government revenues from export and import duties formed a large and increasing component of total government revenues. Import duties, most of which were on imports by the modern export sector, formed the largest source of revenue. About 80 percent of revenue from export duties has been estimated to have been collected from the output of estates. Thus revenues, whether from exports or imports, related to the export sector of the economy. When exports and thus imports increased, government revenues and expenditures also increased. It was therefore to the colonial government's advantage, in terms of increasing future revenues, to allot expenditures in such a way as to expand its export economy. In the late 1890s, Ceylonese government revenues recovered due to increased tea exports, and Ceylon resumed heavy spending on public works projects. The government built several railways, improved Colombo harbor, and constructed irrigation facilities. Government expenditures chiefly provided services to the export sector. Apart from small defense expenditures and heavy ad-

34. Ho [63, ch. 3, pp. 14–21].
35. Rajaratnam [27, pp. 10–20] and Snodgrass [94, pp. 38–39].

ministrative costs, most expenditures—such as those for roads, rail-roads, and electricity—directly or indirectly aided the estates.[36]

Because government infrastructure for one export crop was in-herited by the next, and because of increased revenue from export growth, Ceylon needed to borrow very little from abroad. Thus inter-est on public debt took very little of the central government's expendi-tures.[37] Unlike the case in India, the government was free from heavy debt and defense payments, and had sufficient revenues to export growth.

Despite the role government expenditures played in the expansion of Ceylonese exports, the colonial requirement of a balanced budget limited Ceylon's fiscal policy. Snodgrass concludes that, as a result, "the colonial government took little interest in influencing economic trends via fiscal policy or the composition of its expenditures. Instead, it reacted passively to demands that it attend to the most basic needs of the colony, especially to those of the planters." [38]

Nigeria (1901–37). The previously described lack of modern in-frastructure in Nigeria in 1900 was rapidly corrected by the new British colonial government.[39] Government expenditures were highly concentrated in areas which would help increase exports. Initially, a primary requirement for expanding the export sector was the estab-lishment of British control. Resistance to the establishment of British control did occur, especially in the North until 1909. The mainte-nance of law and order accounted for a large proportion of govern-ment expenditures at first, but with the end of resistance, agricultural production increased as much of the population gradually shifted from fortified cities to villages and small towns.[40]

The government's principal contribution to developing an export economy was the building of infrastructure. In order to encourage the movement of commodities for export, the government built and operated railways to connect the interior and the coastal markets. The government built a railway system that was particularly designed to increase exports from the interior and to open new trading locations and mines. To further aid export development, the government also engaged in considerable construction and improvement of roads, har-

36. Rajaratnam [27, pp. 8–9] and Snodgrass [94, pp. 62–63].
37. Snodgrass [94, p. 63].
38. Snodgrass [94, p. 68].
39. See p. 9.
40. For details on the British conquest of Northern Nigeria, see Geary [57, pp. 210–30].

bors, and communications facilities. Realizing the value of a good harbor to promoting exports, the government began harbor work at Lagos in 1907. The eastern breakwater was completed in 1913, but not until the western breakwater became effective in late 1916 was the harbor opened for year-round use. The outbreak of World War I and a shortage of coal had caused cessation of dredging. However, local supplies of coal became available due to the development of the Udi coal field and the completion of the Eastern Railway in 1916. This local supply of coal enabled the dredgers to resume work on the Lagos bar and to maintain an adequate water depth. Even though opening the coal fields did not initially lead to coal exports, a local supply of coal was indirectly influential in expanding exports. It supplied crucial fuel for the harbor and dredging work in Lagos and for the operation of the railroad, both of which led directly to increases in exports.[41] Thus the Nigerian government used its expenditures to improve conditions in several different areas which, directly or indirectly, stimulated increased exports.

These efforts were quite successful as shown by the rapid growth of exports. Since the oil palm grows wild, the output of palm products increased as transportation costs to market decreased. Thus, road construction in the palm-producing areas of Southern Nigeria made it possible and profitable to export palm products from, and to import consumer goods into, previously remote areas. Government efforts at improving transport and communications thus helped expand the market possibilities for palm products, which acted as a stimulant to their collection for export. The completion of the Lagos-Kano railway line in 1912 and the Jebba bridge on that line in 1916 provided low-cost transportation for the first time between previously remote groundnut growing areas and the coastal markets. The result was that exports increased from prewar levels of less than 2,000 tons per year to over 50,000 tons in 1916. The construction of the railways also helped change the pattern of growing areas. With more areas accessible by good railroads, the great bulk of Nigerian cotton-growing gradually shifted from Western Nigeria to Northern Nigeria. Cotton was displaced in Western Nigeria from about 1905 onward by the more profitable cultivation of cocoa, spurred by strong worldwide demand and by the opening of roads in the cocoa areas. Thus roads and railways made it possible to grow the optimal export commodity in each

41. Geary [57, pp. 141–47, 253–57] and Helleiner [61, pp. 13–15, 228].

region. The railway system also provided low-cost transportation to the tin-producing areas of Nigeria, and as a result, Nigeria became an important tin-producing country.[42] With transportation cheaper and easier, goods could be easily and profitably moved to the coast for export. As a result, Nigeria's real exports continued to grow rapidly from about 7 million pounds in 1913 to 24 million pounds in 1937.[43] These increases can be traced directly to government-built infrastructure which made available low-cost transportation. Thus, its infrastructure was extremely significant in opening up Nigeria for economic development and for the export of its produce.

With this tremendous increase in exports, government revenues also increased. A large portion of government revenue derived, directly and indirectly, from foreign trade. As Helleiner explained, "The most striking feature of the Nigerian fiscal system . . . is the overwhelming share of the total contributed by the sector of the economy participating in foreign trade . . . . Import and export duties, produce sales taxes, and mining royalties other than coal . . . all are unmistakeably taxes on foreign trade." [44] Throughout the period under study, import duties were the most important source of tax revenue. Direct export duties, first imposed in 1916, were also a significant source of revenue.[45] The Nigerian government was willing and able to build its revenues by increased direct and indirect taxation of the trade sector, the most dynamic sector of its economy. These increased revenues were used by the colonial government of Nigeria to further expand its export economy. For example, increased peanut production for export resulted from the constant expansion of the peanut production area as new roads and railroads were completed in Northern Nigeria.[46]

However, governmental efforts to increase exports were not as large as possible. Despite these attempts to develop the export economy, administrative expenses were roughly as large as development expenditures. British control in Nigeria was also a factor limiting exports. We have already described, for example, how British rejection of palm oil plantations caused Nigeria to lose its dominant world position as a supplier of palm oil products by the 1930s.[47]

42. The expansionary effects of railway and road construction are analyzed in Helleiner [61, pp. 4–18; ch. 4] and Pim [25, pp. 16–19].
43. See table A.31, column 1.
44. Helleiner [61, pp. 207–8].
45. See Helleiner [61, pp. 206–30] for an analysis of Nigerian taxation.
46. Helleiner [61, pp. 111–12].
47. See pp. 19–20. See also Helleiner [61. p. 14].

Egypt (1891–1937). Construction of public works in Egypt under Ismail (1863–79) started the development of modern infrastructure in Egypt; the government built canals, harbors, bridges, railroads, and telegraph lines. Railroad construction in particular caused an increase in cotton and sugar exports, as the reduced transport cost to Alexandria provided an incentive to increase cultivation for export.[48]

Recognizing the role of a continuous water supply in increasing exports, Egypt under British control devoted large amounts of expenditures to irrigation. The completion of the Delta Barrage in 1890 and of the first Aswan Dam in 1902 were extremely important in increasing exports. The Delta Barrage was responsible for the cotton crop roughly doubling during the 1890s. At that time almost all Egyptian cotton grew in the delta area, serviced by irrigation from this project built with government funds. Not only did this water supply from the Delta Barrage increase output per acre, but also it increased the number of acres cultivated and, in some cases, the number of harvests per year. The effects of irrigation were obvious in extensions of crop area for all crops. Due to the increased availability of summer irrigation after completion of the Aswan Dam, the crop area for cotton rose by over 50 percent from 1900 to 1910.[49] Increased production of both exported and nonexported crops resulted from government expenditures on irrigation. Increased cultivation of consumption crops was important, because when the internal food supply was inadequate, cultivation of export crops was restricted by the Egyptian government. With an adequate level of consumption crops, the cultivation of export crops could continue without government restrictions.[50] These irrigation projects established a dependable year-round supply of water, and railroads built by the government provided the necessary low-cost transportation for export products.

However, government efforts to increase agricultural output and productivity through irrigation projects became less effective over time due to the increasing cost of extending cultivation to more marginal land and due to drainage problems. After 1900, government expenditures were used to build several large-scale irrigation works to extend perennial agriculture to Middle and Upper Egypt, but these projects resulted in less dramatic increases in agricultural production

48. Infrastructure improvement and export development under Ismail are analyzed by Crouchley [44, pp. 116–25, 131–39].
49. Crouchley [44, pp. 146–50, 264].
50. The relationship between the production of cotton and food crops is explained further in Crouchley [44, pp. 182–99, 210–13].

than did the earlier irrigation projects. Furthermore, from about 1900 to 1925 a decline in average productivity occurred due to soil impoverishment and insufficient drainage on irrigated land. When Egypt increased the water supply and water level with barrages and dams, the natural drainage system of the land was destroyed, and the inadequate drainage which resulted became a major problem when it led to a decrease in productivity. In 1913 Egypt began work on extensive drainage projects. The work was suspended during the war but resumed after it, and productivity began to recover after about 1925.[51] Thus, Egyptian efforts to increase agricultural production were limited by the need to correct drainage problems. In turn, the slower growth of agricultural production adversely affected the growth of exports.

Although government expenditures in building transportation also continued in the twentieth century, they progressed at a much slower pace, to the disadvantage of Egypt's export economy. Because of the influence of railroad interests, road construction was delayed until 1913 and progressed quite slowly. The development of roads to encourage exports was neglected: in 1936 Egypt had only 250 miles of paved roads and another 4,400 miles of dirt roads. The result was a road system often impassible after heavy rains and inadequate for heavy vehicles. Also, Egypt spent very little on railroad improvements between the end of World War I and 1937.[52] The Egyptian government failed to improve transportation services during the twentieth century as effectively as it had during the nineteenth century.

The increase in exports resulting from the government-financed infrastructure in turn brought about an increase in government revenues, the result that the Egyptian government originally sought. The increasing dependence of government revenues on the export sector, which was mainly the export of cotton, tended to tie all Egyptian trade to cotton. Cotton and its by-products accounted for 80 to 90 percent of the value of Egyptian exports, and they indirectly determined the value of imports, which produced a large part of government revenues. Therefore the government was able to increase its revenues through increases in cotton exports. The proportion of government tax receipts from customs duties (both on exports and im-

51. For details on irrigation and productivity changes in Egyptian agriculture, see Crouchley [44, pp. 150–61, 164–69, 219–23].
52. The slow improvement of Egyptian roads and railroads during the period 1900–37 is described in Crouchley [44, pp. 230–31] and Issawi [67, pp. 199–206].

ports) increased from 28 percent in 1900 to nearly 60 percent in 1938–39, and accounted for most of the threefold increase in revenues during this period. The increase in customs revenues before 1930 reflected increased import values, whereas after 1930 they reflected an increase in tariff rates which offset the drop in imports.[53] Until 1930 the government, by international treaty, was not free to alter its rates of customs duties; it could increase revenues only by using its expenditures to encourage an increase in exports. Barring a drop in export price due to supply growing much more rapidly than demand, the export value would thereby increase and would indirectly result in an increase in import value. Although the customs duty rates remained unchanged until 1930, the government increased its revenue by increasing the value to which these rates were applied. Thus, not only did increased exports account for a larger portion of government revenues, but also they became a stimulant for increased revenues in general.

While Egypt did try to expand its exports, debt and tribute payments dominated Egyptian expenditures and absorbed a significant share of its revenue gains from increased exports. Thus the revenue increases resulting from export increases could not freely be reinvested in the export sector, but were sent abroad. Egypt also was not free to increase revenues by taxing her foreign trade sector more heavily. Since international treaties prevented Egypt from increasing tariff rates, it had to depend on increases in the value of its exports and imports.[54] Once increases in the quantity of exports slowed down, Egypt had to depend on the world price for its cotton. Thus because of British limits on Egyptian revenues and the interest payments on debt incurred before 1880, Egypt was unable to reap all the benefits possible from the expansion of her export economy.

India (1890–1936). Before the period of study, the principal transportation improvement in India was the construction of 12,000 miles of railroads between 1859 and 1885. Those routes primarily satisfied military rather than economic considerations.[55]

Realizing the strong effect of transportation on increasing exports, the government during the period under study attempted to develop

53. See Crouchley [44, pp. 169–73, 236–37], Issawi [67, pp. 221–26], and Mead [77, pp. 14–15].
54. See pp. 22–23 for details on debt and tribute payments and on treaty limits on revenues. See also Marlowe [76, pp. 108–9] and USTC [120, pp. 292, 301–4].
55. See p. 7.

an integrated transportation network. Of particular importance is the period between 1885 and 1914, when railroad mileage tripled from 12,000 to 35,000, with construction emphasizing links and feeders to the principal export-producing areas in India. All railroad work stopped during World War I, and some lines were even dismantled to meet British war needs in the Middle East. Following the war the government again used its expenditures to improve rail transport. It repaired existing lines and extended the rail network to 43,000 miles by 1936, opening up large fertile areas for producing export commodities. But railroads were only part of the infrastructure needed to increase exports. Most railways were connected with several port cities and acted as links between the export-producing interior and export markets. Without adequate ports for moving exports out of India, these railways would be of little value. Thus government expenditures on port and harbor construction were necessary to transport the increased volume of exports and imports in the twentieth century.[56]

In response to improvements in infrastructure during the latter nineteenth century and early twentieth century, production for export —especially rice, wheat, coal, cotton, and jute—increased. The railroads were an important cause of increased export production. They were a major force in connecting the interior with world demand, and British investment which followed complemented these government efforts. Besides railroad construction, expenditures on irrigation increased yields, which increased exports.[57]

Customs revenues in India reflected much of the influence of export increases. As specified in the model, growth in imports was caused by growth in exports. In the earlier years under study, customs revenues were only a small portion of total government revenue, accounting for 5 percent in 1890, 7 percent in 1900, and 9 percent in 1910. However, in later years this proportion increased significantly to 14 percent in 1920 and 21 percent in 1930. Thus increased exports and imports, especially during the later years under study, became increasingly important in directly determining total government revenue. By

56. For details on the development of Indian railroads and ports, see Anstey [35, ch. 6, sections 2 and 4], and for railroad mileage see Great Britain, Board of Trade [107]. The western ports, Bombay and Karachi, were greatly improved in the early twentieth century and Bombay, Karachi, and Calcutta were improved after World War I.

57. See Anstey [35, p. 331 and ch. 6, sections 3 and 5] for details on the increased exports resulting from railroads and ports. See Anstey [35, ch. 7, sections 2 and 3] for details on increases in exports resulting from irrigation and miscellaneous government efforts.

1936 customs duties had replaced land taxes as the major source of government revenue.

Although land taxes dropped relative to customs duties, they increased absolutely. This increase resulted primarily from the increased land values generated by government-financed irrigation works. Further, the irrigation works themselves yielded a large profit to the government, and by making food production more stable they also reduced the government's expenditures for famine relief.[58] Thus through its expenditures on infrastructure to increase exports, the government both directly and indirectly brought about the increase in its own revenues. However, the United Kingdom also followed a policy of restricting Indian revenues, which limited expenditures for expansion of exports. The policy aimed at increasing revenues through expenditures to promote exports was not successful. The United Kingdom permitted few export duties and thus restricted India from obtaining revenue directly from exports.[59]

Besides limiting revenues, British controls discussed in chapter 1 limited expenditures and exercised a very conservative influence on India's development. Defense payments, debt payments, and administrative costs absorbed a large portion of Indian expenditures. The result was that Indian railroads and roads were inadequate for Indian needs and were a bottleneck for increased exports.[60]

Besides the direct restrictions imposed by United Kingdom control, the British presence in itself created more subtle pressures against Indian economic improvement. The color line in India and the widespread British assumption that Indians belonged to an inferior race tended to create an environment that discouraged Indian economic incentive. Several other social factors in India itself also worked against the expansion of their export economy. The caste system made it very difficult for certain castes to respond to economic incentives for increased export of products. Also, population growth in India was already becoming a problem by the 1920s. Because of the increase in the population growth rate, internal consumption increased more rapidly in the 1920s and 1930s, which in turn decreased the export of foodstuffs.[61]

58. For a discussion of the development of Indian revenues and expenditures, see Anstey [35, pp. 345–59 and ch. 14]; see also table A.23, column 2.

59. See Lamb [21, pp. 482–88] and USTC [120, pp. 292, 325–36] for details on British restraints on Indian tariffs.

60. See pp. 16–17, Anstey [35, pp. 129, 136, 142–43], and Lamb [21, pp. 488–95].

61. Anstey [35, pp. 40–41, 339] and Lamb [21, p. 479].

Jamaica (1886–1938). After the rebellion of 1865, the Jamaican colonial government undertook a public works program to make up for previous neglect and mismanagement. After 1880, the government substantially increased its expenditures on railroads, irrigation projects, and roads. By about 1890, these expenditures, which induced increased agricultural investment, had the desired effect of increasing exports.[62]

Jamaican government revenues were very dependent on the export economy. Between 1890 and 1930, about 60 percent of government revenue came from customs. The instability in Jamaican exports was the result of periods of poor demand and the adverse effects of hurricanes and earthquakes. Because of the instability in exports and correspondingly in imports, it was difficult to estimate future revenues and to adequately plan public works projects.[63]

Despite its revenue instability problems, the Jamaican colonial government continued work on export-promoting projects throughout the period. Administrative changes in the late nineteenth century resulted in reduced administrative and ecclesiastical expenses, leaving a rising share of expenditures available for development, including basic social services and public works. Public works accounted for about one-fourth of total government expenditures from 1890 to 1930. Jamaica also used foreign loans to help finance infrastructure improvements to aid exports. Government subsidies remained relatively small until the 1930s, when they increased sharply as a result of the huge railway deficit. These subsidies were for operating deficits and not for improvements in transportation. One limit on expenditures in Jamaica was the payment of debt charges. They were 13.6 percent of total expenditures in 1890 and 27.9 percent in 1910. This increase was mainly the result of the government's purchase of two private railroads in 1900 and secondarily due to the use of loans for public works during the nineties. Debt service fell to 14.5 percent of total expenditures by 1930.[64]

Limited revenue affected other government efforts to develop the export economy. For example, after 1902 the government attempted to improve agricultural technology, but agricultural research and extension work suffered from lack of funds and inadequately trained personnel. One way to increase expenditures had been to borrow, but

62. See p. 6.
63. See Eisner [49, pp. 365–71] for details on Jamaican government revenues.
64. See Eisner [49, pp. 358–65] for a disaggregate analysis of government expenditures.

beginning in the middle 1890s government borrowing was curtailed drastically due to the depression in the sugar industry and the cost of the Jamaican railway. After that, several hurricanes and the earthquake of 1907 required rebuilding of damaged public works. However, during the 1920s the government was able to finance further railway improvements, schools, water systems, and sewerage development.[65]

Despite continued efforts to promote exports, a combination of poor investments and natural disasters limited the benefits from these expenditures. For example, the government built roads in the 1890s to encourage exports. However, the foundations of these roads could not carry modern motor traffic. The heavier traffic, particularly after World War I, caused grooving which resulted in increased maintenance costs. The government started a major new road program in 1925, but progress was limited. As a result, in 1930 it prohibited the importing of motor vehicles weighing more than 1.5 tons. Thus the government paid high maintenance costs for roads which could not support heavier equipment for transporting exports.[66]

The Jamaican railway system was another example of poor investment. In August 1900 the railway became government property, and immediately government expenditures had to be used to bring the railway into working order. Even after these expenditures for improvements, railway receipts covered railway debt charges only partially before World War I and not at all after the war. The mountainous nature of the country led to extremely high railway working expense. The most important reason that these railroads failed was that their routes were badly located. The Montego Bay line drew little traffic, and the Annotto Bay to Port Antonio line had to compete with coastal transport.[67] Thus with railroads, as well as with roads, the infrastructure became a financial burden to the government instead of the asset it was intended to be. Further, instead of being able to use expenditures to create more infrastructure to promote exports, Jamaica had to use its expenditures to maintain, but not to correct, past mistakes.

Another major retarding force on Jamaican development, along with these poor investments, was the lack of a strong government commitment to export development: "What was needed was large

65. The fluctuations in government expenditures are described in Eisner [49, pp. 227, 285, 368–70].
66. Eisner [49, pp. 178–79].
67. Eisner [49, pp. 180–81].

public investment in irrigation, reclamation, drainage, terracing, conservation, afforestation, and feeder roads to make land available for the small farmers. Considerable headway was made with the investment in roads, but not much thought was given to other forms of public investment." [68] For example, Jamaica allocated less than 10 percent of its government expenditures for education. Of particular importance was an extreme deficiency in secondary school education. The result was a financial burden on the economy as it meant that most jobs requiring secondary or college graduates had to be filled with expatriate personnel. Eisner sums up the government's attitude: "Behind the government's failure to assume responsibility for economic development lay the failure on the part of Jamaicans to recognize the importance of public expenditure on education, on health and on public works. . . . The dominant creed was laissez-faire. The government's proper function was the maintenance of law and order, while economic development was best left to private enterprise." [69]

Thailand (1902–36). We described in chapter 1 the inadequate development of Thailand's transport prior to 1900.[70] Our period of study begins when government expenditures on railroads began to increase exports. The first major railroad, the Bangkok to Korat line, was completed in 1900. This line became the first major transportation link between the major port city Bangkok and the northeast section of the country. Between 1900 and 1910 the government began construction on lines to the North and to the South. Up through the 1920s railroad construction was the main area of government expenditures for increasing exports. The government-built railroads had quite a positive effect on exports of rice. The completion to Korat of the Northeast line in 1900 resulted in rapid increases in rice exports. When the North line was extended beyond Pitsanukok it also brought about immediate increases in rice from the North. Thus, when these railways brought cheap transportation to these areas for the first time, rice production for export quickly responded. Even in the traditional export area of the Central Plain, railways encouraged exports by transporting much of that area's rice at a lower cost than the water transportation used previously. This government-promoted growth of rice exports was quite significant for Thailand since rice production represented 60 to 70 percent of total exports throughout the period under

68. Eisner [49, pp. xx–xxii].
69. Eisner [49, p. 317].
70. See pp. 10–11. See also Ingram [64, pp. 79–80].

study. The appearance of railways also changed the proportion of the contribution of rice exports from different regions. In 1905–06, soon after the first rail lines were complete, only 2 percent of total rice exports originated outside the Central Plain. But by 1935, 20 percent of total exports came from the Northeast alone, a direct result of the Korat railroad and its extensions. Thailand therefore successfuly expanded exports by using government expenditures to build railroads.[71]

The limitations imposed by the Bowring Treaty (1856–1926) severely limited Thai revenues and expenditures.[72] In 1905 only 11 percent of revenues came from customs duties, while 38 percent came from opium and gambling. By 1926, customs duties were still only 11 percent of revenues. The stimulus to exports and thus imports caused by better rail transportation did not increase the proportion of customs revenues. From 1905 to 1926 the share of revenue from commercial services—the largest being the railroads—increased from 4 percent to 13 percent. However, opium remained the largest single source of revenue, accounting for 20 percent of the total in 1926. Because the tax structure was virtually frozen by the Bowring Treaty, revenue generated from increased exports thus had a limited effect on increasing total revenues. In 1926, the new treaty negotiated to replace the Bowring Treaty gave Thailand financial autonomy. A series of tariff increases from 1926 to 1935 raised import duties from 7 to 25 percent of total government revenue.[73]

Thailand's expenditures had been limited by the restrictions on available revenue. As a result, important projects frequently had to be postponed. For example, the loss in revenue from the abolition of gambling in 1917 meant that certain projects were not undertaken. Lack of funds was the principal factor which delayed the construction of irrigation works before World War I. Although plans were approved in 1913, increased costs during World War I and a lack of funds considerably slowed actual irrigation construction.[74] Thus the limits on revenues imposed by the British in turn limited Thai expenditures on projects, such as irrigation, which would have increased exports and revenues over time.

71. See Ingram [64, pp. 37–52, 85–87] for details on increased exports resulting from railways and irrigation.
72. See pp. 24–26.
73. Ingram [64, pp. 178–83].
74. For details on these postponed expenditures, see Ingram [64, pp. 80–84, 161].

Despite these revenue limitations, government capital expenditures averaged about 11 percent of ordinary expenditures during the period under analysis. These capital expenditures were for infrastructure geared to increasing exports, with railway construction emphasized before 1920, and irrigation work becoming important after 1920. Although limited funds were one cause of the delay of irrigation construction, the low priority it received from the Thai government was perhaps equally important. Funds were scarce, but Ingram concludes that the government could have done much more to encourage irrigation construction. Even after the costly crop failure of 1919–20 irrigation expenditures were not given high priority. As a result, irrigation was much below its potential in Thailand, so that in 1938 less than 7 percent of potentially irrigable land was irrigated.[75]

Another aspect of Thai governmental policy which reduced expenditures for irrigation and other public works was the government's insistence on capital projects paying for themselves. Thus, the government was extremely reluctant to make expenditures on infrastructure from which it could not reap direct revenues. It was therefore eager to build railroads, which yielded direct revenues to the government, but highways and irrigation works could not so directly yield revenues and so their construction was delayed. "Thus it was no accident that highway construction was retarded, and that those highways constructed did not compete with the railway." [76]

Another reason that the government limited expenditures to increase exports was British insistence on maintaining the international convertibility of the baht by having Thailand accumulate large currency reserves in London. These reserves tied up funds that could have been used to promote exports. This stress on stability limited the long-run development of the Thai economy.[77]

The government of Thailand maintained these conservative economic policies because of its fear of foreign intervention. It had been determined ever since 1850 to make sure that no foreign nation would use financial irresponsibility as a justification to intervention.[78] The government was extremely careful not to endanger its political independence by borrowing heavily or by having low currency reserves in case of an emergency. However, by stressing this goal so strongly,

75. Ingram [64, pp. 80–85, 194].
76. Ingram [64, pp. 174, 194].
77. See Ingram [64, pp. 170–81] for an analysis of Thailand's conservative monetary policy.
78. Ingram [64, pp. 195–96].

it allowed itself to lose much sovereignty to the United Kingdom and became subservient to British wishes. Although British control was not explicit, Thailand brought upon itself the foreign intervention which it sought to avoid.

If Thailand had just changed the perspective of its thinking, it could have done much more for its economy in the long run: "The provision of railways and irrigation works represents the major government effort to encourage rice production and export. The government has been severely criticized for not having done more to promote and improve agriculture." [79] The power of the British Financial Advisors in Thailand reinforced Thailand's conservative attitude toward economic development.[80]

Because of British control and the Thai government's outlook, Thailand was unable to take advantage of the dynamic process of productive government expenditures. Some railway construction was motivated by geopolitical considerations; the government was reluctant to build irrigation projects; and increased rice cultivation without improved technology resulted in a long-run decrease in yield per acre.[81] And of course, lack of revenue meant that many projects were delayed or never built, even though they would have been of substantial value in expanding Thailand's export economy.

79. Ingram [64, p. 87].
80. Ingram [64, p. 196]. For a detailed discussion of the British Financial Advisors, see p. 25 of this study.
81. Ingram [64, pp. 48–50, 85, 108].

4

Structural Estimation

The structural estimation of the econometric model described in chapter 2 is analyzed in this chapter. Equations 2.1 through 2.12 constitute a system of twelve equations in twelve unknowns (X_S^R, X_D^R, Px, M^R, X, M, R, P_T, B_T, G, G^R, and $\sum_{i=1}^{\infty} G_{t-i}^R$). Simultaneous equation methods need to be applied to the model in order to obtain consistent estimates of the model's behavioral equations—export supply (2.1), export demand (2.2), real imports (2.4), government revenues (2.9), and government expenditures (2.10). After briefly explaining why a particular econometric method was used, the chapter analyzes the estimated behavioral coefficients.

ESTIMATION METHOD

Initial estimation of the model using instrumental variable techniques revealed a well-defined pattern of serial correlation in the plotted residuals of most equations. This serial correlation posed serious problems for making reliable cross-country comparisons, for distinguishing between distributed lags and autoregressive errors, for dynamically simulating the model, and for judging the performance of the model in explaining the observed development pattern.

The estimation method described in supplement 4.1 was used to solve these problems caused by autocorrelated errors in a simultaneous equation system. All current and lagged endogenous variables in the autoregressive model were treated as endogenous.[1] Therefore,

---

1. This approach differs from the previous theoretical work of Dhrymes [7] and Fair [8]. They treat lagged endogenous variables as exogenous and use them as instrumental variables to adjust the current endogenous variables. Their estimations are consistent if it is assumed that the lagged endogenous variables are uncorrelated with the current errors. However, Fisher [9] has shown that, in general, this assumption is not true for simultaneous equations models.

these variables were instrumentally adjusted, taking into account the structural ordering of the model.[2] In our econometric model, structural ordering emphasizes that lagged exogenous variables rather than current exogenous variables should be used in the instrumental adjustment of lagged endogenous variables. Consistent estimates of the equation parameters were obtained using an iterative method for determining the value of the autoregressive parameter ρ. This method always converged to a value of ρ that satisfied the condition that its absolute value not exceed one, and it actually removed the first order serial correlation pattern in the data.[3] All the signs of the estimated coefficients are correct, and the standard errors of the coefficients and of the equations are rather low.

STRUCTURAL ESTIMATION RESULTS

The estimates of the five structural equations for each of the ten countries are reported in tables 4.1 through 4.7.[4] The definitions of the variables used in these tables are listed in table 2.5 at the end of chapter 2.

Lagged real exports, X_{t-1}^R , appears as an explanatory variable indicating the occurrence of a partial adjustment process in the export supply equations of Ceylon, Cuba, Nigeria, and Taiwan, and in the export demand equations of Chile, Nigeria, and the Philippines. For the remaining export supply and demand equations, lagged real exports was either insignificant or negative and so was dropped as an explanatory variable. It is important to emphasize that our aggregate specification of export supply and demand does not allow for a simple explanation of why distributed lags appear for one country and not for another.[5] The large supply coefficient for lagged real exports for Ceylon, .842, is to be expected since its two principal exports, tea

2. This method, called structurally ordered instrumental variables, was developed by Fisher [9] and by Mitchell and Fisher [24].

3. While this conclusion is based upon examination of the plots of the estimated residuals of the fifty equations estimated, an imperfect indicator of the degree of improvement is given by the Durbin-Watson statistic. Omitting the eight equations for which no autoregressive adjustment was needed, the average D.W. statistic was 1.23 before, and 1.94 after the adjustment.

4. We report the R^2 statistic because it is usually expected, even though its explanatory power in a simultaneous equation system cannot be relied upon.

5. This is not to deny that individual export crops might exhibit a distributed lag structure for land under cultivation. However, our model is for aggregate exports, not for land under cultivation for a particular crop. Chapter 2 explains why we conclude that no country exhibited adaptive price expectations for aggregate exports.

Table 4.1. Export Supply Equation Estimates
(Standard errors of estimated coefficients in parentheses)

	Constant	Logarithmic variables				Dummy variables	R^2	ρ	D.W.	S.E.
		Export price Px_t	Import price Pm_t	Acc. real govt. exp. $\sum_{i=1}^{\infty} G^R_{t-i}$	Lagged real exports X^R_{t-1}					
Ceylon	-4.15 (1.50)	.303 (.083)	-.144 (.096)	.349 (.183)	.842 (.137)	-.191 $LIMIT_t$ (.064)	.987	.000	2.02	.069
Chile	5.59 (2.38)	.321 (.291)	-.429 (.242)	.654 (.108)		-.437 $RESTR_t$ (.307)	.785	.412	1.99	.198
Cuba	.85 (2.28)	.273 (.218)	-.399 (.301)	.547 (.172)	.364 (.225)	-.479 $QUOTA_t$ (.172)	.842	.000	2.23	.129
Egypt	6.02 (0.88)	.267 (.198)	-.454 (.187)	.316 (.065)		.146 WWI_t (.138)	.542	.000	1.88	.111
India	14.89 (3.22)	.422 (.190)	-.286 (.149)	.267 (.127)			.754	.597	1.60	.077
Jamaica	4.10 (1.62)	.536 (.337)	-.665 (.280)	.606 (.095)		-.226 $RESTR_t$ (.151)	.709	.258	1.97	.148
Nigeria	1.76 (0.76)	.142 (.110)	-.233 (.108)	.361 (.129)	.495 (.159)	.268 $INFRA_t$ (.095) -.083 WWI_t (.039)	.982	.000	2.04	.069
Philippines	-.20 (0.92)	.268 (.225)	-.220 (.248)	.921 (.045)		-.173 $QUOTA_t$ (.068)	.965	.257	1.80	.110
Taiwan	-2.01 (2.96)	.363 (.222)	-.482 (.228)	.453 (.328)	.626 (.205)	.108 WWI_t (.041)	.982	-.243	2.11	.086
Thailand	2.52 (.45)	.158 (.217)	-.209 (.211)	.361 (.022)			.918	.000	2.12	.091

Table 4.2. Estimated Long-Run Export Supply Coefficients
for Countries with a Distributed Lag

	Logarithmic variables		
	Export price Px_t	Import price Pm_t	Acc. real govt. exp. $\sum_{i=1}^{\infty} G_{t-1}^R$
Ceylon	1.917	−.914	2.210
Cuba	.430	−.627	.860
Nigeria	.282	−.462	.715
Taiwan	.972	−1.292	1.212

and rubber, require about five years between initial planting and coming into full production. In addition, in order to maintain output quality, tea must be picked continually.[6] The distributed lag for real exports for Nigeria is primarily due to its exports of cocoa, which has about a seven-year lag between planting and production.[7] The distributed lags for real export supply for Cuba and Taiwan probably are caused by the fact that the supply of their principal export, sugar, was dominated by American and Japanese owned sugar companies. These companies, with their substantial fixed investments in sugar land and centrals (refineries), were either unable or unwilling to respond rapidly to changing sugar prices. Further, in both countries, the government and sugar growers' associations actively pursued policies designed to maintain sugar supplies.[8] It is plausible to expect no partial adjustment process for countries exporting annual crops or minerals as was the case for Egypt (whose principal export was cotton), Thailand (whose principal export was rice), and Chile (whose principal exports were copper and nitrates). India and the Philippines both had a more mixed export bundle,[9] and with their greater possibilities of substitution between exports, it is very difficult to

6. Snodgrass [94, pp. 36–39] and Rajaratnam [26, pp. 170–74].
7. Bateman [2].
8. CERP [45, pp. 239–42, 325–48] and Ho [63, ch. 4, pp. 59–63]. See also pp. 28–31, 34, and 59 of this study.
9. India exhibited the most heterogeneous export bundle of any country in our sample. Sugar did not become the principal export of the Philippines until the mid-1920s. Further, unlike Cuba and Taiwan, U.S. corporations did not play a dominant role in the Philippine sugar industry. Resnick [87].

Table 4.3. Export Demand Equation Estimates
(Standard errors of estimated coefficients in parentheses)

	Constant	Export price Px_t	Logarithmic variables: Developed country's real income	Developed country's domestic prices	Lagged real exports X^R_{t-1}	Dummy variables	R^2	ρ	D.W.	S.E.
Ceylon	9.89 (2.11)	-.411 (.084)	.787 $Y^R_{UK_t}$ (.283)	.255 CAR_t (.017)		-.210 $LIMIT_t$ (.078)	.985	.000	2.02	.069
Chile	7.40 (2.86)	-.989 (.237)	.516 Q_{US_t} (.141)	.755 $P^{mm}_{US_t}$ (.196)	.343 (.156)	-.539 $RESTR_t$ (.203)	.831	-.143	2.06	.175
Cuba	10.93 (1.11)	-.789 (.195)	.650 Q_{US_t} (.136)	1.162 $P^m_{US_t}$ (.289)		-.350 $QUOTA_t$ (.106)	.883	.351	1.78	.113
Egypt	3.52 (0.94)	-.228 (.065)	.882 $Y^R_{UK_t}$ (.123)	.169 P_{UK_t} (.077)		-.163 WWI_t (.051)	.687	.000	2.12	.092
India	18.04 (1.22)	-.214 (.167)	.604 Q_{UK_t} (.191)	.151 $P^R_{UK_t}$ (.152)			.716	.752	1.93	.083
Jamaica	10.04 (0.69)	-.451 (.200)	1.031 Q_{UK_t} (.159)	.236 $P^R_{UK_t}$ (.176)		-.121 $RESTR_t$ (.084)	.790	.136	1.94	.125
Nigeria	-.60 (1.18)	-.189 (.076)	.617 $Y^R_{UK_t}$ (.268)	.366 P_{UK_t} (.132)	.735 (.095)	-.097 WWI_t (.043)	.979	.000	2.09	.076
Philippines	3.14 (2.03)	-.498 (.212)	.424 $Y^R_{US_t}$ (.240)	.601 P_{US_t} (.267)	.592 (.179)	-.056 $QUOTA_t$ (.056)	.976	-.216	2.04	.090
Taiwan	2.21 (3.89)	-1.095 (.376)	1.650 $Y^R_{JP_t}$ (.344)	.287 P_{JP_t} (.299)		.171 WWI_t (.083)	.966	.802	2.07	.118
Thailand	-3.66 (1.70)	-.212 (.109)	1.093 $Y^R_{UK_t}$ (.221)	.736 P_{UK_t} (.090)			.899	.251	1.87	.087

Table 4.4. Estimated Long-Run Export Demand Coefficients
for Countries with a Distributed Lag

		Logarithmic variables	
	Export price Px_t	Developed country's real income	Developed country's domestic prices
Chile	−1.506	.785	1.149
Nigeria	−.712	2.329	1.380
Philippines	−1.221	1.039	1.473

measure an aggregate partial adjustment process for these two countries.

The probable cause of the distributed lags for real export demand arises from the importance of these countries as the major worldwide producers of certain commodities—palm oil products in Nigeria, nitrates in Chile and abaca (Manila hemp) in the Philippines. Technically, the partial adjustment process between desired demand and actual demand probably occurs on the demand side either because close substitutes were only developed over time or because alternative sources of supply were not readily available in the short run due to trade ties. Specifically, Nigeria was the world's largest producer of palm oil products until the 1930s, when the Belgian Congo became the principal producer.[10] Chile had a virtual monopoly in nitrates until the 1920s, when synthetic and by-product nitrogen production were developed.[11] Abaca, Manila hemp, was the strongest fiber for ropes until the development of synthetics in the late 1930s.[12] Unlike the Philippines, Cuba was the world's largest producer of sugar, and our results and economic history support the conclusion that the United States was able to shift the burden of the adjustment process onto sugar producers through its trade and tariff policies.[13]

The estimated export price coefficients in the supply equations indi-

10. See pp. 000–000.
11. See pp. 000 and 000. For extensive analyses, see USTC [119] and Stocking and Watkins [96, ch. 4].
12. Resnick [87].
13. U.S. controls, described on p. 000, made this shift possible. Chapters 9 and 10 will describe how Cuba was much more adversely affected than the Philippines during the 1930s by the depression and by U.S. trade restrictions. For further analysis, see CERP [45, chs. 16 and 26].

cate inelastic aggregate export supply schedules in colonial economies. The estimates vary in magnitude from .142 in Nigeria to .536 in Jamaica, with an average of .305. These are short-run supply elasticities for all countries, and also long-run supply elasticities for the six countries where no distributive lag process was discovered. For the four countries in which lagged real exports appear, long-run export price elasticity ranges from .282 in Nigeria to 1.917 in Ceylon, and averages .900. Ceylon's export supply was price inelastic in the short run because of the previously discussed technical conditions that limited short-run output adjustments in its principal exports, tea and rubber. However, its export supply was price elastic in the long run as the number and size of tea and rubber estates responded over time to the profitability of the estates in previous years.[14] Excluding Ceylon, the estimated aggregate export supply elasticity for the other nine countries is inelastic in the long run as well as in the short run. The average long-run export supply elasticity falls to .406 when Ceylon is excluded.[15]

The elasticity of demand for aggregate real exports is also typically inelastic with an average export price coefficient in the demand equation of −.511 in the short run for all ten countries. The long-run elasticity averages −1.145 for the three countries in which an adjustment process is present. If Chile is excluded on the grounds that the demand for its two main exports, copper and nitrate, is elastic, then the average (for Nigeria and the Philippines) falls to −.458 in the short run and −.967 in the long run.

The relatively inelastic export supply and demand schedules for a colonial economy when both curves are quite shiftable produce rather dramatic changes in the price of exports. Shifts in the supply schedule are measured by the coefficients of the import price and accumulated real government expenditures. The average short-run coefficient associated with the government variable is .484, and with the import price, −.352; for the four countries with an adjustment process, the long-run coefficients are respectively 1.251 and −.824. India has the lowest long-run elasticity associated with government expenditures, followed by Egypt and then by Thailand. In fact, these three countries

14. See Rajaratnam [27, pp. 6–20] and Rippy [29].

15. Of course, within the export sector there may be significant shifting of resources out of one export and into another as relative export prices change. This adjustment process would have been slower for the countries with a distributed lag adjustment process and would have been more limited the fewer the possible alternative exports.

seem to be in a relatively low government productivity group compared to the other countries, the average long-run government elasticity being 1.025 for the other seven and .315 for India, Egypt, and Thailand. Chapters 1 and 3 present some historical evidence to support the finding of relatively low government productivity for these three countries. On average, almost one half of the Indian budget in this period was devoted to military expenditures, and thus a low coefficient is not surprising.[16] Egypt had the slowest growth rate of real exports of all ten countries; much of its government expenditures were allocated to the required interest payments on previous international loans rather than devoted toward development.[17] The Thai government was constrained from controlling and utilizing government expenditures for productive investments by British financial control.[18]

The wide range of estimated coefficients of accumulated real government expenditures indicates that these expenditures had different export-promoting effects. Thus, the values of these coefficients are equally important in explaining the low export growth of India (which had the lowest coefficient) as in explaining the high export growth of Ceylon and the Philippines (which had the highest coefficients). This result shows that the government must be included in explaining the development of a colonial export economy and that to ignore or omit this relationship would lead to a major misspecification error. The importance of the government sector will be discussed in more detail in chapter 7.

Shifts in the demand schedule facing the colony are measured by the coefficients of real income and domestic prices in the developed country. The average real income elasticity of demand for colonial exports is .825 in the short run and 1.384 in the long run for Chile, Nigeria, and the Philippines in which lagged real exports appears in their export demand equations. For all ten countries the average long-run income elasticity is 1.085, which indicates the important influence of income growth in the developed countries upon export growth in the colonial countries. The average elasticity of substitution between home and colonial commodities in the developed countries is .391 in the short run and in the three countries with lagged real exports it is 1.334 in the long run. Examining these substitution elas-

16. See pp. 16–17 and 73–75.
17. See pp. 22–24 and 71–73.
18. See pp. 24–26 and 79–81.

ticities by colonial blocs suggests that those countries which were tied to the United States had higher substitution effects than countries tied to the United Kingdom or Japan. For the United States there was more substitution between domestic goods and imports from colonies (copper from Chile and cane sugar from Cuba and the Philippines) than in either the United Kingdom or Japan. The model would predict, then, that ceteris paribus, a fall in U.S. prices would shift the demand schedule for goods from its colonies to the left more than an equivalent fall in prices in the United Kingdom or Japan. For this reason, the world depression of the 1930s had a more dramatic effect on Chile, Cuba, and the Philippines than on the other seven countries.[19] In contrast, table 4.3 indicates that the real income effects of the United Kingdom and Japan were more important than their price levels in influencing real export activity in their trade-dependent countries.

The remaining variables in the supply and demand schedules are the dummy variables. They are specific to the economic history of a particular country and measure the impact of World War I or of an imposed tariff, quota, or restriction scheme. The dummies all have the proper signs and are generally large in magnitude. The depressing effects of the restrictive trade policies pursued by the United States during the 1930s are measured by the dummies *RESTR* for Chile and *QUOTA* for Cuba and the Philippines.[20] Since prices and real income were falling in the United States during the Great Depression,[21] the imposition of these restrictions on trade compounded the difficulties experienced in these three countries tied to the United States as compared with the countries tied to the United Kingdom or Japan. Interestingly enough, the U.S. trade restrictions on the Philippines were less severe and were imposed somewhat later in the depression years than the restrictions on Cuba and Chile.[22] This partial evidence suggests, at least for these countries linked to the United States, that legal colonialism as exemplified by the Philippines acted to mitigate the impact of U.S. trade restrictions pursued during the 1930s.

19. This will be discussed in detail in chapter 9.
20. For Chile, see Reynolds [89, pp. 232–33]. For Cuba, see CCA [41, pp. 61–62] and CERP [45, pp. 333–34]. The imposition of a quota on the Philippines' sugar exports in 1934 led sugar producers to burn their fields. The overall effect of the quota was a 17 percent decline in the Philippines' supply of real exports.
21. See appendix table A.52.
22. Chapter 10 will analyze these U.S. trade restrictions in detail.

The results also indicate that similar dummy variables used in different countries need not have the same sign. For example, World War I increased the supply of real exports from Taiwan because Japan was not a belligerent. Nigerian exports suffered because trade with Germany, one of its main export markets, was completely cut off until 1922.[23] In only two countries, India and Thailand, was there no evidence to suggest the use of appropriate dummy variables reflecting either the impact of World War I or the serious trade restrictions imposed during the depression. The economic changes measured by these dummy variables will be analyzed in greater detail in chapter 9.

In the import equation, the average coefficient of real exports is .981 (table 4.5) which indicates that, ceteris paribus, the growth of real exports in each colony did produce a corresponding increased demand for imported commodities. Moreover, this coefficient indicates that on the average the colonies ran a nominal trade surplus over this historical period. This result agrees with their actual balance of trade. Jamaica is the only country with an estimated coefficient of real exports that is greater than one. Actual trade data supports this result: Jamaica is the only country with a nominal trade deficit, primarily a result of the tourist trade and remittances from emigrant Jamaicans.[24] Thailand's coefficient is the lowest of all ten countries. This result is also supported by the trade data. Thailand had relatively the largest nominal trade surpluses of the ten countries in our sample. Appendix table A.46 shows that Thailand had a large nominal trade surplus in every year except 1920, when a deficit occurred because rice exports were forbidden due to a severe drought.[25] The other eight countries had nominal trade surpluses in most years.[26] In addition, over the sample period, only Jamaica had a cumulative nominal trade deficit. The average import price elasticity of demand is −.418, once again revealing inelastic demand schedules but this time for imports of the developed countries' goods. The average coefficient associated with the export price in the import equation is .454, indicating that increased export earnings due to an export price increase resulted in a relatively smaller increase in imports.

23. See table 2.1 and USTC [120, pp. 340–42].
24. Eisner [49, pp. 283, 288–89]. Appendix table A.26 shows that Jamaica had a commodity trade surplus for 44 out of the 53 years in the sample period.
25. These trade surpluses financed the desired accumulation of exchange reserves in London (see p. 80). The deficit of 1920 is further explained in Ingram [64, pp. 156–57]. For further analysis of the causes of the trade surpluses, see Ingram [64, pp. 202–7].
26. See the appendix tables.

Table 4.5. Import Demand Equation Estimates
(Standard errors of estimated coefficients in parentheses)

| | Logarithmic variables | | | World War I dummy variable WWI_t | R^2 | ρ | D.W. | S.E. |
	Real exports X_t^R	Import price Pm_t	Export price Px_t					
Ceylon	.983 (.007)	−.366 (.147)	.334 (.127)	−.204 (.066)	.946	.903	2.12	.080
Chile	.980 (.004)	−.471 (.231)	.758 (.195)		.779	.297	1.94	.212
Cuba	.985 (.006)	−.135 (.336)	.330 (.246)		.797	.749	1.81	.142
Egypt	.986 (.010)	−.403 (.373)	.277 (.341)	−.177 (.229)	.837	.727	2.30	.174
India	.979 (.003)	−.450 (.278)	.405 (.337)		.815	.666	1.80	.124
Jamaica	1.018 (.010)	−.581 (.319)	.855 (.371)		.869	.850	2.34	.152
Nigeria	.994 (.009)	−.941 (.173)	.750 (.206)	−.259 (.099)	.809	.720	2.02	.119
Philippines	.986 (.003)	−.024 (.242)	.256 (.201)		.941	.421	1.86	.129
Taiwan	.975 (.004)	−.288 (.267)	.182 (.304)		.967	.504	1.52	.114
Thailand	.928 (.025)	−.548 (.316)	.416 (.270)		.903	.822	2.12	.121

The revenue equation shows that the average contribution of real exports to nominal revenues (.564) is slightly higher than that of nominal imports (.435). However, the marginal contribution of real exports varies from a low of .230 in Thailand to a high of .966 in Cuba, and the marginal contribution of nominal imports varies from a low of .151 in Cuba to .813 in India (table 4.6).

A measure of the total tax effort is the sum of the coefficients of real exports and imports in the revenue equation. The average sum for these two coefficients for the ten countries is .999, which suggests in general a constant returns to scale revenue function. For six countries—Ceylon, Chile, Cuba, India, Jamaica, and the Philippines—the sum of these two coefficients is not significantly different from one. We conclude that for these countries there existed a constant returns to scale revenue function. For these six countries, the growth of government revenues paralleled the growth of real exports and imports. However, the average sum of the coefficients for Thailand and Taiwan is .564. Compared with the other eight countries, where the average sum is 1.108, it appears that the colonial tax efforts in Taiwan and Thailand were not strong enough. Thailand's low total tax effort occurred as a result of the tax limitations imposed by the Bowring Treaty with the United Kingdom.[27] Since nearly all of Taiwan's trade was with Japan (see tables 2.1 and 2.2), the Japanese colonial government kept tariffs at low levels. As a result, customs duties were only about 10 percent of government revenues in Taiwan.[28] The rapid growth of real exports and imports of Taiwan[29] far exceeded the growth of its government revenues not only because tariffs were kept low, but also because indirect taxes on the trade sector grew more slowly than the trade sector.[30] In the revenue equation, the sum of Nigeria's coefficients of real exports and imports, 1.376, is the largest of all ten countries. The explanation for Nigeria's increasing tax effort is that as export development proceeded, the Nigerian colonial government was able to both adopt new taxes and increase existing taxes.[31] The sum of Egypt's coefficients, 1.247, is next largest and Egypt's increasing tax effort can be explained by its need to meet interest payments on its large international debt at the same time that it used its revenue to finance dams, irrigation and railroad construc-

27. See pp. 24–26 and 79–81.
28. Ho [63, ch. 3, pp. 8–10] and Ho [62, appendix table IX-I-A].
29. See table A.41, columns 1 and 4.
30. Ho [62, appendix table IX-I-A].
31. Pim [25, pp. 227–37].

Table 4.6. Government Revenue Equation Estimates
(Standard errors of estimated coefficients in parentheses)

		Logarithmic variables		Dummy variables					
	Constant	Real Exports	Imports	Taxation	Accounting	R^2	ρ	D.W.	S.E.
Ceylon	-0.26 (1.24)	.754 (.123)	.192 (.133)		-.037 $WORKS_t$ (.060) -.039 NET_t (.085)	.973	.510	2.01	.088
Chile	-0.98 (2.05)	.830 (.151)	.182 (.092)	.071 $INCOME_t$ (.016)		.935	.444	1.93	.150
Cuba	-3.11 (2.03)	.966 (.128)	.151 (.065)			.860	.230	1.93	.144
Egypt	-2.80 (2.72)	.636 (.238)	.611 (.081)	.032 $TARIFF_t$ (.025)		.945	.650	2.04	.116
India	-1.83 (4.37)	.278 (.224)	.813 (.102)	.564 $TARIFF_t$ (.072)	-.333 NET_t (.089)	.920	.443	1.85	.091
Jamaica	-0.58 (0.94)	.353 (.080)	.627 (.038)		.152 $RAIL_t$ (.040)	.976	.250	2.01	.068
Nigeria	-6.85 (1.21)	.889 (.113)	.487 (.075)		-.262 NET_t (.086)	.979	.441	1.80	.091
Philippines	-0.43 (0.92)	.388 (.074)	.603 (.082)			.964	.313	1.94	.101
Taiwan	5.01 (1.18)	.314 (.172)	.357 (.160)			.940	.411	2.20	.117
Thailand	1.70 (0.86)	.230 (.199)	.325 (.080)	.020 $FIXED_t$ (.010)		.960	.526	2.16	.058

tion, and other infrastructure improvements needed to promote export development.[32]

Some of the dummy variables in the revenue equation measure changes in tax effort. The dummy variable *INCOME* measures the revenue gain from the imposition of increasing income and other taxes on copper in Chile from 1926 to 1938.[33] The dummy variable *FIXED* measures the revenue gain from increasing import duties in Thailand from 1927 to 1938 after the restrictions of the Bowring Treaty were dropped.[34] The dummy variable *TARIFF* measures the revenue gain from increased tariffs in Egypt from 1930 to 1937 and in India from 1931 to 1937.[35] Chapter 10 will analyze in detail these increases in taxes. Accounting dummy variables were also introduced into the revenue equations of Ceylon, India, Jamaica, and Nigeria to reflect changes in accounting practices by their governments. The accounting dummy *NET* in Ceylon, India, and Nigeria indicates a shift from including gross revenue (and expenditure) from railroad operations to including only net revenue from railroads.[36] In Jamaica, the accounting dummy *RAIL* reflects the government takeover of two private railroads in 1900.[37] In Ceylon, revenues from 1916–24 excluded public works expenditures.

The results of the expenditure equation show that all ten colonial governments ran a balanced budget in the long run (table 4.7). The average short-run revenue elasticity is .637 and the average elasticity associated with lagged expenditures is .362. For each of the ten countries, the resulting long-run revenue elasticity is very close to 1. This is consistent with the underlying data reported in the appendix, which indicate that each colonial government did indeed run a balanced budget in the long run. There is, however, significant variation in the distribution between current and recurrent nominal expenditures for the ten countries. India and Taiwan form one bloc where expenditures were financed almost entirely out of current revenues. For the other eight countries, recurrent expenditures were much more important.

32. Crouchley [44, pp. 145–49, 235–37] describes these conflicting claims on Egyptian revenues. See also chapter 3, pp. 106–7.
33. Reynolds [89, pp. 227–36].
34. Ingram [64, pp. 178–83], and pp. 00–00 and 000–00 of this study.
35. Anstey [35, pp. 504–5] and Crouchley [44, pp. 233–34].
36. For details, see the revenue tables covering the years in which changes occurred in the *Statistical Abstract for the British Empire,* Great Britain, Board of Trade [107].
37. See p. 76 and Eisner [49, pp. 180–81, 194].

Table 4.7. Government Expenditures Equation Estimates
(Standard errors of estimated coefficients in parentheses)

	Logarithmic variables		Accounting dummy WORKS$_t$	R^2	ρ	D.W.	S.E.	Estimated long-run coefficient government expenditures G$_t$
	Government revenues R$_t$	Government expenditures G$_t$						
Ceylon	.505 (.137)	.496 (.137)	.029 (.026)	.981	-.203	2.01	.076	1.001
Chile	.710 (.085)	.289 (.086)		.967	.346	1.76	.111	.998
Cuba	.649 (.084)	.353 (.084)		.982	.136	1.89	.053	1.002
Egypt	.556 (.119)	.443 (.119)		.981	.000	2.26	.065	.997
India	.847 (.099)	.153 (.099)		.988	.542	1.74	.037	1.000
Jamaica	.579 (.120)	.421 (.120)		.986	-.209	1.95	.058	1.000
Nigeria	.400 (.096)	.604 (.095)		.971	.296	2.13	.094	1.009
Philippines	.652 (.077)	.348 (.077)		.986	-.389	1.95	.066	1.001
Taiwan	.851 (.119)	.146 (.119)		.973	.332	2.07	.084	.977
Thailand	.626 (.143)	.367 (.146)		.960	.526	2.16	.058	.989

SUMMARY

A key conclusion of this chapter is the quantitative importance of colonial government expenditures in promoting the development of the export economy. The estimates of the government revenue equation indicate that these expenditures were financed from different combinations of taxation of real exports and nominal imports. On average, the colonial revenue equation exhibits constant returns to scale. The estimates of the government expenditure equation indicate that colonial governments ran deficits and surpluses in the short run, but balanced their budgets in the long run. Thus, the government expenditures which promoted the development of the trade sector were financed by the internal taxes falling on that sector.

In general, the supply and demand schedules for colonial real exports were found to be price inelastic. Thus, the explanation of the large historical fluctuations in export price is the shifting of these inelastic supply and demand schedules in response to changes in the developed countries' real income, prices, and trade policies, and to changes in the accumulated stock of colonial government expenditures. The average real income elasticity of demand for colonial exports is approximately equal to one in the long run. On average, the elasticity of substitution between the developed country's domestic goods and their imports from colonies is inelastic, except for Nigeria and the three countries tied to the United States. The estimates of the import equation indicate that on average the colonies ran a nominal export surplus, that import demand by the colonies was price inelastic, and that import demand shifted in response to export price changes.

Structural Estimation Method

The estimation method considers a set of K simultaneous equations

$$Y\Gamma + Y_{-1}A + XB = U \tag{4.1}$$

where there are K endogenous variables, Y; K lagged endogenous variables, Y_{-1}; and M exogenous variables, X. For T observations, then, Y and Y_{-1} are $T \times K$ matrices and X is a $T \times M$ matrix. Γ, A, and B are matrices of coefficients to be estimated with dimensions $K \times K$, $K \times K$, and $M \times K$ respectively.

It is assumed that the error matrix U follows a first order autoregressive pattern

$$U = U_{-1}R + E \tag{4.2}$$

where U_{-1} is the matrix of U lagged, and U, U_{-1}, and E are $T \times K$ matrices. Denoting e_t' as the column components of E, the following assumptions are made:

(i) $E(e_t) = 0$ $t = 1, 2, \ldots, T$

(ii) $E(e_t)(e_t') = \Sigma$ $t = 1, 2, \ldots, T$, Σ positive definite

(iii) $E(e_t)(e_\tau') = 0$ $t, \tau = 1, 2, \ldots, T, t \neq \tau$

(iv) $\text{plim } T^{-1}XE = \text{plim } T^{-1}X_{-1}E = 0$

(v) $\text{plim } T^{-1}Q'Q$ exists as a fixed, nonsingular matrix where $Q = (X, X_{-1})$

(vi) R is a diagonal matrix with elements $|r_{ii}| < 1, i = 1, 2, \ldots, K$

(vii) $(\Gamma + A)$ has an inverse

(viii) the equations of the model are identified

Without any loss of generality, let the equation to be estimated be the first equation:

$$y_1 = Y_1\gamma_1 + Y_{1_{-1}}\alpha_1 + X_1\beta_1 + u_1 \tag{4.3}$$

where y_1 is a column vector of T observations on the first endogenous variable; Y_1 is a $T \times k_1$ matrix of observations on k_1 other included endogenous variables; $Y_{1_{-1}}$ is a $T \times j_1$ matrix of observations on j_1 included lagged endogenous variables; X_1 is a $T \times m_1$ matrix on m_1 included exogenous variables; and β_1, α_1, and γ_1 are vectors of coefficients to be estimated. The T-component column vectors of error terms, u_1, $u_{1_{-1}}$, and e_1, satisfy

$$u_1 = \rho_1 u_{1_{-1}} + e_1 \tag{4.4}$$

where ρ_1 is the first diagonal element of R. As the only lagged endogenous variables appearing in the theoretical model are lagged left-hand variables, equation 4.3 can be simplified to

$$y_1 = Y_1\gamma_1 + y_{1_{-1}}\alpha_1 + X_1\beta_1 + u_1 \tag{4.5}$$

From equations 4.4 and 4.5, the equation to be estimated is

$$y_1 - \rho_1 y_{1_{-1}} = (Y_1 - \rho_1 Y_{1_{-1}})\gamma_1 + (y_{1_{-1}} - \rho_1 y_{1_{-2}})\alpha_1$$
$$+ (X_1 - \rho_1 X_{1_{-1}})\beta_1 + e_1 \tag{4.6}$$

Outline of Estimation Procedure

Equation 4.6 can be consistently estimated using the following limited information method.

1. *Instrumental Adjustment.* Using a set of instrumental variables that include at least X_1 and $X_{1_{-1}}$ and are asymptotically uncorrelated with e_1, instrumentally adjust Y_1, $Y_{1_{-1}}$, $y_{1_{-1}}$, and $y_{1_{-2}}$, and denote their predicted values as $\hat{Y}_1$, $\hat{Y}_{1_{-1}}$, $\hat{y}_{1_{-1}}$, and $\hat{y}_{1_{-2}}$, respectively.

2. *Initial Consistent Estimation.* Equation 4.5 is estimated by ordinary least squares using $\hat{Y}_1$ instead of Y_1 and $\hat{y}_{1_{-1}}$ instead of $y_{1_{-1}}$. The estimated coefficients of this regression are denoted as $\hat{\gamma}_1$, $\hat{\alpha}_1$, and $\hat{\beta}_1$. By the properties of instrumental variables, these estimates are consistent. A consistent estimate of the residuals u_1 is given by

$$\hat{u}_1 = y_1 - Y_1\hat{\gamma}_1 - y_{1_{-1}}\hat{\alpha}_1 - X_1\hat{\beta}_1 \tag{4.7}$$

A consistent estimator of ρ_1 is given by

$$\hat{\rho}_1 = \frac{(\hat{u}_{1_{-1}}{}' \hat{u}_1)}{(\hat{u}_{1_{-1}}{}' \hat{u}_{1_{-1}})} \tag{4.8}$$

An econometric interpretation of $\hat{\rho}_1$ is that it is the estimated coefficient obtained by regressing $\hat{u}_1$ on $\hat{u}_{1_{-1}}$.

3. *Iterative Procedure.* For any consistent estimator $\hat{\rho}_1$ of ρ_1, equation 4.6 is estimated by ordinary least squares using the instrumentally adjusted endogenous variables $\hat{y}_{1_{-1}}$, $\hat{Y}_1$, $\hat{Y}_{1_{-1}}$, and $\hat{y}_{1_{-2}}$ instead of $y_{1_{-1}}$, Y_1, $Y_{1_{-1}}$, and $y_{1_{-2}}$, respectively. The estimated coefficients of this regression are denoted by $\hat{y}_1$, $\hat{\alpha}_1$, and $\hat{\beta}_1$, and these estimates are consistent. These estimates are used to calculate successively $\hat{u}_1$ and $\hat{\rho}_1$ from equations 4.7 and 4.8. Starting from the initial consistent estimates of step 2, this iterative procedure is continued until the estimates converge.

4. *Equation Statistics.* A consistent estimator of e_1 can be calculated as follows

$$\hat{e}_1 = \hat{u}_1 - \rho_1 \hat{u}_{1_{-1}} \tag{4.9}$$

The standard error of the equation is

$$\hat{S}_1 = \sqrt{\frac{\hat{e}_1'\hat{e}_1}{T}} \tag{4.10}$$

The estimated variance-covariance matrix of the estimated coefficients is

$$V(\hat{\delta}_1) = \hat{S}_1^2 (\hat{Z}_1'\hat{Z}_1)^{-1} \tag{4.11}$$

where: $\hat{\delta}_1 = [\hat{\gamma}_1, \hat{\alpha}_1, \hat{\beta}_1]$ and

$$\hat{Z}_1 = [\hat{Y}_1 - \hat{\rho}_1 \hat{Y}_{1_{-1}}, \hat{y}_{1_{-1}} - \hat{\rho}_1 \hat{y}_{1_{-2}}, X_1 - \hat{\rho}_1 X_{1_{-1}}]$$

and the standard errors of the estimated coefficients are the square roots of the diagonal elements of the variance-covariance matrix.

Characteristics of the Estimation Procedure

This procedure has the desirable property of consistency because the three conditions for consistency of an instrumental variable estimator are satisfied. First, all the included predetermined variables appearing in equation 4.6, namely X_1 and $X_{1_{-1}}$, appear in the list of instruments used in step 1. Second, the equation is assumed to be identified. Third, the set of instrumental variables used are asymptotically uncorrelated with e_1.

In this estimation procedure, the lagged endogenous variables in equation 4.6, $Y_{1_{-1}}$, $y_{1_{-1}}$, and $y_{1_{-2}}$, are treated as endogenous rather than exogenous. Recalling the discussion by Franklin Fisher [9], the endogeneity of these lagged variables arises from the fact that they are correlated with the error term, e_1. This argument is particularly applicable here, since the lagged left-hand variables appear because of both a distributed lag process and an autoregressive process. If $Y_{1_{-1}}$, $y_{1_{-1}}$, and $y_{1_{-2}}$ are endogenous, then the estimation methods proposed by Fair [8][38] and Dhrymes [7] will yield inconsistent estimators since their methods treat lagged endogenous variables as exogenous.

The instrumental adjustment was done using the structurally ordered instrumental variable method described by Fisher [9] and by Mitchell and Fisher [24]. In our econometric model, structural ordering emphasizes lagged exogenous variables rather than current exogenous vari-

---

38. We attempted unsuccessfully to estimate the model using Fair's method, but the estimates often failed to converge. When convergence did occur, the estimated coefficients often had incorrect signs and the residuals still exhibited a first-order serial correlation pattern.

ables in the instrumental adjustment of lagged endogenous variables, while still satisfying the consistency requirement of using X_1 and $X_{1_{-1}}$ as instruments. First Y_1, $Y_{1_{-1}}$, $y_{1_{-1}}$, and $y_{1_{-2}}$ are regressed on instrument lists of different exogenous variables. The fitted values of these regressions are denoted as $\tilde{Y}_1$, $\tilde{Y}_{1_{-1}}$, $\tilde{y}_{1_{-1}}$, and $\tilde{y}_{1_{-2}}$. For consistent estimators, then Y_1, $Y_{1_{-1}}$, $y_{1_{-1}}$, and $y_{1_{-2}}$ are instrumentally adjusted using $\tilde{Y}_1$, $\tilde{Y}_{1_{-1}}$, $\tilde{y}_{1_{-1}}$, $\tilde{y}_{1_{-2}}$, X_1, and $X_{1_{-1}}$ to obtain the predicted values $\hat{Y}_1$, $\hat{Y}_{1_{-1}}$, $\hat{y}_{1_{-1}}$, and $\hat{y}_{1_{-2}}$ of the first step of the estimation procedure. It should be noted that the theoretical model is block triangular. The highest block consists of the export sector, and the lower blocks, in declining order, are the import, revenue, and expenditure sectors.

5

Degree of Similarity in Colonial Development

The previous chapter yielded the important conclusion that the same econometric model can be used to explain the process of colonial development for all ten countries in our sample. We found that the structure of this model depended on identifying and measuring the common internal and external forces that produced this similar development process. In discussing these results, we noted differences in the coefficient estimates of the structural model and attributed these differences mainly to colonial bloc behavior and government productivity in promoting the export economy.

This chapter first investigates whether these differences in the structural coefficient estimates are significant. Using covariance analysis, we show that the same structural estimates of an equation cannot be used for a pair or a block of countries. While rejecting the hypothesis of identical structural equations, the covariance analysis does suggest varying degrees of similarity and difference within the structure of colonial development. However, the F-tests computed by covariance analysis cannot be used to measure this degree of similarity or diversity.

The technique appropriate for analyzing the degree of similarity within the development process is cluster analysis. The second part of this chapter explains how cluster analysis can be used to identify countries having the most similar characteristics. The technique of cluster analysis is applied in turn to the short-run estimated coefficients and to the long-run estimated coefficients. An important conclusion of this cluster analysis is that it is possible to quantitatively identify blocs of countries having similar colonial characteristics.

COVARIANCE ANALYSIS

This section uses covariance analysis to test the hypothesis that a bloc of countries had the same subset of structural coefficients for a

102

behavioral equation. Supplement 5.1 extends the covariance analysis method of Chow, Fisher, and Johnston[1] to handle two additional requirements of our equation estimates. These requirements are that the estimation period for each country can differ and that the number of right-hand variables in the equation for each country can also differ.

The results of the covariance test indicate that the structure of colonial development was not homogeneous. Table 5.1 summarizes the F-tests for the coefficients of the ten countries classified by the behavioral equations of the model. It indicates the number of acceptances of either homogeneity or heterogeneity at the 5 percent, 10 percent, and 25 percent significance levels. Even though it is not usual practice to report acceptances at the 25 percent level or even at the 10 percent level, we include these levels in order to indicate the broader relative range of similarity and diversity within the structural estimates. The need for examining this broader range of significance levels is clearly evident from the last two columns of table 5.1. These columns report the large number of pairs of countries which cannot be accepted as either homogeneous or heterogeneous at the 25 percent and 10 percent significance levels. In the discussion that follows we analyze first the hypothesis of homogeneity in the structure of colonial development, and then the alternative of heterogeneity.

The hypothesis of equality of the export price coefficient in the supply equation for any two countries in the model is easily rejected at the 5 percent level. Even at the 25 percent level, out of 45 possible country combinations, the hypothesis of equality is accepted for only 2 pairs, Chile-India and Chile-Jamaica. Similarly, we reject at the 5 percent level the hypotheses that the import price elasticity in the supply equation is the same for any two countries, and that the coefficient of accumulated real government expenditures in the supply equation is the same for any two countries. At the 25 percent level the hypothesis of equality is accepted in only one out of 45 combinations for the import price coefficient and also only one time for the government coefficient. A covariance analysis was performed testing whether all three coefficients in the supply equation were the same between any two countries. The results of this test (given in table 5.1) indicate that we reject this hypothesis at the 5 percent level

1. Chow [5] developed the tests suitable for application to two countries. The Fisher [11] and Johnston [65, pp. 192–207] extensions of the tests are applicable to more than two countries.

Table 5.1. Covariance Analysis Test Results

Equation	Variable(s) with common coefficient(s)	Total number of pairs of countries	Homogeneous pairs of countries at significance level of			Heterogeneous pairs of countries at significance level of			Pairs neither homogeneous nor heterogeneous at significance level of	
			5%	10%	25%	5%	10%	25%	25%	10%
Export supply, $X_{S_t}^R$	Px, export price	45	0	1	2	23	31	37	6	13
	Pm, import price	45	0	0	1	22	28	34	10	17
	$\sum_{i=1}^{\infty} G_{t-i}^R$, acc. real govt.exp.	45	0	0	1	32	33	36	8	12
	Px, Pm, $\sum_{i=1}^{\infty} G_{t-1}^R$	45	0	0	3	21	26	34	8	19
Export demand, $X_{D_t}^R$	Px, export price	45	0	0	2	34	37	41	2	8
	y^R, real income	45	0	0	2	26	32	36	7	13
	Pd, domestic price	45	0	0	1	30	32	36	8	13
	Px, Y^R, Pd	45	0	0	0	33	36	45	0	9
Import demand, M_t^R	X^R, real exports	45	1	2	8	10	12	23	14	31
	Pm, import price	45	1	2	5	9	9	16	14	34
	Px, export price	45	0	1	5	13	14	20	10	30
	X^R, Pm, Px	45	2	2	10	14	17	22	13	26
Government revenues, R_t	X^R, real exports	45	0	1	1	23	24	30	14	20
	M, imports	45	2	2	3	29	30	33	9	13
	X^R, M	45	0	1	1	32	37	40	4	7
Government expenditures, G_t	R_t, govt. revenue	45	1	1	2	19	24	31	12	20
	R_t, G_{t-1}	45	0	0	1	19	25	31	13	20

for any two countries, and accept it at the 25 percent level for only 3 pairs, Chile-India, Chile-Jamaica and Nigeria-Thailand. Thus, in general, export supply behavior was not homogeneous across countries.

Covariance analysis of the demand equation indicates a similar result. We reject the hypothesis of equality of the three demand coefficients taken separately or together across countries at the 10 percent level (table 5.1). We conclude that homogeneity does not characterize colonial supply and demand behavior.

The remaining three equations show more homogeneity between pairs of countries than did the supply and demand equations. Specifically, the colonial import equation has the largest number of accepted hypotheses of equality between sets of coefficients. Table 5.1 indicates that we can accept at the 5 percent level the hypothesis of equality of import behavior in 2 pairs, Ceylon-Egypt and Ceylon-India. At the 25 percent level, however, we have ten combinations that show homogeneous import behavior. Examining the individual coefficients of the import equations, we can accept at the 25 percent level the hypothesis of equal real export coefficients in eight pairs, of equal import price coefficients in five pairs, and of equal export price coefficients in five pairs. The number of individual coefficient acceptances decreases markedly when we consider the criterion of a 10 or 5 percent level of significance.

We reject at the 5 percent level the hypothesis of equal revenue or expenditure behavior across the ten countries (table 5.1). There are, however, some acceptances of individual coefficients even at the 5 percent level. In the revenue equation, the tax coefficient for nominal imports is accepted as the same at the 5 percent level for Cuba and Ceylon and for the Philippines and Egypt. There is one acceptance at the 10 percent level for the tax coefficient for real exports. In the government expenditure equation, we accept the hypothesis at the 5 percent level of equal revenue coefficients only for Jamaica and Egypt, and there is only one additional acceptance at the 25 percent level. We also tested the hypothesis that the government's expenditure equation was the same for all ten countries in the long run. This hypothesis is accepted at the 5 percent level. In general, then, the government expenditure equation is heterogeneous in the short run, but homogeneous in the long run.

Covariance analysis by pairs thus indicates that even at the 25 percent level we can reject for each equation most of the hypotheses of equality of coefficients or equality of sets of coefficients across the ten countries. It is still possible, however, to find homogeneous blocs of countries for a particular equation's coefficients. Covariance analysis was used to test if a coefficient or a set of coefficients was equal for selected blocs of countries. The selection of the countries comprising these blocs was suggested by the results of our pair wise covariance analyses. For example, the hypothesis that Ceylon, Egypt, Chile, India, Jamaica, Taiwan, and Thailand all had the same coefficient of the import price in the import equation is accepted at the 1 percent level. The hypothesis that Egypt, Jamaica, and the Philippines had the same nominal import coefficient in the revenue equation is accepted at the 5 percent level, and the hypothesis that Taiwan, Thailand, Jamaica, India, and the Philippines had the same real export coefficient in the revenue equation is accepted at the 10 percent level. For blocs of three or more countries, these three hypotheses of homogeneity are the only ones which we accepted at 10 percent significance level or better. All the acceptances are for a particular coefficient of an equation, rather than for sets of coefficients of an equation.

While homogeneity does not characterize the structure of colonial development, the alternative hypothesis of heterogeneity cannot, in general, be accepted at a reasonable level of significance. For all five behavioral equations, we find that the hypothesis of heterogeneity for combinations of coefficients of an equation is accepted at the 5 percent level for less than 50 percent of the possible country combinations. And if we take a significance level of 5 percent for the acceptance of the hypothesis of either homogeneity or of heterogeneity, we reject both hypotheses for 49 percent of the combinations. Even at the 10 percent significance level, about 36 percent of the possible combinations cannot be accepted as either homogeneous or heterogeneous.

A breakdown by individual equations indicates some differences. Of the five behavioral equations, using the 5 percent significance level, the hypothesis of heterogeneity is accepted most often for the export demand equation. The next most heterogeneous equation is that for government revenue. This ordering is somewhat surprising, since we had originally expected that tax behavior would have been more homogeneous across the colonial world. In terms of the proportion of acceptances of the hypothesis of heterogeneity, export supply and government expenditures follow the revenue equation and, finally, the import equation has the lowest proportion of acceptances. In fact, the hypothesis of either homogeneity or heterogeneity for the import equation is inconclusive since 64 percent of the country combinations fall outside the 5 percent level of significance. Only for the export demand and revenue equations do a majority of the possible cases fall within the 5 percent significance level.

To summarize the results of the covariance analysis: We accepted many hypotheses of heterogeneity. However, we did not have enough acceptances at a reasonable level of significance to conclude confidently that the structure of colonial development could be described as heterogeneous. Indeed, table 5.1 (particularly its last two columns) suggests a wide range of diversity within the colonial development process. Thus, in general, neither homogeneity nor heterogeneity characterizes the structure of colonial development.

Therefore, our covariance analysis provides only partial evidence on the question of how similar or different was the structure of colonial development. Even though the results of the covariance analysis suggested degrees of similarity for the coefficient estimates, the computed F-statistics cannot be used to measure the distance between countries or to classify the countries into groups. For example, the hypothesis of identical export price coefficient in the supply equation for some pairs of countries may have been rejected, but the price coefficients for these two countries may have been closer in magnitude than the export price coefficients for any other pair of countries.

CLUSTER ANALYSIS

The covariance analysis indicated the need for a method which measures the degree of similarity within the process of colonial development. Supplement 5.1 explains how cluster analysis calculates this measure as the squared distance between the countries' estimated parameters. Cluster analysis then uses this measure to classify the countries that are closest together into groups. The classification criterion is to minimize the loss, caused by aggregation, in the variance of the data being analyzed. The groups are calculated using a special case of Fisher's progressive merger procedure.[2] A country is correctly classified if the distance to its own group is the minimum of the distance to any group; otherwise it is misclassified.

In applying cluster analysis to the estimates of structural coeffi-

----

2. Fisher [12 and 52].

cients, we consider first the short-run behavior and then the long-run behavior of the colonial development process. One principal advantage of cluster analysis is that it can be applied simultaneously to all the common coefficients of all five behavioral equations. Once cluster analysis has identified blocs of countries, we can examine how individual coefficients explain the differences between the blocs.

Short-Run Estimates

A cluster analysis of the estimated short-run coefficients of all five behavioral equations classifies the countries into three colonial blocs: those countries tied to the United Kingdom, the United States, and Japan. Table 5.2 indicates that all ten countries are correctly classified by the cluster analysis. The relative cost of this classification is a 9.88 percent reduction in the total variance of the estimated short-run coefficients. The cluster analysis merges the six countries tied to the United Kingdom into a bloc at a relative cost of 6.88 percent. The procedure merges the three countries tied to the United States into a bloc at a relative cost of 3.00 percent. As the relative cost per country is about the same for the two blocs, the larger United Kingdom bloc is about as homogeneous as the smaller U.S. bloc. This conclusion is supported by the small squared distance of each country from its own bloc mean (table 5.2). Taiwan, a Japanese colony, remains quite distinct from either bloc (table 5.2, last line). If we were to

Table 5.2. Distance Classification for Short-Run Estimated Coefficients

| Merged colonial bloc | Country | Squared distance from bloc mean | | | Bloc classification by minimum distance criterion |
		United Kingdom	United States	Japan	
	Ceylon	.295	.787	1.793	United Kingdom
	Egypt	.147	1.208	1.749	United Kingdom
United	India	.424	·1.567	2.249	United Kingdom
Kingdom	Jamaica	.455	1.441	1.651	United Kingdom
	Nigeria	.515	1.541	3.524	United Kingdom
	Thailand	.418	2.077	1.649	United Kingdom
United	Chile	1.170	.265	2.263	United States
States	Cuba	1.563	.251	2.479	United States
	Philippines	.976	.471	2.476	United States
Japan	Taiwan	1.727	2.077	.000	Japan

force Taiwan into one of the other two colonial blocs, then Taiwan would join the United Kingdom bloc at a high relative cost of 4.52 percent.

Table 5.3 reports the average short-run coefficients for the three colonial blocs. These average coefficients indicate the differences in the short-run behavioral characteristics of the blocs. Taiwan is distinct from the other two blocs because it has higher coefficients for the export and import prices in the supply equation, for the export price in the demand equation, and for current revenue in the expenditure equation; and it has lower coefficients for real exports and export

Table 5.3. Bloc Means for Short-Run Estimated Coefficients

Behavioral equation	Coefficient	Variable (logarithm)	Short-run estimated coefficient means of colonial blocs		
			United Kingdom[a]	United States[b]	Japan[c]
Export supply (2.1)	a_1	Px, export price	.305	.288	.363
	a_2	Pm, import price	-.332	-.350	-.482
	a_3	$\sum_{i=1}^{\infty} G_{t-1}^R$, acc. real govt. exp.	.377	.707	.453
Export demand (2.2)	b_1	Px, export price	-.289	-.759	-1.095
	b_2	Y^R, real income	.836	.530	1.650
	b_3	Pd, domestic price	.319	.839	.287
Real imports (2.4)	c_1	X^R, real exports	.981	.984	.975
	c_2	Pm, import price	-.548	-.210	-.288
	c_3	Px, export price	.506	.448	.182
Government revenue (2.9)	d_1	X^R, real exports	.523	.728	.314
	d_2	M, imports	.509	.312	.357
Government expenditure (2.10)	e_1	R, revenue	.585	.670	.851
	e_2	G_{t-1}, lagged expenditure	.414	.330	.146

[a]Ceylon, Egypt, India, Jamaica, Nigeria, and Thailand.
[b]Chile, Cuba, and the Philippines.
[c]Taiwan.

price in the import equation, for real exports in the revenue equation, and for lagged expenditures in the expenditure equation. In addition, Taiwan is distinguished from the U.S. bloc alone because it has lower coefficients for accumulated real government expenditures in the supply equation and for the developed country's domestic price in the demand equation. In comparison to the United Kingdom bloc alone, Taiwan has a higher coefficient for accumulated real government expenditures in the supply equation and lower coefficients for the import price in the import equation and for nominal imports in the revenue equation. On balance, Taiwan is quite distinct from the other colonial blocs, but it is somewhat closer to the U.K. bloc than the U.S. bloc.

A comparison of the average short-run coefficients of the U.S. and U.K. blocs indicates that the U.S. bloc has a more robust short-term behavioral response in both its supply and demand equations, except for the developed country's real income variable in the demand equation. In contrast, the United Kingdom countries have higher coefficients for all the price variables in the import equation. In the government sector, the U.S. bloc relies more heavily on the taxation of real exports and less on the taxation of imports. The average coefficients for lagged expenditures in the government expenditures equation indicate that Uinted Kingdom bloc countries were less likely to balance their government budgets in the short run than were the countries tied to the United States.

Long-Run Estimates

The cluster analysis of the short-run and long-run behavioral coefficients differ not only because the coefficients are different but also because the relative variance contained in the five behavioral equations changes. The possibility of a distributed lag process was included in the specification of the equations for export supply and demand. When these equations were estimated, the use of distributed lags was found to be appropriate in the supply equations of four countries (Ceylon, Cuba, Nigeria, and Taiwan) and in the demand equations of three countries (Chile, Nigeria, and the Philippines). A comparison of the estimated short-run and long-run coefficients of these two equations indicates that the long-run coefficients contain more variance than do the short-run coefficients.[3] As no distributed lag

3. See tables 4.1–4.4.

process was specified for the import and revenue equations, the short-run and long-run coefficients for these equations are the same. A distributed lag process in the government expenditure equation was estimated for all ten countries. The estimated short-run coefficients of this equation vary considerably in value, while the estimated long-run coefficients for the revenue variable vary by only a small fraction from 1,[4] indicating that all ten countries balanced their budgets in the long run. Thus the estimated short-run expenditure coefficients have much more variance than the long-run estimates. Therefore, a cluster analysis of the long-run coefficients of all five behavioral equations, as compared to that of all the short-run coefficients, puts more emphasis upon the supply and demand equation estimates, both of which contain more variance in the long run, and places very little emphasis on the expenditure equation, which contains much less variance in the long run.

A cluster analysis of the estimated long-run coefficients of all five behavioral equations classifies the countries into two groups (table 5.4). The first group consists of four countries—Egypt, India, Jamaica, and Thailand—which we call the low productivity bloc. The second group consists of six countries—Ceylon, Chile, Cuba, Nigeria, the Philippines, and Taiwan—which we call the high productivity bloc. This terminology is used because the most important difference between these two blocs is the productivity of the government in promoting the export economy. This difference is measured by the average long-run coefficient for the variable, accumulated real government expenditures, in the export supply equation: it is 1.095 for the high productivity bloc and only .388 for the low productivity bloc (table 5.5). Further, the four low productivity bloc countries individually have the lowest long-run estimated coefficients for accumulated real government expenditures (table 4.1 and 4.2).

The relative cost of this classification into two productivity blocs is a 19.60 percent reduction in the total variance of the long-run estimated coefficients. The cluster analysis forms the low productivity countries into a single bloc at a relative cost of 1.93 percent, whereas the relative cost of forming the high productivity bloc is 17.67 percent. Thus the low productivity bloc is much more homogeneous than the high productivity bloc, since formation of the latter bloc has a much higher relative cost. Table 5.4 indicates that the cluster analysis

4. See table 4.7.

Table 5.4. Distance Classification for Long-Run Estimated Coefficients
(Countries Classified by Merger Procedure)

| Merged bloc | Country | Squared distance from bloc mean | | Bloc classification by minimum distance criterion |
		Low	High	
Low productivity bloc	Egypt	.162	2.002	Low
	India	.223	2.674	Low
	Jamaica	.352	1.316	Low
	Thailand	.388	1.859	Low
High productivity bloc	Ceylon	6.442	3.588	High
	Chile	2.730	1.130	High
	Cuba	2.012	.858	High
	Nigeria	4.002	2.486	High
	Philippines	2.833	1.253	High
	Taiwan	3.287	1.198	High

correctly classifies all ten countries. This table also supports the conclusion of relatively greater homogeneity in the low productivity bloc.
The squared distance of each country in that bloc from the bloc mean
is smaller than the corresponding squared distance for the high productivity bloc.

The average estimated long-run coefficients for the two blocs, reported in table 5.4, show the substantial differences between them.
Comparing these average coefficients, the high productivity bloc has
much larger long-run coefficients for all the variables in both the
supply and the demand equations and for the taxation of real exports
in the revenue equation. The low productivity bloc has larger coefficients only for the three variables in the import equation and for imports in the revenue equation. For each of the coefficients in the import equation, the differences between the blocs are relatively small.
The higher taxation of imports by the low productivity bloc is more
than offset by the higher taxation of real exports by the high productivity bloc.

If we consider the next to last step of the cluster analysis classification, then Ceylon and Taiwan form a group separate from Nigeria
and the three countries tied to the United States. Ceylon and Taiwan
have the highest estimated long-run supply equation coefficients of all
the countries in the sample, and they have an average coefficient of
.272 for developed country's domestic price in the demand equation,
which is very different from the average coefficient of 1.291 for Ni-

Table 5.5. Bloc Means for Long-Run Estimated Coefficients
(Countries Classified by Merger Procedure)

Behavioral equation	Coefficient	Variable (logarithm)	Long-run estimated coefficient means of merged productivity blocs	
			Low[a]	High[b]
Export supply (2.1)	a_1	Px, export price	.346	.698
	a_2	Pm, import price	−.403	−.658
	a_3	$\sum_{i=1}^{\infty} G_{t-i}^{R}$, acc. real govt. exp.	.388	1.095
Export demand (2.2)	b_1	Px, export price	−.276	−.961
	b_2	Y^R, real income	.903	1.207
	b_3	Pd, domestic price	.323	.951
Real imports (2.4)	c_1	X^R, real exports	.978	.984
	c_2	Pm, import price	−.495	−.371
	c_3	Px, export price	.488	.435
Government revenue (2.9)	d_1	X^R, real exports	.374	.690
	d_2	M, imports	.594	.329
Government expenditures (2.10)	e_1	R, revenue	.997	1.001

[a]Egypt, India, Jamaica, and Thailand.
[b]Ceylon, Chile, Cuba, Nigeria, the Philippines, and Taiwan.

geria and the countries tied to the United States.[5] Also, with an average coefficient of .534 for real exports in the revenue equation, Ceylon and Taiwan taxed real exports much less than did Nigeria and the countries tied to the United States, for which the average is .763.[6] The relative cost of making this classification into three groups is a 10.88 percent reduction in the total variance of the long-run coefficients.

By comparison, if the previously derived short-run classification of countries into the three colonial blocs is used instead to group the

5. Averages calculated using tables 4.3 and 4.4.
6. Averages calculated using table 4.6.

Table 5.6. Distance Classification for Long-Run Estimated Coefficients
(Countries Classified by Colonial Blocs)

Colonial bloc	Country	*United Kingdom*	*United States*	*Japan*	*Bloc classification by minimum distance criterion*
		Squared distance from bloc mean			
	Ceylon	4.446	6.284	1.728	Japan
	Egypt	.572	2.502	3.545	United Kingdom
United	India	.885	3.034	4.379	United Kingdom
Kingdom	Jamaica	.295	2.294	2.365	United Kingdom
	Nigeria	3.382	2.157	2.389	United States
	Thailand	.645	1.920	3.984	United Kingdom
United	Chile	2.185	.342	3.800	United States
States	Cuba	1.430	.340	3.231	United States
	Philippines	2.270	.424	3.665	United States
Japan	Taiwan	2.064	3.197	.000	Japan

long-run coefficients, the relative cost increases to 18.46 percent. Moreover, a classification test for this nonoptimal grouping by colonial blocs reveals that both Nigeria and Ceylon are misclassified (see table 5.6). The test confirms that Ceylon should be grouped with Taiwan, and Nigeria with the U.S.-tied countries. If these two reclassifications are made, then the correct classification of countries into three blocs is obtained. An important question is why Ceylon and Nigeria are classified differently from the rest of the United Kingdom bloc in the long run, but not in the short run. The explanation lies in the distributed lags for export supply and demand for Ceylon and Nigeria. The short-run coefficients of Ceylon and Nigeria are quite similar to the other four United Kingdom–tied countries in the short run, but quite different in the long run. For example, these four United Kingdom countries (the low productivity bloc) had an average short-run and long-run coefficient of .388 for accumulated real government expenditures. However, the coefficients for this variable for Ceylon and Nigeria are .349 and .361 in the short run, which are very close to the low productivity bloc average, but they are quite different in the long run, taking on values of 2.210 and .715 respectively.[7]

7. See tables 4.1 and 4.2 for estimates.

Table 5.7. Bloc Means for Long-Run Equilibrium Coefficients
(Countries Classified by Colonial Blocs)

Behavioral equation	Coefficient	Variable (logarithm)	Long-run estimated coefficient means of colonial blocs		
			United Kingdom[a]	United States[b]	Japan[c]
Export supply (2.1)	a_1	Px, export price	.597	.340	.972
	a_2	Pm, import price	−.498	−.426	−1.292
	a_3	$\sum_{i=1}^{\infty} G_{t-i}^{R}$, acc. real govt. exp.	.746	.812	1.212
Export demand (2.2)	b_1	Px, export price	−.376	−1.172	−1.095
	b_2	Y^R, real income	1.121	.825	1.650
	b_3	Pd, domestic price	.488	1.261	.287
Real imports (2.4)	c_1	X^R, real exports	.981	.984	.975
	c_2	Pm, import price	−.548	−.210	−.288
	c_3	Px, export price	.506	.448	.182
Government revenue (2.9)	d_1	X^R, real exports	.523	.728	.314
	d_2	M, imports	.509	.312	.357
Government expenditures (2.10)	e_1	R, revenue	.999	1.000	.997

[a]Ceylon, Egypt, India, Jamaica, Nigeria, and Thailand.
[b]Chile, Cuba, and the Philippines.
[c]Taiwan.

SUMMARY

The cluster analysis indicates the existence of well-defined blocs of countries for the short-run and long-run estimated coefficients. Two colonial characteristics—the developed country to which a colony was tied and the productivity of government expenditures directed toward export development—are the key explanations for the degree of similarity and difference within the structural process of colonial development. The ten countries were classified into the three colonial blocs—countries tied to the United Kingdom, the United States or

Japan—when the short-run estimated coefficients were used as the data for the cluster analysis. The countries are classified into low and high government productivity blocs when the long-run estimated coefficients are used.

Covariance Analysis and Cluster Analysis

Covariance Analysis Method

The covariance analysis test used in this chapter can be developed using the following notation:[8]

N = number of countries,

n_i = number of observations for country i $(i = 1, 2, \ldots, N)$,

k_i = number of right-hand variables in the equation for country i $(i = 1, 2, \ldots, N)$,

q = number of common variables, where $q \leqq k_i$ for all i,

y_i = column vector of actual values of left-hand variables for country i $(i = 1, 2, \ldots, N)$,

$\hat{y}_i$ = column vector of fitted values of separately estimated regression equation for country i $(i = 1, 2, \ldots, N)$,

$$y = \begin{bmatrix} y_1 \\ y_2 \\ \vdots \\ y_n \end{bmatrix} \quad \text{and} \quad \hat{y} = \begin{bmatrix} \hat{y}_1 \\ \hat{y}_2 \\ \vdots \\ \hat{y}_n \end{bmatrix}, \text{ and}$$

$\hat{\hat{y}}$ = column vector of fitted values of pooled regression equation with q common variates.

The pooled regression is estimated using the econometric method outlined in supplement 4.1 with a separate instrumental and autoregressive adjustment for each country.[9]

The sum of squared residuals of the pooled regression with q common variables is

$$Q_1 = (\hat{\hat{y}} - y)'(\hat{\hat{y}} - y),$$

where Q_1 has $\sum_{i=1}^{N} (n_i - k_i) + (N - 1)q$ degrees of freedom. The sum of squared residuals of the separately estimated regressions is

$$Q_2 = (\hat{y} - y)'(\hat{y} - y)$$

---

8. The reasoning used to derive the covariance analysis test is similar to the argument in Chow [5], Fisher [11], and Johnston [69, pp. 192–207].

9. Thus we are adopting the added assumption that the autoregressive process is the same for each country. Separate instrumental adjustment is sufficient to assume consistency of the estimators.

where Q_2 has $\sum\limits_{i=1}^{N} (n_i - k_i)$ degrees of freedom. The increment in the sum of squared residuals due to pooling is

$$Q_3 = Q_1 - Q_2$$

where Q_3 has $(N - 1)q$ degrees of freedom. Then the F-test for the hypothesis that the N countries have the same q coefficients is given by

$$F = \frac{Q_3/(N-1)q}{Q_2/\left(\sum\limits_{i=1}^{N} (n_i - k_i)\right)}$$

with $\left((N-1)q, \sum\limits_{i=1}^{N} (n_i - k_i)\right)$ degrees of freedom.

Cluster Analysis Method

This section outlines how cluster analysis can be used to classify the ten countries into distinct groups using either a set of estimated structural coefficients or a set of estimated dynamic multipliers.[10] Let P be a data matrix where each of the H rows is a parameter and each of the ten columns is a country in our sample. Let J be the number of distinct groups and n_j be the number of countries in group j ($j = 1, 2, \ldots, J$). Then define a classification matrix T with J rows and ten columns as:

$$\underset{(J \times 10)}{T} = \begin{bmatrix} 1 \ldots 1 & 0 & \ldots 0 \\ 0 & 1 \ldots 1 \ldots 0 \\ \vdots & \vdots & \ddots & \vdots \\ 0 & 0 \ldots 1 \ldots 1 \end{bmatrix} \tag{5.1}$$

where the number of 1s in the jth row is the number of countries n_j in the jth group, and where a 0 is a row vector of zeros. Each group of countries is weighted by the number of countries in that group, as specified by the group-weighting matrix $\overline{M}$:

$$\underset{(J \times J)}{\overline{M}} = TT' = \begin{bmatrix} n_1 & 0 \ldots 0 \\ 0 & n_2 \ldots 0 \\ \vdots & \vdots & \vdots \\ 0 & 0 \ldots n_J \end{bmatrix} \tag{5.2}$$

10. Dynamic multipliers will be derived and analyzed in the next three chapters.

The countries are then grouped using the classification matrix T and the group-weighting matrix $\overline{M}$ to form an aggregate data matrix $\overline{P}$, where

$$\underset{(H \times J)}{\overline{P}} = PT'\overline{M}^{-1} \tag{5.3}$$

Thus, the countries classified into a particular group form a single column of the aggregate matrix $\overline{P}$, which has as a typical element

$$\overline{p}_{ij} = \frac{1}{n_j} \sum_{k \in j} p_{ik}$$
$$i = 1, 2, \ldots, H$$
$$j = 1, 2, \ldots, J \tag{5.4}$$

$\overline{p}_{ij}$ is the mean of the ith parameter for all the countries in the jth group. Each column, $\overline{p}_j$, of the matrix $\overline{P}$ is a vector of the means of all the parameters for the countries in the jth group.

The objective of cluster analysis is to minimize the loss, caused by aggregation, in the total variance of the original data matrix P. The cost function which measures this loss in classifying the countries into J groups is

$$C_J = \sum_{i=1}^{H} \sum_{j=1}^{J} \sum_{k \in j} ((p_{ik})^2 - (\overline{p}_{ij})^2) \tag{5.5}$$

The cost function thus measures the cost of disregarding the variance in the data between countries in a particular group.[11]

The procedure for obtaining the classification into groups using this cost function is a special case of the progressive merger procedure described by Walter Fisher [12, 52]. In each step of this procedure, pairs of countries or country groups are merged together to form a single new country group. This stepwise procedure is continued until a final classification is obtained. Equation 5.3 specifies that column vectors are merged together. Each of these column vectors, p_j, can contain either the data for an individual country or the vector of the means of the data for a group of countries. The additional cost of merging together two column vectors p_i and p_j is obtained from equation 5.5 as[12]

11. This formula follows directly from the mathematical cost function specified by Fisher [52] as $C = \operatorname{tr} PP' - \operatorname{tr} \overline{P}\overline{M}\overline{P}'$.
12. For the derivation of equations 5.6 through 5.8 see Fisher [12 and 52].

$$dc_{ij} = \frac{(p_i - p_j)'(p_i - p_j)}{\dfrac{1}{n_i} + \dfrac{1}{n_j}} \tag{5.6}$$

The numerator is the squared distance between the two points, and the denominator weights this distance in proportion to the number of countries in group i and group j. The particular column vectors p_i and p_j for which equation 5.6 is minimized are then merged together to form a single column vector $\bar{p}_j$. Then from 5.3, the merged vector is

$$\bar{p}_j = \frac{n_i p_k + n_j p_j}{n_i + n_j} \tag{5.7}$$

which is the weighted average of the columns, where the weights are the number of countries in each column. All the remaining columns of P remain unchanged. From 5.2, the diagonal element of the weighting matrix for this merged point is the number of countries merged together:

$$\bar{m}_j = n_i + n_j \tag{5.8}$$

All the remaining elements of the group-weighting matrix remain unchanged.

The stepwise procedure then employs the revised P and M matrices as the original matrices for the next step in the procedure. The revised P is without the merged column p_i and the revised M is now a square matrix without the diagonal element n_i for the number of countries comprising the merged group i. The next merger is obtained by using equations 5.6–5.8 for the revised P and M matrices.

The cluster analysis results report the relative cost of a set of mergers. Let V be the total variance of the data matrix P about its grand mean, and let dc_k be the cost of the kth merger as specified by equation 5.6. After K mergers, the variance lost is given by equation 5.5 as

$$C_J = \sum_{k=1}^{K} dc_k$$

The relative cost of these K mergers is then

$$RC_K = 100 \frac{C_J}{V} = 100 \frac{\sum_{k=1}^{K} dc_k}{V} \tag{5.9}$$

which is the percentage of the total variance lost due to aggregation. Since the cost of each progressive merger increases, blocs formed earlier in the procedure are relatively more homogeneous than blocs formed later.

This stepwise procedure does not guarantee that the final classification minimizes the cost function. All the procedure assures is that at each step the minimum-cost merger is performed. However, the proper classification of countries can be checked by calculating the squared distance of each country k from each group j,

$$d_{kj} = \sum_{i=1}^{H} (p_{ik} - \bar{p}_{ij})^2$$

$$k = 1, 2, \ldots, 10$$
$$j = 1, 2, \ldots, J \tag{5.10}$$

A country is correctly classified if the distance to its own group is smaller than the distance to any other group. If not, the country is misclassified. In that case reclassifying the country to a group for which the distance is smaller will reduce the cost of classification.[13] The matrix of distances calculated using equation 5.10 measures the degree of similarity between a country and each group, and this matrix will be reported for each cluster analysis. Furthermore, the classification procedure assures that a country will be classified into that group to which it is most similar.

13. Alternative classifications can be obtained by two methods. First, at a specified stage in the clustering, alternative combinations of countries can be specified. Second, the combining of certain country pairs can be forbidden.

6

Impact Multipliers, Basic Dynamic Simulations, and Historical Accuracy

Using the estimates of the equations derived in chapter 2, the full twelve-equation simultaneous equation system can now be used to analyze the process of colonial development in the short, intermediate and long run. The first section of this chapter describes the method used to calculate the impact or short-run reduced form multipliers. The calculated short-run reduced form multipliers are then used to analyze the initial effects of an assumed change in either an exogenous variable or a lagged endogenous variable on the process of colonial development. However, analysis of the development impact over time of these assumed changes requires the calculation of dynamic multipliers. The second section outlines the dynamic simulation method used to calculate these multipliers and to perform simulation experiments; it also derives a suitable method for calculating long-run balanced growth multipliers. The actual values of the dynamic and long-run balanced growth multipliers will be analyzed in the next two chapters. The dynamic simulation method will also be used in later chapters to perform simulation experiments to investigate the quantitative impact of World War I, the Great Depression, U.S. trade restrictions, and tax changes. The third section reports and evaluates the basic dynamic simulations of the countries for their full estimation periods. These simulations explain quite well both the long-term trends and cyclical fluctuations of the endogenous variables of the model. These results provide important support for the conclusion that the specified model explains the historical process of colonial development from the late nineteenth century to the beginning of World War II. The final section evaluates stability properties of the model and finds that the process of colonial development exhibited strong stability in response to exogenous shocks.

SHORT-RUN REDUCED FORM MULTIPLIERS

Supplement 6.1 shows how short-run reduced form multipliers can be derived. The short-run reduced form is calculated as a matrix solution of the first eleven log-linear structural equations. The reduced form for the variable, accumulated real government expenditures, can be calculated separately using the linear equation 2.12′. The short-run reduced form multipliers, also called impact multipliers, are then shown to be the difference quotient of the short-run reduced form with respect to either a current exogenous or lagged endogenous variable (see supplement 6.1).

The short-run reduced form multipliers reported in table 6.1 illustrate the initial steps of the circular process of colonial development. A 1 percent change in any of the exogenous variables or lagged endogenous variables causes a computed percentage change in each of the endogenous variables. For example, reading down the first column of table 6.1A, a 1 percent increase in the import price of Ceylon decreases its real exports by .086 percent, increases its export price by .194 percent, decreases its real imports by .386 percent, and so forth.

Table 6.1 can also be used to examine a simultaneous change in both the external and the internal forces affecting the process of colonial development. For example, the effects upon Chile's real exports and terms of trade of a 1 percent increase in real income in the developed country (the external force) and a corresponding 1 percent increase in lagged accumulated real government expenditures (the internal force) can be calculated using columns 2 and 5 of table 6.1B. For these assumed changes, Chile's real exports would increase by .619 percent, since

$$\frac{\Delta \ln X_t^R}{\Delta \ln Y_t^R} + \frac{\Delta \ln X_t^R}{\Delta \sum_{i=1}^{\infty} \ln G_{t-i}^R} = .126\% + .493\% = .619\%$$

and its terms of trade would decrease by .106 percent, since

$$\frac{\Delta \ln P_{T_t}}{\Delta \ln Y_t^R} + \frac{\Delta \ln P_{T_t}}{\Delta \sum_{i=1}^{\infty} \ln G_{t-i}^R} = .393\% - .499\% = -.106\%$$

The terms of trade fall in this case because the rightward shift of export supply is greater than the rightward shift of export demand. A similar analysis for Ceylon would yield the opposite result, a rise in

Table 6.1. Short-Run Reduced Form Multipliers

Endogenous variable (logarithm)	Current exogenous variables			Lagged endogenous variables	
	Import price Pm	Developed country's real income Y^R	Developed country's domestic price Pd	Real exports X^R	Accumulated real government expenditures $\sum_{i=1}^{\infty} G^R_{t-i}$
6.1A. Ceylon					
X^R, real exports	-.086	.320	.104	.749	.207
Px, export price	.194	1.059	.343	-.306	-.469
M^R, real imports	-.385	.668	.216	-.253	.047
X, exports	.108	1.379	.446	.443	-.262
M, imports	.614	.668	.216	-.253	.047
P_T, terms-of-trade	-.806	1.058	.343	-.306	-.469
B_T, trade balance	-.506	.711	.230	.697	-.309
R, government revenue	.053	.370	.120	.132	.165
G, government expenditures	.027	.187	.060	.066	.083
G^R, real government expenditures	-.973	.187	.060	.066	.083
6.1B. Chile					
X^R, real exports	-.325	.126	.185	.084	.493
Px, export price	.328	.393	.576	.262	-.499
M^R, real imports	-.541	.422	.618	.281	.105
X, exports	.004	.526	.761	.346	-.005

M,	imports	.459	.422	.618	.281	.105
P_T,	terms-of-trade	-.672	.393	.576	.262	-.499
B_T,	trade balance	-.455	.098	.143	.065	-.110
R,	government revenue	-.186	.182	.266	.121	.429
G,	government expenditures	-.132	.129	.189	.086	.304
G^R,	real government expenditures	-1.132	.129	.189	.086	.304

6.1C. Cuba

X^R,	real exports	-.296	.167	.299	.270	.406
Px,	export price	.376	.612	1.094	-.342	-.515
M^R,	real imports	-.303	.367	.656	.153	.230
X,	exports	.079	.780	1.393	-.072	-.109
M,	imports	.697	.367	.656	.153	.230
P_T,	terms-of-trade	-.624	.612	1.094	-.342	-.515
B_T,	trade balance	-.618	.413	.737	-.225	-.339
R,	government revenue	-.181	.217	.388	.284	.427
G,	government expenditures	-.118	.141	.251	.184	.277
G^R,	real government expenditures	-1.118	.141	.251	.184	.277

6.1D. Egypt

X^R,	real exports	-.209	.477	.092	.000	.146
Px,	export price	.917	1.781	.343	.000	-.639
M^R,	real imports	-.355	.962	.185	-.716	-.033

(Continued)

Table 6.1—Continued

Endogenous variable (logarithm)	Current exogenous variables			Lagged endogenous variables	
	Import price Pm	Developed country's real income Y^R	Developed country's domestic price Pd	Real exports X^R	Accumulated real government expenditures $\sum_{i=1}^{\infty} G^R_{t-i}$
X, exports	.708	2.258	.435	.000	−.493
M, imports	.645	.962	.185	−.716	−.033
P_T, terms-of-trade	−.083	1.781	.343	.000	−.639
B_T, trade balance	.063	1.296	.249	.716	−.461
R, government revenue	.261	.890	.171	−.851	.071
G, government expenditures	.145	.495	.095	−.473	.040
G^R, real government expenditures	−.855	.495	.095	−.473	.040
6.1E. India					
X^R, real exports	−.096	.401	.100	.700	.090
Px, export price	.451	.951	.238	.243	−.420
M^R, real imports	−.362	.778	.195	.132	−.082
X, exports	.355	1.352	.338	.457	−.330
M, imports	.638	.778	.195	.132	−.082
P_T, terms-of-trade	−.549	.951	.238	.243	−.420
B_T, trade balance	−.284	.575	.144	.325	−.248

R,	government revenue	.492	.744	.186	.179	-.042
G,	government expenditures	.417	.630	.158	.151	-.035
G^R,	real government expenditures	-.583	.630	.158	.151	-.035

6.1F. Jamaica

X^R,	real exports	-.304	.560	.128	.517	.277
Px,	export price	.673	1.045	.239	.485	-.614
M^R,	real imports	-.315	1.463	.335	.076	-.243
X,	exports	.369	1.604	.368	1.002	-.337
M,	imports	.685	1.463	.335	.076	-.243
P_T,	terms-of-trade	-.327	1.045	.239	.485	-.614
B_T,	trade balance	-.316	.141	.032	.926	-.094
R,	government revenue	.322	1.114	.255	.142	-.054
G,	government expenditures	.187	.646	.148	.082	-.032
G^R,	real government expenditures	-.813	.646	.148	.082	-.032

6.1G. Nigeria

X^R,	real exports	-.133	.265	.157	.598	.206
Px,	export price	.704	1.863	1.104	.726	-1.091
M^R,	real imports	-.544	1.661	.984	.424	-.614
X,	exports	.571	2.128	1.261	1.324	-.885
M,	imports	.456	1.661	.984	.424	-.614
P_T,	terms-of-trade	-.296	1.863	1.104	.726	-1.091

(Continued)

Table 6.1–Continued

Endogenous variable (logarithm)	Current exogenous variables			Lagged endogenous variables	
	Import price Pm	Developed country's real income Y^R	Developed country's domestic price Pd	Real exports X^R	Accumulated real government expenditures $\sum_{i=1}^{\infty} G^R_{t-i}$
B_T, trade balance	.116	.467	.277	.901	-.271
R, government revenue	.104	1.045	.691	.346	-.116
G, government expenditures	.041	.418	.248	.138	-.046
G^R, real government expenditures	-.959	.418	.248	.138	-.046
6.1H. Philippines					
X^R, real exports	-.143	.148	.210	.299	.599
Px, export price	.287	.553	.784	.156	-1.201
M^R, real imports	-.092	.288	.408	-.080	.282
X, exports	.144	.701	.994	.455	-.603
M, imports	.908	.288	.408	-.080	.282
P_T, terms-of-trade	-.713	.553	.784	.156	-1.201
B_T, trade balance	-.764	.413	.586	.535	-.885
R, government revenue	.492	.231	.328	-.054	.403
G, government expenditures	.321	.151	.214	-.035	.263
G^R, real government expenditures	-.679	.151	.214	-.035	.263

6.1I. Taiwan

X^R, real exports	-.362	.411	.071	.488	.340
Px, export price	.331	1.131	.197	.287	-.311
M^R, real imports	-.581	.606	.105	.037	.275
X, exports	-.031	1.542	.268	.775	.030
M, imports	.419	.606	.105	.037	.275
P_T, terms-of-trade	-.660	1.131	.197	.287	-.311
B_T, trade balance	-.451	.936	.163	.738	-.245
R, government revenue	.036	.346	.060	.037	.205
G, government expenditures	.031	.294	.051	.032	.175
G^R, real government expenditures	-.969	.294	.051	.032	.175

6.1J. Thailand

X^R, real exports	-.120	.467	.314	.107	.207
Px, export price	.564	2.954	1.988	.678	-.976
M^R, real imports	-.425	1.661	1.118	-.382	-.214
X, exports	.444	3.421	2.303	.785	-.769
M, imports	.575	1.661	1.118	-.382	-.214
P_T, terms-of-trade	-.436	2.954	1.988	.678	-.976
B_T, trade balance	-.131	1.760	1.185	1.166	-.555
R, government revenue	.159	.647	.435	-.254	-.022
G, government expenditures	.100	.405	.272	-.159	-.014
G^R, real government expenditures	-.900	.405	.272	-.159	-.014

the terms of trade of .590 percent. An important implication of this result is that the same set of assumed changes can cause the terms of trade to move either in favor of or against a colony depending upon the actual values of the impact multipliers. This analysis indicates clearly how the terms of trade for these countries were endogenously determined by both external and internal forces. International development models have often attempted to explain this price behavior in terms of external forces alone and have rarely, if ever, been concerned with the importance of the government in promoting exports.

As the coefficients in the export demand curve for the developed country's real income and domestic prices are positive, an increase in either of these two variables shifts the export demand curve to the right. Thus, for every country, the short-run reduced form multipliers for real exports and export prices are positive. The result is a short-run expansion of both the colonial trade and government sectors, and all the other impact multipliers are positive (columns 2 and 3 of table 6.1). Therefore, an increase (decrease) in real income or domestic prices in the developed world would have a short-run expansionary (depressing) effect on the colonial trade and government sectors.

The analysis for the other multipliers is more complicated. An increase in the colonial import price shifts the supply curve to the left, so that real exports fall and export prices rise in the short run (column 1, table 6.1). Nominal exports then would rise in every country except Chile, which is the only country with an elastic short-run export demand curve.[1] As colonial import demand is inelastic, real imports would increase. The terms of trade would shift in the short-run against every colony, and the trade balance would shift against them also, except in Egypt and Nigeria where export prices and thus nominal exports would increase the most due to their inelastic short-run export demand.[2] Nominal government revenues and expenditures could rise or fall in the short-run due to an import price increase depending on whether increased taxes from increased nominal imports were, respectively, smaller or larger than the decreased taxes from lowered real exports. Most important, however, is that short-run real government expenditures fall in every country because even if nominal government expenditures rise, they do not rise as much as the assumed increase in import prices. Thus, a rise in import prices would

1. See table 4.3.
2. See table 4.3.

act as a depressing force on real colonial economic activity. Alternatively, a short-run decrease in the import price would increase real government expenditures in every country.

The short-run reduced form multipliers for lagged real exports depend in part upon the existence of distributed lag adjustments in export supply and demand. They also depend on whether there is an autoregressive process in those two equations and in the import equations as well.[3] Thus, since the estimated export supply and demand curves for Egypt do not have either distributed lags or autoregressive adjustment,[4] then the lagged real exports multipliers for Egypt's real exports, export price, and terms of trade are zero (column 4, table 6.1D). For the other nine countries the current real exports multipliers for lagged real exports are positive (column 4, table 6.1). This indicates that an increase in real exports in one year caused by favorable export supply or demand conditions would carry over into the next year. Alternatively, a decrease in real exports in one year caused by unfavorable supply conditions such as drought, flood or hurricane, or unfavorable demand conditions such as a real income decline in the developed world, would cause a decline in real exports in the following year. Excluding Egypt, the export price and the terms of trade multipliers for lagged real exports can be positive or negative depending on the relative importance of the adjustments measured by distributed lags and autoregressive processes in export supply and demand. The results are mixed, with negative export price multipliers in Ceylon, Chile, and Cuba and positive multipliers in six countries. The real and nominal import multipliers, which are equal in this case, are always less than those for nominal exports, and thus the trade balance multipliers are all positive. The multipliers for government revenues and expenditures can be negative provided not only that the nominal imports multipliers due to a short-run increase in real exports are negative, but also that the resulting fall in revenue from nominal imports is greater than the increase in revenue from increased real exports. The government revenues and expenditures multipliers of three countries—Egypt, the Philippines, and Thailand—are negative, indicating that a short-run increase in real exports has a depressing effect on the government sectors of these three countries (column 4, table 6.1).

We found that the marginal productivity of accumulated real gov-

3. See equation 6.6 in this chapter's supplement.
4. See tables 4.1 and 4.3.

ernment expenditures in increasing export supply was positive in every country. Thus an increase in lagged accumulated government expenditures would shift real export supply to the right so that real exports would rise and the export price would fall in the short run (column 5, table 6.1). As a result, real nominal imports can either rise or fall, but in every country the short-run multiplier for nominal imports is less than that for nominal exports, so that the trade balance would have shifted in the short run against all ten countries. As is the case for lagged real exports, current government revenues and expenditures can either rise or fall. The short-run government multipliers are very small or negative for Egypt, India, Jamaica, Nigeria, and Thailand, indicating that an increase in lagged accumulated real government expenditures would have had initially a depressing or a very limited positive effect on the government sectors of these countries.[5]

We wish to emphasize that the short-run reduced form multipliers explain only the initial steps of the circular process of colonial development. The analysis of the development impact over time of an assumed change in either exogenous or lagged endogenous variables requires the calculation of dynamic multipliers. The analysis of the values of these multipliers not only will yield results about the development impact over time, but also will yield further information about the differences in the short-run reduced form multipliers.

DYNAMIC AND LONG-RUN BALANCED GROWTH MULTIPLIERS

The calculation of dynamic multipliers requires that a basic dynamic simulation be performed first. For this dynamic simulation, all the actual values of the exogenous variables and only the initial actual values of the lagged endogenous variables are used. Then, successively for each year of the dynamic simulation, the simulated values of the current endogenous variables are calculated using the short-run reduced form solution, and then accumulated real government expenditures are found using the inventory equation (2.12′). Except for the initial year, the dynamic simulation does not use the actual lagged endogenous variables in this solution. Instead, the simulated values of the lagged endogenous variables which have already been calculated are used.

The dynamic multipliers can then be calculated directly by performing a new dynamic simulation in which a change in the value of either an exogenous variable or a lagged endogenous variable is speci-

5. This important result will be further analyzed in the next chapter.

fied. For each year, the dynamic multiplier of an endogenous variable is the difference between its value from the new dynamic simulation and its value from the basic dynamic simulation. The dynamic multipliers for the first year are exactly the same as the short-run reduced form multipliers. The dynamic multipliers take into account all the features of the model including the possible distributed lags in equations for export supply, export demand, and government expenditures; the autoregressive process in each behavioral equation, and the fact that the inventory equation for calculating accumulated real government expenditures (2.12′) is not log-linear like the other structural equations (2.1 through 2.11).

The calculation of the long-run balanced growth multipliers assumes that in long-run equilibrium the endogenous variables of the model are growing at constant, but not necessarily equal, rates.[6] However, the stock variable, accumulated real government expenditures, will grow at a steady rate if and only if it grows at the same rate as the flow variable, real government expenditures. Using these two conditions, the long-run reduced form is derived. The long-run balanced growth multipliers are the difference quotients of the long-run reduced form with respect to the exogenous variables. An important property of these estimated multipliers is that they do not require estimates of any of the long-run growth rates of the variables in the model.

HISTORICAL ACCURACY OF THE MODEL

Before we analyze the dynamic properties of this system, we examine the quality of its basic dynamic simulation; to have confidence in these multipliers, the historical explanatory power of the model must be high. For this evaluation we performed a dynamic simulation for each country for its full estimation period. Figures 6.1 through 6.10 and table 6.2 give the results of these simulations for the three most important endogenous variables—real exports, export price, and government expenditures. For the dynamic simulations, the standard error of each endogenous variable is calculated as the sum of squares of the difference between the actual and simulated values of the logarithm of that variable, divided by the number of years simulated. This method is comparable to the method described in chapter 4 for cal-

---

6. Since the endogenous variable, accumulated real government expenditures, is increasing, the equilibrium assumption that these rates are all zero is impossible. Thus, we cannot use the long-run equilibrium condition that the current and lagged values of the endogenous variables are equal.

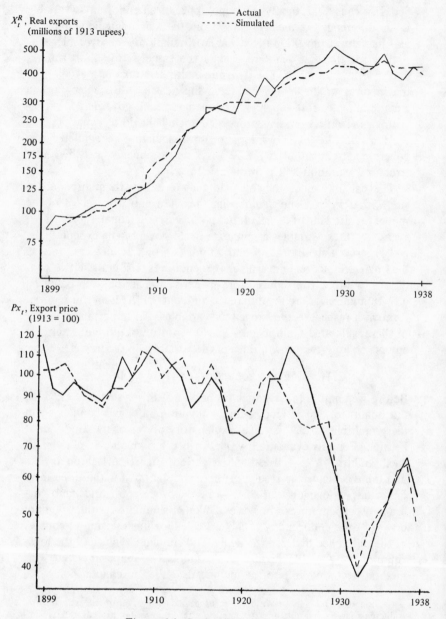

Figure 6.1. Ceylon Simulation Plots

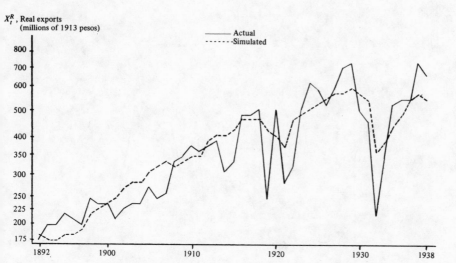

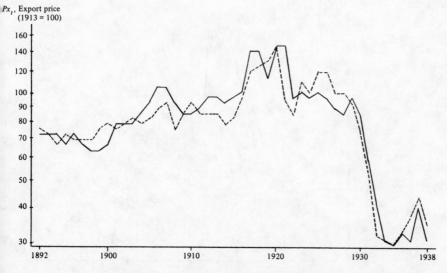

Figure 6.2. Chile Simulation Plots

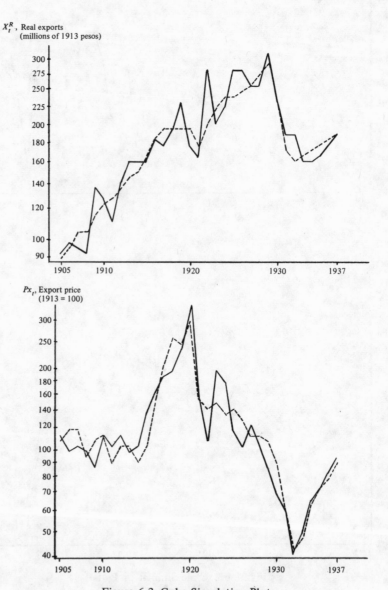

Figure 6.3. Cuba Simulation Plots

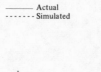

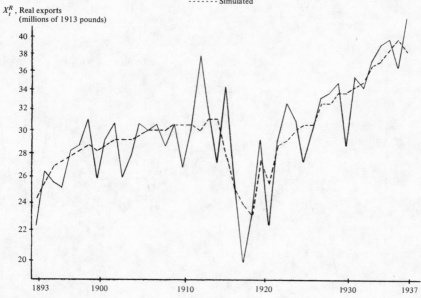

X_t^R, Real exports
(millions of 1913 pounds)

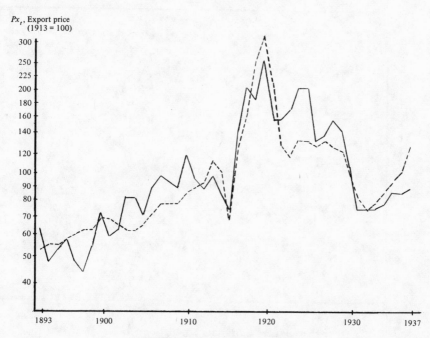

Px_t, Export price
(1913 = 100)

Figure 6.4. Egypt Simulation Plots

137

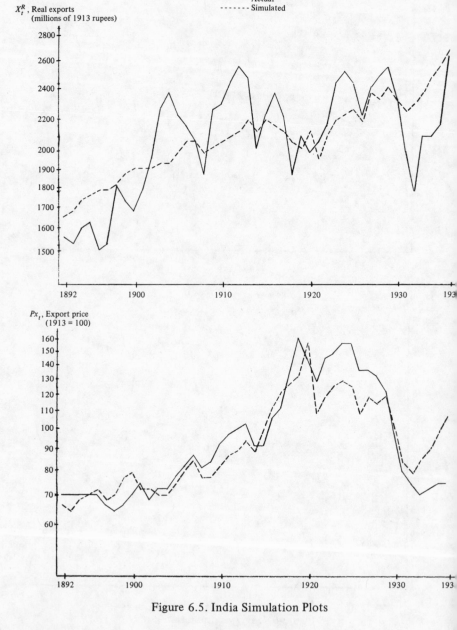

Figure 6.5. India Simulation Plots

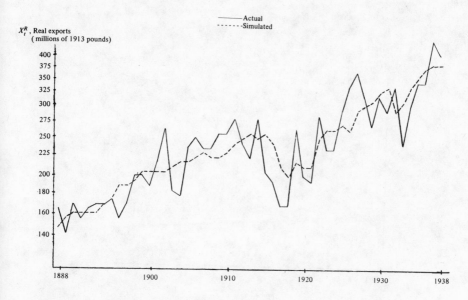

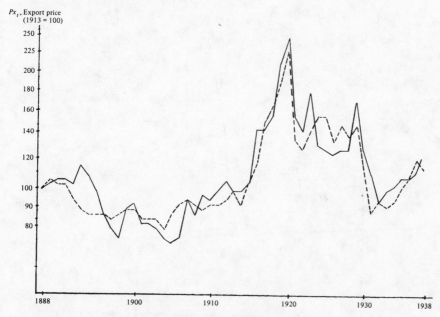

Figure 6.6. Jamaica Simulation Plots

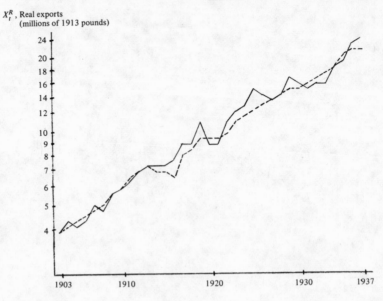

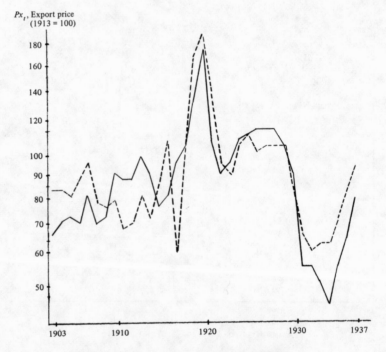

Figure 6.7. Nigeria Simulation Plots

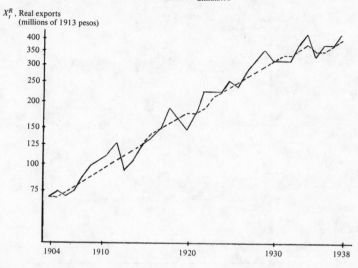

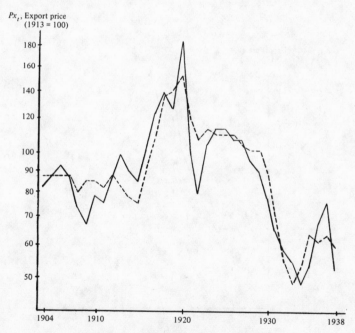

Figure 6.8. Philippines Simulation Plots

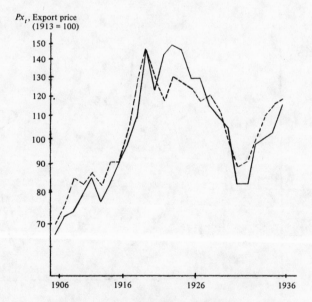

Figure 6.9. Taiwan Simulation Plots

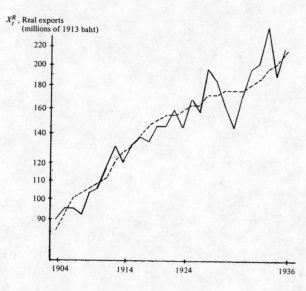

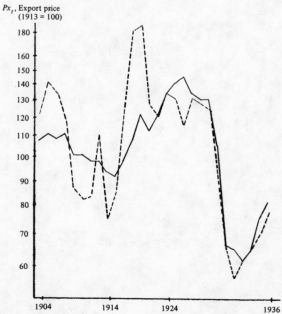

Figure 6.10. Thailand Simulation Plots

Table 6.2. Measures of Historical Accuracy of the Model

	Standard Errors					Residual of acc. real govt. exp. in final year of simulation
	Export supply equation	Export demand equation	Simulated exports	Simulated export price	Simulated acc. real govt. exp.	
	(1)	(2)	(3)	(4)	(5)	(6)
Ceylon	.069	.075	.087	.114	.017	.0076
Chile	.198	.175	.196	.136	.044	.0697
Cuba	.129	.113	.105	.168	.013	.0090
Egypt	.111	.092	.088	.217	.053	.0611
India	.077	.083	.107	.126	.031	.0028
Jamaica	.148	.126	.128	.110	.035	-.0001
Nigeria	.069	.076	.078	.189	.077	-.0172
Philippines	.110	.090	.092	.125	.033	.0181
Taiwan	.086	.118	.097	.087	.020	.0058
Thailand	.091	.087	.079	.183	.043	-.0103
Average	.1088	.1035	.1057	.1463	.0370	.0202[a]

[a] Average absolute residual

culating the standard error of each behavioral equation in the model.[7] As the variables being considered are in logarithmic form, the standard errors when multiplied by 100 can be interpreted as percentage standard errors.[8]

Real Export Development

The model dynamically explains the long-term trends and cyclical fluctuations of real exports. This conclusion can be seen in figures 6.1 through 6.10, which plot the actual and simulated values of real exports. Columns 1–3 in table 6.2 compare the standard errors of each country's estimated export supply and demand equations with the standard error of its exports from its dynamic simulation. The dynamic simulations had an average standard error of .1057 for real exports. This compares quite well with the average standard errors of .1088 in the estimated supply equations and .1035 in the estimated demand equations. Thus we conclude that the model accurately explains export development.

The simulation plots (figures 6.1–6.10) also support the conclusion that the model explains quite well the pattern of export development. These plots illustrate the degree to which the model explains both the long-term trend in export development and important deviations from that trend. For example, the dynamic simulation shows the model's power of historical prediction; it explains the sharp decreases in real exports in Chile and Cuba during the Great Depression (figures 6.2 and 6.3), as well as the large drop in real exports during World War I in Egypt and Jamaica (figures 6.4 and 6.6). Another example is the explanation of the fall in the growth rates of real exports in Ceylon and Taiwan after about 1914 (figures 6.1 and 6.9). In the following chapters, further use of these dynamic simulations will be made to analyze historical changes in colonial export development.

Export Price Fluctuations

We have previously shown that colonial development requires specifying endogenously both export prices and government expendi-

7. See equations 6.10 and 6.11 in this chapter's supplement.
8. This interpretation is a close approximation of the following exact formula

$$SE(\%) = 100 \, (e^{SE} - 1)$$

where SE = reported standard error of a logarithmic variable
$SE(\%)$ = standard error in percentage terms

For example, a .10 reported standard error corresponds to a standard error in percentage terms of 10.52 percent.

tures. As we have found, the pattern of export prices was historically very volatile[9] due to relatively price-inelastic and quite shiftable colonial supply and demand schedules. The relatively low standard errors of the simulated export prices shown in column 4 of table 6.2 are a favorable test of the model, for they show that the simulations explain quite well the historical pattern of cyclical fluctuations in the export prices of each country. Figures 6.1 through 6.10 indicate that the dynamic simulations also explain the long-term trends in export prices. For the period before World War I, for example, the dynamic simulations explain not only the long-term upward trend in export prices in Chile, Egypt, India, Nigeria, and Taiwan but also the long-term relatively stable trend in export prices in Ceylon, Cuba, Jamaica, and the Philippines, and the downward trend in export prices in Thailand.

Since chapter 9 will use dynamic simulation experiments to analyze the impact of two major events—the Great Depression and World War I—on the development of these ten countries, the validity of the analysis depends on these simulations being able to explain the substantial fluctuations in export prices that occurred. Figures 6.1–6.10 show that the simulations explain quite well the major export price decreases that occurred in every country during the Great Depression. The dynamic simulation also explains the export price increases that started with the outbreak of World War I in 1914 and reached a peak about 1920, and the export price decreases that occurred as a result of the depression of 1921–22. An exception to this pattern is Ceylon, where export prices first dropped and then rose (see figure 6.1); the dynamic simulation also exhibits this pattern.[10]

Accumulated Real Government Expenditures

Since the government sector is an important part of our model, an important check of the model is how accurately the simulations explain the stock variable, accumulated real government expenditures. If this stock variable were inaccurately simulated, then we would have incorrectly described government promotion of exports over time. However, columns 5 and 6 of table 6.2 show that the dynamic simulations accurately explain accumulated real government expenditures and

9. For an analysis of the volatility of export prices, see United Nations [117].
10. This unusual export price pattern will be explained in chapter 9's discussion of World War I.

thus are a favorable check of the method of calculating this stock variable.

Favorable simulation results were obtained for the remaining endogenous variables of the model. These basic simulations thus fail to reveal any systematic divergence in the simulation plots between the calculated and observed values for each endogenous variable in the model. Perhaps most important, they testify to the historical accuracy of the specified model in describing the process of colonial development from the late nineteenth century to the beginning of World War II. These favorable simulation results provide the necessary empirical support to use the model to analyze the dynamic properties of colonial development during this period, and to draw certain important conclusions about this colonial development process.

STABILITY PROPERTIES

One question of historical interest was whether the process we are describing was stable or not. Would a major shock in the external forces or the error term produce a different long-run development path in the colonies? To answer this question, we investigated the stability properties of the model by analyzing the impact of exogenous shocks on the endogenous variables. These shocks ranged in magnitude from a unit increase to a unit decrease in a given year in the value of each exogenous variable appearing in the equation system. For the exogenous variable appearing as logarithms, this was equivalent respectively to a 172 percent increase or to a 63 percent decrease. We emphasize that these changes were larger than any that appeared in the data. For each dummy variable appearing in a behavioral equation, this one-year change in the dummy was equivalent to the same change in the error term of that behavioral equation. Such an error was much larger than any of the residuals for the fifty equations we estimated.

For every country, we found the important result that the dynamic simulations of the model with these one-year exogenous shocks converged without oscillation toward the country's original long-run path. Thus, we conclude that the development process we have described was very stable. This result also suggests that to change this process of colonial development in a fundamental way required a major structural change. Perhaps the changes in the developed world caused by World War II would meet this criterion, but this war likely led to a different economic structure that would require a different model.

Methods for Calculating Multipliers

Short-Run Reduced Form Multipliers

The method of calculating the impact multipliers from the short-run reduced form employs the first eleven double logarithmic equations, 2.1 through 2.11, of the structural model. Using matrix notation for T observations, these equations can be written as

$$y_t\Gamma + y_{t-1}A + x_tB + \ln \sum_{i=1}^{\infty} G_{t-i}^{R} \, c = u_t \qquad t = 1, 2, \ldots, T$$

(6.1)

where y_t is a vector of the logarithms of all the endogenous variables except lagged accumulated real government expenditures, $\sum_{i=1}^{\infty} G_{t-i}^{R}$; c is a vector whose first element is the coefficient a_3 of the variable $\sum_{i=1}^{\infty} G_{t-i}^{R}$ in the supply equation (2.1) and whose remaining elements are zero; x_t is a vector of both exogenous logarithmic and dummy variables; and Γ, A, and B are the coefficient matrices. The estimation procedure used assumes that the error vector u_t follows a first order autoregressive pattern:

$$u_t = u_{t-1} R + e_t$$

(6.2)

where the e_t's satisfy the usual assumptions and R is a diagonal matrix whose diagonal elements have absolute values less than one.[11]

From equations 6.1 and 6.2, the model becomes:

$$y_t\Gamma = -y_{t-1}A - x_tB - \ln \sum_{i=1}^{\infty} G_{t-i}^{R} \, c + e_t$$

$$+ (y_{t-1}\Gamma + y_{t-2}A + x_{t-1}B + \ln \sum_{i=2}^{\infty} G_{t-i}^{R} \, c)R \qquad t = 1, 2, \ldots, T$$

(6.3)

Let $\hat{\Gamma}$, $\hat{A}$, $\hat{B}$, $\hat{c}$, $\hat{R}$, and $\hat{e}_t$ be estimates of Γ, A, B, c, R, and e_t, respectively. Solving for y_t yields the short-run reduced form:

$$y_t = (-y_{t-1}\hat{A} - x_t\hat{B} - \ln \sum_{i=1}^{\infty} G_{t-i}^{R} \, \hat{c} + \hat{e}_t)\hat{\Gamma}^{-1}$$

$$+ (y_{t-1}\hat{\Gamma} + y_{t-2}\hat{A} + x_{t-1}\hat{B} + \ln \sum_{i=2}^{\infty} G_{t-i}^{R} \, \hat{c})\hat{R}\hat{\Gamma}^{-1} \quad (6.4)$$

11. See supplement 4.1.

Then the short-run reduced form multipliers for the exogenous variables x_t are the difference quotient of y_t with respect to x_t:

$$\frac{\Delta y_t}{\Delta x_t} = -\hat{B}\hat{\Gamma}^{-1} \tag{6.5}$$

The calculated values of these multipliers for import price, real income, and domestic price are reported for each country in columns 1–3 of table 6.1. The short-run reduced form multipliers for the lagged endogenous variables y_{t-1} are the difference quotient:

$$\frac{\Delta y_t}{\Delta y_{t-1}} = -(\hat{A} - \hat{\Gamma}\hat{R})\hat{\Gamma}^{-1} \tag{6.6}$$

The first term of equation 6.6 measures the possible distributed lag effects, while the second term of equation 6.6 occurs because of the autoregressive adjustment. The calculated multipliers for lagged real exports are reported in column 4 of table 6.1. The short-run reduced form multipliers for the lagged endogenous variable $\ln \sum_{i=1}^{\infty} G_{t-i}^R$ are the difference quotient:

$$\frac{\Delta y_t}{\Delta \ln \sum\limits_{i=1}^{\infty} G_{t-i}^R} = -\hat{c}\hat{\Gamma}^{-1} \tag{6.7}$$

which, unlike equation 6.6, do not depend on the autoregressive adjustment. The calculated values of these multipliers are reported in column 5 of table 6.1. This matrix algebra solution for the short-run reduced form multipliers is possible even though the inventory equation for calculating accumulated real government expenditures (2.12) is not log-linear. The solution is possible because the model is ordered so that the current value of this stock variable is the last determined variable.

Long-Run Balanced Growth Multipliers

The calculation of the long-run balanced growth multipliers requires that the accumulation equation (2.12′) be replaced by a log-linear equation. To derive this equation, we begin with the long-run equilibrium condition that the stock variable, accumulated real government expenditures, grows at a constant annual rate $r_{\Sigma G}$ where:

$$\bar{r}_{\Sigma G} = \frac{G_t^R}{\sum\limits_{i=0}^{\infty} G_{t-i}^R} = \frac{G_{t-1}^R}{\sum\limits_{i=1}^{\infty} G_{t-i}^R} > 0 \tag{6.8}$$

The growth rate $\bar{r}_{\Sigma G}$ must be positive since accumulated real government expenditures increases over time. This equation implies, of course, that the flow variable G_t^R grows at the same positive rate as the stock variable $\sum\limits_{i=1}^{\infty} G_{t-i}^R$. Taking logarithms, and letting $\bar{g}_{\Sigma G} = \ln \bar{r}_{\Sigma G}$, where $\bar{g}_{\Sigma G}$ is the corresponding constant continuous growth rate of accumulated real government expenditures, yields

$$\ln \sum_{i=1}^{\infty} G_{t-i}^R = \ln G_{t-1}^R - \bar{g}_{\Sigma G} \tag{6.9}$$

Thus, for long-run balanced growth, equation 2.12' can be replaced by equation 6.9.

On the long-run balanced growth path, the endogenous variables are growing at a vector of constant rates $\bar{g}_y$, where

$$\bar{g}_y = y_t - y_{t-1} \tag{6.10}$$

The equilibrium assumption that these growth rates are zero is impossible, since real government expenditures increase over time. Further, this long-run balanced growth path has no deviations and, therefore, no autoregressive process. Thus, this path can be derived from equation 6.1 with no error term after successive substitution of the two conditions in equations 6.9 and 6.10. First, substituting equation 6.9 into equation 6.1, we obtain the following eleven-equation system:

$$y_t\Gamma + y_{t-1}A + x_tB + (\ln G_{t-1}^R - \bar{g}_{\Sigma G})c = 0 \tag{6.11}$$

As the last of the eleven lagged endogenous variables is $\ln G_{t-1}{}^R$, this expression can be simplified by defining a new coefficient matrix for y_{t-1}:

$$A^* = A + u_{11}c \tag{6.12}$$

where u_{11} is an eleven-component column vector with the last element one and the remaining elements zero. Substituting equation 6.12, equation 6.11 simplifies to

$$y_t\Gamma + y_{t-1}A^* + x_tB - \bar{g}_{\Sigma G}c = 0 \tag{6.13}$$

Now substituting equation 6.10 into equation 6.13 yields the following long-run balanced growth structural model:

$$y_t(\Gamma + A^*) + x_tB - \bar{g}_yA^* - \bar{g}_{\Sigma G}c = 0 \tag{6.14}$$

Now, partition B into a column vector of constant terms b_1 and a remaining matrix B*, and denote x_t* as the vector of exogenous variables omitting the constant term. Then equation 6.14 becomes

$$y_t(\Gamma + A^*) + x_t*B^* + b_1 - \bar{g}_yA^* - \bar{g}_{\Sigma G}c = 0 \qquad (6.15)$$

Solving 6.15 for the endogenous variables, we obtain the long-run balanced growth reduced form as

$$y_t = -x_t*B^*(\Gamma + A^*)^{-1} + (b_1 - \bar{g}_yA^* - \bar{g}_{\Sigma G}c)(\Gamma + A^*)^{-1} \qquad (6.16)$$

Taking difference quotients, the long-run balanced growth multipliers are

$$\frac{\Delta y_t}{\Delta x_t*} = -B^*(\Gamma + A^*)^{-1} \qquad (6.17)$$

The estimates of these multipliers are obtained by replacing B*, Γ, and A* with the corresponding estimated coefficient matrices $\hat{B}^*$, $\hat{\Gamma}$, and $\hat{A}^*$. To estimate these multipliers does not require estimates of the long-run growth rates $\bar{g}_y$ and $\bar{g}_{\Sigma G}$, because these growth rates enter only into the determination of a vector of constants on the right-hand side of equation 6.16 and not into equation 6.17.

7

Government Reflection Ratio

This chapter and the following chapter investigate the dynamic properties of colonial development for the ten countries in our sample using the short-run, dynamic, and long-run balanced growth multipliers. These multipliers provide the proper framework for analyzing the circular structure of the colonial development process by tracing the effects over time of an assumed change in an exogenous variable or in the initial value of a lagged endogenous variable. This development process was dependent not only upon the external forces of changes in real income and prices in the developed world; but also it was determined by the internal force of real government expenditures in the colonial world. This chapter investigates the dynamic properties of this internal force and the next chapter analyzes the external forces.

The importance of the government in promoting the export economy was described in chapters 2 and 3 and was confirmed by the estimates in chapter 4. A simulation of the model in which accumulated real government expenditures are increased in some initial base year T yields multipliers which measure the impact of these expenditures on all the endogenous variables of the colonial economy. One of the most important of these multipliers is called the government reflection ratio,[1]

$$\frac{\Delta \ln G_t}{\Delta \ln \left(\sum_{i=0}^{\infty} G_{T-i}{}^R \right)}$$

where $t > T$. Ceteris paribus, this ratio measures the productivity of past government expenditures directed toward promoting export development in generating current expenditures through the circular process of colonial development. Thus, at each point of time the

1. For the theoretical model deriving this concept, see Hymer and Resnick [16].

higher the ratio, the more productive was the government in allocating its own resources to increase real exports and, through the specified dynamic process of the model, to generate future expenditures by the government itself.

The first section of this chapter describes the multipliers for an increase in accumulated real government expenditures. The second section uses cluster analysis to classify these countries into two blocs. The two blocs are distinguished by the size of their government reflection ratio and are identical to the classification into productivity blocs obtained from the analysis of the long-run estimates in chapter 5. In the third section an analysis of the multipliers will be used to explain the causes of the differences in these productivity blocs. The fourth section derives some development implications from these differences.

Dynamic Multiplier Tables

Table 7.1 reports the multipliers associated with an assumed 1 percent increase in the initial value of the stock variable, accumulated real government expenditures. For each country, reading across a row in table 7.1, this initial increase causes computed percentage changes in each of the endogenous variables for selected years. For example, table 7.1A reports the real export multipliers for this initial 1 percent increase in the government stock variable. For example, Egyptian real exports increase by .146 percent in the first year, by .140 percent in the second year, by .135 percent in the third year, and so on. We reemphasize that the impact or short-run multipliers, which are the multipliers for the first year, do not take into account the dynamic features of the specified model. The importance of the dynamic features can be clearly seen when multipliers change signs.[2]

Table 7.1 includes all the multipliers for the first five years to allow for the analysis of the transition from the impact multipliers to the intermediate or dynamic multipliers. This table also reports the dynamic multipliers for 10, 15, 20, and 25 years. There are important reasons why we wish to analyze these longer-period dynamic multipliers. First, while we are interested in the short- to intermediate-run adjustment process, we are also very much interested in the long-term development impact that is measured by these multipliers. Second, we will use these multipliers to analyze the approach toward

2. For example, the impact multiplier for Nigeria in table 7.1G is negative, while all of its other dynamic multipliers are positive.

Table 7.1. Dynamic Multipliers for 1 Percent Increase in the Initial Value of Accumulated Real Government Expenditures

7.1A. Real Exports

	Years								
	1	2	3	4	5	10	15	20	25
Egypt	0.146	0.140	0.135	0.129	0.123	0.101	0.084	0.073	0.066
India	0.090	0.087	0.085	0.082	0.079	0.067	0.056	0.053	0.049
Jamaica	0.278	0.264	0.249	0.237	0.223	0.177	0.136	0.110	0.093
Thailand	0.207	0.175	0.149	0.123	0.109	0.054	0.035	0.028	0.021
Bloc average	0.180	0.166	0.154	0.144	0.133	0.100	0.078	0.066	0.057
Ceylon	0.206	0.301	0.342	0.354	0.354	0.316	0.272	0.229	0.200
Chile	0.493	0.516	0.504	0.493	0.481	0.421	0.365	0.325	0.285
Cuba	0.404	0.481	0.481	0.467	0.449	0.381	0.334	0.308	0.276
Nigeria	0.206	0.311	0.349	0.361	0.359	0.265	0.222	0.198	0.177
Philippines	0.598	0.691	0.690	0.674	0.658	0.584	0.523	0.476	0.426
Taiwan	0.339	0.487	0.546	0.566	0.565	0.410	0.328	0.290	0.249
Bloc average	0.374	0.464	0.485	0.486	0.478	0.396	0.341	0.304	0.269
Average, all 10 countries	0.297	0.345	0.353	0.349	0.340	0.278	0.235	0.209	0.184

Table 7.1.–*Continued*

7.1B. Export Price and Terms of Trade

	Years								
	1	2	3	4	5	10	15	20	25
Egypt	−0.639	−0.616	−0.592	−0.566	−0.542	−0.443	−0.370	−0.321	−0.292
India	−0.420	−0.408	−0.397	−0.385	−0.373	−0.319	−0.278	−0.250	−0.229
Jamaica	−0.614	−0.583	−0.552	−0.525	−0.495	−0.389	−0.305	−0.247	−0.205
Thailand	−0.976	−0.828	−0.703	−0.602	−0.516	−0.256	−0.166	−0.130	−0.101
Bloc average	−0.662	−0.609	−0.561	−0.519	−0.481	−0.352	−0.280	−0.237	−0.207
Ceylon	−0.468	−0.686	−0.778	−0.811	−0.810	−0.717	−0.614	−0.519	−0.458
Chile	−0.498	−0.351	−0.331	−0.323	−0.316	−0.276	−0.239	−0.213	−0.187
Cuba	−0.515	−0.609	−0.609	−0.590	−0.570	−0.482	−0.424	−0.391	−0.350
Nigeria	−1.090	−0.846	−0.636	−0.552	−0.498	−0.309	−0.290	−0.269	−0.230
Philippines	−1.201	−0.677	−0.562	−0.533	−0.519	−0.467	−0.416	−0.378	−0.336
Taiwan	−0.311	−0.447	−0.502	−0.518	−0.517	−0.376	−0.303	−0.265	−0.230
Bloc average	−0.681	−0.603	−0.570	−0.554	−0.538	−0.438	−0.381	−0.339	−0.298
Average, all 10 countries	−0.673	−0.605	−0.566	−0.540	−0.516	−0.403	−0.340	−0.298	−0.262

Table 7.1.—*Continued*
7.1C. Nominal Exports

					Years				
	1	2	3	4	5	10	15	20	25
Egypt	-0.494	-0.476	-0.457	-0.437	-0.419	-0.342	-0.286	-0.248	-0.225
India	-0.331	-0.320	-0.313	-0.305	-0.293	-0.250	-0.220	-0.194	-0.180
Jamaica	-0.337	-0.320	-0.302	-0.288	-0.272	-0.215	-0.168	-0.136	-0.111
Thailand	-0.769	-0.652	-0.554	-0.475	-0.406	-0.204	-0.131	-0.103	-0.078
Bloc average	-0.483	-0.442	-0.406	-0.376	-0.347	-0.253	-0.201	-0.170	-0.148
Ceylon	-0.262	-0.383	-0.438	-0.453	-0.456	-0.397	-0.342	-0.287	-0.255
Chile	-0.006	0.165	0.174	0.169	0.165	0.145	0.128	0.111	0.096
Cuba	-0.110	-0.131	-0.130	-0.125	-0.121	-0.101	-0.090	-0.081	-0.073
Nigeria	-0.884	-0.536	-0.287	-0.191	-0.141	-0.044	-0.070	-0.070	-0.053
Philippines	-0.603	0.014	0.127	0.140	0.139	0.121	0.108	0.099	0.089
Taiwan	0.027	0.040	0.046	0.046	0.047	0.037	0.027	0.026	0.018
Bloc average	-0.306	-0.138	-0.085	-0.069	-0.061	-0.040	-0.040	-0.034	-0.030
Average, all 10 countries	-0.377	-0.260	-0.213	-0.192	-0.176	-0.125	-0.104	-0.088	-0.077

Table 7.1—*Continued*
7.1D. Real and Nominal Imports

					Years				
	1	2	3	4	5	10	15	20	25
Egypt	-0.033	-0.032	-0.031	-0.029	-0.028	-0.023	-0.019	-0.017	-0.015
India	-0.082	-0.081	-0.079	-0.075	-0.075	-0.058	-0.056	-0.049	-0.049
Jamaica	-0.243	-0.230	-0.218	-0.207	-0.197	-0.156	-0.122	-0.095	-0.081
Thailand	-0.214	-0.181	-0.154	-0.132	-0.113	-0.056	-0.037	-0.029	-0.022
Bloc average	-0.143	-0.131	-0.120	-0.111	-0.103	-0.073	-0.058	-0.047	-0.042
Ceylon	0.049	0.070	0.081	0.084	0.084	0.075	0.061	0.053	0.044
Chile	0.104	0.238	0.243	0.238	0.230	0.206	0.179	0.157	0.139
Cuba	0.230	0.273	0.273	0.266	0.256	0.215	0.189	0.174	0.156
Nigeria	-0.613	-0.325	-0.131	-0.057	-0.018	0.011	0.004	0.004	0.004
Philippines	0.282	0.508	0.536	0.526	0.516	0.459	0.409	0.375	0.334
Taiwan	0.275	0.395	0.443	0.458	0.458	0.331	0.269	0.235	0.201
Bloc average	0.054	0.193	0.241	0.252	0.254	0.216	0.185	0.166	0.146
Average, all 10 countries	-0.025	0.063	0.096	0.107	0.111	0.100	0.088	0.081	0.071

Table 7.1—*Continued*
7.1E. Trade Balance

	Years								
	1	2	3	4	5	10	15	20	25
Egypt	-0.461	-0.444	-0.426	-0.408	-0.391	-0.319	-0.267	-0.232	-0.210
India	-0.249	-0.240	-0.233	-0.230	-0.218	-0.192	-0.163	-0.145	-0.131
Jamaica	-0.095	-0.090	-0.084	-0.081	-0.075	-0.058	-0.046	-0.041	-0.031
Thailand	-0.555	-0.471	-0.400	-0.343	-0.293	-0.147	-0.094	-0.074	-0.056
Bloc average	-0.340	-0.311	-0.286	-0.265	-0.244	-0.179	-0.142	-0.123	-0.107
Ceylon	-0.310	-0.452	-0.517	-0.537	-0.540	-0.473	-0.403	-0.340	-0.299
Chile	-0.110	-0.073	-0.069	-0.069	-0.066	-0.061	-0.050	-0.046	-0.044
Cuba	-0.340	-0.404	-0.404	-0.389	-0.375	-0.316	-0.279	-0.256	-0.229
Nigeria	-0.271	-0.210	-0.156	-0.134	-0.123	-0.075	-0.073	-0.066	-0.056
Philippines	-0.887	-0.493	-0.409	-0.386	-0.377	-0.339	-0.301	-0.276	-0.246
Taiwan	-0.247	-0.356	-0.397	-0.412	-0.409	-0.294	-0.241	-0.209	-0.183
Bloc average	-0.361	-0.331	-0.325	-0.321	-0.315	-0.260	-0.224	-0.199	-0.176
Average, all 10 countries	-0.352	-0.323	-0.309	-0.299	-0.287	-0.227	-0.192	-0.168	-0.148

Table 7.1—*Continued*
7.1F. Government Revenues

				Years					
	1	*2*	*3*	*4*	*5*	*10*	*15*	*20*	*25*
Egypt	0.072	0.070	0.067	0.064	0.061	0.050	0.042	0.036	0.033
India	-0.043	-0.040	-0.040	-0.040	-0.038	-0.031	-0.029	-0.027	-0.026
Jamaica	-0.055	-0.052	-0.049	-0.047	-0.043	-0.033	-0.027	-0.021	-0.018
Thailand	-0.022	-0.019	-0.016	-0.014	-0.012	-0.006	-0.004	-0.003	-0.003
Bloc average	-0.012	-0.010	-0.010	-0.009	-0.008	-0.005	-0.004	-0.004	-0.003
Ceylon	0.163	0.240	0.273	0.285	0.284	0.253	0.215	0.183	0.159
Chile	0.427	0.470	0.461	0.453	0.443	0.388	0.336	0.299	0.262
Cuba	0.427	0.505	0.505	0.490	0.471	0.400	0.352	0.323	0.290
Nigeria	-0.116	0.119	0.247	0.295	0.312	0.250	0.199	0.175	0.159
Philippines	0.404	0.577	0.594	0.580	0.565	0.508	0.452	0.412	0.363
Taiwan	0.204	0.296	0.331	0.342	0.340	0.247	0.198	0.175	0.150
Bloc average	0.251	0.368	0.402	0.407	0.402	0.341	0.292	0.261	0.230
Average, all 10 countries	0.146	0.217	0.237	0.241	0.238	0.203	0.173	0.155	0.137

Table 7.1—*Continued*

7.1G. Nominal and Real Government Expenditures

	Years								
	1	2	3	4	5	10	15	20	25
Egypt	0.040	0.056	0.062	0.063	0.062	0.052	0.043	0.037	0.033
India	-0.035	-0.040	-0.040	-0.037	-0.037	-0.032	-0.031	-0.024	-0.023
Jamaica	-0.032	-0.043	-0.047	-0.046	-0.046	-0.037	-0.029	-0.023	-0.018
Thailand	-0.014	-0.017	-0.016	-0.014	-0.012	-0.006	-0.004	-0.003	-0.002
Bloc average	-0.010	-0.011	-0.010	-0.008	-0.008	-0.006	-0.005	-0.003	-0.002
Ceylon	0.082	0.162	0.218	0.252	0.269	0.259	0.223	0.191	0.165
Chile	0.304	0.423	0.450	0.450	0.444	0.394	0.339	0.301	0.267
Cuba	0.276	0.424	0.478	0.485	0.478	0.407	0.356	0.327	0.294
Nigeria	-0.046	0.019	0.110	0.184	0.236	0.270	0.215	0.186	0.164
Philippines	0.262	0.467	0.549	0.571	0.568	0.513	0.458	0.415	0.372
Taiwan	0.175	0.278	0.320	0.337	0.339	0.249	0.198	0.174	0.151
Bloc average	0.175	0.295	0.354	0.380	0.389	0.349	0.298	0.266	0.235
Average, all 10 countries	0.101	0.173	0.208	0.224	0.230	0.207	0.177	0.158	0.140

Table 7.1—*Continued*

7.1H. Accumulated Real Government Expenditures

	Years								
	1	2	3	4	5	10	15	20	25
Egypt	0.964	0.925	0.886	0.849	0.812	0.666	0.562	0.491	0.454
India	0.972	0.945	0.916	0.888	0.861	0.739	0.644	0.584	0.536
Jamaica	0.949	0.900	0.854	0.806	0.766	0.604	0.473	0.386	0.323
Thailand	0.848	0.720	0.617	0.529	0.459	0.243	0.162	0.127	0.096
Bloc average	0.933	0.872	0.818	0.768	0.724	0.563	0.460	0.397	0.352
Ceylon	0.963	0.931	0.899	0.865	0.832	0.722	0.609	0.523	0.464
Chile	0.961	0.934	0.912	0.891	0.871	0.761	0.659	0.589	0.516
Cuba	0.914	0.864	0.827	0.797	0.769	0.656	0.587	0.536	0.481
Nigeria	0.912	0.790	0.739	0.697	0.589	0.458	0.410	0.363	0.327
Philippines	0.948	0.912	0.887	0.865	0.845	0.755	0.677	0.613	0.548
Taiwan	0.966	0.937	0.908	0.879	0.848	0.597	0.488	0.430	0.372
Bloc average	0.944	0.895	0.862	0.832	0.792	0.658	0.572	0.509	0.451
Average, all 10 countries	0.940	0.886	0.844	0.807	0.765	0.620	0.527	0.464	0.412

the long-run equilibrium. These multipliers show that this approach during the colonial period was quite gradual. Third, some important results only become apparent over a longer time span.

CLUSTER ANALYSIS

An important application of cluster analysis is that it can also be applied to these dynamic multipliers to identify and describe groups of countries which had similar multipliers for an increase in accumulated real government expenditures. A cluster analysis of these multipliers[3] classifies the ten countries into two groups. In actual fact, we identified these two blocs first by direct examination of the multiplier tables. This early classification of the countries into blocs was thus confirmed by the cluster analysis. The first group is the previously identified low productivity bloc consisting of Egypt, India, Jamaica, and Thailand. The second group includes the remaining six countries, which form the high productivity bloc. This classification is the same as that found for the long-run structural coefficients. This result is consistent with our conclusion about the major importance of increases in government expenditures on the long-run growth of the export economy. Comparing the average multipliers for these two groups in table 7.1 shows that the low productivity bloc has a much smaller increase in real exports, a decrease rather than an increase in real imports, and a more rapid decline over time in the multipliers for accumulated real government expenditures. For both blocs, the decline in export prices and the shift toward a trade deficit are roughly the same.

For all the multipliers associated with this change in the initial value of accumulated real government expenditures, the relative cost of the classification into two groups is a 9.07 percent reduction in the total variance of the multipliers. The low productivity bloc is more homogeneous; the relative cost of forming this bloc is 2.07 percent. The relative cost of forming the more heterogeneous high productivity bloc of six countries is 7.00 percent. However, this cost arises primarily from including the Philippines and Nigeria in this bloc at rela-

3. The multipliers for nominal exports were excluded from the cluster analysis since they are by definition exactly the sum of the multipliers for real exports and the export price. The multipliers for government revenues were also excluded, since the government expenditure multipliers follow the same pattern of values due to the specification of the government expenditure equation 2.10.

tive costs of 1.84 percent and 2.77 percent, respectively. Furthermore, the Philippines and Nigeria have the largest squared distance from the high productivity bloc mean (see table 7.2). The difference between the Philippines and the rest of the high productivity bloc is that it has, in general, the largest multipliers. Nigeria's negative multipliers for real imports in the first five years (table 7.1D) and for government revenues and expenditures in the first year (tables 7.1F and 7.1G) are the most important differences between Nigeria and the rest of the high productivity bloc. Further explanation of the differences between these countries will require a dynamic analysis of the multipliers.

DYNAMIC ANALYSIS OF MULTIPLIERS

The arrow diagram (figure 7.1) is a graphic description of the changes caused by a 1 percent increase in lagged accumulated real government expenditures. We are assuming that the first period (or current) exogenous variables are unchanged. Thus the export demand schedule is unchanged, while the increase in accumulated real government expenditures shifts the export supply function rightward. As a result, real exports rise and the export price falls (figure 7.1). The actual impact multipliers for real exports and the export price can be derived from the structural equations (2.1–2.3) as:

Table 7.2. Distance Classification for Accumulated Real
Government Expenditure Multipliers

Merged bloc	Country	Squared distance from bloc means		Bloc classification by minimum distance criterion
		Low	*High*	
Low government reflection ratio bloc	Egypt	.334	1.906	Low
	India	.404	3.037	Low
	Jamaica	.390	3.231	Low
	Thailand	.869	3.971	Low
High government reflection ratio bloc	Ceylon	2.199	1.087	High
	Chile	3.690	.886	High
	Cuba	3.466	.196	High
	Nigeria	2.232	1.414	High
	Philippines	7.779	1.808	High
	Taiwan	3.645	.561	High

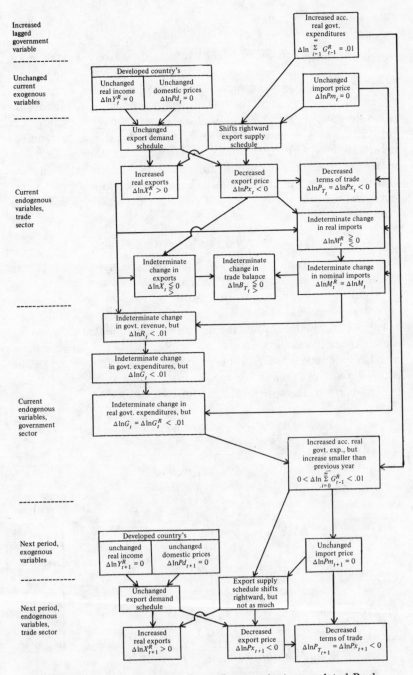

Figure 7.1. Arrow Diagram for an Increase in Accumulated Real
Government Expenditures

$$\frac{\Delta \ln X_t^R}{\Delta \ln \sum_{i=1}^{\infty} G_{t-i}^R} = -\frac{a_3 b_1}{a_1 - b_1} > 0$$

$$\frac{\Delta \ln P_x}{\Delta \ln \sum_{i=1}^{\infty} G_{t-i}^R} = -\frac{a_3}{a_1 - b_1} < 0$$

where $a_1 > 0$, $a_3 > 0$, $b_1 < 0$. The larger is a_3, the coefficient measuring the export-promoting productivity of government expenditures, the larger are these multipliers; the larger are the supply and demand price elasticities—a_1 and b_1 respectively—the smaller are these multipliers. Tables 7.1A and 7.1B give the values of these impact multipliers and their associated dynamic multipliers. The signs of these impact multipliers are as already derived. For nominal exports, the impact multiplier is

$$\frac{\Delta \ln X}{\Delta \ln \sum_{i=1}^{\infty} G_{t-i}^R} = \frac{-a_3(b_1 + 1)}{a_1 - b_1} \gtreqless 0, \qquad \text{when } |b_1| \gtreqless 1$$

Thus, nominal exports rise if the demand schedule is price elastic and fall if the schedule is price inelastic. As Taiwan is the only country with a demand schedule that is price elastic in the short run (table 4.1), it is the only country with an increase in nominal exports in the first period (table 7.1A).

Because real exports rise while the export price falls as a result of this rightward shift of the supply schedule, the impact multiplier for real imports can be either positive or negative (figure 7.1):

$$\frac{\Delta \ln M_t^R}{\Delta \ln \sum_{i=1}^{\infty} G_{t-i}^R} = -\frac{a_3(c_1 b_1 + c_3)}{a_1 - b_1} \gtreqless 0, \qquad \text{when } (c_1 b_1 + c_3) \lesseqgtr 0$$

where $c_1 > 0$ and $c_3 > 0$. Note that the magnitude but not the sign of this multiplier depends on the marginal productivity of export-promoting government expenditures measured by a_3. The sign of this multiplier depends only on the price elasticity of export demand, b_1, and on the coefficients c_1 and c_3 of the import equation. The more price inelastic is the demand for real exports, the more likely is it that this multiplier will be negative. Correspondingly, the change in nominal imports cannot be predicted because, with an assumed unchanged import price, the nominal import multiplier equals the real import multiplier. Therefore, even though real exports have increased, the multiplier for government revenue can be either positive or negative as the nominal import multiplier's sign is indeterminate (figure 7.1). The impact multiplier for government revenue is

$$\frac{\Delta \ln R_t}{\Delta \ln \sum_{i=1}^{\infty} G_{t-i}^R} = \frac{-a_3(d_1b_1 + d_2(c_1b_1 + c_3))}{a_1 - b_1} \gtreqless 0,$$

$$\text{when} \quad d_1b_1 + d_2(c_1b_1 + c_3) \lesseqgtr 0$$

where $d_1 > 0$ and $d_2 > 0$.

The sign of the reflection ratio for the first year, like that of the revenue multiplier, is indeterminate, because the reflection ratio for the first year is

$$\frac{\Delta \ln G_t}{\Delta \ln \sum_{i=1}^{\infty} G_{t-i}} = e_1 \frac{\Delta \ln R}{\Delta \ln \sum_{i=1}^{\infty} G_{t-i}^R}$$

where e_1 is a positive coefficient measuring the expenditures of the government out of current revenue. According to table 7.1F, there are four countries whose government expenditures fall in the first year as a result of an increase in the stock of real government expenditures. There is one country, Egypt, where there is only a small rise in government expenditures. Government expenditures increase significantly in the other five countries.

The impact multiplier for accumulated real government expenditures itself can be derived from equation 2.12′ as[4]

---

4. This result can be derived by taking the difference quotient of equation 2.12′ with respect to lagged accumulated real government expenditures:

$$\frac{\Delta \ln \sum_{i=1}^{\infty} G_{t-i}^R}{\Delta \ln \sum_{i=1}^{\infty} G_{t-i}^R} = \frac{e^{\ln \sum_{i=1}^{\infty} G_{t-i}^R} + e\ln G_t^R \left(\dfrac{\Delta \ln G_t^R}{\Delta \ln \sum_{i=1}^{\infty} G_{t-i}^R} \right)}{e^{\ln \sum_{i=1}^{\infty} G_{t-i}^R} + e\ln G_t^R}$$

Simplifying:
$$\frac{\Delta \ln \sum_{i=0}^{\infty} G_{t-i}^R}{\Delta \ln \sum_{i=1}^{\infty} G_{t-i}^R} = \frac{\sum_{i=1}^{\infty} G_{t-i}^R + G_t^R \left(\dfrac{\Delta \ln G_t^R}{\Delta \ln \sum_{i=1}^{\infty} G_{t-i}^R} \right)}{\sum_{i=0}^{\infty} G_{t-i}^R}$$

Rearranging, we obtain the desired result.

$$\frac{\Delta \ln \sum\limits_{i=0}^{\infty} G_{t-i}^R}{\Delta \ln \sum\limits_{i=1}^{\infty} G_{t-i}^R} = 1 + \frac{G_t^R}{\sum\limits_{i=0}^{\infty} G_{t-i}^R} \left(\frac{\Delta \ln G_t^R}{\Delta \ln \sum\limits_{i=1}^{\infty} G_{t-i}^R} - 1 \right)$$

This multiplier thus depends both on the government reflection ratio and on the growth rate of accumulated real government expenditures at time t, which is defined as

$$g_t = \frac{G_t^R}{\sum\limits_{i=0}^{\infty} G_{t-i}^R}$$

Furthermore, since g_t is positive,

$$\frac{\Delta \ln \sum\limits_{i=0}^{\infty} G_{t-i}^R}{\Delta \ln \sum\limits_{i=1}^{\infty} G_{t-i}^R} \gtreqless 1 \quad \text{when} \quad \frac{\Delta \ln G_t^R}{\Delta \ln \sum\limits_{i=1}^{\infty} G_{t-i}^R} \gtreqless 1$$

then the multipliers for accumulated real government expenditures can theoretically increase over time when the government reflection ratio is greater than one. For all countries in our sample, however, the multipliers decrease monotonically over time because their government reflection ratios are always less than one (see tables 7.1G and 7.1H).

This result means that in the long run no colonial country could maintain an initial 1 percent increase in the real stock of its government capital. These countries were characterized by a marginal productivity of an initial increase in government expenditures which diminished over time toward zero. For each succeeding period, the increase in accumulated real government expenditures is smaller than in the previous period, and as a result the shift in export supply decreases over time (table 7.1H and the next period of figure 7.1). Thus, all the other dynamic multipliers for a change in initial value of the endogenous government stock variable must also decrease toward zero.[5] These results, which occur because the government reflection ratio is less than one, explain our earlier conclusion about the stability of the model—the simulation path for an exogenous shock

5. This result can also be derived by using equation 5.15 for the long-run balanced growth reduced form. As this equation does not involve the initial value of accumulated real government expenditures, an increase in this initial value will have no effect on the long-run balanced growth path.

converges toward each country's original growth path in the long run.[6]

The dynamic government reflection ratios in table 7.1G thus clearly distinguish the two blocks of countries: the low productivity bloc consisting of Egypt, India, Jamaica, and Thailand, in which the government expenditure multipliers are close to zero; and the high productivity bloc of the remaining six countries, in which the multipliers are significantly greater than zero.[7] Nigeria is considered to be a member of the latter bloc because its reflection ratio becomes positive in the second year. Of the ten countries, the Philippines stands out as having the highest reflection ratio. This result is quite consistent with its economic history under U.S. rule; much of the colonial government's effort was directed toward development expenditures on transport, education, health, and so forth.[8] The countries with the highest government reflection ratios were associated with U.S. influence (Chile and Cuba), direct U.S. control (the Philippines), or Japanese control (Taiwan). One might conclude that dependence on the United States or Japan resulted in relatively efficient development of an export economy.[9]

The story for British colonialism is mixed. In previous chapters we have already seen how British control in Egypt, India, Jamaica, and Thailand limited their development and resulted in the lowest export productivity of government expenditures.[10] Historical factors may have acted to establish economic and social barriers which were difficult to overcome, such as the caste system in India or the British

6. The theoretically possible case of the reflection ratio exceeding one can also yield stability, but with the simulation path converging toward a new long-run balanced growth path.

7. This result differs from that of Hymer and Resnick [16], where the reflection ratio had a positive partial derivative. The negative ratio found in our analysis results from a different specification of the model.

8. See pp. 62–64; see also Resnick [26]. It is interesting to note that the empirical results of the present model confirm the historical analysis in Resnick's paper, which suggested that the Thai government was not as productive as the Philippine government.

9. It is possible to argue that the United States and Japan were latecomers to the colonial process and thus could draw from and improve upon the experiences of the older colonial powers in running or influencing a colonial government.

10. Chile, Cuba, and the Philippines also had long histories of Spanish influence. Chile was a colony of Spain until the early nineteenth century. Cuba and the Philippines remained colonies of Spain until the Spanish-American War. One could argue, however, that Spanish colonialism rested on an inferior mode of development as compared with British colonialism with its more favorable history of British industrial development.

emphasis on financial controls in Egypt that were intended to repay its previous loans. Thailand did have a much higher growth rate of real exports than did these three countries, but the possibility of increased government development expenditures was constrained by the Bowring Treaty and the British Financial Advisors.[11]

DEVELOPMENT IMPLICATIONS

These results suggest that although the process of export development may have been similar, the effects of colonialism differed among the ten countries in terms of the governmental effort to promote an export economy. This conclusion does not depend on the size of the government reflection ratio, for it is equally important in explaining the low growth rate of India (which had the lowest ratio) as in explaining the high growth rate of the Philippines (which had the highest ratio).

For the low productivity bloc, the real export multipliers (table 7.1A) fall over time while for the rest of the countries an increasing pattern is observed from the short-run to the intermediate-run. The multipliers of the latter group of countries fall in magnitude only as the end of the first decade is approached.

The relative gains from colonial export-promoting government expenditures can be measured by the multipliers for real imports. Table 7.1D shows that over time a negative or low reflection ratio has, as its dual, a negative import multiplier, while a country with a positive reflection ratio has a positive import multiplier. Thus, the Philippines was able to capture some of the real benefits associated with having the highest reflection ratio by also having the highest real import multiplier.

Table 7.1E shows that the nominal balance of trade shifts over time toward a nominal trade deficit as a result of an increase in the stock of real government capital. If we assume that such an increase in the stock of accumulated real government expenditures was made possible by grants of foreign aid from the developed country to its

11. See pp. 24–26; see Ingram [64] for further historical examples of this financial control. One could also argue that if the Thai government had attempted to alter its foreign-enforced tax rates or refused to build up its enormous foreign reserve position, then these actions might have caused the British to establish direct colonial rule. Thus, to preserve the integrity of Thai institutions, the government was effectively constrained from controlling and utilizing the gains from its export trade.

colony,[12] then over time the developed country would find it necessary to continue to finance its colony's trade deficit, although at a diminishing rate. Although colonial foreign aid would create a nominal trade deficit, colonial real exports would increase.

A very important difference between the low and high productivity blocs is the effectiveness over time of the government in promoting the export economy. To analyze the implications of this difference, we use the government reflection ratio for the first year:

$$\frac{\Delta \ln G_t}{\Delta \ln \sum_{i=1}^{\infty} G_{t-i}^R} = \frac{-a_3(d_1 b_1 + d_2(c_1 b_1 + c_3))}{a_1 - b_1} e_1$$

Even if the low productivity countries were able to increase a_3, which measures the productivity of their export-promoting government expenditures, the difference between the government reflection ratios of the two blocs need not narrow. In fact, the government reflection ratios of India, Jamaica, and Thailand would become even more negative as a result of this increased productivity. This paradoxical result is a result of the dynamic properties of the model, and can be shown by differentiating the equation for the government reflection ratio for the first year with respect to a_3:

$$\frac{\partial}{\partial a_3} \left(\frac{\Delta \ln G_t}{\Delta \ln \sum_{i=1}^{\infty} G_{t-i}^R} \right) = \frac{-[d_1 b_1 + d_2(c_1 b_1 + c_3)] e_1}{a_1 - b_1} \gtrless 0$$

The sign of this expression is the same as that for the first-year equation.

Since the low productivity bloc placed a greater reliance on the taxation of nominal imports than real exports,[13] it can be shown that a change in their pattern of taxation would have raised their reflection ratios and thus led to a more successful circular process of colonial development. A shift from the taxation of nominal imports to the taxation of real exports obtained by increasing d_1 by .01 and decreasing d_2 by .01 yields the following change in the impact multiplier:

$$\Delta \left(\frac{\Delta \ln G_t}{\Delta \ln \sum_{i=1}^{\infty} G_{t-i}^R} \right) = \frac{-.01 \, a_3(b_1 - c_1 b_1 - c_3)}{a_1 - b_1} e_1$$

12. Nigeria received decreasing British grants-in-aid from 1900 to 1918 (see Geary [57, p. 236] and Kibuka [20, p. 10]), and Taiwan received decreasing Japanese grants from 1900 to 1915 (Ho [62, appendix table 9, Government]).
13. See table 5.5.

Since c_1 is approximately 1,[14]

$$\Delta \left(\frac{\Delta \ln G_t}{\Delta \ln \sum\limits_{i=1}^{\infty} G_{t-i}^R} \right) \cong \frac{.01 \, a_3 c_3 e_1}{a_1 - b_1} > 0$$

so that a shift in taxation from nominal imports to real exports raises the government reflection ratio. Substituting into this equation the actual average short-run coefficients for the low productivity bloc, such a tax shift of 1 percent would cause an increase of .18 percent in the government reflection ratio for the first year. Furthermore, if the low productivity bloc had the average short-run coefficient of accumulated real government expenditures of the high productivity bloc, then this 1 percent shift would result in a .48 percent increase in the reflection ratio. Thus, the low productivity bloc would have raised their government reflection ratios if they had simultaneously shifted their taxation from nominal imports to real exports, and increased the proportion of their expenditures directed toward the promotion of exports.

14. See table 4.5.

8

Dynamic Properties of External Forces

This chapter investigates the developmental impact of changes in the model's external forces—the colony's import price and the developed country's real income and domestic prices. Dynamic multipliers calculated for these exogenous variables are used to measure the quantitative linkages, through the international trade mechanism, between each of the endogenous variables and the changes in these variables whose values are determined in the developed world. We find that these exogenous changes had an uneven impact on the colonial world, both initially and over time. Further, the analysis of these multipliers indicates that colonial history more than regional history is needed to explain the differences in these multipliers. The government productivity blocs identified in the previous chapter will be used to help explain the dynamic effects of these exogenous changes.

Tables 8.1, 8.3, and 8.5 report the multipliers associated with an assumed 1 percent sustained change in the colonies' import prices, the developed countries' real incomes, and the developed countries' domestic prices. For each country, a row in tables 8.1, 8.3, and 8.5 reports the percentage changes in a particular endogenous variable caused by the increase of an exogenous variable. Thus, table 8.1B shows that a 1 percent sustained increase in Ceylon's exogenous import price causes a .194 percent increase in its export price in the initial year, a .310 percent increase after 2 years, a .382 percent increase after 3 years, and so on. For long-run balanced growth (LRBG) this real export multiplier is 1.807 percent. In all cases, the dynamic multipliers for the exogenous variables are correctly moving toward the long-run balanced growth multipliers.

CHANGE IN COLONY'S IMPORT PRICE

A change in import price, determined in the developed world, has an effect in five different equations of our model (figure 8.1 and table

172

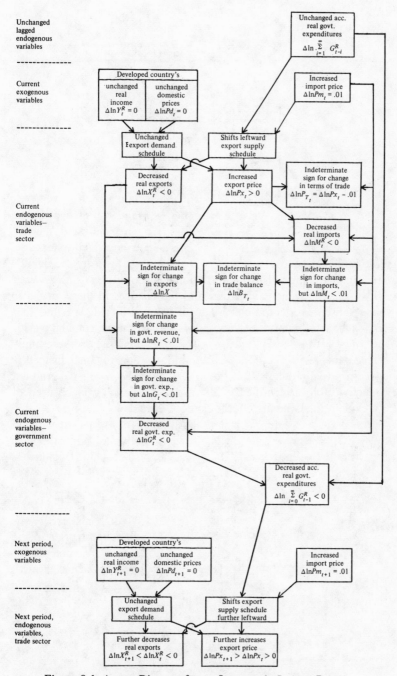

Figure 8.1. Arrow Diagram for an Increase in Import Prices

Table 8.1. Dynamic Multipliers for a 1 Percent Increase in All Years in the Colony's Import Price

8.1A. Real Exports

	Years									$LRBG$[a]
	1	2	3	4	5	10	15	20	25	
Egypt	-0.209	-0.213	-0.218	-0.223	-0.227	-0.245	-0.258	-0.267	-0.272	-0.325
India	-0.096	-0.098	-0.098	-0.101	-0.102	-0.108	-0.116	-0.116	-0.116	-0.140
Jamaica	-0.304	-0.314	-0.325	-0.331	-0.338	-0.366	-0.390	-0.408	-0.419	-0.482
Thailand	-0.120	-0.152	-0.178	-0.200	-0.217	-0.243	-0.248	-0.261	-0.271	-0.290
Bloc average	-0.182	-0.194	-0.205	-0.214	-0.221	-0.240	-0.253	-0.263	-0.270	-0.309
Ceylon	-0.085	-0.136	-0.166	-0.191	-0.209	-0.276	-0.342	-0.404	-0.438	-0.797
Chile	-0.325	-0.383	-0.415	-0.446	-0.473	-0.616	-0.755	-0.861	-0.951	-1.660
Cuba	-0.296	-0.430	-0.513	-0.578	-0.635	-0.864	-1.021	-1.115	-1.221	-2.151
Nigeria	-0.133	-0.230	-0.302	-0.360	-0.407	-0.546	-0.664	-0.719	-0.755	-1.492
Philippines	-0.143	-0.198	-0.237	-0.267	-0.293	-0.415	-0.513	-0.600	-0.681	-1.392
Taiwan	-0.363	-0.548	-0.650	-0.713	-0.761	-0.912	-0.999	-1.091	-1.202	-1.893
Bloc average	-0.224	-0.321	-0.380	-0.426	-0.463	-0.605	-0.716	-0.798	-0.875	-1.564
Average, all 10 countries	-0.207	-0.270	-0.310	-0.341	-0.366	-0.459	-0.531	-0.584	-0.633	-1.062

[a] Long Run Balanced Growth Multipliers

Table 8.1 – *Continued*
8.1B. Export Price

	Years									$LRBG^a$
	1	2	3	4	5	10	15	20	25	
Egypt	0.917	0.937	0.958	0.978	0.998	1.077	1.134	1.173	1.196	1.426
India	0.451	0.457	0.463	0.470	0.476	0.501	0.519	0.531	0.543	0.655
Jamaica	0.673	0.697	0.718	0.735	0.751	0.812	0.862	0.902	0.930	1.068
Thailand	0.565	0.719	0.837	0.941	1.023	1.147	1.171	1.234	1.280	1.329
Bloc average	0.651	0.702	0.744	0.781	0.812	0.884	0.921	0.960	0.987	1.119
Ceylon	0.194	0.310	0.382	0.432	0.473	0.632	0.775	0.916	0.995	1.807
Chile	0.328	0.275	0.288	0.305	0.323	0.420	0.512	0.578	0.638	1.102
Cuba	0.375	0.548	0.652	0.733	0.804	1.097	1.292	1.413	1.548	2.726
Nigeria	0.704	0.702	0.705	0.727	0.758	0.859	1.006	1.036	1.096	2.094
Philippines	0.287	0.233	0.239	0.257	0.276	0.362	0.443	0.510	0.575	1.140
Taiwan	0.331	0.498	0.590	0.648	0.692	0.831	0.907	0.995	1.096	1.729
Bloc average	0.370	0.428	0.476	0.517	0.554	0.700	0.822	0.908	0.991	1.766
Average, all 10 countries	0.482	0.538	0.583	0.623	0.657	0.774	0.862	0.929	0.990	1.508

[a] Long Run Balanced Growth Multipliers

Table 8.1—*Continued*
8.1C. Nominal Exports

	Years									$LRBG^a$
	1	2	3	4	5	10	15	20	25	
Egypt	0.708	0.724	0.740	0.756	0.770	0.832	0.876	0.906	0.924	1.101
India	0.354	0.360	0.363	0.369	0.375	0.395	0.406	0.418	0.427	0.515
Jamaica	0.369	0.382	0.393	0.402	0.411	0.445	0.473	0.494	0.511	0.586
Thailand	0.444	0.565	0.660	0.744	0.807	0.904	0.923	0.971	1.007	1.039
Bloc average	0.469	0.508	0.539	0.568	0.591	0.644	0.669	0.697	0.717	0.810
Ceylon	0.108	0.171	0.212	0.243	0.264	0.356	0.435	0.514	0.557	1.010
Chile	0.005	-0.110	-0.130	-0.139	-0.150	-0.198	-0.243	-0.284	-0.316	-0.558
Cuba	0.079	0.114	0.137	0.156	0.169	0.232	0.272	0.301	0.327	0.575
Nigeria	0.571	0.471	0.403	0.369	0.350	0.314	0.342	0.319	0.342	0.602
Philippines	0.143	0.034	0.002	-0.011	-0.020	-0.050	-0.072	-0.089	-0.105	-0.252
Taiwan	-0.031	-0.049	-0.060	-0.064	-0.067	-0.079	-0.090	-0.096	-0.105	-0.164
Bloc average	0.146	0.105	0.094	0.092	0.091	0.096	0.107	0.111	0.117	0.202
Average, all 10 countries	0.275	0.266	0.272	0.282	0.291	0.315	0.332	0.345	0.357	0.445

[a] Long Run Balanced Growth Multipliers

Table 8.1—*Continued*
8.1D. Terms of Trade

	Years									$LRBG^a$
	1	2	3	4	5	10	15	20	25	
Egypt	-0.083	-0.063	-0.042	-0.022	-0.002	0.077	0.134	0.173	0.196	0.426
India	-0.549	-0.543	-0.537	-0.530	-0.524	-0.499	-0.481	-0.469	-0.457	-0.345
Jamaica	-0.327	-0.303	-0.282	-0.265	-0.249	-0.188	-0.138	-0.098	-0.070	0.068
Thailand	-0.435	-0.281	-0.163	-0.059	0.023	0.147	0.171	0.234	0.280	0.329
Bloc average	-0.349	-0.297	-0.256	-0.219	-0.188	-0.116	-0.078	-0.040	-0.013	0.119
Ceylon	-0.806	-0.690	-0.618	-0.568	-0.527	-0.368	-0.225	-0.084	-0.005	0.807
Chile	-0.672	-0.725	-0.712	-0.695	-0.677	-0.580	-0.488	-0.422	-0.362	0.102
Cuba	-0.625	-0.452	-0.348	-0.267	-0.196	-0.097	0.292	0.413	0.548	1.726
Nigeria	-0.296	-0.298	-0.295	-0.273	-0.242	-0.141	0.006	0.036	0.096	1.094
Philippines	-0.713	-0.767	-0.761	-0.743	-0.724	-0.638	-0.557	-0.490	-0.425	0.140
Taiwan	-0.669	-0.502	-0.410	-0.352	-0.308	-0.169	-0.093	-0.005	0.096	0.729
Bloc average	-0.630	-0.572	-0.524	-0.483	-0.446	-0.300	-0.177	-0.092	-0.009	0.766
Average, all 10 countries	-0.517	-0.462	-0.417	-0.377	-0.343	-0.226	-0.138	-0.071	-0.010	0.508

[a] Long Run Balanced Growth Multipliers

Table 8.1—*Continued*
8.1E. Real Imports

| | | | | | *Years* | | | | | |
	1	*2*	*3*	*4*	*5*	*10*	*15*	*20*	*25*	*LRBG*[a]
Egypt	−0.355	−0.354	−0.353	−0.352	−0.351	−0.347	−0.344	−0.342	−0.341	−0.329
India	−0.362	−0.360	−0.362	−0.359	−0.359	−0.349	−0.348	−0.346	−0.343	−0.322
Jamaica	−0.314	−0.304	−0.296	−0.292	−0.287	−0.261	−0.241	−0.226	−0.218	−0.159
Thailand	−0.425	−0.391	−0.365	−0.342	−0.324	−0.297	−0.292	−0.278	−0.268	−0.249
Bloc average	−0.364	−0.352	−0.344	−0.336	−0.330	−0.313	−0.306	−0.298	−0.292	−0.265
Ceylon	−0.385	−0.395	−0.403	−0.407	−0.412	−0.430	−0.446	−0.458	−0.464	−0.547
Chile	−0.542	−0.638	−0.661	−0.679	−0.691	−0.757	−0.827	−0.876	−0.920	−1.262
Cuba	−0.304	−0.380	−0.426	−0.464	−0.496	−0.623	−0.713	−0.764	−0.824	−1.352
Nigeria	−0.544	−0.642	−0.712	−0.752	−0.776	−0.840	−0.847	−0.877	−0.868	−0.853
Philippines	−0.093	−0.163	−0.198	−0.223	−0.244	−0.339	−0.420	−0.482	−0.546	−1.105
Taiwan	−0.580	−0.729	−0.812	−0.864	−0.903	−1.027	−1.094	−1.172	−1.259	−1.819
Bloc average	−0.408	−0.491	−0.535	−0.565	−0.587	−0.669	−0.724	−0.771	−0.813	−1.156
Average, all 10 countries	−0.390	−0.436	−0.459	−0.473	−0.484	−0.527	−0.557	−0.582	−0.605	−0.800

[a] Long Run Balanced Growth Multipliers

Table 8.1—*Continued*
8.1F. Nominal Imports

	Years									$LRBG^{\text{a}}$
	1	2	3	4	5	10	15	20	25	
Egypt	0.645	0.646	0.647	0.648	0.649	0.653	0.656	0.658	0.659	0.671
India	0.638	0.641	0.638	0.642	0.642	0.650	0.653	0.653	0.658	0.678
Jamaica	0.685	0.696	0.703	0.709	0.715	0.738	0.760	0.775	0.782	0.841
Thailand	0.575	0.609	0.635	0.658	0.676	0.703	0.708	0.722	0.732	0.751
Bloc average	0.636	0.648	0.656	0.664	0.670	0.686	0.694	0.702	0.708	0.735
Ceylon	0.613	0.604	0.597	0.592	0.587	0.571	0.554	0.540	0.536	0.453
Chile	0.459	0.362	0.339	0.322	0.308	0.243	0.174	0.124	0.082	−0.262
Cuba	0.697	0.620	0.575	0.536	0.504	0.377	0.287	0.235	0.175	−0.352
Nigeria	0.456	0.358	0.288	0.248	0.224	0.160	0.153	0.124	0.131	0.147
Philippines	0.908	0.835	0.803	0.778	0.755	0.661	0.580	0.517	0.453	−0.105
Taiwan	0.418	0.272	0.188	0.136	0.096	−0.027	−0.093	−0.172	−0.259	−0.819
Bloc average	0.592	0.508	0.465	0.435	0.412	0.331	0.276	0.228	0.186	−0.156
Average, all 10 countries	0.609	0.564	0.541	0.527	0.516	0.473	0.443	0.418	0.395	0.200

[a] Long Run Balanced Growth Multipliers

Table 8.1—*Continued*

8.1G. Trade Balance

					Years					
	1	2	3	4	5	10	15	20	25	LRBG[a]
Egypt	0.063	0.078	0.093	0.108	0.122	0.179	0.219	0.248	0.264	0.430
India	-0.284	-0.281	-0.275	-0.273	-0.267	-0.255	-0.247	-0.235	-0.230	-0.163
Jamaica	-0.316	-0.313	-0.310	-0.307	-0.304	-0.293	-0.287	-0.280	-0.271	-0.255
Thailand	-0.131	-0.043	0.025	0.086	0.131	0.201	0.216	0.250	0.275	0.328
Bloc average	-0.167	-0.140	-0.117	-0.096	-0.080	-0.042	-0.025	-0.004	0.009	0.085
Ceylon	-0.505	-0.433	-0.385	-0.349	-0.323	-0.215	-0.119	-0.026	0.021	0.557
Chile	-0.455	-0.471	-0.468	-0.461	-0.458	-0.441	-0.417	-0.407	-0.398	-0.296
Cuba	-0.618	-0.505	-0.438	-0.380	-0.334	-0.145	-0.015	0.066	0.151	0.927
Nigeria	0.116	0.114	0.114	0.121	0.127	0.153	0.189	0.195	0.211	0.455
Philippines	-0.764	-0.801	-0.801	-0.789	-0.775	-0.711	-0.652	-0.606	-0.558	-0.147
Taiwan	-0.449	-0.320	-0.247	-0.200	-0.163	-0.052	0.003	0.076	0.154	0.655
Bloc average	-0.446	-0.403	-0.371	-0.343	-0.321	-0.235	-0.168	-0.117	-0.070	0.358
Average, all 10 countries	-0.334	-0.297	-0.269	-0.244	-0.224	-0.158	-0.111	-0.072	-0.038	0.249

[a] Long Run Balanced Growth Multipliers

Table 8.1—*Continued*

8.1H. Government Revenues

	Years									$LRBG^a$
	1	2	3	4	5	10	15	20	25	
Egypt	0.261	0.259	0.257	0.254	0.252	0.243	0.236	0.232	0.230	0.203
India	0.491	0.494	0.494	0.496	0.494	0.497	0.496	0.496	0.497	0.513
Jamaica	0.322	0.323	0.326	0.329	0.329	0.335	0.338	0.343	0.342	0.357
Thailand	0.159	0.163	0.165	0.168	0.170	0.172	0.173	0.174	0.175	0.177
Bloc average	0.308	0.310	0.310	0.312	0.311	0.312	0.311	0.311	0.311	0.312
Ceylon	0.053	0.014	-0.014	-0.032	-0.046	-0.099	-0.151	-0.201	-0.229	-0.513
Chile	-0.186	-0.253	-0.287	-0.311	-0.334	-0.467	-0.597	-0.693	-0.774	-1.425
Cuba	-0.180	-0.322	-0.410	-0.479	-0.539	-0.780	-0.943	-1.041	-1.154	-2.131
Nigeria	0.104	-0.030	-0.128	-0.198	-0.253	-0.407	-0.515	-0.577	-0.607	-1.256
Philippines	0.493	0.427	0.391	0.363	0.339	0.240	0.151	0.084	0.008	-0.604
Taiwan	0.037	-0.075	-0.134	-0.172	-0.203	-0.298	-0.348	-0.404	-0.468	-0.888
Bloc average	0.053	-0.040	-0.097	-0.138	-0.173	-0.302	-0.400	-0.472	-0.537	-1.136
Average, all 10 countries	0.155	0.100	0.066	0.042	0.021	-0.056	-0.116	-0.159	-0.198	-0.557

[a]Long Run Balanced Growth Multipliers

Table 8.1–*Continued*
8.1I. Government Expenditure

				Years						$LRBG^a$
	1	2	3	4	5	10	15	20	25	
Egypt	0.145	0.208	0.235	0.245	0.248	0.243	0.237	0.232	0.229	0.203
India	0.417	0.481	0.490	0.494	0.494	0.497	0.494	0.502	0.499	0.513
Jamaica	0.186	0.267	0.300	0.315	0.323	0.334	0.338	0.341	0.343	0.357
Thailand	0.100	0.138	0.154	0.162	0.165	0.170	0.171	0.172	0.173	0.175
Bloc average	0.212	0.273	0.295	0.304	0.307	0.311	0.310	0.312	0.311	0.312
Ceylon	0.026	0.020	0.005	-0.014	-0.031	-0.089	-0.142	-0.189	-0.223	-0.514
Chile	-0.133	-0.217	-0.264	-0.298	-0.325	-0.452	-0.586	-0.682	-0.766	-1.423
Cuba	-0.117	-0.250	-0.352	-0.436	-0.504	-0.757	-0.929	-1.031	-1.141	-2.136
Nigeria	0.041	0.013	-0.043	-0.106	-0.165	-0.369	-0.486	-0.565	-0.604	-1.267
Philippines	0.320	0.391	0.391	0.374	0.351	0.252	0.160	0.090	0.017	-0.605
Taiwan	0.031	-0.060	-0.124	-0.168	-0.200	-0.293	-0.345	-0.401	-0.467	-0.885
Bloc average	0.028	-0.017	-0.064	-0.108	-0.146	-0.285	-0.388	-0.463	-0.531	-1.138
Average, all 10 countries	0.102	0.099	0.079	0.057	0.036	-0.046	-0.109	-0.153	-0.194	-0.558

[a] Long Run Balanced Growth Multipliers

Table 8.1—*Continued*

8.1J. Real Government Expenditures

	Years									$LRBG$[a]
	1	*2*	*3*	*4*	*5*	*10*	*15*	*20*	*25*	
Egypt	−0.855	−0.792	−0.766	−0.755	−0.752	−0.757	−0.763	−0.768	−0.771	−0.797
India	−0.583	−0.519	−0.510	−0.507	−0.505	−0.504	−0.505	−0.497	−0.502	−0.487
Jamaica	−0.813	−0.734	−0.699	−0.683	−0.678	−0.667	−0.661	−0.658	−0.657	−0.643
Thailand	−0.900	−0.862	−0.846	−0.838	−0.835	−0.830	−0.829	−0.828	−0.827	−0.825
Bloc average	−0.788	−0.727	−0.705	−0.696	−0.692	−0.689	−0.689	−0.688	−0.689	−0.688
Ceylon	−0.972	−0.980	−0.995	−1.013	−1.030	−1.088	−1.143	−1.190	−1.222	−1.514
Chile	−1.132	−1.218	−1.265	−1.297	−1.326	−1.451	−1.585	−1.683	−1.765	−2.423
Cuba	−1.118	−1.251	−1.353	−1.436	−1.501	−1.756	−1.930	−2.031	−2.142	−3.136
Nigeria	−0.959	−0.987	−1.044	−1.106	−1.165	−1.367	−1.487	−1.565	−1.605	−2.267
Philippines	−0.679	−0.610	−0.610	−0.627	−0.648	−0.748	−0.841	−0.911	−0.984	−1.605
Taiwan	−0.969	−1.059	−1.123	−1.167	−1.199	−1.292	−1.344	−1.402	−1.466	−1.855
Bloc average	−0.971	−1.017	−1.065	−1.108	−1.145	−1.284	−1.388	−1.464	−1.531	−2.133
Average, all 10 countries	−0.898	−0.901	−0.921	−0.943	−0.964	−1.046	−1.109	−1.153	−1.194	−1.555

[a] Long Run Balanced Growth Multipliers

Table 8.1—*Continued*

8.1K. Accumulated Real Government Expenditures

	Years									$LRBG$[a]
	1	2	3	4	5	10	15	20	25	
Egypt	-0.032	-0.064	-0.097	-0.126	-0.155	-0.271	-0.353	-0.410	-0.439	-0.797
India	-0.015	-0.029	-0.044	-0.058	-0.072	-0.130	-0.175	-0.203	-0.227	-0.487
Jamaica	-0.038	-0.072	-0.101	-0.125	-0.148	-0.243	-0.322	-0.381	-0.424	-0.643
Thailand	-0.158	-0.281	-0.388	-0.470	-0.535	-0.626	-0.636	-0.696	-0.740	-0.825
Bloc average	-0.061	-0.111	-0.157	-0.195	-0.227	-0.317	-0.371	-0.422	-0.457	-0.688
Ceylon	-0.035	-0.069	-0.104	-0.137	-0.169	-0.322	-0.478	-0.616	-0.684	-1.514
Chile	-0.064	-0.122	-0.174	-0.224	-0.272	-0.545	-0.798	-0.972	-1.147	-2.423
Cuba	-0.133	-0.249	-0.354	-0.449	-0.540	-0.916	-1.151	-1.331	-1.517	-3.136
Nigeria	-0.087	-0.154	-0.223	-0.288	-0.310	-0.543	-0.729	-0.772	-0.880	-2.267
Philippines	-0.047	-0.089	-0.127	-0.162	-0.195	-0.343	-0.471	-0.580	-0.687	-1.605
Taiwan	-0.040	-0.082	-0.131	-0.185	-0.241	-0.423	-0.537	-0.697	-0.858	-1.855
Bloc average	-0.068	-0.127	-0.185	-0.241	-0.288	-0.515	-0.694	-0.828	-0.962	-2.133
Average, all 10 countries	-0.065	-0.121	-0.174	-0.222	-0.264	-0.436	-0.565	-0.666	-0.760	-1.555

[a]Long Run Balanced Growth Multipliers

2.4). This increase shifts leftward the export supply curve and decreases the demand for real exports. For a 1 percent increase in the import price, the terms of trade multiplier is 1 percent less than the export price multiplier. Similarly, the multipliers for nominal imports and nominal government expenditures are 1 percent less than their corresponding real variables (figure 8.1 and table 8.1).[1]

A cluster analysis for a 1 percent change in the import price of a colony classifies the ten countries into the same two groups as for a change in the initial value of accumulated real government expenditures. The low productivity bloc consisting of Egypt, India, Jamaica, and Thailand would have been far less affected by an increase in the import price than the remaining six countries. The differences in the blocs are clearly evident in table 8.1. First, real exports fall over time much less for the low productivity bloc than for the high productivity bloc (table 8.1A). Export prices increase for both blocs; the increase is initially larger for the low productivity bloc, but over time it becomes larger for the high productivity bloc (table 8.1B). The combined effects of falling real exports and rising export prices cause real imports to fall much less for the low productivity bloc (table 8.1E). As a result, nominal government expenditures rise for the low productivity bloc and fall for the high productivity bloc (table 8.1H). The low productivity bloc thus has the smallest decrease over time in accumulated real government expenditures (table 8.1K), which in turn explains why it has the smallest drop in real exports over time.

For all the multipliers associated with a 1 percent increase in the import price, the relative cost of this classification into two groups is a 14.48 percent reduction in the total variance of the multipliers. Table 8.2 indicates that the countries are correctly classified. Using this table, we conclude that the low productivity bloc is much more homogeneous, since the squared distance of each country from its own bloc mean is uniformly lower for the countries in the low productivity bloc. Furthermore, the low productivity bloc is more homogeneous since the relative cost of forming this bloc is only 2.69 percent. In comparison, the more heterogeneous high productivity bloc forms at the larger relative cost of 11.79 percent. A cluster analysis of only

1. We are assuming an unchanged import price for the other three tables of dynamic multipliers (tables 7.1, 8.3, and 8.5). These other tables have three less parts than table 8.1; not only are the export price and the terms of trade multipliers the same, but the multipliers for nominal imports and nominal government expenditures are the same as for their corresponding real variables.

Table 8.2. Distance Classification for Import Price Multipliers

| Merged bloc | Country | Squared distance from bloc means | | Bloc classification by minimum distance criterion |
		Low	High	
Low government productivity bloc	Egypt	1.192	13.912	Low
	India	2.520	19.404	Low
	Jamaica	.866	13.507	Low
	Thailand	1.124	12.756	Low
High government productivity bloc	Ceylon	5.219	3.663	High
	Chile	20.901	2.524	High
	Cuba	36.909	8.098	High
	Nigeria	14.746	2.658	High
	Philippines	10.358	7.399	High
	Taiwan	19.091	2.846	High

the long-run balanced growth multipliers yields the same classification at a relative cost of 11.14 percent. The relative cost of forming the quite homogeneous low productivity bloc is only 1.08 percent, while the relative cost of forming the remaining bloc of six countries is 10.06 percent.

A change in the import price, determined exogenously in the developed world, initially has a depressing effect upon the colonial economy of all ten countries. Ceteris paribus, a rise in import prices shifts the real export supply schedule leftward, while the export demand schedule is unchanged. As a result, real exports decrease and the import price increases (figure 8.1).[2] In the first year real exports would fall by .207 percent and the export price would rise by .482 percent (tables 8.1A and 8.1B). Over time, however, a sustained 1 percent increase in the import price has a further depressing effect on colonial exports and eventually leads after 25 years to an average .990 percent export price increase for all the countries, and for the long-run balanced growth path, to a 1.508 percent increase in export

2. The impact multipliers for real exports and the export price are:

$$\frac{\Delta \ln X^R}{\Delta \ln P_M} = -\frac{a_2 b_1}{a_1 - b_1} < 0$$

$$\frac{\Delta \ln P_X}{\Delta \ln P_M} = -\frac{a_2}{a_1 - b_1} > 0$$

where $a_1 > 0$, $a_2 > 0$, and $b_1 < 0$.

prices (tables 8.1A and 8.1B). With import prices changing by 1 percent, the terms-of-trade multiplier is 1 percent less than the export price multipliers. Thus, for an import price increase, the results of the model indicate that the average terms of trade first move against the colonies and then, as the long run is approached, move in their favor (table 8.1D). India is the one exception to this long-run finding.[3] This empirical result suggests that the specific value of India as a colony to the United Kingdom was that even in the long run the resulting shift in terms of trade caused by an import price rise remained adverse to India. In the case of all other United Kingdom colonies, on the other hand, initial unfavorable shifts in their terms of trade were substantially reversed.

This surprising result about the time pattern of the terms of trade can be understood only by examining the dynamic properties of the model (figure 8.1). Basically, the key effect is a decrease in real government expenditures that then feeds back onto the export sector as a leftward shift over time of the export supply schedule. Because of the assumed 1 percent increase in the import price and the resulting decline in real exports, real imports are always falling for all ten countries (table 8.1F and figure 8.1). The multipliers for nominal imports are obtained by adding 1 to the multipliers for real imports. While, in theory, the sign of the nominal import multiplier in the first year is indeterminate (figure 8.1), in actual practice nominal imports initially rise for all ten countries (table 8.1F). However, nominal imports can fall over time, as seen in the case of Taiwan after 10 years, and in the cases of Cuba, Chile, and the Philippines as the long-run balanced growth path is approached (table 8-1F). These four countries have the highest government reflection ratios (table 8.1H) and it is not surprising that their import sectors are most depressed over time by an increase in the import price.

Since real exports are falling, the signs of the multipliers for government revenue and expenditure are indeterminate when nominal imports rise (figure 8.1). These government multipliers definitely become negative over time for the four countries whose nominal imports fall over time, since both sources of government revenues have decreased (tables 8.1H and 8.1I). Table 8.1I shows that the government's nominal expenditures never rise as much as the assumed 1

3. India experienced the smallest leftward shift in its export supply schedule (figure 8.1) and thus the smallest decrease in real exports and the smallest increase in export price (tables 8.1 and 8.1B).

percent increase in the import price for any country in the sample. Therefore, the real government expenditure multipliers are always negative for all ten countries (table 8.1J). As a result, accumulated real government expenditures decrease over time (table 8.1K). This implies, in turn, a further dynamic leftward shift of the export supply curve and thus a downward trend over time in the real export multipliers (table 8.1A and figure 8.1) and, finally, an upward trend in export prices. Table 8.1K indicates that India has the smallest loss over time in terms of the trend of accumulated real government expenditures and thus the smallest recovery in its export price. The other three members of the low productivity bloc—Egypt, Jamaica, and Thailand—also had small decreases over time in accumulated real government expenditures and thus small drops in real exports over time (table 8.1A). Here, for an increase in the import price, the dynamic effects of the government reflection ratio are working in reverse, with the low productivity bloc having the smallest decreases in accumulated real government expenditures over time and the high productivity bloc having the largest decreases. As a result, an increase in import prices would have had the least depressing effect on the export development of the low productivity bloc. Conversely, a decrease in import prices would have had the most expansionary effect on the export development of the high productivity bloc.

CHANGE IN DEVELOPED COUNTRY'S REAL INCOME

The arrow diagram (figure 8.2) traces the changes caused by a 1 percent increase in the developed country's real income. Ceteris paribus, this increase in real income shifts the export demand schedule to the right so that both real exports and export price initially rise, as shown by the impact multipliers in tables 8.3A and 8.3B.[4] Since both of these impact multipliers are positive, all the remaining impact multipliers are also positive (figure 8.2 and table 8.3). While figure 8.2 indicates that the impact multiplier for the commodity trade balance can theoretically be negative, table 8.3E shows that this impact multiplier is actually positive.

4. The impact multipliers for real exports and the export price are:

$$\frac{\Delta \ln X_t^R}{\Delta \ln Y_t^R} = \frac{a_1 b_2}{a_1 - b_1} > 0$$

$$\frac{\Delta \ln Px_t}{\Delta \ln Y_t^R} = \frac{b_2}{a_1 - b_1} > 0$$

where $a_1 > 0$, $b_1 < 0$, and $b_2 > 0$.

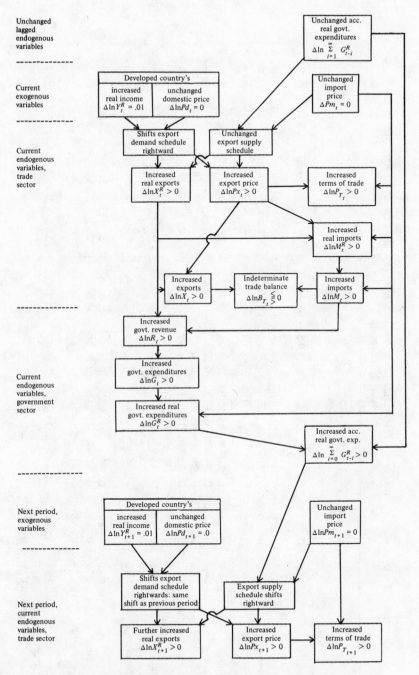

Figure 8.2. Arrow Diagram for an Increase in Developed Country
Real Income

Table 8.3. Dynamic Multipliers for a 1 Percent Increase in All Years in the Developed Country's Real Income

8.3A. Real Exports

	\multicolumn{9}{c}{Years}									LRBG[a]
	1	2	3	4	5	10	15	20	25	
Nigeria	0.265	0.432	0.544	0.627	0.693	0.902	1.079	1.157	1.216	2.302
Ceylon	0.320	0.482	0.566	0.610	0.636	0.694	0.735	0.775	0.798	1.026
Taiwan	0.410	0.606	0.705	0.758	0.795	0.882	0.922	0.967	1.022	1.365
Bloc average	0.365	0.544	0.635	0.684	0.715	0.788	0.828	0.871	0.910	1.195
Chile	0.127	0.140	0.146	0.150	0.154	0.179	0.201	0.218	0.235	0.348
Cuba	0.168	0.221	0.243	0.259	0.270	0.323	0.354	0.378	0.403	0.610
Philippines	0.148	0.186	0.203	0.218	0.232	0.291	0.348	0.389	0.435	0.813
Bloc average	0.148	0.182	0.197	0.209	0.219	0.264	0.301	0.328	0.358	0.590
India	0.401	0.404	0.406	0.407	0.407	0.414	0.423	0.429	0.432	0.465
Jamaica	0.560	0.569	0.580	0.592	0.604	0.655	0.690	0.719	0.741	0.853
Bloc average	0.480	0.486	0.493	0.499	0.505	0.534	0.556	0.574	0.586	0.659
Egypt	0.476	0.479	0.484	0.489	0.494	0.516	0.533	0.544	0.550	0.616
Thailand	0.467	0.482	0.499	0.516	0.530	0.556	0.561	0.572	0.580	0.596
Bloc average	0.471	0.480	0.492	0.502	0.512	0.536	0.547	0.558	0.565	0.606
Average, all 10 countries	0.334	0.400	0.438	0.463	0.481	0.541	0.585	0.615	0.641	0.899

[a] Long Run Balanced Growth Multipliers

Table 8.3—*Continued*

8.3B. Export Price and Terms of Trade

	Years									$LRBG^{a}$
	1	2	3	4	5	10	15	20	25	
Nigeria	1.862	2.012	2.070	2.065	2.037	1.859	1.644	1.596	1.503	0.038
Ceylon	1.059	0.694	0.506	0.403	0.343	0.211	0.117	0.029	-0.027	-0.540
Taiwan	1.131	0.951	0.861	0.811	0.779	0.701	0.663	0.620	0.572	0.260
Bloc average	1.095	0.822	0.683	0.607	0.561	0.456	0.390	0.324	0.272	-0.140
Chile	0.393	0.423	0.423	0.420	0.417	0.401	0.386	0.375	0.365	0.290
Cuba	0.612	0.548	0.518	0.498	0.481	0.415	0.372	0.345	0.316	0.052
Philippines	0.553	0.655	0.664	0.655	0.645	0.596	0.553	0.519	0.483	0.185
Bloc average	0.519	0.542	0.535	0.524	0.514	0.471	0.437	0.413	0.388	0.176
India	0.951	0.944	0.936	0.928	0.920	0.881	0.847	0.831	0.814	0.651
Jamaica	1.045	1.026	1.001	0.973	0.947	0.839	0.752	0.687	0.642	0.395
Bloc average	0.998	0.985	0.969	0.950	0.933	0.860	0.799	0.759	0.728	0.523
Egypt	1.781	1.769	1.750	1.727	1.705	1.606	1.535	1.486	1.457	1.169
Thailand	2.954	2.884	2.803	2.723	2.656	2.537	2.510	2.459	2.421	2.343
Bloc average	2.368	2.326	2.276	2.225	2.181	2.071	2.023	1.972	1.939	1.756
Average, all 10 countries	1.234	1.191	1.153	1.120	1.093	1.005	0.938	0.895	0.855	0.484

[a] Long Run Balanced Growth Multipliers

Table 8.3–*Continued*
8.3C. Nominal Exports

	Years									
	1	2	3	4	5	10	15	20	25	LRBG[a]
Nigeria	2.129	2.443	2.614	2.692	2.729	2.761	2.722	2.754	2.721	2.340
Ceylon	1.379	1.172	1.070	1.013	0.978	0.905	0.856	0.807	0.772	0.486
Taiwan	1.543	1.558	1.567	1.572	1.573	1.582	1.585	1.590	1.593	1.625
Bloc average	1.461	1.365	1.318	1.292	1.275	1.243	1.220	1.198	1.182	1.055
Chile	0.520	0.563	0.569	0.571	0.572	0.577	0.591	0.594	0.598	0.638
Cuba	0.780	0.766	0.760	0.757	0.754	0.739	0.729	0.725	0.717	0.662
Philippines	0.700	0.839	0.867	0.874	0.876	0.890	0.899	0.909	0.919	0.998
Bloc average	0.667	0.723	0.732	0.734	0.734	0.735	0.740	0.743	0.745	0.766
India	1.352	1.347	1.340	1.335	1.328	1.299	1.268	1.260	1.247	1.116
Jamaica	1.604	1.594	1.581	1.565	1.552	1.492	1.443	1.407	1.384	1.248
Bloc average	1.478	1.470	1.460	1.450	1.440	1.395	1.355	1.333	1.315	1.182
Egypt	2.258	2.248	2.233	2.217	2.200	2.122	2.067	2.029	2.007	1.785
Thailand	3.421	3.366	3.302	3.238	3.185	3.091	3.071	3.030	3.001	2.939
Bloc average	2.839	2.807	2.767	2.727	2.693	2.606	2.569	2.530	2.504	2.362
Average, all 10 countries	1.569	1.590	1.590	1.583	1.575	1.546	1.523	1.510	1.496	1.384

[a]Long Run Balanced Growth Multipliers

Table 8.3—*Continued*
8.3D. Real and Nominal Imports

	Years									LRBG[a]
	1	2	3	4	5	10	15	20	25	
Nigeria	1.661	1.938	2.093	2.173	2.217	2.289	2.307	2.347	2.339	2.316
Ceylon	0.668	0.705	0.723	0.732	0.737	0.749	0.755	0.768	0.772	0.828
Taiwan	0.607	0.766	0.847	0.891	0.919	0.986	1.021	1.057	1.102	1.378
Bloc average	0.637	0.735	0.785	0.811	0.828	0.867	0.888	0.912	0.937	1.103
Chile	0.421	0.458	0.464	0.464	0.465	0.479	0.487	0.497	0.505	0.638
Cuba	0.366	0.394	0.406	0.415	0.423	0.458	0.475	0.488	0.502	0.617
Philippines	0.287	0.349	0.369	0.383	0.395	0.441	0.485	0.520	0.554	0.998
Bloc average	0.358	0.400	0.413	0.421	0.428	0.459	0.482	0.502	0.520	0.751
India	0.778	0.777	0.775	0.774	0.771	0.764	0.754	0.755	0.751	0.719
Jamaica	1.463	1.457	1.447	1.434	1.424	1.381	1.347	1.323	1.302	1.206
Bloc average	1.120	1.117	1.111	1.104	1.097	1.072	1.050	1.039	1.026	0.963
Egypt	0.962	0.961	0.960	0.959	0.958	0.953	0.949	0.947	0.945	0.930
Thailand	1.661	1.646	1.628	1.610	1.595	1.569	1.563	1.552	1.544	1.527
Bloc average	1.311	1.303	1.294	1.284	1.276	1.261	1.256	1.249	1.244	1.228
Average, all 10 countries	0.887	0.945	0.971	0.983	0.990	1.007	1.014	1.025	1.032	1.116

[a] Long Run Balanced Growth Multipliers

Table 8.3—*Continued*
8.3E. Trade Balance

	Years									$LRBG$[a]
	1	2	3	4	5	10	15	20	25	
Nigeria	0.468	0.504	0.521	0.519	0.512	0.473	0.416	0.407	0.383	0.024
Ceylon	0.711	0.467	0.346	0.281	0.241	0.156	0.101	0.040	-0.002	-0.342
Taiwan	0.937	0.792	0.720	0.681	0.655	0.597	0.565	0.533	0.491	-0.247
Bloc average	0.824	0.629	0.533	0.481	0.448	0.377	0.333	0.286	0.244	-0.048
Chile	0.099	0.105	0.105	0.107	0.107	0.098	0.102	0.095	0.092	0.077
Cuba	0.414	0.372	0.352	0.342	0.333	0.282	0.255	0.237	0.215	0.054
Philippines	0.412	0.490	0.497	0.491	0.481	0.449	0.415	0.389	0.365	0.0
Bloc average	0.308	0.322	0.318	0.313	0.307	0.276	0.257	0.240	0.224	0.044
India	0.574	0.571	0.565	0.562	0.557	0.534	0.514	0.505	0.496	0.397
Jamaica	0.140	0.137	0.134	0.131	0.128	0.113	0.096	0.084	0.081	0.042
Bloc average	0.357	0.354	0.350	0.346	0.342	0.323	0.305	0.294	0.288	0.220
Egypt	1.296	1.286	1.272	1.258	1.241	1.169	1.118	1.082	1.062	0.855
Thailand	1.760	1.720	1.674	1.627	1.590	1.522	1.508	1.478	1.456	1.412
Bloc average	1.528	1.503	1.473	1.443	1.415	1.345	1.313	1.280	1.259	1.133
Average, all 10 countries	0.681	0.644	0.619	0.600	0.584	0.539	0.509	0.485	0.464	0.277

[a]Long Run Balanced Growth Multipliers

Table 8.3—*Continued*
8.3F. Government Revenues

	Years									$LRBG^{a}$
	1	2	3	4	5	10	15	20	25	
Nigeria	1.045	1.329	1.504	1.617	1.696	1.918	2.083	2.173	2.221	3.176
Ceylon	0.369	0.497	0.563	0.600	0.620	0.668	0.700	0.732	0.749	0.932
Taiwan	0.346	0.465	0.525	0.557	0.578	0.629	0.655	0.684	0.714	0.921
Bloc average	0.358	0.481	0.544	0.578	0.599	0.648	0.677	0.708	0.731	0.926
Chile	0.182	0.200	0.204	0.211	0.214	0.233	0.256	0.270	0.287	0.391
Cuba	0.217	0.272	0.294	0.310	0.323	0.380	0.417	0.439	0.462	0.682
Philippines	0.232	0.284	0.304	0.314	0.325	0.381	0.426	0.468	0.500	0.828
Bloc average	0.210	0.252	0.267	0.278	0.287	0.331	0.366	0.392	0.416	0.634
India	0.745	0.745	0.743	0.740	0.740	0.737	0.729	0.729	0.728	0.714
Jamaica	1.114	1.113	1.110	1.108	1.107	1.096	1.088	1.084	1.078	1.057
Bloc average	0.930	0.929	0.926	0.924	0.924	0.916	0.908	0.906	0.903	0.885
Egypt	0.890	0.892	0.894	0.897	0.899	0.910	0.918	0.924	0.927	0.960
Thailand	0.647	0.645	0.644	0.642	0.640	0.637	0.637	0.636	0.635	0.633
Bloc average	0.768	0.768	0.769	0.769	0.769	0.773	0.777	0.780	0.781	0.796
Average, all 10 countries	0.579	0.644	0.678	0.700	0.714	0.759	0.791	0.814	0.830	1.029

[a] Long Run Balanced Growth Multipliers

Table 8.3—*Continued*

8.3G. Nominal and Real Government Expenditures

	Years									LRBG[a]
	1	2	3	4	5	10	15	20	25	
Nigeria	0.418	0.784	1.074	1.295	1.460	1.863	2.050	2.170	2.226	3.206
Ceylon	0.186	0.343	0.455	0.528	0.575	0.661	0.691	0.729	0.748	0.932
Taiwan	0.293	0.438	0.510	0.548	0.571	0.624	0.652	0.681	0.711	0.918
Bloc average	0.239	0.391	0.482	0.538	0.573	0.642	0.671	0.705	0.729	0.925
Chile	0.128	0.180	0.198	0.204	0.209	0.235	0.253	0.272	0.284	0.391
Cuba	0.140	0.226	0.273	0.298	0.316	0.374	0.412	0.438	0.462	0.683
Philippines	0.151	0.237	0.279	0.302	0.319	0.377	0.424	0.461	0.499	0.828
Bloc average	0.140	0.214	0.250	0.268	0.281	0.329	0.363	0.390	0.415	0.634
India	0.630	0.725	0.739	0.742	0.740	0.737	0.732	0.734	0.732	0.714
Jamaica	0.645	0.916	1.029	1.073	1.092	1.098	1.090	1.083	1.080	1.057
Bloc average	0.637	0.820	0.884	0.907	0.916	0.917	0.911	0.908	0.906	0.885
Egypt	0.495	0.714	0.813	0.858	0.879	0.905	0.914	0.920	0.923	0.957
Thailand	0.405	0.552	0.605	0.624	0.630	0.630	0.630	0.629	0.628	0.626
Bloc average	0.450	0.633	0.709	0.741	0.754	0.767	0.772	0.774	0.775	0.791
Average, all 10 countries	0.349	0.511	0.597	0.647	0.679	0.750	0.785	0.812	0.829	1.031

[a] Long Run Balanced Growth Multipliers

Table 8.3–*Continued*

8.3H. Accumulated Real Government Expenditures

	Years									LRBG[a]
	1	2	3	4	5	10	15	20	25	
Nigeria	0.040	0.098	0.175	0.258	0.304	0.661	0.934	1.007	1.170	3.206
Ceylon	0.006	0.018	0.035	0.055	0.073	0.169	0.270	0.362	0.407	0.932
Taiwan	0.011	0.029	0.053	0.079	0.107	0.200	0.256	0.333	0.412	0.918
Bloc average	0.008	0.023	0.044	0.067	0.090	0.184	0.263	0.347	0.410	0.925
Chile	0.008	0.015	0.023	0.031	0.038	0.084	0.125	0.154	0.183	0.391
Cuba	0.017	0.038	0.061	0.082	0.102	0.188	0.238	0.281	0.322	0.683
Philippines	0.011	0.027	0.046	0.064	0.082	0.160	0.227	0.287	0.343	0.828
Bloc average	0.012	0.027	0.043	0.059	0.074	0.144	0.197	0.241	0.283	0.634
India	0.017	0.037	0.056	0.076	0.096	0.185	0.253	0.296	0.334	0.714
Jamaica	0.031	0.072	0.117	0.159	0.197	0.366	0.497	0.598	0.670	1.057
Bloc average	0.024	0.055	0.086	0.117	0.146	0.275	0.375	0.447	0.502	0.885
Egypt	0.019	0.048	0.084	0.119	0.155	0.299	0.402	0.473	0.510	0.957
Thailand	0.071	0.155	0.238	0.307	0.362	0.452	0.468	0.516	0.553	0.626
Bloc average	0.045	0.101	0.161	0.213	0.258	0.376	0.435	0.494	0.531	0.791
Average, all 10 countries	0.023	0.054	0.089	0.123	0.152	0.276	0.367	0.431	0.490	1.031

[a]Long Run Balanced Growth Multipliers

The principal effect over time of a sustained increase in the developed country's real income is a rightward shift in the colonial export supply schedule in response to the sustained rightward shift in real export demand. The response mechanism is the increase in government expenditures, which increases the stock of accumulated real government expenditures used to promote exports. With rightward shifts of both supply and demand, the dynamic multipliers for real exports are positive and increase monotonically over time for all countries, as can be seen in table 8.3A and figure 8.2.

A sustained increase in real income in the developed world produces uneven development in the growth of real colonial exports both over time and between countries. This process of uneven development is quantitatively measured by the dynamic multipliers for real exports, which show that the average gap between the colonial real export multipliers and the increase in the developed country's real income narrows over time, but that the average multiplier is always less than 1. In only three countries—Nigeria, Ceylon, and Taiwan—does the real export multiplier increase over time to a value of more than 1, indicating that for these countries the increase in real exports exceeds the increase in real income of the developed countries. The Nigerian multiplier first exceeds 1 after 13 years, while it takes 23 years for Taiwan,[5] and only in the approach to the long-run balanced growth path does Ceylon's multiplier exceed 1 (table 8.3A). For all points in time up to 30 years the smallest multipliers are for the three countries tied to the United States. The explanation is that the U.S. bloc had the lowest coefficients for real income in the export demand equation and therefore the smallest initial increase in export demand.[6] However, the Philippines has a much larger long-run coefficient for real income.[7] Thus the Philippines' multiplier increases substantially and then exceeds those of the United Kingdom colonies, Egypt, India, and Thailand, whose multipliers increase relatively little over time.

These already described differences in the real export multipliers are consistent with a cluster analysis of the multipliers for a 1 percent increase in the developed country's real income. The analysis classifies the ten countries into one distinct country and four groups of countries. The distinct country, Nigeria, has the largest increases over time in its multipliers not only for real exports but also for real imports,

5. Exact year figures are from the actual simulations which are summarized in table 8.3A.
6. See table 4.3.
7. See table 4.4.

government revenues and expenditures, and accumulated real government expenditures (table 8.3). Nigeria's distinctiveness is evident in table 8.4, which indicates very large square distances for Nigeria from the other groups. This situation is explained by the fact that Nigeria had by far the largest long-run estimated coefficient for the variable, developed country's real income, in the export demand equation, resulting in large increases in real exports. Further, the second group, consisting of Ceylon and Taiwan, had the next largest long-run coefficients for real incomes, and thus they also experienced substantial increases over time in their real exports, although not as large as the increases for Nigeria. The third group consists of the three colonies tied to the United States—Chile, Cuba, and the Philippines—which had the smallest coefficients for real income in their demand functions and thus the smallest initial real income multipliers.[8] The fourth and fifth groups divide the low productivity bloc into two groups.

The distinctive characteristic of the fifth group, Egypt and Thailand, is that their multipliers for increases in both export price and nominal exports are the largest in our sample. In the short run, the explanation for these increases is the combination of very inelastic demand functions with their relatively high coefficients for real income in that function.[9] These large increases change very little over time because these two countries are members of the low productivity bloc. As a result, these two countries have exceptionally large multipliers for their commodity trade balance (table 8.3E).

For all the multipliers associated with an increase in the developed country's real income, the relative cost of this classification into five groups is an 8.56 percent reduction in the total variance of the multipliers. The relative cost of joining Ceylon and Taiwan is 1.38 percent; of joining Chile, Cuba, and the Philippines is .75 percent; of joining India and Jamaica is 1.99 percent; and of joining Egypt and Thailand is 4.34 percent. Thus, the U.S. group forms a very homogeneous group in terms of their multipliers for a change in U.S. real income. The two groups closest in distance are groups two and four (table 8.4). Combining these two groups raises the relative cost to 10.85 percent. However, we would be combining two high productivity countries, Ceylon and Taiwan, with two low productivity countries, India and Jamaica. The economic interpretation of this combination is difficult, so we preferred the classification into five groups.

8. See tables 4.3 and 4.4.
9. See table 4.3.

Table 8.4. Distance Classification for Developed Country's Real Income Multipliers

Merged group	Country	Squared distance from group means					Group classification by minimum distance criterion
		1 Nigeria	2 Ceylon Taiwan	3 Chile Cuba Philippines	4 India Jamaica	5 Egypt Thailand	
1	Nigeria	.000	56.037	83.020	43.638	46.205	1
2	Ceylon	65.889	1.353	5.024	7.341	51.902	2
	Taiwan	48.891	1.353	9.069	4.323	28.000	2
3	Chile	92.724	9.015	.755	12.065	56.631	3
	Cuba	82.112	4.901	.124	9.211	49.430	3
	Philippines	75.690	4.631	.587	8.454	42.900	3
4	India	57.327	4.628	5.472	1.944	25.698	4
	Jamaica	33.837	8.218	17.258	1.944	33.815	4
5	Egypt	44.121	19.842	27.419	13.061	4.346	5
	Thailand	56.982	66.047	79.604	51.257	4.346	5

Whereas initially the export price and the terms of trade move substantially in favor of the colonial countries, over time this price gain diminishes as real export supply increases. The fall from this initial increase in the export price is the least for the low productivity bloc countries because the export supply curve is shifted least by the increase in accumulated real government expenditures. Ceylon is an exceptional case because it is the only country for which the export price increase turns into a decrease; this happens after 20 years. This is because Ceylon has the highest long-run estimated coefficient of accumulated real government expenditures in its export supply equation[10] and thus the largest long-run shift in its export supply curve.

Table 8.3H shows that the trend of accumlated real government expenditure multipliers is always positive, which causes the downward trend in export prices as export supply shifts rightward. Interestingly enough, only in the long run are the colonies able to capture the increase of income in the developed countries, the average long-run expenditure multiplier being 1.032. Nigeria stands out as the one colony in our sample best able to capture real growth in the developed world, with a long-run multiplier of 3.206. The average long-run balanced growth multiplier for the nine countries excluding Nigeria is .792. After 25 years the average multiplier excluding Nigeria is only .408, indicating that it takes a very long time for income changes in the developed world to be reflected in the colonial world. A similar pattern can be seen in the real export multipliers (table 8.3A). The time trend of these multipliers is obviously increasing, but the average long-run multiplier for all ten countries is .899, and excluding Nigeria it is .743.

The real import gains to the colonial countries from an assumed increase in real income in the developed world are measured by the multipliers in table 8.3D. On average, the increase in colonial real imports is about equal to the increase in the developed country's real income. Over time, however, there is a downward trend in the real import multipliers for the low productivity group, while the multipliers increase for the rest of the countries. These opposite trends are the result of the corresponding trends for real exports and export price for both blocs (tables 8.3A and 8.3B). Comparing the long-run balanced growth multipliers with those after five years, the Philippines shows the largest increase in its real import multiplier, due to the previously described large increase in its real export multiplier (table

10. See tables 4.1 and 4.2.

8.3D). Consistent with the small magnitude of their real export multipliers, the U.S. bloc countries show the smallest real import multipliers (except as the Philippines approaches the long run). In fact, Chile and Cuba stand out as having the smallest real import gains of all ten countries.

Table 8.3E reveals that an income increase in the developed world always leads to a shift in the nominal trade balance of the colonies toward an export surplus. Ceylon is the one exception to this trend. It has a nominal export deficit after 25 years, due to the previously explained adverse movement of its terms of trade (table 8.3B). Although the average shift for all countries toward a nominal trade surplus diminishes through time, the average shift remains positive even in the long run, indicating that income increases in the developed countries lead to the accumulation of reserves in either London, New York, or Tokyo. In fact, the larger the increase of real income, the larger the accumulation of reserves that results from this income expansion. As previously explained, the two countries where this accumulation is the largest are Egypt and Thailand. A 1 percent increase in the real income of the United Kingdom leads to a more than 1 percent shift in the nominal trade balance toward an export surplus in the short-, intermediate-, and long-run positions of these two countries. This pattern is consistent with the economic history of Egypt and Thailand, where British influence led to substantial increases in their reserves held in London, rather than in Cairo or Bangkok.[11]

CHANGE IN DEVELOPED COUNTRY'S DOMESTIC PRICES

An assumed change in domestic prices in the developed countries produces a set of impact multipliers which only differ in magnitude by a scalar from those produced by a change in real income. This scalar equals the ratio of the domestic price coefficient to the real income coefficient in the estimated demand equation for the colony's real exports. Thus, the pattern of changes summarized in figure 8.2 is the same, except that now we are analyzing a 1 percent increase in the developed country's domestic prices rather than a 1 percent increase in its real income.

11. See Feis [51], Ingram [64, pp. 152–62, 170–74], and pp. 00–00 of this study. This result suggests that British colonial policy with regard to accumulation of reserves was more conservative in its two de facto colonies, Egypt and Thailand, than in its four de jure colonies.

A cluster analysis of the multipliers for a 1 percent increase in the developed country's domestic prices divides the ten countries into two distinct countries and two groups of countries. The distinctiveness of both Nigeria and Thailand is evident in the classification matrix of table 8.6. The squared distances of these two countries from each other and from the other two groups are very large. By comparison, the squared distance of each country in the other two groups from its own group mean is much smaller.

The first distinct country, Nigeria, is the colony whose trade and government sectors were most influenced by price and income changes in the developed country. Nigeria has the largest increases overtime in its multipliers for real exports, real imports, government expenditures, and accumulated real government expenditures (table 8.5). These large multipliers for Nigeria indicate that it was the colony most influenced by both price and income changes in the developed world.[12] The second distinct country is Thailand; its export price and therefore its terms of trade and its balance of trade improved the most as the result of domestic price changes in the developed world (table 8.5).

The first group of countries consists of the three countries tied to the United States—Chile, Cuba, and the Philippines. Previously, we found that for up to 30 years the U.S. bloc countries had the smallest real export multipliers produced by a change in the developed country's real income. A reverse ordering is apparent if we examine the effects on real exports of a change in the developed country's domestic prices (table 8.5A). This suggests, in contrast to the United Kingdom and Japan, that U.S. prices were more important than its real income in determining real export activity in its trade-dependent countries. Increases in U.S. domestic prices caused a substantial expansion of these countries' trade and government sectors in a pattern similar to, but not as large as, the expansion in Nigeria caused by United Kingdom domestic price increases. These substantial multipliers for the U.S. bloc reflect the greater internal substitution within the U.S. economy.[13] For example, the long-run real export multiplier for the Philippines is greater than 1 and is nearly 1 for Cuba, suggesting strong competition in the United States between imported cane sugar and domestically produced beet sugar. The long-run co-

12. These large multipliers for Nigeria are caused by the combined effects of the large long-run coefficients for the developed country's real income and domestic prices.

13. See tables 4.3 and 4.4 and the discussion of this result on pp. 89–90.

Table 8.5. Dynamic Multipliers for a 1 Percent Increase in All Years in the Developed Country's Domestic Price

8.5A. Real Exports

	Years									$LRBG^a$
	1	2	3	4	5	10	15	20	25	
Nigeria	0.157	0.256	0.322	0.371	0.410	0.533	0.638	0.684	0.719	1.364
Thailand	0.314	0.324	0.336	0.347	0.357	0.374	0.378	0.385	0.390	0.401
Chile	0.185	0.206	0.214	0.220	0.229	0.259	0.294	0.320	0.343	0.510
Cuba	0.299	0.392	0.432	0.459	0.482	0.575	0.636	0.676	0.716	1.089
Philippines	0.211	0.266	0.290	0.310	0.331	0.414	0.494	0.552	0.620	1.152
Bloc Average	0.232	0.288	0.312	0.330	0.347	0.416	0.475	0.516	0.560	0.917
Ceylon	0.104	0.156	0.182	0.194	0.203	0.227	0.241	0.253	0.259	0.332
Egypt	0.092	0.092	0.093	0.094	0.095	0.099	0.103	0.105	0.106	0.119
India	0.101	0.102	0.102	0.102	0.104	0.102	0.105	0.108	0.107	0.117
Jamaica	0.128	0.130	0.131	0.136	0.138	0.150	0.156	0.165	0.170	0.195
Taiwan	0.070	0.102	0.119	0.130	0.136	0.153	0.159	0.168	0.177	0.237
Bloc average	0.099	0.116	0.125	0.131	0.135	0.146	0.153	0.160	0.164	0.200
Average, all 10 countries	0.166	0.203	0.222	0.236	0.248	0.289	0.320	0.342	0.361	0.552

[a] Long Run Balanced Growth Multipliers

Table 8.5—Continued

8.5B. Export Price and Terms of Trade

	Years									LRBG[a]
	1	2	3	4	5	10	15	20	25	
Nigeria	1.104	1.193	1.227	1.226	1.208	1.104	0.978	0.947	0.894	0.023
Thailand	1.988	1.941	1.887	1.832	1.787	1.707	1.689	1.655	1.628	1.577
Chile	0.576	0.619	0.618	0.614	0.610	0.587	0.564	0.548	0.534	0.424
Cuba	1.094	0.977	0.925	0.889	0.861	0.743	0.665	0.615	0.564	0.092
Philippines	0.784	0.928	0.940	0.928	0.913	0.846	0.784	0.735	0.687	0.262
Bloc Average	0.818	0.841	0.828	0.810	0.795	0.725	0.671	0.633	0.595	0.259
Ceylon	0.342	0.224	0.163	0.130	0.111	0.070	0.039	0.006	−0.014	−0.175
Egypt	0.343	0.340	0.337	0.333	0.328	0.309	0.296	0.286	0.280	0.225
India	0.238	0.236	0.235	0.233	0.231	0.221	0.211	0.209	0.203	0.163
Jamaica	0.239	0.235	0.230	0.223	0.218	0.192	0.170	0.158	0.149	0.091
Taiwan	0.196	0.165	0.149	0.140	0.135	0.121	0.112	0.105	0.098	0.045
Bloc average	0.272	0.240	0.223	0.212	0,205	0.183	0.166	0.153	0.143	0.070
Average, all 10 countries	0.690	0.686	0.671	0.655	0.640	0.590	0.551	0.526	0.502	0.273

[a] Long Run Balanced Growth Multipliers

Table 8.5—*Continued*
8.5C. Nominal Exports

	Years									$LRBG$[a]
	1	2	3	4	5	10	15	20	25	
Nigeria	1.261	1.448	1.550	1.598	1.617	1.636	1.614	1.633	1.613	1.387
Thailand	2.303	2.266	2.222	2.179	2.144	2.079	2.067	2.040	2.020	1.978
Chile	0.761	0.824	0.833	0.836	0.836	0.847	0.864	0.871	0.876	0.934
Cuba	1.392	1.367	1.357	1.350	1.344	1.317	1.303	1.292	1.282	1.181
Philippines	0.993	1.190	1.231	1.237	1.242	1.263	1.277	1.288	1.306	1.414
Bloc Average	1.049	1.127	1.140	1.141	1.141	1.142	1.148	1.150	1.155	1.176
Ceylon	0.447	0.380	0.345	0.328	0.314	0.298	0.279	0.266	0.250	0.157
Egypt	0.435	0.433	0.430	0.427	0.424	0.408	0.398	0.391	0.387	0.344
India	0.339	0.337	0.336	0.333	0.334	0.327	0.317	0.320	0.310	0.280
Jamaica	0.366	0.366	0.363	0.358	0.357	0.341	0.328	0.323	0.316	0.286
Taiwan	0.269	0.269	0.270	0.269	0.272	0.276	0.275	0.272	0.276	0.282
Bloc average	0.371	0.357	0.349	0.343	0.340	0.330	0.319	0.314	0.308	0.270
Average, all 10 countries	0.857	0.888	0.894	0.891	0.888	0.879	0.872	0.870	0.864	0.824

[a] Long Run Balanced Growth Multipliers

Table 8.5—*Continued*
8.5D. Real and Nominal Imports

| | Years | | | | | | | | | |
	1	2	3	4	5	10	15	20	25	$LRBG$[a]
Nigeria	0.984	1.148	1.240	1.288	1.314	1.355	1.365	1.391	1.387	1.372
Thailand	1.118	1.108	1.095	1.083	1.073	1.056	1.052	1.044	1.039	1.028
Chile	0.616	0.671	0.679	0.677	0.681	0.700	0.717	0.731	0.740	0.821
Cuba	0.655	0.706	0.731	0.748	0.761	0.813	0.848	0.873	0.896	1.103
Philippines	0.407	0.496	0.525	0.543	0.558	0.627	0.688	0.737	0.786	1.204
Bloc Average	0.559	0.624	0.645	0.656	0.667	0.713	0.751	0.780	0.807	1.043
Ceylon	0.217	0.229	0.237	0.240	0.241	0.246	0.244	0.249	0.250	0.268
Egypt	0.185	0.185	0.185	0.185	0.185	0.184	0.183	0.182	0.182	0.179
India	0.195	0.195	0.194	0.197	0.197	0.194	0.188	0.191	0.186	0.180
Jamaica	0.336	0.335	0.332	0.330	0.327	0.316	0.307	0.304	0.303	0.276
Taiwan	0.105	0.133	0.146	0.154	0.160	0.171	0.179	0.182	0.194	0.276
Bloc average	0.208	0.215	0.219	0.221	0.222	0.222	0.220	0.222	0.223	0.228
Average, all 10 countries	0.482	0.521	0.536	0.544	0.550	0.566	0.577	0.588	0.596	0.667

[a] Long Run Balanced Growth Multipliers

Table 8.5—*Continued*
8.5E. Trade Balance

	Years									$LRBG$[a]
	1	2	3	4	5	10	15	20	25	
Nigeria	0.277	0.300	0.310	0.310	0.304	0.281	0.248	0.243	0.227	0.015
Thailand	1.185	1.158	1.127	1.096	1.070	1.023	1.015	0.996	0.981	0.950
Chile	0.145	0.154	0.154	0.157	0.157	0.148	0.146	0.140	0.134	0.113
Cuba	0.737	0.661	0.624	0.604	0.584	0.505	0.455	0.420	0.386	0.079
Philippines	0.584	0.694	0.706	0.694	0.684	0.636	0.589	0.551	0.522	0.210
Bloc Average	0.489	0.503	0.495	0.485	0.475	0.430	0.397	0.370	0.347	0.134
Ceylon	0.232	0.153	0.110	0.089	0.073	0.050	0.035	0.017	−0.002	−0.111
Egypt	0.250	0.248	0.246	0.242	0.239	0.224	0.216	0.209	0.205	0.165
India	0.143	0.142	0.142	0.136	0.137	0.133	0.130	0.130	0.124	0.100
Jamaica	0.031	0.031	0.031	0.028	0.030	0.027	0.020	0.019	0.013	−0.030
Taiwan	0.163	0.136	0.124	0.116	0.111	0.107	0.096	0.089	0.082	0.043
Bloc average	0.164	0.142	0.131	0.122	0.118	0.108	0.099	0.093	0.084	0.033
Average, all 10 countries	0.375	0.368	0.357	0.347	0.339	0.313	0.295	0.281	0.267	0.153

[a] Long Run Balanced Growth Multipliers

Table 8.5—*Continued*
8.5F. Government Revenues

	Years									$LRBG^a$
	1	2	3	4	5	10	15	20	25	
Nigeria	0.619	0.788	0.890	0.958	1.005	1.135	1.232	1.285	1.314	1.882
Thailand	0.435	0.434	0.433	0.432	0.431	0.429	0.428	0.427	0.427	0.426
Chile	0.266	0.293	0.299	0.307	0.313	0.345	0.377	0.401	0.418	0.573
Cuba	0.388	0.485	0.528	0.557	0.580	0.677	0.743	0.784	0.826	1.218
Philippines	0.328	0.401	0.429	0.447	0.464	0.542	0.607	0.662	0.710	1.173
Bloc Average	0.327	0.393	0.419	0.437	0.452	0.521	0.576	0.616	0.651	0.988
Ceylon	0.119	0.160	0.182	0.194	0.198	0.217	0.227	0.240	0.244	0.302
Egypt	0.171	0.172	0.172	0.173	0.173	0.175	0.177	0.178	0.179	0.185
India	0.186	0.186	0.186	0.186	0.186	0.186	0.182	0.182	0.180	0.179
Jamaica	0.255	0.255	0.253	0.253	0.253	0.252	0.248	0.248	0.247	0.242
Taiwan	0.061	0.079	0.093	0.099	0.104	0.108	0.113	0.122	0.124	0.160
Bloc average	0.158	0.170	0.177	0.181	0.183	0.188	0.189	0.194	0.195	0.214
Average, all 10 countries	0.283	0.325	0.346	0.361	0.371	0.407	0.433	0.453	0.467	0.634

[a] Long Run Balanced Growth Multipliers

Table 8.5—*Continued*

8.5G. Nominal and Real Government Expenditures

	Years									$LRBG$[a]
	1	2	3	4	5	10	15	20	25	
Nigeria	0.248	0.464	0.636	0.767	0.865	1.102	1.213	1.285	1.318	1.900
Thailand	0.272	0.372	0.408	0.420	0.424	0.424	0.424	0.423	0.422	0.421
Chile	0.188	0.262	0.290	0.301	0.310	0.343	0.371	0.401	0.418	0.572
Cuba	0.252	0.403	0.487	0.531	0.565	0.668	0.740	0.781	0.826	1.221
Philippines	0.214	0.336	0.395	0.429	0.453	0.534	0.601	0.653	0.706	1.174
Bloc Average	0.218	0.334	0.391	0.420	0.443	0.515	0.571	0.612	0.650	0.989
Ceylon	0.060	0.110	0.148	0.172	0.185	0.217	0.224	0.238	0.241	0.302
Egypt	0.095	0.137	0.156	0.165	0.169	0.174	0.176	0.177	0.178	0.184
India	0.159	0.182	0.185	0.188	0.188	0.182	0.182	0.188	0.183	0.179
Jamaica	0.148	0.210	0.235	0.245	0.250	0.251	0.248	0.248	0.248	0.242
Taiwan	0.050	0.075	0.089	0.096	0.099	0.107	0.116	0.121	0.124	0.160
Bloc average	0.102	0.143	0.163	0.173	0.178	0.186	0.189	0.194	0.195	0.213
Average, all 10 countries	0.169	0.255	0.303	0.331	0.351	0.400	0.429	0.451	0.466	0.635

[a] Long Run Balanced Growth Multipliers

Table 8.5—*Continued*

8.5H. Accumulated Real Government Expenditures

	Years									$LRBG$[a]
	1	2	3	4	5	10	15	20	25	
Nigeria	0.023	0.056	0.102	0.151	0.179	0.388	0.549	0.594	0.691	1.900
Thailand	0.048	0.104	0.160	0.207	0.244	0.304	0.315	0.347	0.372	0.421
Chile	0.011	0.023	0.035	0.047	0.058	0.125	0.185	0.227	0.270	0.572
Cuba	0.029	0.069	0.110	0.146	0.183	0.334	0.427	0.500	0.574	1.221
Philippines	0.015	0.040	0.066	0.092	0.117	0.227	0.322	0.406	0.485	1.174
Bloc Average	0.018	0.044	0.070	0.095	0.119	0.229	0.311	0.378	0.443	0.989
Ceylon	0.002	0.005	0.009	0.017	0.023	0.055	0.087	0.119	0.136	0.302
Egypt	0.004	0.009	0.016	0.023	0.030	0.057	0.077	0.091	0.098	0.184
India	0.005	0.009	0.014	0.018	0.023	0.046	0.064	0.075	0.084	0.179
Jamaica	0.006	0.015	0.026	0.035	0.043	0.084	0.114	0.136	0.153	0.242
Taiwan	0.002	0.005	0.009	0.014	0.018	0.037	0.047	0.061	0.073	0.160
Bloc average	0.004	0.009	0.015	0.021	0.027	0.056	0.078	0.096	0.109	0.213
Average, all 10 countries	0.014	0.033	0.055	0.075	0.092	0.166	0.219	0.256	0.294	0.635

[a] Long Run Balanced Growth Multipliers

Table 8.6. Distance Classification for Developed Country's Domestic Price Multipliers

| Merged group | Country | Squared distance from group means | | | | Group classification by minimum distance criterion |
		1 Nigeria	2 Thailand	3 Chile Cuba Philippines	4 Ceylon Egypt India Jamaica Taiwan	
1	Nigeria	.000	22.940	8.890	33.741	1
2	Thailand	22.940	.000	18.391	42.804	2
3	Chile	15.128	24.709	2.167	4.618	3
	Cuba	6.070	17.550	.893	15.618	3
	Philippines	9.212	16.655	.680	13.300	3
	Ceylon	33.203	46.047	10.126	.304	4
	Egypt	33.484	38.024	9.222	.324	4
4	India	34.719	42.183	10.355	.070	4
	Jamaica	31.025	42.579	9.252	.229	4
	Taiwan	37.339	46.248	11.766	.136	4

efficient of .563 for Chile demonstrates the ability of the United States to produce domestic copper.

The second group of countries—Ceylon, Egypt, India, Jamaica, and Taiwan—experienced the smallest impact on their trade and government sectors as a result of domestic price changes in the developed world. The explanation for this grouping is that these five countries had the smallest coefficients for the developed country's domestic price in the demand equation. The average short-run and also long-run coefficients for these five countries are only .220. For the other five countries, the averages are .722 in the short run and 1.200 in the long run.[14]

For all the multipliers associated with a change in the developed country's domestic price, the relative cost of this classification into four groups is a 5.42 percent reduction in the total variance of the multipliers. The U.S. bloc is more heterogeneous than the five-country bloc. The relative cost of forming the U.S. bloc is 4.22 percent, while the relative cost for the five-country bloc is 1.20 percent. The best classification into three groups would add Nigeria to the U.S. bloc and increase the cost to 12.97 percent. For only the long-run balanced growth multipliers, the same classification into four groups occurs with a relative cost of 5.05 percent. Adding Nigeria to the U.S. bloc increases the relative cost to 15.79 per cent.

Table 8.5B shows that an increase in prices in the developed world spills over into the colonial world by raising export prices. Export prices, and thus the terms of trade, shift in favor of each colony. However, the export price multipliers diminish over time, reflecting the rightward shift in the supply schedule as the colony responds to the increase in demand for its exports.[15]

SUMMARY

An increase in import prices was shown to lead initially to an unfavorable shift in the colonies' terms of trade, but over time to a favorable shift (except in the case of India). This terms of trade reversal was a result of increased import prices, which decreased real government expenditures, which, over time, shifted the export supply curve leftward.

There were considerable differences in the ability of colonial coun-

14. Calculations based on tables 4.3 and 4.4.
15. However, as described previously, Ceylon is an exception; after 20 years its export price multiplier becomes negative.

tries to capture income increases in the developed countries. Only in Ceylon, Nigeria, and Taiwan did an increase in the developed country's income finally lead to a greater increase in these countries' real exports. Although the U.S. bloc was in general less able to capture a real income increase in the developed country, there was variation here as well. The Philippines stood out as the one country whose real export multiplier substantially increased over time such that it even exceeded that of some of the United Kingdom colonies.

Since colonial export prices were endogenously determined in the model, we were able to show how an increase in demand initially led to a rise in export price but, as the colonial economy responded to this increased macro-profitability of export trade, the supply curve shifted dynamically to the right and thus, over time, the increase in the export price diminished. The crucial relationship within this dynamic adjustment of export supply to a change in price was the role of the government sector in taxing the expanding trade sector and spending that increased revenue on further export development.

The cluster analysis selected well-defined blocs of countries for the set of dynamic multipliers for external forces. Two colonial characteristics—the developed country to which a colony was tied and the value of the colony's government reflection ratio—were found to be the key explanations for the degree of similarity and difference within the process of colonial development. Countries were classified into the previously identified low and high productivity blocs by cluster analysis of dynamic multipliers for a change in the colony's import price. For the dynamic multipliers associated with a change in the developed country's real income or domestic prices, different classifications were obtained. These classifications depended upon a combination of short-run impacts (explained by colonial bloc differences) and long-run adjustments to these short-run impacts (explained by differences in government productivities). In summary, the existence of well-defined blocs of countries depended upon identifying external forces associated with the colonial relationship and internal forces associated with government productivity.

9

Dynamic Effects of World War I and the Great Depression

In this chapter we investigate the net percentage gains and losses from two major historical events, World War I and the Great Depression, using the dynamic simulation method described in chapter 5. The net effect of a major historical event on the economy of a country can be found by first calculating a new dynamic simulation that assumes that the event did not occur. For example, to examine the impact of World War I, the new dynamic simulation of the country assumes that the exogenous variables continued to grow at their prewar rates and omits the dummy variables for World War I. For each year, the estimated net increase or decrease for each endogenous variable caused by the historical event is the difference between the value of the variable obtained from the new basic simulation and the value obtained from the basic dynamic simulation discussed in chapter 5.

WORLD WAR I AND ITS AFTERMATH

Table 9.1 reports the estimated net effects of World War I on the trade and government sectors of each country obtained by dynamically simulating its model from 1915 onwards.[1] We assume that the exogenous variables grew at their prewar rates and we omit the dummy variables for World War I. The uneven impact of the war is measured by the estimated percentage changes in real exports reported in table 9.1A. The three countries associated with the United States (Chile, Cuba and the Philippines), the Japanese colony (Taiwan), and Thailand all had increased real exports as a result of the war. These net increases were caused by war-induced demand for both war materials and food, as measured in the model by the in-

1. Since the war began in August 1914, its impact becomes apparent in 1915, and the simulations begin to show its effects at the later date.

215

Table 9.1. Simulated Percentage Changes Caused by World War I and Its Aftermath

	Ceylon	Chile	Cuba	Egypt	India	Jamaica	Nigeria	Philippines	Taiwan	Thailand
9.1A. Real Exports										
1915	-3.2	-2.0	4.1	-10.9	1.6	1.2	-15.5	1.0	16.2	1.8
1916	-6.2	8.3	12.0	-20.0	-.9	-5.8	-19.7	3.7	20.1	3.7
1917	-8.9	22.0	12.6	-24.5	-3.6	-18.3	-22.8	5.5	16.8	5.4
1918	-10.2	13.1	9.1	-26.7	-6.3	-22.8	-26.0	6.0	9.5	n.s.a
1919	n.s.	-10.2	2.3	-14.7	-3.0	-19.2	-27.0	3.6	5.1	n.s.
1920	-15.0	-15.4	-1.1	n.s.	-.5	-21.0	-32.7	2.9	n.s.	n.s.
1921	-21.2	-27.0	-12.6	-20.0	-13.0	-22.6	-39.1	1.0	n.s.	10.5
1922	-24.4	-10.8	-4.5	-11.2	-7.9	-9.6	-36.8	2.5	1.9	5.8
1923	-26.6	-10.8	1.2	-10.3	-5.7	-7.2	-35.6	6.0	-1.1	4.0
1924	-25.8	-11.1	1.1	-7.2	-2.2	-6.6	-35.3	6.8	-1.5	4.3
1925	-25.9	-8.5	.5	-6.0	-1.5	-5.5	-35.7	7.1	-5.6	4.4
9.1B. Export Prices										
1915	-8.1	2.9	14.1	-33.1	11.1	12.0	13.5	-.7	11.0	16.5
1916	-5.0	21.7	64.8	12.0	22.8	23.2	42.1	17.0	21.0	72.7
1917	-3.2	48.7	127.5	48.5	32.7	55.8	84.7	39.9	42.5	157.4
1918	6.5	51.6	177.4	113.5	44.3	69.1	187.0	73.9	71.9	n.s.
1919	n.s.	60.0	172.4	236.5	57.2	91.4	329.1	81.1	102.1	n.s.
1920	18.5	80.0	220.1	n.s.	85.3	145.7	455.8	96.9	n.s.	n.s.
1921	4.6	13.9	67.8	69.4	10.0	33.2	234.8	55.6	n.s.	228.2
1922	15.4	19.8	51.3	-5.3	17.0	24.0	126.7	37.6	77.4	127.2
1923	18.0	26.6	62.7	-17.3	23.4	33.4	117.4	43.2	65.1	116.3
1924	32.4	17.4	43.9	-9.8	30.4	44.7	152.7	41.0	84.9	139.3
1925	32.6	37.4	53.2	-14.9	22.5	40.4	162.0	39.9	81.6	133.2

9.1C. Real Imports

1915	-24.5	.8	8.8	-41.7	1.3	6.8	-42.8	0.9	18.2	6.5
1916	-28.4	27.8	30.1	-51.2	-7.2	-3.2	-44.4	7.8	17.2	13.9
1917	-31.0	22.4	40.3	-55.6	-15.1	-18.8	-44.8	14.4	10.3	22.0
1918	-32.1	15.4	41.3	-57.1	-22.6	-24.4	-45.4	20.9	26.2	n.s.
1919	n.s.	-2.2	30.1	-21.0	-17.2	-12.8	-37.3	19.0	-3.8	n.s.
1920	-31.6	-8.2	30.9	n.s.	-15.1	-7.5	-52.1	20.4	n.s.	n.s.
1921	-36.2	-42.9	-3.9	-31.5	-31.0	-29.3	-66.6	12.0	n.s.	47.1
1922	-36.5	-15.6	7.5	-18.3	-21.2	-7.5	-54.3	10.8	0.2	26.3
1923	-36.4	-7.3	16.9	-17.3	-17.3	0.2	-51.0	15.8	-3.0	19.2
1924	-31.7	-10.1	12.5	-11.4	-10.6	4.8	-47.6	16.3	-2.6	21.5
1925	-31.9	2.3	13.2	-9.6	-7.2	5.9	-46.2	16.4	-8.5	22.5

9.1D. Terms of Trade

1915	-12.2	.3	15.2	-52.3	.05	4.0	-10.8	4.8	11.9	13.0
1916	-17.2	26.7	49.2	-53.2	-12.0	-4.8	-4.5	12.7	0.2	36.0
1917	-18.8	15.5	56.5	-53.3	-22.7	-19.3	4.2	16.8	-5.4	65.3
1918	-18.6	8.2	55.7	-48.6	-32.5	-24.0	17.7	14.9	-9.5	n.s.
1919	n.s.	-10.5	39.1	20.5	-26.5	-15.6	50.2	5.2	-4.4	n.s.
1920	-44.3	-17.4	47.3	n.s.	-25.4	-13.5	29.4	3.3	n.s.	n.s.
1921	-44.2	-45.8	-5.9	-20.4	-40.0	-24.7	-11.4	3.9	n.s.	127.5
1922	-37.9	-12.6	31.3	-20.6	-28.5	-5.7	-16.6	14.8	16.8	69.7
1923	-32.5	-6.5	43.8	-23.2	-23.9	-0.3	-12.8	29.4	12.6	55.4
1924	-19.3	-7.5	30.7	-14.1	-15.8	2.5	-3.8	30.2	20.5	64.0
1925	-19.8	4.1	30.8	-13.7	-10.8	3.8	0.2	29.0	11.3	65.4

[a] n.s. = year not in country's simulation

Table 9.1–Continued

9.1E. Trade Balance

	Ceylon	Chile	Cuba	Egypt	India	Jamaica	Nigeria	Philippines	Taiwan	Thailand
1915	12.6	-0.7	10.2	-27.2	0.8	-1.5	31.7	4.9	9.9	8.0
1916	8.6	7.3	28.4	-23.3	-5.9	-7.4	38.0	8.4	2.6	23.9
1917	7.3	-3.7	25.7	-20.7	-12.2	-18.7	45.7	7.7	0.2	42.8
1918	7.7	-7.5	20.3	-12.1	-18.2	-22.4	59.6	0.8	-1.1	n.s.
1919	n.s.	-17.7	9.4	30.0	-18.9	-21.7	74.8	-8.4	4.4	n.s.
1920	-30.8	-23.9	11.3	n.s.	-12.5	-26.1	82.0	-11.7	n.s.	n.s.
1921	-31.1	-30.8	-14.5	-7.0	-24.4	-17.5	61.4	-6.3	n.s.	70.9
1922	-26.1	-7.6	16.6	-13.6	-16.4	-7.8	15.3	6.3	18.7	42.2
1923	-22.0	-10.0	24.5	-16.8	-13.3	-7.6	14.7	18.5	14.8	35.6
1924	-12.4	-8.6	17.4	-9.9	-8.0	-8.6	18.7	19.6	21.8	40.8
1925	-12.7	-6.9	16.1	-10.4	-5.2	-7.3	19.8	18.7	14.8	40.9

9.1.F. Government Expenditures

	Ceylon	Chile	Cuba	Egypt	India	Jamaica	Nigeria	Philippines	Taiwan	Thailand
1915	-3.5	3.2	3.3	-10.3	8.5	5.5	-16.9	-1.5	9.3	2.2
1916	-5.9	7.7	12.5	-7.1	20.7	9.6	-20.3	4.9	18.2	9.2
1917	-8.1	9.8	20.4	-1.5	32.2	17.4	-20.8	16.7	24.7	18.6
1918	-9.0	8.5	23.4	8.3	45.3	22.5	-17.5	35.8	28.7	n.s.
1919	n.s.	3.3	19.7	28.1	55.8	33.5	-10.8	48.8	30.5	n.s.
1920	-6.9	0.2	17.3	n.s.	78.6	52.9	-6.7	60.4	n.s.	n.s.
1921	-10.3	-15.0	2.5	17.2	24.4	23.1	-15.9	44.8	n.s.	25.8
1922	-13.4	-11.0	.1	2.0	20.8	14.8	-20.2	28.0	18.8	22.0
1923	-16.4	-6.9	3.6	-6.7	24.4	16.1	-22.4	21.9	13.8	19.9
1924	-17.4	-7.0	4.1	-7.9	28.7	21.0	-21.8	19.2	14.7	20.8
1925	-17.9	-3.4	4.6	-9.2	22.3	22.0	-21.3	18.6	13.5	20.5

9.1G. Accumulated Real Government Expenditures

1915	-0.4	-.1	.3	-0.8	-0.0	-0.1	-2.8	0.3	0.6	-0.1
1916	-1.3	.5	.4	-2.3	-0.3	-0.5	-5.5	0.3	0.4	-1.3
1917	-2.5	-.2	-.7	-3.8	-0.7	-1.5	-8.5	0.1	-0.5	-3.1
1918	-4.0	-1.3	-2.6	-5.4	-1.3	-2.7	-11.8	-0.5	-2.2	n.s.
1919	n.s.	-3.2	-4.9	-6.5	-1.7	-3.7	-15.5	-1.3	-4.1	n.s.
1920	-6.7	-5.5	-7.3	n.s.	-2.1	-4.9	-19.6	-2.2	n.s.	n.s.
1921	-9.2	-8.0	-9.3	-7.3	-2.6	-5.5	-23.6	-2.2	n.s.	-3.4
1922	-11.6	-8.7	-9.5	-7.4	-3.0	-5.7	-26.3	-1.7	-4.6	-3.8
1923	-13.9	-9.6	-9.5	-7.6	-3.4	-5.9	-29.2	-1.0	-5.4	-4.5
1924	-15.9	-10.4	-9.3	-7.6	-3.6	-6.1	-32.1	-0.4	-6.3	-5.3
1925	-17.9	-11.0	-9.3	-7.7	-3.7	-6.2	-34.2	0.2	-7.3	-5.8

[a] n.s. = year not in country's simulation

crease of domestic prices in the developed countries and by the increase of real income and industrial output in the United States and Japan (see tables A.51 through A.53). Chile, as the world's largest producer of nitrates, benefited substantially from the war-increased demand for nitrates to be used to produce explosives.[2] The war also increased the demand for sugar, since the principal European beet-sugar production areas were either in battle areas or isolated by shipping shortages and by the Allied naval blockade. The resulting war-increased demand for sugar favored the cane-sugar exporting countries in our sample—Cuba, the Philippines, and Taiwan. Cuba was able to become the world's principal sugar producer.[3] The Philippines benefited from the war-increased demand for its exports of abaca for ropes and coconut oil to be processed to yield glycerin for explosives. High worldwide prices for rice benefited both Taiwan and Thailand.[4]

In contrast, the five countries under direct control of the United Kingdom incurred real export losses as a result of the war. Egypt, Nigeria, and Jamaica suffered large losses; Ceylon and India experienced small ones (table 9.1A). Unlike Thailand, which was under indirect British control, exports for each of these five countries were adversely affected by controls established to meet British war requirements. The large fall in Egyptian real exports occurred while it was under direct British control during the war and was the principal supply base for British troops in the Near East.[5] Egyptian real exports dropped markedly due to shipping shortages, restrictions on cotton production, and the reduced availability of imported goods. To provide food for British troops in Egypt and to offset decreases in food imports, the British administration sharply restricted cotton acreage and thereby increased land for food crops.[6] As a result Egyptian real exports fell sharply (table 9.1A and appendix table 16). A large net fall in real exports occurred in Nigeria because it was cut off from its German export market. Germany accounted for

2. USTC [119, pp. 86, 105] and Stocking and Watkins [96, pp. 119–21].
3. The Cuban sugar industry during World War I is described in CERP [45, pp. 233–39, 243–49], Jenks [68, pp. 177–84, 193–202], Rowe [90, pp. 78–79], and Wright [101, pp. 70–72]. U.S. control of the Cuban sugar industry during World War I is analyzed on p. 29 of this study.
4. Ingram [64, p. 125].
5. The United Kingdom disposed of the Egyptian Khedive after the outbreak of World War I and assumed direct rule of Egypt as a military protectorate. Issawi [66, p. 47].
6. See Crouchley [44, pp. 182–88].

about 50 percent of Nigeria's prewar exports and for about 75 percent of its principal export, palm products. Shipping restrictions and a discriminatory export duty which forced export of palm products to the United Kingdom also adversely affected Nigeria's exports.[7] Jamaican real exports fell, primarily due to the lack of shipping space for its bulky exports, particularly bananas, and, as a result, many banana estates were converted to sugar production. However, the increase in sugar exports was much less than the decrease in banana exports, and therefore, real exports fell during World War I.[8] Ceylon's and India's tea exports were restricted by the colonial administration because of shipping shortages and by the purchase of tea crop in bulk at an average prewar price.[9] However, war demand for Ceylonese rubber was very strong, and as a war-priority good it had first claim on scarce shipping space.[10] In India, shipping shortages caused the British to restrict most exports, but war requirements did produce an increase in some exports, particularly jute and leather.[11] Thus, as a result of specific war requirements, real exports of Ceylon and India were less adversely affected by British colonial policy than were those of Egypt, India, and Jamaica. However, in comparison with the export gains of Taiwan, Thailand, and the three countries tied to the United States, all five of these colonies were adversely affected by British wartime controls.

Export prices rose in every country except Ceylon, where the price of its major export, tea, was controlled by the government (table 9.1B). War-induced demand for raw materials and food shifted rightward the demand for exports. This shift is measured by the rise in domestic prices of the developed countries; it is also measured for some colonies by the dummy variable for World War I. For some colonies, however, the shortage of shipping limited the export of bulky products and therefore limited this rightward shift of

7. See table 2.2 for data on Germany's share of Nigerian exports. See also USTC [120, pp. 308–9, 340–42] for an analysis of the German role in the palm products trade and of the effects of World War I. We describe the discriminatory export duty on p. 20.

8. Besides being adversely affected by World War I, banana exports were also reduced by three hurricanes during the war. Exports of bananas decreased from an average of 14 million stems in 1911–13 to an average of 3 million stems in 1916–18. For details on wartime changes in the sugar and banana industries, see Eisner [49, pp. 206–9, 242–43, 250–53, 256–57].

9. Rajaratnam [26, pp. 190–92] and Snodgrass [94, p. 34].

10. Rajaratnam [27, pp. 11–16].

11. Bhattacharyya [38, p. 136].

the demand schedule. Shortages of shipping space were reflected in dramatic increases in freight rates and insurance. For example, freight rates from India to the United Kingdom were about ten to fifteen times greater in 1918 than in 1913.[12] On the export supply side, the rapid increase in the price of imports during the war shifted leftward the export supply schedule. As explained in chapter 2, this leftward shift occurred because the short-run costs of export production increased sharply due to the increased costs of imports, particularly imports of fuels, fertilizers, and other intermediate goods on which the colonial countries were dependent.[13] From 1913 to 1918, import prices rose an average of 164 percent for the five colonies under United Kingdom control and 78 percent for Taiwan, Thailand, and the three countries tied to the United States.[14] With the demand schedule shifting rightwards and the supply schedule shifting leftwards, real exports could have either risen or fallen as a result of the war. As the estimated supply and demand schedules are both relatively price inelastic, war-induced shifts in these schedules caused the observed relatively large increases in export prices in every country except Ceylon (table 9.1B).

During the war, real imports in the five countries under direct United Kingdom control, Ceylon, Egypt, India, Jamaica, and Nigeria, were substantially reduced (table 9.1C). These reductions were caused by the previously analyzed drops in the real exports of these British colonies, by the very sharp rise in import prices, and by the restrictions on imports because of lack of shipping. These results agree with the actual data for these five countries, which show that their real imports fell an average of 49 percent from 1913 to 1918.[15] This analysis indicates that the United Kingdom was able to shift part of the substantial costs of its war effort onto its direct colonies by substantially reducing their real imports. In contrast, real imports increased in Thailand, which was not under direct British colonial control; in Taiwan, which benefited from the war-induced

12. For data, see Ray [86, p. 274]. For further discussion about the adverse effects of shipping shortages, see Snodgrass [94, pp. 34, 39], Rajaratnam [27, pp. 11–13], and Rowe [90, p. 132–33] on Ceylon; Issawi [66, p. 40] on Egypt; Anstey [35, pp. 334–35] and Bhattacharyya [38, p. 274] on India; Eisner [49, pp. 207, 256] on Jamaica; and USTC [120, pp. 340–42] on Nigeria.

13. Import data indicate that colonial goods imported dropped to very low levels during the war due to high prices or unavailability as a result of war needs.

14. Calculated using actual import price data reported in the appendix.

15. See Real Imports, M^R, in tables A.1, A.16, A.21, A.26, and A.31.

expansion of Japan (Japan was not a direct participant in the war);[16] and in the three countries tied to the United States, all of which benefited because the U.S. economy expanded during the war (table 9.1C).[17]

Accumulated real government expenditures were reduced in all ten countries as a result of the war (table 9.1G). In terms of our model, every country suffered a long-term development loss. This reduction in the stock of government capital was caused mainly by the sharp rise in import prices during the war in all ten countries, which led to a decline in the flow of real government expenditures. Although nominal imports rose for all countries, real exports, as shown above, could have risen or fallen as a result of the war; correspondingly, nominal revenues and expenditures could have moved in either direction. Nominal expenditures fell for three United Kingdom colonies, Ceylon, Egypt, and Nigeria (table 9.1F). For these three countries, the revenue lost from the fall in real exports exceeded the gain in revenue from the increase in nominal imports. For these three countries, the dummy variable *WWI* in their import equations measures the impact of special war-related reduction in tax revenues. In Egypt, the restrictions on cotton acreage caused by the war reduced government revenues directly because of the decrease in export duties and also reduced them indirectly because half of the land taxes were deferred when many cotton farmers could not meet their land tax payments.[18] In Ceylon, a particular reason for the government revenue loss was that wartime restrictions favored the importing of essential foods to feed plantation workers and of raw materials, all of which either entered free or were taxed at low rates.[19] In Nigeria, government revenues were adversely affected by the reduced growth of real exports. Furthermore, before the war, imports of "trade spirits" (liquor for consumption by Nigerians) came mostly from Germany and were a major source of tariff revenue. These imports were first sharply reduced by an almost prohibitive tariff in 1916, and then forbidden in 1919. Export duties were

16. See table A.53.
17. See table A.52.
18. The dummy variable *WWI* in the import equation measures this revenue loss at almost 20 percent. Land tax revenue was directly dependent on cotton exports and they accounted for about 40 percent of total government revenues. Crouchley [44, pp. 182–83] and Mead [77, p. 380].
19. USTC [120, p. 325].

added in 1916, but not until after the war did they fully offset the
revenue losses from the taxation of trade spirits.[20]

On the other hand, the United Kingdom colonies, India and
Jamaica, experienced a rise in nominal expenditures because the
revenue increase from the gain in nominal imports exceeded the
revenue decrease from the fall in real exports. In both countries,
import tariff rates were increased to offset the revenue losses from
restricted imports.[21] For the three countries tied to the United States,
and also for Taiwan and Thailand, both real exports and nominal
imports rose as a result of the war and, therefore, government revenues and expenditures increased. The gains in nominal government
expenditures of these seven countries were, however, less than the
substantial increases in import prices during the war. Thus, real expenditures fell in these seven countries as well as in the three countries whose nominal expenditures fell. Therefore, as a result of the
war, accumulated real government expenditures fell for all the
colonial countries in our sample. In this sense we conclude that this
war among the developed countries produced a common long-run
development loss for these ten countries.

The international price inflation that began with the war increased
to a peak in 1919–20. This inflation was followed in 1921–22 by a
short, but severe, worldwide depression and deflation. In order to
identify the dynamic impact of these postwar events as well as the
long-run impact of the war itself, we have reported our simulation
results in table 9.1 up to the mid-1920s. With the exception of small
increases in the Philippines, Thailand, and Cuba after 1922, real
export losses occurred in this period (table 9.1A). However, by the
mid-1920s, when prices had stabilized and economic growth had
resumed in the developed countries, only two countries—Ceylon
and Nigeria—had large net real export losses as a result of the war
and the postwar inflation and deflation. Ceylon's three major
exports all had difficulties. Exports of tea were restricted because
the excess tea purchased in bulk during the war was being released
onto the postwar market, so that tea was in excess supply.[22] Exports
of coconut products were adversely affected by the loss of the U.S.

20. See Geary [57, pp. 258–62], Helleiner [61, pp. 209, 212–18], Pim [25,
p. 234], and USTC [120, pp. 311–13].
21. See Anstey [35, pp. 347–49, 385–86, 394–95] on India, and USTC
[120, pp. 318–19] on Jamaica.
22. See Rajaratnam [26, pp. 190–96] for details on British control of the
Ceylonese tea industry during and following World War I.

market to the Philippines, which had received a preferential tariff from the United States.[23] Due to unfavorable demand for rubber as a result of the depression of 1921–22, exports of rubber from Ceylon were restricted, starting in late 1922, by the Stevenson scheme.[24] Thus, the export growth of Ceylon's three major exports—tea, coconut products, and rubber—was adversely affected by the war and its aftermath. The continued net loss in Nigeria's real exports occurred not only because it regained very little of its prewar German market and had to shift to a more slowly growing United Kingdom market,[25] but also because it experienced the largest sustained increase in import prices of the ten countries in our sample.[26] In Jamaica, the adverse effects of the postwar period were eased by British preferential duties and direct subsidies, which kept the prices paid Jamaican export producers above world prices.[27] As a result Jamaican real export losses became substantially smaller beginning in 1922. Chile shifted from a real export gain during the war to a loss after the war because of the development of competing supplies of synthetic and by-product nitrate production. By 1921–22, production of by-product nitrogen was greater than that of Chilean natural sodium nitrate, and by 1925 German production alone of synthetic and by-product nitrogen was 30 percent greater than Chilean nitrate production.[28]

In the postwar period, actual colonial export prices were higher than the simulated level of export prices based upon prewar trends. This export price increase continued in every country except in Egypt where the simulated export price change is negative beginning in 1922 (table 9.1B). The estimated increases in export prices reached a peak at the same time as did the worldwide inflation of 1919–20 and then began a relative decline. This pattern of international price inflation and deflation is clearly shown by the simulations in table 9.1B. However, even at the trough of the 1921–22 deflation, the war's inflationary influence resulted in export prices that were still higher than their simulated level based upon prewar

23. Snodgrass [94, p. 44].
24. Rajaratnam [27, pp. 15–16], Rowe [90, pp. 132–34], and Snodgrass [94, pp. 39, 44]. Rowe [30] gives an excellent and detailed account of the rubber industry in general, emphasizing events preceding and during the Stevenson scheme.
25. See table 2.2.
26. See table A.32.
27. Eisner [49, pp. 251–52, 287].
28. Reynolds [89, pp. 214–15] and Stocking and Watkins [96, pp. 125–29].

trends. For the one exception, Egypt, export prices had been growing before the war at the very high rate of 4.6 percent, and the
decline in prices after 1922 reflected the decrease in demand for
Egyptian cotton as a result of the British colonial policy of expanding
other cotton-producing areas within the British Empire.[29]

Those countries which showed real export gains from the impact
of World War I had a continued favorable shift in their terms of
trade after the war. The only exception is Chile, whose declining export market for nitrates and rising import prices produced an adverse
shift in the terms of trade. The terms of trade moved against the five
United Kingdom colonies—Ceylon, Egypt, India, Jamaica, and Nigeria—all of which showed real export losses from the war. The main
reason for this was the rapid rise in import prices after the war which,
combined with the lack of growth in British export demand from
the effects of the war,[30] shifted the terms of trade against these five
countries. Egypt's terms of trade were further adversely affected by
the decline in price of its principal export, cotton.[31] The trend in
Jamaica's terms of trade improved in the 1920s because of stronger
Canadian demand for Jamaican products.[32]

Although World War I and its aftermath had an uneven impact
upon the colonial countries—causing expansions of real exports and
real imports in some countries and declines in others (table 9.1C)
—all but one of the countries in the sample sustained a long-term
development loss as measured by the decrease in their accumulated
real government expenditures (table 9.1G). The one exception is
the Philippines, which had fully recovered by 1925. Thus, World
War I together with the postwar inflation and the 1921 deflation
placed the other nine countries on a lower development path than
would have been the case had this series of major events, produced
in the developed world, not occurred.

THE GREAT DEPRESSION

The impact of the Great Depression upon the economies of the
colonial countries was mixed: quite large real export losses occurred
in the U.S. colonial bloc countries and Ceylon; real exports changed
very little for the United Kingdom colonial bloc, excluding Ceylon;

29. See p. 15 about the efforts of the Empire Cotton Growing Association.
30. Table A.51 shows that British industrial production did not recover from
the war until the mid-1920s and that British real income did not recover until
the late 1920s.
31. See previous discussion and Issawi [67, p. 32].
32. See p. 19 and Eisner [49, pp. 270, 274–76].

and Taiwan's real exports actually increased. The calculated percentage decreases or increases in real exports caused by the depression are reported in table 9.2A. This table and the rest of table 9.2 provide measures of the real costs or benefits incurred by the colonial countries as a result of this major worldwide depression. For example, the cost of the depression to Cuba in 1932 was a 52 percent reduction in real exports from the level that would have been reached if U.S. income and prices had grown at predepression rates and if the United States had not imposed trade restrictions on Cuba. At the other extreme, the effect of the depression in Taiwan in 1932 was an estimated increase in real exports of 15 percent. During the depression, Taiwan's real exports increased because export supply increased, due to the fall in Taiwan's import price and to technical improvements in Taiwanese agriculture, while export demand did not decline. In fact, Japan's real income continued to rise during the depression, partly due to Japanese war preparations and to successful efforts to isolate Japan and its colonies from the depression.[33]

The large real export losses of Chile, Cuba, the Philippines, and Ceylon were primarily due to the fact that the United States was the center of the world depression. Real income, industrial production, and domestic prices declined most severely in the United States, and export demand fell sharply as a result.[34]

Thus, the substantial decline in real exports of the U.S. bloc countries as compared to United Kingdom bloc countries was a result of the more serious decline of real income, industrial production, and domestic prices experienced by the United States than by the United Kingdom. In addition, the restrictive trade policies employed by the United States during the 1930s increased the decline in the real exports of Chile, Cuba, and the Philippines.[35] The large decline in Ceylon's real exports was due to the depressed state of the U.S. automobile industry, the primary purchaser of Ceylonese rubber.[36]

33. For Taiwan's import price decrease, see table A.42, column 2. Ho argues that this technical change was the result of the combined effects of improved seeds, greater fertilizers, expanded irrigation, and agricultural research and extension. Not until the late 1920s and 1930s were all of these necessary factors there at the same time. Ho [63, ch. 4, p. 64]. Japan's real income increase is shown in table A.53.

34. See table A.52.

35. The effects of these U.S. trade restrictions will be discussed on pp. 234–239.

36. This effect is measured by the variable CAR. See also Rajaratnam [27, pp. 16–20], Bauer [37, pp. 45–47], and Snodgrass [94, pp. 39–40].

Table 9.2. Simulated Percentage Changes Caused by The Great Depression

	Ceylon	Chile	Cuba	Egypt	India	Jamaica	Nigeria	Philippines	Taiwan	Thailand
				9.2A. Real Exports						
1930	-5.5	-5.3	-24.7	-.9	-3.8	3.4	-.2	-2.7	4.6	-1.3
1931	-11.8	-12.5	-45.8	-1.5	-8.4	2.8	.1	-4.9	14.7	-2.9
1932	-20.7	-46.7	-52.4	-2.7	-9.1	-14.0	.0	-8.3	15.2	-3.1
1933	-21.2	-43.5	-52.3	-.7	-8.4	-10.4	1.4	-9.7	12.2	-1.6
1934	-18.9	-39.4	-53.0	-1.1	-6.4	-6.6	4.0	-10.0	13.6	-.3
1935	-30.0	-37.1	-53.2	-.7	-4.0	-4.8	5.8	-21.0	9.1	2.3
1936	-33.9	-33.8	-53.4	.4	-2.2	-2.0	7.7	-23.1	6.4	5.0
1937	-35.9	-34.7	-54.4	-4.7	n.s.[a]	-3.2	7.4	-24.3	n.s.	n.s.
1938	-42.6	-40.0	n.s.	n.s.	n.s.	-5.3	n.s.	-27.4	n.s.	n.s.
				9.2B. Export Price						
1930	-24.1	-20.7	-15.5	-16.9	-14.6	-21.9	-17.7	-10.7	-9.7	-23.0
1931	-36.3	-44.4	-40.2	-32.2	-27.5	-38.6	-36.7	-28.1	-20.1	-44.0
1932	-47.8	-66.8	-55.7	-38.4	-31.6	-35.4	-43.5	-43.6	-16.3	-54.0
1933	-33.0	-71.6	-47.5	-35.1	-27.9	-38.5	-41.4	-49.0	-5.8	-49.0
1934	-33.7	-68.4	-27.3	-30.0	-21.3	-35.7	-42.5	-43.3	4.3	-46.0
1935	-16.8	-65.1	-13.3	-22.8	-15.8	-30.9	-34.5	-30.7	13.3	-42.0
1936	1.7	-60.1	0.9	-17.6	-7.3	-26.4	-27.2	-31.7	17.7	-36.0
1937	8.4	-52.7	18.5	3.9	n.s.	-17.9	-15.9	-28.2	n.s.	n.s.
1938	-16.0	-61.7	n.s.	n.s.	n.s.	-22.8	n.s.	-30.4	n.s.	n.s.
				9.2C. Real Imports						
1930	-7.5	-18.6	-28.5	-2.3	-5.6	-3.2	-4.1	-5.4	7.7	-4.5
1931	-12.3	-40.3	-52.0	-4.3	-13.2	-12.9	-7.4	-12.2	22.8	-10.5

Year										
1932	−24.6	−72.0	−60.7	−6.8	−13.7	−23.1	−11.0	−20.4	18.6	−11.8
1933	−17.6	−70.0	−58.2	−3.1	−13.7	−18.6	−5.1	−23.2	12.8	−8.3
1934	−13.2	−63.8	−55.6	−3.8	−11.1	−10.4	3.8	−21.6	15.6	−5.1
1935	−24.4	−59.2	−53.6	−2.7	−7.3	−4.7	8.0	−27.6	7.6	3.3
1936	−22.2	−52.3	−51.8	−0.5	−5.6	3.0	14.6	−29.8	5.0	11.8
1837	−23.6	−50.7	−51.2	−9.2	n.s.	4.7	10.4	−30.1	n.s.	n.s.
1938	−37.8	−62.0	n.s.	n.s.	n.s.	−2.1	n.s.	−33.6	n.s.	n.s.

9.2D. Terms of Trade

Year										
1930	−8.3	−14.3	−15.1	−9.1	−5.9	0.3	−7.9	−9.3	7.0	−11.9
1931	−6.1	−32.3	−20.1	−17.7	−14.3	−5.5	−16.1	−13.9	17.9	−25.4
1932	−18.6	−42.6	−27.7	−23.0	−14.8	1.9	−21.3	−24.7	4.9	−30.6
1933	7.8	−34.6	−12.1	−17.9	−15.6	7.1	−16.3	−27.5	0.7	−25.5
1934	16.2	−21.1	−4.1	−16.4	−13.3	14.9	−10.8	−29.9	9.2	−21.4
1935	19.4	−11.9	5.4	−12.3	−9.3	19.5	−6.2	−16.5	0.6	−10.9
1936	53.1	1.5	14.4	−7.9	−8.4	26.0	0.3	−22.3	2.0	0.9
1937	59.4	0.2	18.4	−10.2	n.s.	25.8	−0.5	−24.1	n.s.	n.s.
1938	19.5	−19.3	n.s.	n.s.	n.s.	19.9	n.s.	−32.3	n.s.	n.s.

9.2E. Balance of Trade

Year										
1930	−6.3	−3.2	−10.8	−7.7	−4.0	7.1	−4.1	−6.7	4.0	−8.9
1931	−5.5	−7.5	−9.8	−15.3	−9.7	11.6	−9.3	−6.7	10.2	−19.1
1932	−14.4	−7.5	−12.4	−19.6	−10.2	13.9	−11.6	−13.5	1.9	−23.7
1933	3.1	3.1	0.3	−15.8	−10.4	17.8	−10.6	−14.6	0.1	−20.1
1934	8.6	11.0	1.5	−14.1	−8.7	19.7	−10.6	−19.5	7.3	−17.5
1935	10.5	14.4	6.3	−10.5	−6.0	19.4	−8.0	−9.0	2.0	−11.7
1936	30.1	19.0	10.8	−7.1	−5.1	19.9	−5.8	−14.9	3.3	−5.2
1937	33.7	13.0	10.6	−5.8	n.s.	16.2	−3.2	−17.8	n.s.	n.s.
1938	10.2	5.0	n.s.	n.s.	n.s.	16.0	n.s.	−26.0	n.s.	n.s.

[a] n.s. = year not in country's simulation

Table 9.2—Continued

	Ceylon	Chile	Cuba	Egypt	India	Jamaica	Nigeria	Philippines	Taiwan	Thailand
9.2F. Government Expenditures										
1930	-4.6	-6.3	19.0	-4.1	-11.0	-9.1	-3.0	-3.4	-1.7	-3.9
1931	-11.4	-16.5	42.8	-8.3	25.5	-21.4	-8.4	-13.7	-2.1	-9.6
1932	-19.6	-47.1	-55.1	-10.6	26.7	-32.5	-13.1	-24.2	1.8	-14.0
1933	-23.2	-53.2	-58.6	-8.4	32.7	-37.1	-14.8	-30.6	5.1	-14.2
1934	-23.3	-52.4	-59.0	-4.3	43.0	-36.9	-14.9	-28.3	7.4	-13.6
1935	-28.1	-50.4	-58.7	1.6	52.1	-34.3	-12.4	-31.3	9.6	-12.5
1936	-31.9	-47.3	-58.2	8.1	65.7	-30.6	-8.5	-32.1	9.3	-10.8
1937	-34.5	-45.3	-58.1	17.4	n.s.	-25.8	-4.1	-30.8	n.s.	n.s.
1938	-39.4	-48.9	n.s.	n.s.	n.s.	-26.2	n.s.	-30.2	n.s.	n.s.
9.2G. Accumulated Real Government Expenditures										
1930	0.6	-1.7	-1.1	0.1	-0.0	0.5	0.3	-0.1	0.7	0.5
1931	1.8	-3.7	-2.4	0.4	0.9	1.0	1.0	0.1	2.5	1.6
1932	2.8	-5.1	-3.8	0.7	1.9	1.2	1.8	0.2	3.6	3.0
1933	3.6	-5.6	-5.4	1.1	2.9	1.4	2.5	0.1	3.9	4.2
1934	4.2	-6.0	-7.8	1.5	4.0	1.7	3.7	-0.7	4.3	5.4
1935	4.1	-6.3	-10.3	1.8	5.2	2.1	4.7	-1.7	4.0	6.9
1936	4.1	-6.6	-12.9	2.3	6.3	2.6	5.7	-3.1	3.6	8.6
1937	3.7	-7.0	-15.6	2.3	n.s.	2.9	6.0	-4.7	n.s.	n.s.
1938	2.9	-7.4	n.s.	n.s.	n.s.	3.3	n.s.	-6.5	n.s.	n.s.

[a] n.s. = year not in country's simulation

The large contraction of real exports for the U.S. bloc countries and Ceylon had a corresponding depressing effect upon real imports (table 9.2C). Once again, there was a relatively small decline for the United Kingdom bloc, excluding Ceylon, while Taiwan experienced a net increase in real imports during the entire period. Real imports for the United Kingdom bloc began to recover in 1933, especially in Nigeria and Thailand, which both showed gains from 1935 to 1938. There is no evidence suggesting a similar recovery for any of the U.S. bloc countries or Ceylon; for these countries, the cost of the Great Depression continued until at least the start of World War II, when our simulation period ends. The largest decline in real imports occurred in Chile, primarily because of the effects of the sharp drop in real exports and export price in Chile after the imposition of the U.S. copper tariff in 1932. In addition, increased export and import taxation, measured by the dummy *INCOME,* also decreased Chile's real imports. The sharp drop in Cuba's real imports was caused by the reduction in its sugar export earnings.[37]

Because of the drop in export demand, the depression caused an unambiguous fall in export prices from 1930 to 1935 for all countries except Taiwan which, because of favorable Japanese demand, showed an improvement after 1933.[38] The recovery in export prices after 1935 reflects the corresponding recovery in the United Kingdom and the United States from the depths of the depression. Export price recovered sharply in Ceylon after 1936 due to the International Rubber Restriction Scheme, as measured by the dummy variable *LIMIT.*[39] From 1930 to 1932, the terms of trade moved against all countries with the exception of Taiwan and Jamaica (table 9.2D). Ceylon, Cuba, Nigeria, and Thailand experienced a recovery in their terms of trade after 1932 due mainly to the more rapid recovery in their export prices than their import prices. Chile, Egypt, India, and

37. For details on Chile during the depression, see Ellsworth [50, pp. 1–58]. The analysis of the dummy *INCOME* is on pp. 243–44 of this study. For details on the decrease in Cuba's imports, see CCA [41, pp. 54–58] and CERP [45, pp. 347–48, 358–76, 402–3, and 409–11]. Cuban exports were also reduced as a result of restrictions by the Cuban government on sugar exports [see pp. 235, 238 of this study].

38. See figures 6.1 through 6.10 and table 9.2B. For the analysis of some specific countries, see Anstey [35, p. 497] on India; Helleiner [61, pp. 19, 80–81, 85–86, 103–4, 114–16, 124] on Nigeria; Rowe [90, pp. 80–90] and Stocking and Watkins [96, pp. 32–41] on Cuba; and Snodgrass [94, pp. 35, 41, 44, 357–61] on Ceylon.

39. See pp. 239–41 for an analysis of this dummy variable, and tables A.51 and A.52 for movement in prices.

the Philippines did not experience a similar terms of trade improvement.[40]

Table 9.2G measures the cost of the depression in terms of accumulated real government expenditures. Ceylon's accumulated real government expenditures increased because while its nominal expenditures were falling, its import prices fell even faster, and as a result real expenditures rose. The steady rise in accumulated real government expenditures for the rest of the United Kingdom bloc acted to offset the actual, but small, fall in export demand due to the depression. For all these countries, the shift of the export supply curve to the right tended to offset the shift of the export demand curve to the left and as a result there was only a small change in real exports.[41] In fact, the change in Nigeria's real exports remained slightly positive throughout the period; this suggests that the rightward shift of its export supply outweighed the leftward shift of its export demand. Of these countries, only India showed a rise in nominal government revenues and expenditures for nearly the whole period. These expenditures should have fallen due to the decline in both real exports and nominal imports, which should have produced a corresponding decline in nominal revenues. The explanation for the rise in Indian government expenditures was that the Indian tariff, established in 1931, counteracted the effects of the depression. As a result real government expenditures in India actually increased during the depression.[42]

Only Taiwan and Jamaica showed improved trade balances throughout the Great Depression (table 9.2E). This result agrees with the fact that only these two countries had improved terms of trade throughout the depression. Taiwan's large trade surpluses reflected the Japanese policy of making Taiwan serve its economic and increasingly its military needs, as mentioned in chapters 1 and 3. Net improvement in trade balances occurred in Ceylon in 1933 because the decline in its terms of trade was reversed; in Chile in 1933 because of exchange controls; and in Cuba in 1934 because of a substantial reduction in both shipping charges and remittances

40. See also the actual terms of trade data in the appendix for these countries.

41. For movement in Ceylon's prices, see table A.3, column 3. For the remainder of the United Kingdom bloc, see table 9.2A.

42. For a detailed analysis of the effect of this tariff in India, see the discussion of the dummy *TARIFF* on pp. 243–44. See also table A.23 and Anstey [35, pp. 510, 630–31].

abroad by sugar workers. While the remaining five countries—Egypt, India, Nigeria, the Philippines, and Thailand—all ran trade surpluses, table 9.2E indicates that these surpluses were reduced as a result of the depression.[43]

SUMMARY

The results of our simulations show that World War I and the Great Depression had different patterns of impact upon colonial development. The economic losses from World War I were greatest for the countries under the direct control of the United Kingdom, while the largest losses from the Great Depression were for countries linked to the United States.

43. For details on each country, see Ho [63, ch. 6, pp. 1–16] and table A.41 on Taiwan; table A.2 on Ceylon; Reynolds [89, pp. 232–36] on Chile; CERP [45, pp. 400–402] on Cuba; and the appendix and the discussion in chapter 4 for the remaining six countries.

10

Trade Restrictions and Tax Changes

This chapter measures the impact of specific trade restrictions and tax increases on the process of colonial development. These exogenous changes are measured by the dummy variables for trade restrictions in the export supply and demand equations and for taxation in the government revenue equations.[1] For each country, the developmental effects of a particular change can be measured by resimulating that country's model after dropping the specific dummy variable or after starting it at a different year.

U.S. TRADE RESTRICTIONS

The first set of simulations focuses upon the effects of the restrictive trade policies of the United States during the 1930s upon Chile, Cuba, the Philippines, and Jamaica, as measured by the dummy variables *QUOTA* and *RESTR*. U.S. restrictive trade policies affecting Chile were the result of the 1932 Tariff Act, which imposed a four-cents-per-pound tariff on imported copper.[2] Cuban exports were adversely affected by several U.S. trade restrictions. First, the Hawley-Smoot Tariff of 1930 substantially increased the import duty on Cuban sugar. Second, the Jones-Costigan Act of 1934 applied a quota on imported Cuban sugar based on the average imports of the period 1931–33. Since Cuban sugar exports to the United States had already been cut substantially during this base period due to the Hawley-Smoot Tariff, the result was to limit Cuban sugar exports to this low base period level.[3] Philippine exports of sugar to the United

1. The definitions of these dummy variables are listed in table 2.5. The World War I dummies have already been analyzed, and the dummy variables reflecting changes in accounting practices need no special analysis.
2. Reynolds [89, pp. 232–33, 265]. He notes that "this tax was, in effect, a 70 percent ad valorem duty on copper, based on the average world price during the year [1932]."
3. CCA [41, pp. 52–53, 61–62, 225] and CERP [45, pp. 333–34]. For details on the various restraints on the Cuban sugar industry, see CERP [45, ch. 28].

States were also made subject to the Jones-Costigan Act, but since Philippine sugar exports had not been subject to the Hawley-Smoot Tariff, the Philippines received a much more favorable quota than did Cuba. The Hawley-Smoot Tariff cut Jamaican exports to the United States to very low levels.[4]

Table 10.1 measures the effect of these U.S. trade restrictions on the trade and government sectors of these four countries. As a result of these restrictions, real exports were reduced in all four countries (table 10.1A). Chile and Cuba's real exports were at about half the level that would have prevailed if there had been no restrictions on their export trade. In Chile, the 1932 tariff caused U.S. imports of Chilean refined copper to decrease from 87,000 tons in 1931 to 5,000 tons in 1933 and to 2,000 tons in 1938.[5] As a result of the U.S. trade restrictions, Cuban sugar exports to the United States were cut about in half during the 1930s.[6]

Real exports of the Philippines and Jamaica were much less adversely affected by U.S. trade restrictions. The trade restrictions directed toward the Philippines were not as severe as those for Chile and Cuba and were imposed somewhat later in the depression years (1935). The reduction in Jamaica's trade with the United States was partially offset by an increase in the demand for its exports from the United Kingdom and its colonies,[7] a market that was much less depressed than that of the United States during this period.[8] Trade ties with the U.S. economy caused economic difficulties for these four countries during the 1930s, but our evidence suggests that legal colonialism, as exemplified by the Philippines and Jamaica, helped to mitigate the impact of U.S. trade policies.

The export supply curves as well as the export demand curves shifted leftward in the four countries affected by restrictive U.S. trade policies. These leftward supply shifts occurred in Chile because multinational U.S. copper companies reallocated production from their mines in Chile to their mines in the United States.[9] In Cuba, this leftward shift occurred because the government employed various internal methods to restrict sugar production. In response to the

4. Table 2.2 shows that the U.S. share of Jamaican exports dropped from 40.7 percent in 1925 to 3.5 percent in 1938.
5. Reynolds [89, pp. 232–33].
6. CCA [41, pp. 53, 61–62, 225, 250–51, 256] and CERP [45, pp. 283, 330–34].
7. See table 2.2.
8. See tables A.51 and A.52.
9. Reynolds [89, p. 233].

Table 10.1. Simulated Percentage Changes Caused by U.S. Trade Restrictions

	1930	1931	1932	1933	1934	1935	1936	1937	1938
10.1A. Real Exports									
Chile			-37.0	-40.0	-41.2	-42.5	-43.9	-45.3	-46.5
Cuba	-20.0	-40.0	-45.0	-46.8	-48.1	-49.0	-49.8	-50.5	
Jamaica			-15.5	-15.6	-15.6	-15.7	-15.8	-15.9	-15.9
Philippines						-12.4	-14.9	-15.8	-16.3
10.1B. Export Prices									
Chile			-7.5	-17.3	-16.9	-15.6	-14.2	-12.7	-11.4
Cuba	6.2	22.4	36.6	43.0	47.4	50.7	53.7	56.6	
Jamaica			11.2	11.3	11.5	11.7	12.0	12.2	12.4
Philippines						16.4	5.6	4.1	4.2
10.1C. Real Imports									
Chile	-18.1	-35.3	-40.0	-47.5	-48.3	-48.9	-49.4	-50.0	-50.6
Cuba			-38.4	-39.6	-40.4	-41.0	-41.5	-42.0	
Jamaica			-7.8	-7.7	-7.7	-7.6	-7.5	-7.5	-7.4
Philippines						-8.7	-13.5	-14.7	-15.2
10.1D. Trade Balance									
Chile	3.8	13.5	-2.8	-5.5	-5.4	-5.1	-4.8	-4.4	-4.1
Cuba			22.1	25.8	28.3	30.2	31.9	33.6	
Jamaica			1.9	1.9	1.9	1.9	2.0	2.0	2.0
Philippines						11.7	3.9	2.8	2.9

10.1E. Government Expenditures

Chile	-44.7	-28.7	-38.2	-41.6	-43.3	-44.7	-46.0	-47.2
Cuba	-34.1	-43.3	-47.6	-49.8	-51.2	-52.2	-53.0	
Jamaica		-6.2	-8.7	-9.7	-10.1	-10.3	-10.3	-10.4
Philippines					-6.7	-11.5	-13.8	-14.9

10.1F. Accumulated Real Government Expenditures

Chile	-.8	-1.8	-5.1	-9.0	-13.1	-17.2	-20.6	-23.5
Cuba	-3.1	-6.1	-9.2	-11.8	-14.1	-16.3	-18.2	
Jamaica		-.2	-.5	-.8	-1.1	-1.4	-1.7	-2.0
Philippines					-.4	-1.1	-1.8	-2.5

Hawley-Smoot Tariff, Cuba limited sugar output first under its own Sugar Stabilization Act of 1930 and then under an international agreement, the Chadbourne Plan, in 1931.[10] In Jamaica the leftward supply shift occurred because producers reacted to the loss of the U.S. market by reducing their banana tree plantings;[11] and it occurred in the Philippines because producers actually burned their sugar fields. For each country the export price rose or fell depending on whether the leftward supply shift was respectively larger or smaller than the leftward demand shift. Thus, Chile's export price fell because the coefficient of the trade restriction dummy was larger in the demand equation than in the supply equation. The opposite result holds for Cuba, Jamaica, and the Philippines.[12]

The reduction in real exports for these countries and the resulting fall in both real and nominal imports caused a decline in nominal revenues and expenditures and, therefore, a reduction in accumulated real government expenditures. The most substantial reduction in the real stock of government expenditures occurred in Chile. This reduction resulted in a further leftward shift in its export supply curve, dampening the falling pattern of Chile's export prices (table 10.1B). In Cuba and Jamaica, the reduction in the real stock of government expenditures and the resulting further leftward shift in their supply curves caused a further rise in export prices. A similar pattern should hold for the Philippines, but because of the underlying auto-regressive structure and the late imposition of the quota, there are only enough observations just to start this dynamic pattern, as measured by the small rise in its export price from 1937 to 1938.

The pattern of the terms of trade is the same as that of the export price; a favorable shift occurred in the terms of trade for Cuba, the Philippines, and Jamaica, and an adverse shift for Chile. Correspondingly, there was a deficit in the nominal balance of trade for Chile and nominal surpluses for the other three countries (table

10. CCA [41, pp. 250–51] and CERP [45, pp. 325–35].

11. Conclusion based on Jamaica trade data [107].

12. This conclusion can be derived by using the same dummy variable D in equations 2.1 and 2.2 so that $D = D_S = D_D$. Then the impact multiplier for the trade restrictions, with $\Delta D = $ one, is

$$\Delta \ln P_x = \frac{b_5 - a_5}{a_1 - b_1}$$

Since b_5 and a_5 are both negative,

$$\Delta \ln P_x \gtreqless 0, \text{ when } |a_5| \gtreqless |b_5|$$

10.1D). The restrictive trade policies pursued during the 1930s by the United States led, then, to an improvement in its nominal balance of trade only with Chile.

We have noted that the Philippines suffered much less of an export loss than did Chile and Cuba from restrictive U.S. policies during the 1930s. One way to measure this difference is to assume that the more favorable Philippine trade restrictions were imposed upon Chile and Cuba. These simulations show that real exports for Chile and Cuba would have increased an average of 81 percent and 70 percent respectively over the level of real exports that occurred under their actual trade restrictions. Both countries would also have had higher accumulated real government expenditures, the average increase being about 9 percent for Cuba and a dramatic 32 percent for Chile. These results suggest that the restrictive effects of U.S. trade policies could have been mitigated for Cuba and Chile if they had been under formal colonial control. Like the Philippines, they might have had a stronger bargaining position in Washington; as a consequence, less of the burden of the U.S. depression might have been passed onto their economies.

The trade advantages of Philippine sugar over Cuban sugar are especially noticeable. The main competition for Cuban sugar selling in the U.S. market was cane sugar from the Philippines, Hawaii, and Puerto Rico, and beet sugar produced in the continental United States. These alternative sources were not subject to the Hawley-Smoot Tariff. The result was a sharp decline in U.S. demand for Cuban sugar, as the United States protected these other producers at Cuba's expense. Further, as the sugar quotas of 1934 were based upon export levels of the previous three years, the Philippines were subject to a much more favorable quota than was Cuba.[13]

RUBBER EXPORT LIMITATION AGREEMENT

The impact of the International Rubber Regulation Scheme on Ceylon is measured by the dummy variable *LIMIT*. This agreement was signed by producers of 98 percent of the world's rubber and became effective in late 1934. The purpose of the rubber agreement was to restrict exports from all the important rubber-producing countries and thus to raise the price of rubber. Countries signed with the purpose of "reducing world stocks to a normal figure and adjusting in an

13. CCA [41, pp. 235, 249] and CERP [45, pp. 330–33].

orderly manner supply to demand and maintaining a fair and equitable price level which will be reasonably remunerative to efficient producers." Control was achieved by regulating exports from participating countries, prohibiting new planting, and prohibiting exports of rubber seedlings.[14] The simulation results in table 10.2 measure the effectiveness of this scheme for Ceylon. Real exports fell by 18 percent in 1935 and by 31.5 percent in 1938. Because of the distributed lag process in the supply equation of Ceylon, export prices fell by 2.5 percent in 1935 but thereafter increased steadily until, in 1938, they were 46.7 percent above the level which would have prevailed without the limitation agreement. Thus, the rubber limitation agreement did in fact restrict real exports and raise export prices. The effect of the restricted rubber exports was strengthened by the recovery of U.S. automobile production[15] and by German rearmament.[16] With limited supply and increasing demand, rubber in 1937 had reached its highest price since 1927.[17]

The restriction scheme led to improved terms of trade and generated a nominal trade surplus for Ceylon. However, the limit on rubber exports also depressed Ceylon's government sector, measured by an increasingly large decline in government revenues and expenditures and a small decline in accumulated real government expenditures. Thus, the benefit to the export sector in the short run was obtained at the cost of long-run export development in Ceylon. One method of describing this possible trade-off is to start the *LIMIT* dummy in 1931, near the beginning of the world depression, instead of in 1935. Our results indicate that the terms of trade would have started to improve in 1932, and that nominal trade surpluses would have been generated from this date onward. Thus, starting the restriction scheme earlier would have benefited Ceylon in terms of export prices and nominal trade balance. The cost, however, would have been that the reduction in accumulated real government expenditures began in 1931 rather than 1935, and therefore, in 1938, it would have been 7.3 percent lower for the longer period of export restriction as compared to a 3.4 percent reduction for the shorter period.

14. Bauer [37, pp. 84–86] and Rowe [90, ch. 6].
15. See table A.52.
16. Snodgrass [94, p. 40].
17. See Bauer [37, pp. 124–38] for a detailed analysis of price fluctuations and export control under the International Rubber Regulation Scheme.

Table 10.2. Ceylon: Simulated Percentage Changes Caused by
Rubber Limitation Agreement

	1935	1936	1937	1938
X^R	−18.0	−25.8	−29.6	−31.5
Px	−2.5	22.4	37.6	46.7
M^R	−18.4	−20.2	−21.2	−21.7
B_T	−2.0	13.8	23.0	28.2
G	−9.1	−16.7	−21.9	−25.2
$\sum\limits_{i=1}^{\infty} G^R_{t-i}$	−.4	−1.3	−2.3	−3.4

CHANGES IN TAX POLICY

As we explained in the section on political controls in chapter 1, Thailand's customs duties were fixed at low rates until 1926 by the Bowring Treaty with the United Kingdom. In 1926, new treaties gave Thailand control over its tax structure. With its new fiscal autonomy, Thailand abolished inland transit duties and raised tariff rates. The effect of the increased tariffs was immediate, causing revenues from import duties to more than double by the next year, 1927. From 1927 to 1935, further increases raised the average import duty rate from 8.5 percent to 22 percent.[18] The dummy variable *FIXED* was included in Thailand's revenue equation to explain the revenue increases in Thailand when tariff rates were no longer limited by the Bowring Treaty. Dynamic simulation of the model for Thailand omitting the dummy *FIXED* shows that government revenues and expenditures were over 20 percent higher by 1936 than they would have been if the Bowring Treaty had remained in force. This simulation result agrees with the actual data, which show that import duties as a percentage of total revenue increased from 7 percent in 1926 to 25 percent in 1935.[19]

As a result of this new taxing power, accumulated real government expenditures were almost 5 percent higher by 1936, and real

18. Ingram [64, pp. 180–85].
19. Ingram [64, p. 183].

Table 10.3. Thailand: Simulated Percentage Changes Caused by
End of Bowring Treaty Restrictions

	Real exports X^R	Export price P_X	Trade balance B_T	Govt. exp. G	Acc. real govt. exp. $\sum_{i=1}^{\infty} G^R_{t-i}$
1927				1.25	.06
1928	.01	-.06	-.04	2.99	.21
1929	.04	-.20	-.12	4.93	.44
1930	.09	-.42	-.24	6.97	.77
1931	.16	-.75	-.43	9.08	1.23
1932	.25	-1.19	-.68	11.23	1.80
1933	.37	-1.73	-.99	13.42	2.43
1934	.50	-2.31	-1.32	15.66	3.14
1935	.64	-2.97	-1.70	17.94	3.96
1936	.81	-3.72	-2.13	20.26	4.87

exports were almost 1 percent higher by this date. The terms of
trade, however, turned against Thailand and the country ran a
smaller nominal trade surplus. Basically, the increased revenues led
to a rightward shift in the supply curve, a fall in export prices, and a
greater fall in nominal exports than in nominal imports. If the
Bowring Treaty had been eliminated earlier—say in 1923 rather
than in 1926—there would have been a steadily rising pattern of
real exports, nominal revenues and expenditures, and accumulated
real government expenditures. Conversely, the terms of trade and
the nominal trade balance would have moved against Thailand from
1923 onward. Thus, the real export gains and higher stock of government capital as a result of the elimination of this aspect of United
Kingdom control on the Thai government sector must be balanced
against adverse export price movements and reduced accumulation
of foreign exchange reserves. Thailand historically had been accumulating vast foreign exchange reserves, so on balance its welfare
was probably improved by the elimination of the Bowring Treaty in
1926, and its economy would have been even better off had the
elimination come earlier.[20]

Egypt's tariffs, like Thailand's, were fixed at low rates by a series
of international treaties. In 1930, after the last treaties with the

20. For details on Thailand's government revenues and expenditures prior to
and following the 1926 tariff changes, see pp. 78–80.

United Kingdom and Italy expired, Egypt adopted a new customs tariff that generally increased import duties.[21] India also increased its tariff rates substantially in 1931 to balance its government budget, which was in deficit as a result of the Great Depression.[22] Further minor tariff increases were adopted in both countries during succeeding years. These tariff increases, measured by the dummy *TARIFF*, while significant in their revenue equations, had only limited effects upon their export sectors. Dynamic simulations with the omission of the *TARIFF* dummy indicate that real exports for Egypt were only .21 percent higher by 1937, and exports for India were only .51 percent higher by 1936, than they would have been had the tariffs not been imposed. The terms of trade moved against Egypt by 1.0 percent in 1937 and against India by 2.3 percent in 1936. Thus, real and nominal imports were somewhat lower in both countries.

Both tariff increases were somewhat protective and did in fact encourage import substitution of cotton, clothing, and some foods in both countries and of iron and steel products in India.[23] The basic reason for higher real exports in both countries was a higher stock of government capital as a result of the tariff's generation of increased revenues. The export supply curve shifted rightward, resulting in a lower export price. Perhaps the most interesting result is not that these effects on the export sector are small, but rather that a change in the tariff schedule did have some effect, through the government sector, on the growth of real exports.

The income tax on copper production imposed in Chile in 1926 and its subsequent increases provide a good example of the importance of the government sector in promoting the growth of the export economy. As mentioned in chapter 3, the Chilean government began in 1927 to use these increased revenues to finance an increased public works program.[24] Simulation analysis yields the conclusion that copper producers in Chile had higher, not lower, real and nominal exports because the government imposed an income tax on copper production. By 1938, these tax increases measured by the dummy *INCOME* raised real exports by 13.8 percent, lowered the terms of trade and the export price by 8.9 percent, raised real imports by 5.7

21. Crouchley [44, pp. 232–34] and League of Nations [113, ch. 32, p. 7].
22. See Anstey [35, pp. 398–99, 505–12] and Thomas [33, pp. 473–81] for details on these tariff rate increases and their financial impact on India.
23. For further analysis of the results of tariffs in India, see Anstey [35, pp. 398–99, 504–5]; in Egypt, see Crouchley [44, pp. 233–34].
24. See also Reynolds [89, pp. 233–34].

Table 10.4. Egypt: Simulated Percentage Changes Caused by Tariff Increases

	Real exports X^R	Export price Px	Real imports M^R	Trade balance B_T	Govt. expenditures G	Acc. real govt. exp. $\sum_{i=1}^{\infty} G^R_{t-1}$
1931					1.8	.05
1932	.01	−.03	−.001	−.02	4.5	.15
1933	.02	−.10	−.005	−.07	7.6	.35
1934	.05	−.22	−.01	−.16	11.1	.61
1935	.09	−.39	−.02	−.28	14.6	.96
1936	.14	−.61	−.03	−.44	18.4	1.41
1937	.21	−.90	−.05	−.64	22.3	1.87

Table 10.5. India: Simulated Percentage Changes Caused by Tariff Increases

	Real exports X^R	Export price Px	Real imports M^R	Trade balance B_T	Govt. exp. G	Acc. real govt. exp. $\sum_{i=1}^{\infty} G^R_{t-i}$
1931					61.2	.95
1932	.08	−.40	−.08	−.23	73.4	2.11
1933	.19	−.87	−.17	−.52	75.3	3.29
1934	.29	−1.35	−.27	−.80	75.5	4.50
1935	.40	−1.84	−.36	−1.09	75.5	5.79
1936	.51	−2.34	−.46	−1.39	75.4	7.10

percent, and shifted the nominal trade balance toward a deficit position by 2.0 percent. Like some of the previously analyzed effects, the tax produced not only the benefits of higher real exports and imports but also the costs of adverse terms of trade movement and possible balance of payments problems. But what is most interesting about this simulation is that copper producers in Chile increased their real and nominal exports because the government imposed an income tax on copper production. These increases occurred because the government used the increased tax revenues to increase expenditures that promoted the growth of exports, particularly copper.

The final simulation uses the dummy variable *INFRA* to measure the effect upon Nigerian export development of the completion by 1916 of major infrastructure projects—the railroad to Northern Nigeria, port facilities in Lagos, and the railroad to the Udi coalfields in Eastern Nigeria. The completion of the Lagos-Kano railway line in 1912 and of the Jebba bridge over the Niger River on that line in 1916 opened up the previously remote peanut (groundnut) growing areas of Northern Nigeria to the coastal export markets, causing peanut exports to increase from less than 2,000 tons yearly before World War I to over 50,000 tons in 1916.[25] Before the port of Lagos was completed in 1916, all cargo had to be transshipped at substantial cost between ocean-going steamers and small beach boats.[26] The completion of the railroad to the Udi coalfields in Eastern Nigeria opened up an assured supply of low-cost coal for railroads, tin mines, harbor dredgers, electric generators, and other Nigerian coal users.[27] Here, the real export growth effects are substantial and serve to confirm the importance of infrastructure in colonial development. Transportation costs were substantially lower as a result of the railroads and the port, so that the differential between export prices and prices paid export producers narrowed. Reduced transportation costs were directly responsible for increased exports of peanuts, cocoa, cotton, tin, and palm products.[28] The increase in export supply was such that in only ten years real exports were estimated to be 50 percent higher than they would have been had the railroads and the port not been constructed. Export prices decreased substantially—by 44 percent in ten years—as a result of the increased export supply. Increased export supplies at a lower price was a clear gain to Nigeria's main export buyers. However, since the completed infrastructure reduced internal transportation costs, the prices paid export producers could remain at higher levels than they would have otherwise or even increase. Furthermore, transportation costs for some areas, particularly Northern Nigeria, were previously so high that export production was unprofitable. Due to the large fall in export prices, real imports changed very little, and Nigeria's trade balance shifted toward a surplus. By 1926, government revenues and expenditures had increased 40 percent as a result of the completion of the raliroads and the ports.

25. Helleiner [61, pp. 109–12].
26. Geary [57, pp. 145–47].
27. Geary [57, pp. 254–55].
28. For a complete analysis of the real export growth effects of infrastructure in Nigeria, see pp. 68–70.

TAX EFFORT

The results derived in the previous section suggest that in general an increase in the colonial tax effort could have considerable effects on the development of the colonial trade and government sectors. Evidence on the magnitude of these possible tax effects for all ten countries is reported in table 10.6, where we calculate the dynamic multipliers for an assumed .01 increase in the constant term of the revenue equation.[29] Over time, real exports for all ten countries would increase monotonically: the export supply curve shifts to the right as increased tax revenue leads to increased accumulated real government expenditures. As might be expected, the low productivity group—Egypt, India, Jamaica, and Thailand—would experience the smallest gain in real exports from a possible tax increase. The U.S. bloc countries—the Philippines, Cuba, and Chile—stand out as having the largest increases in real exports due to increased taxes. We might conclude that there should have been an increased tax effort in the U.S. bloc countries, given the previously identified productivity of their government sectors in promoting export expansion. This conclusion is confirmed by table 10.6E. Under the condition of increased taxes, the U.S. bloc countries are clearly identified as the countries that would have had both the greatest increase in accumulated real government expenditures and the largest rightward shift in their export supply curves.

In general, increased taxes on the trade sector would have expanded, rather than contracted, the export economy. This conclusion depends, of course, on the colonial government spending that revenue on export-promoting activities. It seems then that the developed country would have benefited by higher colonial taxes since real exports would expand and export prices would fall. In the colonial world, however, the fall in export prices could lead to a fall in colonial real imports even though real exports were expanding. In fact, only the U.S. bloc countries, Ceylon, and Taiwan show an expansion in real imports due to increased taxes. For the other five colonies, the cost of increased taxes would have been a fall in their real imports. Increased taxes would have had a negative effect on the nominal balance of trade (table 10.6D). Nonetheless, this shift in the trade balance due to a tax increase would have been possible since historically, except for Jamaica, each country ran a trade deficit.

29. The first year multipliers in table 10.6 are zero for the trade variables because of the structural order of the model.

Table 10.6. Dynamic Multipliers for a .01 Increase in the Constant Terms
of the Revenue Equation

	Years				
	1	5	10	20	30

10.6A. Real Exports

Ceylon	0.000	0.024	0.085	0.215	0.290
Chile	0.000	0.069	0.186	0.392	0.520
Cuba	0.000	0.146	0.328	0.528	0.682
Egypt	0.000	0.012	0.036	0.069	0.079
India	0.000	0.008	0.019	0.034	0.041
Jamaica	0.000	0.036	0.080	0.143	0.178
Nigeria	0.000	0.048	0.143	0.286	0.366
Philippines	0.000	0.145	0.357	0.694	0.983
Taiwan	0.000	0.068	0.189	0.346	0.458
Thailand	0.000	0.058	0.109	0.147	0.170
Averages	0.000	0.061	0.153	0.285	0.377

10.6B. Export Price

Ceylon	0.000	−0.054	−0.193	−0.488	−0.658
Chile	0.000	−0.053	−0.132	−0.266	−0.348
Cuba	0.000	−0.186	−0.417	−0.671	−0.863
Egypt	0.000	−0.052	−0.157	−0.302	−0.349
India	0.000	−0.035	−0.088	−0.157	−0.193
Jamaica	0.000	−0.079	−0.178	−0.318	−0.393
Nigeria	0.000	−0.143	−0.278	−0.428	−0.556
Philippines	0.000	−0.174	−0.338	−0.606	−0.837
Taiwan	0.000	−0.062	−0.173	−0.316	−0.418
Thailand	0.000	−0.273	−0.513	−0.695	−0.804
Averages	0.000	−0.111	−0.247	−0.425	−0.542

10.6C. Real Imports

Ceylon	0.000	0.005	0.019	0.049	0.066
Chile	0.000	0.026	0.084	0.185	0.249
Cuba	0.000	0.084	0.189	0.298	0.385
Egypt	0.000	−0.003	−0.008	−0.016	−0.018
India	0.000	−0.007	−0.017	−0.031	−0.038
Jamaica	0.000	−0.031	−0.070	−0.126	−0.156
Nigeria	0.000	−0.059	−0.066	−0.037	−0.054
Philippines	0.000	0.099	0.266	0.529	0.755
Taiwan	0.000	0.055	0.153	0.280	0.370
Thailand	0.000	−0.060	−0.112	−0.152	−0.176
Averages	0.000	0.011	0.044	0.098	0.138

(Continued)

Table 10.6–*Continued*

	Years				
	1	5	10	20	30

10.6D. Trade Balance

	1	5	10	20	30
Ceylon	0.000	−0.036	−0.127	−0.321	−0.434
Chile	0.000	−0.009	−0.031	−0.058	−0.075
Cuba	0.000	−0.124	−0.276	−0.438	−0.568
Egypt	0.000	−0.037	−0.113	−0.217	−0.251
India	0.000	−0.021	−0.052	−0.093	−0.114
Jamaica	0.000	−0.012	−0.027	−0.049	−0.060
Nigeria	0.000	−0.035	−0.068	−0.105	−0.137
Philippines	0.000	−0.127	−0.246	−0.441	−0.609
Taiwan	0.000	−0.049	−0.137	−0.250	−0.330
Thailand	0.000	−0.155	−0.292	−0.395	−0.457
Averages	0.000	−0.060	−0.137	−0.237	−0.303

10.6E. Government Expenditures

	1	5	10	20	30
Ceylon	0.247	0.902	1.053	1.163	1.226
Chile	0.395	1.019	1.160	1.355	1.472
Cuba	0.499	1.122	1.329	1.547	1.712
Egypt	0.194	0.812	0.989	1.030	1.036
India	0.472	0.975	0.991	0.985	0.981
Jamaica	0.434	0.971	0.985	0.973	0.966
Nigeria	0.223	0.865	1.069	1.234	1.301
Philippines	0.448	1.080	1.281	1.575	1.826
Taiwan	0.502	1.020	1.108	1.203	1.270
Thailand	0.205	0.797	0.952	0.973	0.971
Averages	0.362	0.956	1.092	1.204	1.276

10.6F. Accumulated Real Government Expenditures

	1	5	10	20	30
Ceylon	0.009	0.112	0.266	0.575	0.739
Chile	0.021	0.168	0.395	0.755	0.977
Cuba	0.058	0.363	0.664	0.993	1.250
Egypt	0.007	0.115	0.276	0.486	0.555
India	0.013	0.111	0.232	0.385	0.466
Jamaica	0.020	0.164	0.317	0.534	0.646
Nigeria	0.021	0.177	0.382	0.578	0.772
Philippines	0.032	0.269	0.540	0.972	1.344
Taiwan	0.020	0.190	0.355	0.593	0.756
Thailand	0.036	0.363	0.569	0.728	0.833
Averages	0.024	0.203	0.400	0.660	0.834

SUMMARY

In this chapter we analyzed the specific impact of trade restrictions and tax changes. U.S. trade restrictions imposed during the 1930s were shown to adversely affect Chile, Cuba, the Philippines, and Jamaica. As a result of these restrictions, real exports fell by about 50 percent in Chile and Cuba and by about 15 percent in the Philippines and Jamaica. These differences suggest that legal colonialism mitigated the impact of U.S. trade policies.

The international agreement to restrict rubber exports was found to have the desired result in Ceylon; exports declined by 31.5 percent and export prices increased by 46.7 percent in 1938 and its trade balance shifted toward a surplus position. These benefits were offset by somewhat lower accumulated real government expenditures, which diminished Ceylon's long-run development potential.

Changes in tax policy were found to have a varying impact on colonial development. In Thailand, the fixing of tariffs until 1926 by the Bowring Treaty limited the growth of Thailand's real exports and accumulated real government expenditures and induced Thailand to accumulate vast foreign exchange reserves. In Egypt and India, new tariff schedules introduced in 1931 had significant, but slight, effects on their economies. In Chile, the imposition of an income tax on copper was found to actually benefit copper producers by causing higher real and nominal exports. In Nigeria, the completion of infrastructure projects in 1916 was found to substantially accelerate the growth of Nigeria's trade and government sectors. In every country, increased taxes on the trade sector would have expanded, rather than contracted, the export sector. This expansion occurs because the taxes would have financed government expenditures directed toward the promotion of the colonial export economy.

11

Conclusions

Economic development is often taken to be synonymous with attempts by governments to organize national industry and to develop indigenous manufacturers. Not only is this approach historically inaccurate —it ignores the complex social and economic changes that occurred during the international colonial system—it also obscures the concept of economic development by confusing it with industrialization, especially the import-substitution programs of recent decades. Curiously, even within this approach, the explicit role of the government is often completely removed when development models are constructed showing only the relationship between an agricultural and an industrial sector, or the relationship between effective protection and industrialization. It almost seems that the more important the government becomes in fostering development, the less important it becomes in these abstract models of development. Great emphasis may be placed, for example, on the necessity of a growing agricultural surplus to finance industrialization, or the need to reduce market imperfections, thereby allowing prices of commodities and factors to better reflect their true opportunity costs; but to ignore the state that helps to shape the development environment through its expenditures and taxes is to omit one of the most important sectors in the economy, and thus to omit crucial economic linkages in the development process. Of course, in reality, it is difficult to conceive of generating a growing agricultural surplus without also being aware of the need for expenditures for infrastructure such as transport systems, irrigation and power facilities, for social intermediate services such as health and education, and even expenditures to maintain peace and order. Yet, development models rarely, if ever, introduce these expenditures or the sector that carries them out. Perhaps the very contribution of Keynesian economics in showing how government expenditures and taxes can help control effective demand has paradoxically limited our perspective of how the government can also influence supply.

The most important implication of the results of this book for the study of economic development is the explicit role of government expenditures in promoting economic growth. By examining the historical record of a range of countries, we have shown how the growth of their trade and government sectors were dependent on the accumulation of government capital, defined in this book as the variable accumulated real government expenditures. Using econometric analysis, the model has empirically provided a measure of these expenditures in promoting the growth of export supply. It is worth emphasizing that these expenditures were shown not to be a proxy for time, but rather to reflect the colonial government's decisions and ability to foster the development of the economy in a particular way, namely, the promotion of export supply. Simply put, the economic development of these countries did not proceed independently of the state. Therefore, to omit the government sector from studies of colonial trade patterns is to omit important equations and thus to derive biased conclusions due to a major misspecification error. This is true not only for the analysis of exports and imports, but also for terms of trade. All of these trade variables were shown to be endogenously determined. What a country exports and imports, then, and at what terms of trade, depend not only upon factor endowments and comparative costs, but also upon what the government does (or does not do) in developing the trade sector or, indirectly, in developing the country's factor endowments.

Historical analysis has been at the core of this book, but our results suggest a new line of research emphasizing the importance of the government in promoting economic development during any period. Basically, the government should be included on the right-hand side of behavioral equations. Clearly, the model as used in this book may not be appropriate in describing a development process where industrialization is emphasized and a different international economy operates. What may be required, however, is not the omission of the government sector, but rather a new economic specification that shows how the role of government has changed.

How political control of government is exercised then becomes crucial to determining how economic development proceeds. Although we have examined qualitative evidence on how this control operated in these countries, we did not give a full political history of colonial control, nor was it our purpose to do so. What we have demonstrated by our econometric model and results, however, is the necessity of specifying both political and economic relationships if the historical development of these countries is to be truly understood. To understand the importance of the government in explaining colonial development requires, then, the econometrics of political economy. This book only begins this type of study.

One of our major goals was to show how both internal and external forces acted together to determine what has been called a colonial development process. Our analysis of the model and its dynamic properties indicated that not only was the record of colonial development dependent upon external forces—the developed countries' growth of income and prices as well as their differing trade policies—but that it was also determined by the historical pattern of the internal force, government expenditures, in the colonies. Using dynamic simulations, we were able to show that our model, specified and estimated in earlier chapters of this book, describes accurately the actual process of colonial development and that this process was stable.

These two conclusions—that the government is important and that external and internal forces combine in the development process—also have applications to the analysis of the post–World War II development process. No doubt a more sophisticated model is required to show how government expenditures promote the development of both agriculture and industry or how taxes and tariffs are used to foster import substitution and industrialization. There is a different government reflection ratio for each new sector of the economy that the government seeks to promote. The conclusion, however, remains the same: the government sector must be identified to have a properly specified model. Similarly, different external conditions in the international economy may imply that the colonial process as we have defined it no longer operates. Yet, that external forces may have changed does not necessarily imply that these forces no longer have any impact on the development process. We have described the dependent development of the export economy; what may now be required is the dependent development of the industrial economy. However one may describe current development characteristics, the econometric model and research presented in this book indicate that a historical perspective is necessary for a proper understanding of any period in the development process.

What we have defined to be the process of colonial development for these ten countries depended on specifying a model of their trade and government sectors that operated in a particular historical fashion: exports were developed to be sold to a developed country in exchange for imports of manufactures, and government expenditures were directed to facilitate and foster this international exchange. Obviously, this relationship historically contained several features that our highly aggregate model could not capture. Colonies served the political and economic needs of the developed countries not only by providing assured sources of food and raw materials and markets for their manufactures, but also by providing profitable areas for foreign investment, greater control over markets, and spheres of influence and control in response to economic and political rivalry among the countries of the developed world itself.[1] Our purpose in this book, however, was not to analyze all these factors. Rather, it was to focus on the essential features of the new international economy that emerged from the late nineteenth century onwards.

Within our period of study, all ten countries experienced profound changes as the expansion of external trade fostered by the growth of capitalism in the developed world acted directly and indirectly to transform their agrarian economies by commercializing their lands, fragmenting their rural industry, and gradually producing a social division of labor tied more to the impersonal world market forces of supply and demand relationships than to tradition or custom. Our model explained the essential properties of this economic development by focusing on its supply and demand characteristics. The growth of the supply and demand of exports, the growth of colonial import demand, and the changes in the price of exports were shown to be a function of income, price, and trade policies in the developed world, as well as a function of the accumulation of government capital in the colonial world. In turn, we demonstrated how the variables associated with the colonial government sector itself were dependent upon this same set of external forces. Therefore, in the long run the

1. Furthermore, this rivalry was not restricted to so-called third world countries; even territory within Europe, such as Alsace-Lorraine, has been a major source of conflict.

internal force, expenditures by the government, is endogenous to the colonial process.

These external and internal forces caused a reallocation of resources within the agrarian sector from a variety of nonagrarian tasks (rural industry) to increased specialization of export products.[2] This reallocation of resources, and especially of labor, was accomplished under a variety of social organizations ranging from plantation labor to different tenure arrangements, and even to the development of wage labor in the agrarian sectors. Imports of manufactures from the developed world replaced the rural industry of the colonial world as organized industrial expansion fragmented the traditional unity of agricultural and industrial production based on the household. Corresponding to the shift of labor out of rural industry and into export production in the colonial world, there was a shift of labor out of agricultural production into manufacturing production in the developed world. Thus, an international division of labor emerged where changes in the developed and colonial world became duals of one another. Our model focused on the products of these changes in the social and economic organization of production in the colonies: the growth of raw materials and food for the markets of the developed countries; the growth of demand for these colonial products resulting from real income and price changes in the developed countries to which the colonies were tied; and the growth in colonial import demand for a variety of manufactures produced by industrial expansion in the developed world. We have shown how the macro profitability of this exchange (the terms of trade) was determined by these external changes in the developed countries. Finally, we explained how, to facilitate and foster this type of development process, government capital was used to increase exports in the colonial world, and what economic forces determined its accumulation.

The bilateral political and economic relationships that we observed characterizing this process of development had clear historical origins. Competition was keen among the developed countries; each sought to achieve a dominant position for sources of food and raw materials for its industry and markets for the goods produced by that industry. Although this dominance often took the form of de jure colonialism, the degree of political control ranged from occupation (as in the case

2. See Resnick [28] for a formal model explaining this development and Hymer and Resnick [16] for a general historical explanation of this transformation.

of the Philippines) to the use of political or military influence or more subtle economic controls to obtain special trading privileges, financial monopolies, and the exclusion of foreign competition (as in the case of Cuba). As we have shown, both Cuba and the Philippines were dependent on the United States. Therefore, the form of control varied with the particular historical circumstances of the country in question. Rather than use terms like "semicolonies" or "dependent countries" to describe the relationship of Cuba or Chile to the United States or of Egypt or Thailand to the United Kingdom, we have described them as colonies. Distinctions between de jure colonialism and various degrees of de facto control are pointless in these cases, since their development depended upon external supply and demand forces effectively outside their control.

From this standpoint, the question of whether our model is applicable to other processes of development has no simple answer. For example, the model as specified in this book would not accurately describe the current development record of many countries even if external political and economic controls were as strong as or stronger than ever before. First, the development of an industrial sector requires a new set of variables and additional relationships and, therefore, a different model from the one specified in this book. Second, the development and growth of multinational corporations in the developed countries has produced a different international economy from that which existed prior to World War II.[3] Even though these new internal and external forces require new sets of relationships, this does not imply that government expenditures are no longer important in determining economic activity, that economic and political changes in the developed countries no longer have any effect on developing countries, or that government promotion of exports has stopped. Finally, the model as specified may be quite useful in analyzing the relationship between regions within a country which may, at some particular time, have taken on characteristics similar to the colonial relationship described in this book. This situation might be especially true for developing countries today where the relationship between the agricultural and industrial sectors might be described as one of internal colonialism.

Our model does not fit every economy that exports food and raw materials and imports manufactures. For example, a country may

3. See, for example, Hymer [15] and Hymer and Resnick [16].

very well continue to have this trade pattern while its government successfully promotes industrialization and import substitution.[4] As already explained, applying our model in this situation would cause a major specification error. Thus we conclude that the trade pattern characteristic of colonial development is a necessary but not sufficient condition for an economy to fit our model for a particular period. Instead, it is first necessary to examine the economic and political history of a country to determine whether or not its economy satisfies the specification of our model.

The final contribution of this book is in showing how the same model applies to a wide range of countries. Qualitatively these ten countries did start out with rather different initial conditions, but they ended up looking rather alike in terms of economic structure. We were able to demonstrate that the dynamic properties of colonial development were similar over countries because the same internal and external forces transformed these countries over time. However, these external and internal forces did not influence colonial development evenly. Thus we concluded that there was a similar but not identical process of colonial development.

Our analysis of the colonial development process yielded the important cross-sectional conclusion that colonial history is the most important factor in explaining the differences in the historical development of the ten countries studied. Four countries economically linked to the United Kingdom—Egypt, India, Jamaica, and Thailand —were found to have the lowest productivity of government expenditures directed toward export development and thus the least dynamic development process. The Japanese colony—Taiwan—and the three countries linked to the United States—Chile, Cuba, and the Philippines—had the highest productivity. However, the three countries tied to the United States were least able to capture the benefits of real income increases in the developed world. Furthermore, the United States found it easiest to substitute between domestic production and imports from these three countries.

In terms of the major international events during our period of study, the economic losses from World War I were shown to be the highest for countries under the direct colonial control of the United Kingdom, while the largest losses from the Great Depression were for

4. However, the import bundle of manufactures is shifting from consumer goods to capital goods needed for the import substitution and industrialization program.

countries linked to the United States. In spite of these very important historical differences, the same model worked well in explaining the wide range of observed growth rates of exports in these ten countries, the large shifts in their terms of trade and trade balances, and the dramatic growth in their government revenues and expenditures. We were able to derive these important cross-sectional results by identifying and measuring the external forces associated with the developed world and the internal forces associated with productive government expenditures in the developing world. An analysis of how both of these forces operate is necessary not only to explain how these colonial countries experienced economic development, but also to understand and analyze current development problems.

Appendix

The following tables present the data sets used for each of the ten countries in our sample and for each of the three developed countries. We provide more detailed information on the export and import price series since these data are often of great importance to economists studying the economic history of these ten countries. For these price series, we provide a listing of all the commodities used to construct them and report the Laspeyres and Fisher Ideal, as well as the Paasche, price series. Our data for each country came from the following sources: Ceylon [107, 115]; Chile [103, 104, 108, 109, 110, 111]; Cuba [45, 83, 105, 106, 109, 110, 111, 115]; Egypt [6, 44, 107, 108, 109, 110, 111, 115]; India [107]; Jamaica [107]; Nigeria [107]; Philippines [88]; Taiwan [62]; Thailand [19, 64, 109, 110, 111, 114]; Japan [81]; United Kingdom [47, 78, 79]; and the United States [74, 118].

Table A.1. Ceylon: Trade Variables (Millions of rupees)

	1913 prices		Current prices		
	Real Exports X^R	Real Imports M^R	Exports X	Imports M	Trade Balance X - M
1895	67.66	73.49	77.45	76.11	1.34
1896	72.66	73.40	77.35	76.57	0.78
1897	78.19	81.06	75.80	85.16	-9.35
1898	87.66	83.59	84.08	87.52	-3.45
1899	87.14	90.97	101.09	101.54	-0.46
1900	96.46	102.54	92.04	114.54	-22.50
1901	96.12	100.11	87.25	104.05	-16.30
1902	100.83	99.40	98.23	97.88	0.35
1903	107.22	102.71	102.23	100.89	1.34
1904	109.55	106.21	101.11	105.34	-4.24
1905	114.34	110.64	102.19	108.35	-6.16
1906	115.81	115.19	109.71	112.77	-3.06
1907	118.36	121.86	129.37	120.06	9.31
1908	126.32	121.60	128.96	122.42	6.54
1909	137.33	123.51	146.90	125.46	21.44
1910	142.05	151.39	166.47	150.01	16.46
1911	158.65	160.24	180.53	156.78	23.74
1912	185.55	177.14	198.95	174.89	24.06
1913	232.98	185.53	232.98	185.53	47.46
1914	252.57	165.82	218.35	171.84	46.52
1915	294.29	151.03	273.37	163.29	110.08
1916	297.11	177.22	297.51	209.72	87.78
1917	317.37	150.12	304.16	184.03	120.13
1918	271.76	132.38	211.33	177.72	33.61
1919	404.59	123.35	367.05	239.32	127.73
1920	354.33	147.63	268.46	321.60	-53.14
1921	343.57	136.26	256.60	260.83	-4.23
1922	392.30	147.96	297.75	280.28	17.47
1923	350.16	161.86	353.84	287.80	66.04
1924	390.28	181.79	388.75	302.42	86.33
1925	421.45	209.72	492.49	351.03	141.46
1926	454.39	242.85	503.23	395.03	108.20
1927	458.86	250.09	447.74	406.11	41.62
1928	472.86	254.14	388.57	400.12	-11.55
1929	532.21	266.29	390.72	403.05	-12.33
1930	501.09	247.95	299.89	302.13	-2.24
1931	485.29	224.33	212.22	218.34	-6.13
1932	457.68	209.65	170.09	187.65	-17.56
1933	450.15	209.97	182.39	177.15	5.24
1934	499.90	249.97	244.77	217.00	27.77
1935	422.42	253.96	234.68	227.51	7.17
1936	407.23	257.89	250.45	214.33	36.12
1937	465.94	293.02	314.95	242.60	72.35
1938	462.36	282.50	266.95	235.53	31.41

Table A.2. Ceylon: Price Variables

	1913 = 100			Exchange rate (rupees per Pound)
	Export price Px (1)	Import price Pm (2)	Terms of trade P$_T$ (3)	π (4)
1895	114.473	103.561	110.537	18.113
1896	106.457	104.328	102.041	16.696
1897	96.944	105.058	92.277	15.824
1898	95.911	104.702	91.604	15.118
1899	116.008	111.618	103.932	15.000
1900	95.417	111.703	85.420	15.000
1901	90.773	103.935	87.337	15.000
1902	97.430	98.471	98.943	15.000
1903	95.345	98.227	97.065	15.000
1904	92.293	99.186	93.050	15.000
1905	89.374	97.928	91.265	15.000
1906	94.730	97.906	96.757	15.000
1907	109.304	98.517	110.949	15.000
1908	102.095	100.674	101.411	15.000
1909	106.970	101.572	105.315	15.000
1910	117.195	99.086	118.276	15.000
1911	113.791	97.841	116.302	15.000
1912	107.224	98.731	108.602	15.000
1913	100.000	100.000	100.000	15.000
1914	86.453	103.627	83.427	15.000
1915	92.890	108.121	85.913	15.000
1916	100.133	118.342	84.613	15.000
1917	95.836	122.586	78.179	15.000
1918	77.763	134.250	57.924	15.000
1919	90.722	194.016	46.760	10.000
1920	75.765	217.847	34.779	10.000
1921	74.687	191.428	39.016	15.000
1922	75.900	189.436	40.066	15.000
1923	101.050	177.811	56.830	15.000
1924	99.608	166.358	59.876	15.000
1925	116.856	167.379	69.815	13.333
1926	110.747	162.664	68.083	13.333
1927	97.576	162.387	60.088	13.333
1928	82.175	157.441	52.194	13.333
1929	73.414	151.361	48.503	13.333
1930	59.848	121.853	49.115	13.333
1931	43.730	97.330	44.930	13.333
1932	37.164	89.509	41.520	13.333
1933	40.517	84.366	48.025	13.333
1934	48.965	86.812	56.403	13.333
1935	55.557	89.585	62.016	13.333
1936	61.501	83.111	73.999	13.333
1937	67.594	82.793	81.642	13.333
1938	57.735	83.373	69.249	13.333

Table A.3. Ceylon: Government Variables (Millions of rupees)

	Current prices		1913 prices	
	Government revenues R (1)	Government expenditures G (2)	Real govt. expenditures G^R (3)	Acc. real govt. exp. $\Sigma_{i=1}^{\infty} G_{t-i}^R$ (4)
1895	20.98	21.52	20.78	506.49
1896	21.97	21.27	20.39	529.08
1897	24.01	21.64	20.60	551.22
1898	25.14	22.85	21.82	574.71
1899	25.91	24.95	22.36	598.84
1900	27.33	28.95	25.92	626.52
1901	26.44	29.22	28.11	657.67
1902	27.20	28.04	28.48	692.62
1903	29.42	27.08	27.57	728.60
1904	30.85	32.02	32.28	763.16
1905	34.40	29.74	30.37	795.93
1906	35.03	32.64	33.34	831.16
1907	36.57	32.59	33.08	866.95
1908	35.57	35.03	34.80	904.52
1909	39.33	35.79	35.24	944.70
1910	42.79	35.71	36.04	980.81
1911	45.34	42.49	43.43	1029.27
1912	50.16	45.67	46.25	1079.18
1913	52.48	50.27	50.27	1134.68
1914	52.88	58.90	56.84	1196.24
1915	51.55	50.15	46.38	1245.74
1916	66.01	56.10	47.41	1293.15
1917	66.98	64.34	52.48	1345.63
1918	63.93	64.94	48.38	1394.01
1919	70.07	70.84	36.51	1430.52
1920	81.20	84.88	38.96	1469.49
1921	70.62	91.77	47.94	1517.43
1922	79.27	77.36	40.84	1558.26
1923	93.72	85.58	48.13	1606.40
1924	102.36	100.69	60.53	1666.94
1925	115.54	105.00	62.73	1730.49
1926	124.52	110.00	67.62	1799.92
1927	129.36	121.05	74.54	1876.05
1928	134.13	152.11	96.61	1972.85
1929	107.82	121.90	80.53	2053.55
1930	110.93	110.28	90.50	2154.42
1931	101.97	100.29	103.04	2275.30
1932	84.84	96.87	108.22	2386.36
1933	106.09	92.69	109.87	2498.05
1934	104.11	93.44	107.63	2606.79
1935	99.00	107.31	119.78	2728.37
1936	102.77	109.75	132.05	2861.24
1937	119.19	108.79	131.40	3014.25
1938	116.93	134.73	161.60	3182.17

Table A.4. Ceylon: Price Index Components

Commodity	Years Included in Index
Export Price Index Components (12 Commodities)	
Areca nuts	1891 to 1938
Cinnamon	1891 to 1938
Plantation coffee	1891 to 1906
Other coffees	1891 to 1906
Coconut oil	1891 to 1938
Plumbago	1891 to 1938
Tea	1891 to 1938
Cocoa	1891 to 1938
Coconuts	1903 to 1938
Copra	1891 to 1938
Poonac	1891 to 1938
Rubber	1903 to 1938
Import Price Index Components (25 Commodities)	
Coal	1891 to 1938
Curry stuffs	1891 to 1938
Fish	1891 to 1938
Paddy	1891 to 1938
Rice	1891 to 1938
Livestock	1891 to 1914
Poonac	1891 to 1938
Whiskey	1891 to 1914
Brandy	1891 to 1914
Gin	1891 to 1914
Sugar	1891 to 1938
Malt liquors	1891 to 1914
Onions	1891 to 1938
Potatoes	1891 to 1922
Tea lead	1893 to 1914
Sheep and lambs	1891 to 1914
Kerosene	1893 to 1938
Bleached cotton	1922 to 1938
Dyed cotton	1922 to 1938
Grey cotton	1922 to 1938
Printed cotton	1922 to 1938
Wheat, flour, and meal	1922 to 1938
Motor spirit oil	1922 to 1938
Petroleum	1922 to 1938
Motor cars	1922 to 1938

Table A.5. Ceylon: Price Indexes (1913 = 100)

	Export price index			
	Laspeyres	Paasche	Fisher Ideal	Paasche as a percentage of Laspeyres
1891	93.539	104.271	98.760	111.5
1892	95.761	104.783	100.171	109.4
1893	102.492	114.275	108.223	111.5
1894	108.830	120.931	114.721	111.1
1895	102.904	114.473	108.535	111.2
1896	97.367	106.457	101.811	109.3
1897	90.765	96.944	93.804	106.8
1898	91.402	95.911	93.629	104.9
1899	108.752	116.008	112.321	106.7
1900	94.695	95.417	95.055	100.8
1901	90.039	90.773	90.405	100.8
1902	94.610	97.430	96.010	103.0
1903	88.631	95.345	91.927	107.6
1904	86.213	92.293	89.201	107.1
1905	84.260	89.374	86.779	106.1
1906	88.230	94.730	91.422	107.4
1907	101.574	109.304	105.368	107.6
1908	96.315	102.095	99.163	106.0
1909	100.064	106.970	103.459	106.9
1910	108.396	117.195	112.710	108.1
1911	106.986	113.791	110.336	106.4
1912	103.043	107.224	105.113	104.1
1913	100.000	100.000	100.000	100.0
1914	88.290	86.453	87.367	97.9
1915	95.124	92.890	94.001	97.7
1916	100.528	100.133	100.330	99.6
1917	95.323	95.836	95.579	100.5
1918	79.693	77.763	78.722	97.6
1919	94.542	90.722	92.612	96.0
1920	80.623	75.765	78.156	94.0
1921	88.816	74.687	81.446	84.1
1922	98.470	75.900	86.451	77.1
1923	118.884	101.050	109.605	85.0
1924	116.863	99.608	107.891	85.2
1925	137.424	116.856	126.724	85.0
1926	127.878	110.747	119.005	86.6
1927	114.700	97.576	105.792	85.1
1928	97.650	82.175	89.579	84.2
1929	87.462	73.414	80.131	83.9
1930	72.465	59.848	65.855	82.6
1931	52.187	43.730	47.772	83.8
1932	43.811	37.164	40.351	84.8
1933	49.088	40.517	44.597	82.5
1934	60.434	48.965	54.398	81.0
1935	66.024	55.557	60.565	84.1
1936	72.310	61.501	66.687	85.1
1937	80.513	67.594	73.771	84.0
1938	69.041	57.735	63.135	83.6

Appendix

	Import price index		
Laspeyres	Paasche	Fisher Ideal	Paasche as a percentage of Laspeyres
95.280	97.500	96.384	102.3
92.735	95.239	93.979	102.7
100.377	103.061	101.710	102.7
100.866	103.598	102.223	102.7
100.483	103.561	102.010	103.1
101.747	104.328	103.030	102.5
100.761	105.058	102.887	104.3
100.829	104.702	102.747	103.8
107.696	111.618	109.640	103.6
108.194	111.703	109.935	103.2
102.325	103.935	103.127	101.6
97.987	98.471	98.229	100.5
97.865	98.227	98.046	100.4
98.955	99.186	99.071	100.2
97.497	97.928	97.712	100.4
97.831	97.906	97.868	100.1
98.454	98.517	98.486	100.1
100.755	100.674	100.715	99.9
101.149	101.572	101.360	100.4
103.232	99.086	101.138	96.0
97.593	97.841	97.717	100.3
98.484	98.731	98.608	100.3
100.000	100.000	100.000	100.0
103.377	103.627	103.502	100.2
107.896	108.121	108.008	100.2
118.512	118.342	118.427	99.9
127.141	122.586	124.843	96.4
146.354	134.250	140.171	91.7
190.958	194.016	192.481	101.6
219.537	217.847	218.691	99.2
190.748	191.428	191.088	100.4
189.776	189.436	189.606	99.8
178.147	177.811	177.979	99.8
166.807	166.358	166.582	99.7
168.070	167.379	167.724	99.6
163.692	162.664	163.177	99.4
163.970	162.387	163.177	99.0
158.023	157.441	157.732	99.6
153.020	151.361	152.188	98.9
124.855	121.853	123.345	97.6
101.383	97.330	99.336	96.0
93.712	89.509	91.586	95.5
88.727	84.366	86.519	95.1
91.996	86.812	89.367	94.4
91.975	89.585	90.772	97.4
85.539	83.111	84.317	97.2
84.941	82.793	83.860	97.5
86.992	83.373	85.163	95.8

Table A.6. Chile: Trade Variables (Millions of pesos)

	1913 prices		Current prices		
	Real Exports X^R	Real Imports M^R	Exports X	Imports M	Trade Balance X - M
1888	171.12	88.78	154.22	128.11	26.11
1889	175.01	98.90	139.18	137.34	1.84
1890	184.21	97.99	138.63	143.25	-4.62
1891	201.41	93.01	142.80	134.37	8.43
1892	180.55	116.24	135.47	164.59	-29.11
1893	204.71	102.60	152.44	143.98	8.46
1894	203.94	82.78	152.01	114.96	37.04
1895	225.49	107.78	153.86	146.03	7.84
1896	215.16	115.48	156.90	156.31	0.58
1897	201.36	99.85	136.63	138.21	-1.58
1898	254.66	97.61	168.07	102.23	65.84
1899	245.44	98.78	161.48	106.26	55.22
1900	242.86	122.76	166.31	128.54	37.77
1901	216.63	131.57	171.84	139.30	32.54
1902	231.64	134.90	185.88	132.43	53.45
1903	236.96	141.14	194.28	142.47	51.81
1904	245.06	150.12	216.00	157.15	58.85
1905	277.93	189.22	265.21	188.60	76.61
1906	246.43	216.43	271.45	225.27	46.18
1907	258.33	273.60	280.08	293.68	-13.60
1908	332.45	236.93	319.12	267.92	51.20
1909	353.43	218.65	306.43	262.08	44.35
1910	377.06	239.69	328.83	297.49	31.34
1911	363.30	271.30	339.41	348.99	-9.58
1912	378.50	340.30	383.23	334.45	48.77
1913	396.31	329.52	396.31	329.52	66.79
1914	308.82	273.04	299.67	269.76	29.92
1915	333.59	150.40	327.48	153.21	174.27
1916	494.51	232.52	513.58	222.52	291.06
1917	495.14	275.42	712.29	355.08	357.21
1918	523.85	309.52	763.62	436.07	327.55
1919	256.65	222.38	301.48	401.32	-99.84
1920	513.73	205.98	778.88	455.08	323.81
1921	288.47	178.27	433.76	381.30	52.46
1922	331.06	198.96	331.61	237.18	94.43
1923	522.64	236.84	537.21	329.31	207.90
1924	629.56	277.42	637.46	363.26	274.20
1925	618.67	298.51	635.67	407.67	228.00
1926	551.42	333.33	560.00	431.00	129.00
1927	618.26	318.39	571.00	357.66	213.34
1928	741.36	328.68	663.33	400.00	263.33
1929	764.01	474.30	775.00	539.33	235.67
1930	511.42	438.37	448.66	466.67	-18.01
1931	472.14	243.72	279.67	235.33	44.33
1932	221.48	97.13	94.00	71.33	22.67
1933	357.27	110.51	111.67	60.67	51.00
1934	541.65	144.49	153.67	71.33	82.33
1935	557.90	205.14	155.00	98.33	56.67
1936	570.05	248.07	183.00	115.67	67.33
1937	762.95	261.92	311.33	143.00	168.33
1938	702.37	298.32	225.00	166.33	58.67

Table A.7. Chile: Price Variables (1913 = 100)

	Export Price Px	Import Price Pm	Terms of Trade P_T
1888	90.125	144.301	62.456
1889	79.527	138.865	57.269
1890	75.258	146.180	51.483
1891	70.901	144.472	49.076
1892	75.032	141.592	52.992
1893	74.464	140.323	53.066
1894	74.534	138.883	53.667
1895	68.233	135.481	50.364
1896	72.921	135.361	53.872
1897	67.855	138.421	49.021
1898	65.999	104.730	63.018
1899	65.790	107.569	61.160
1900	68.478	104.707	65.400
1901	79.327	105.876	74.924
1902	80.245	98.167	81.743
1903	˙81.989	100.942	81.224
1904	88.140	104.687	84.194
1905	95.424	99.670	95.741
1906	110.153	104.084	105.830
1907	108.420	107.341	101.006
1908	95.992	113.083	84.887
1909	86.701	119.866	72.332
1910	87.209	124.115	70.265
1911	93.423	128.636	72.626
1912	101.248	98.282	103.018
1913	100.000	100.000	100.000
1914	97.038	98.799	98.218
1915	98.167	101.872	96.364
1916	103.857	95.700	108.523
1917	143.857	128.923	111.584
1918	145.770	140.887	103.466
1919	117.469	180.469	65.091
1920	151.615	220.934	68.624
1921	150.366	213.887	70.302
1922	100.166	119.211	84.024
1923	102.788	139.045	73.925
1924	101.255	130.940	77.329
1925	102.747	136.566	75.237
1926	101.557	129.303	78.542
1927	92.355	112.335	82.214
1928	89.475	121.697	73.522
1929	101.438	113.711	89.207
1930	87.729	106.454	82.409
1931	59.234	96.558	61.345
1932	42.441	73.438	57.792
1933	31.255	54.898	56.933
1934	28.370	49.369	57.465
1935	27.783	47.935	57.960
1936	32.102	46.626	68.850
1937	40.806	54.598	74.740
1938	32.034	55.756	57.455

Table A.8. Chile: Government Variables (Millions of pesos)

	Current prices		1913 prices	
	Government revenues R (1)	Government expenditures G (2)	Real govt. expenditures G^R (3)	Acc. real govt. exp. $\Sigma_{i=1}^{\infty} G_{t-i}^R$ (4)
1888	67.35	59.57	41.29	844.67
1889	69.23	77.44	55.77	900.44
1890	75.16	91.05	62.29	962.72
1891	91.52	98.18	67.96	1030.68
1892	67.96	67.55	47.71	1078.39
1893	62.30	49.82	35.51	1113.90
1894	62.54	48.74	35.10	1149.00
1895	83.99	74.11	54.70	1203.70
1896	99.35	102.76	75.91	1279.61
1897	72.32	71.74	51.82	1331.43
1898	109.27	88.30	84.31	1415.75
1899	98.44	82.35	76.56	1492.30
1900	109.76	92.37	88.22	1580.53
1901	91.79	103.33	97.59	1678.12
1902	86.39	103.12	105.05	1783.17
1903	101.37	90.63	89.78	1872.95
1904	116.80	110.25	105.32	1978.26
1905	115.06	103.97	104.32	2082.58
1906	146.57	119.13	114.45	2197.03
1907	144.40	120.86	112.59	2309.62
1908	138.32	107.48	95.04	2404.67
1909	135.00	125.77	104.92	2509.59
1910	154.87	163.25	131.53	2641.12
1911	165.85	153.17	119.07	2760.19
1912	210.97	186.00	189.26	2949.45
1913	182.86	165.25	165.25	3114.69
1914	139.39	172.83	174.93	3289.62
1915	128.17	153.92	151.09	3440.71
1916	185.21	161.89	169.17	3609.88
1917	213.61	192.31	149.17	3759.05
1918	249.91	221.62	157.30	3916.35
1919	125.08	183.01	101.41	4017.76
1920	220.29	264.17	119.57	4137.33
1921	202.09	209.73	98.06	4235.38
1922	200.46	198.64	166.63	4402.01
1923	285.90	214.07	153.96	4555.96
1924	307.84	215.69	164.72	4720.69
1925	340.17	274.00	200.63	4921.32
1926	251.80	298.17	230.60	5151.91
1927	303.04	297.22	264.58	5416.49
1928	340.35	327.58	269.18	5685.67
1929	367.76	402.53	354.00	6039.67
1930	351.73	377.16	354.29	6393.96
1931	260.83	342.37	354.57	6748.25
1932	171.59	234.54	319.37	7067.62
1933	315.32	314.71	573.26	7640.88
1934	347.66	324.95	658.21	8299.09
1935	469.88	430.32	897.72	9196.81
1936	489.44	460.87	988.43	10185.25
1937	507.47	492.84	902.68	11087.92
1938	559.61	554.63	994.75	12082.67

Table A.9. Chile: Price Index Components

Commodity	Years Included in Index
Export Price Index Components **(7 Commodities)**	
Wheat	1888 to 1929
Nitrate of soda	1888 to 1938
Copper ore	1888 to 1938
Copper in bars	1888 to 1938
Iodine	1888 to 1929
Iodine super	1936 to 1938
Raw wool	1888 to 1938
Import Price Index Components **(26 Commodities)**	
Horses	1888 to 1912
Cows	1888 to 1938
Sheep	1888 to 1938
Candles	1888 to 1912
Coal	1888 to 1929
Cotton piece goods	1888 to 1912
Iron bars	1888 to 1938
Iron sheets	1888 to 1938
Iron tubing	1888 to 1938
Iron rails	1888 to 1912
Mineral oil	1888 to 1912
Empty sacks	1888 to 1938
Steel in bars	1888 to 1902
Sugar	1888 to 1938
Tea	1888 to 1912
Coffee	1892 to 1912
Yerba mate	1892 to 1912
Wire of all kinds	1892 to 1912
Crude mineral oil	1912 to 1938
Cotton thread	1915 to 1938
Cotton	1912 to 1938
Cement	1915 to 1938
Tea, coffee, and cocoa	1922 to 1938
Edible oils	1912 to 1937
Woolen fabric	1927 to 1938
Other fabrics	1925 to 1927

Table A.10. Chile: Price Indexes (1913 = 100)

	Export price index			
	Laspeyres	*Paasche*	*Fisher Ideal*	*Paasche as a percentage of Laspeyres*
1888	88.138	90.125	89.126	102.3
1889	76.479	79.527	77.988	104.0
1890	72.173	75.258	73.700	104.3
1891	70.372	70.901	70.636	100.8
1892	74.870	75.033	74.951	100.2
1893	73.941	74.464	74.202	100.7
1894	72.193	74.534	73.354	103.2
1895	66.329	68.233	67.274	102.9
1896	70.617	72.921	71.760	103.3
1897	66.470	67.855	67.159	102.1
1898	65.258	65.999	65.628	101.1
1899	67.132	65.790	66.458	98.0
1900	70.082	68.479	69.276	97.7
1901	81.987	79.327	80.646	96.8
1902	82.879	80.245	81.551	96.8
1903	85.505	81.989	83.729	95.9
1904	93.246	88.140	90.657	94.5
1905	97.625	95.425	96.518	97.7
1906	111.131	110.153	110.641	99.1
1907	110.187	108.421	109.300	98.4
1908	98.928	95.992	97.449	97.0
1909	86.355	86.701	86.528	100.4
1910	87.450	87.209	87.329	99.7
1911	92.460	93.423	92.940	101.0
1912	102.314	101.248	101.779	99.0
1913	100.000	100.000	100.000	100.0
1914	99.590	97.038	98.306	97.4
1915	101.719	98.168	99.927	96.5
1916	105.967	103.857	104.907	98.0
1917	151.232	143.857	147.498	95.1
1918	155.769	145.770	150.687	93.6
1919	128.404	117.469	122.815	91.5
1920	163.926	151.615	157.650	92.5
1921	157.124	150.366	153.708	95.7
1922	108.729	100.166	104.360	92.1
1923	112.721	102.789	107.640	91.2
1924	111.833	101.256	106.413	90.5
1925	112.083	102.748	107.314	91.7
1926	110.530	101.557	105.949	91.9
1927	101.014	92.356	96.588	91.4
1928	98.670	89.475	93.960	90.7
1929	112.268	101.438	106.716	90.4
1930	97.632	87.729	92.548	89.9
1931	67.898	59.234	63.418	87.2
1932	56.046	42.441	48.772	75.7
1933	36.554	31.256	33.801	85.5
1934	32.598	28.370	30.411	87.0
1935	32.307	27.783	29.960	86.0
1936	35.446	32.102	33.733	90.6
1937	43.804	40.807	42.279	93.2
1938	35.105	32.034	33.534	91.3

	Import price index		
Laspeyres	Paasche	Fisher Ideal	Paasche as a percentage of Laspeyres
119.192	144.301	131.147	121.1
116.288	138.866	127.076	119.4
121.236	146.180	133.125	120.6
119.082	144.473	131.164	121.3
118.227	141.592	129.383	119.8
117.852	140.322	128.597	119.1
117.559	138.883	127.777	118.1
113.570	135.481	124.043	119.3
113.826	135.361	124.127	118.9
117.566	138.421	127.568	117.7
90.691	104.730	97.458	115.5
90.165	107.569	98.483	119.3
93.565	104.707	98.979	111.9
84.889	105.876	94.803	124.7
81.661	98.167	89.534	120.2
83.978	100.943	92.070	120.2
87.137	104.686	95.509	120.1
84.398	99.670	91.717	118.1
88.303	104.084	95.869	117.9
92.119	107.341	99.439	116.5
100.506	113.083	106.609	112.5
98.798	119.866	108.824	121.3
108.701	124.115	116.153	114.2
111.480	128.637	119.751	115.4
98.230	98.282	98.256	100.1
100.000	100.000	100.000	100.0
99.383	98.799	99.091	99.4
105.987	101.871	103.909	96.1
100.967	95.701	98.298	94.8
137.778	128.922	133.277	93.6
159.370	140.887	149.844	88.4
181.125	180.470	180.797	99.6
245.095	220.934	232.701	90.1
225.504	213.887	219.619	94.8
131.809	119.211	125.352	90.4
149.096	139.045	143.983	93.3
158.037	130.940	143.852	82.9
157.852	136.566	146.824	86.5
146.166	129.302	137.476	88.5
129.217	112.335	120.481	86.9
147.104	121.697	133.799	82.7
144.121	113.711	128.016	78.9
135.699	106.454	120.191	78.4
122.160	96.558	108.607	79.0
97.902	73.438	84.792	75.0
72.491	54.898	63.084	75.7
68.099	49.369	57.983	72.5
62.690	47.934	54.818	76.5
63.725	46.626	54.509	73.2
69.542	54.598	61.618	78.5
71.708	55.755	63.231	77.8

Table A.11. Cuba: Trade Variables (Millions of pesos)

	1913 prices		Current prices		
	Real Exports X^R	Real Imports M^R	Exports X	Imports M	Trade Balance X - M
1902	78.61	67.32	64.33	60.58	3.75
1903	89.85	79.66	77.25	63.46	13.79
1904	92.87	92.32	89.01	77.03	11.99
1905	93.11	114.03	110.17	94.97	15.20
1906	101.16	111.58	103.91	98.02	5.89
1907	98.55	113.68	104.17	104.46	-0.29
1908	93.82	91.76	94.60	85.22	9.39
1909	138.03	98.78	124.72	91.45	33.27
1910	130.64	110.86	150.82	103.68	47.15
1911	114.18	118.62	122.94	113.06	9.89
1912	146.54	122.87	172.98	123.20	49.77
1913	164.61	140.13	164.61	140.13	24.48
1914	164.80	116.06	174.04	118.20	55.84
1915	166.50	136.97	236.23	140.88	95.34
1916	188.11	184.45	321.79	215.96	105.83
1917	184.01	162.89	356.43	256.08	100.34
1918	201.92	149.81	407.28	294.63	112.65
1919	239.18	161.75	574.62	356.63	217.99
1920	184.86	223.11	794.04	557.02	237.03
1921	171.70	169.52	279.79	354.40	-74.61
1922	290.93	130.87	327.65	180.30	147.35
1923	205.14	194.82	422.60	268.85	153.75
1924	231.86	211.50	434.86	289.83	145.03
1925	291.12	200.00	352.98	297.32	55.66
1926	285.80	177.57	301.71	260.83	40.88
1927	259.09	189.41	324.37	257.38	66.98
1928	259.81	175.23	278.07	212.82	65.25
1929	313.13	178.81	272.44	216.21	56.22
1930	239.64	137.36	167.41	162.45	4.96
1931	197.24	91.96	118.87	80.11	38.76
1932	191.58	72.86	80.67	51.02	29.65
1933	166.46	63.24	84.39	42.36	42.03
1934	163.27	88.07	107.75	73.42	34.33
1935	170.56	107.50	128.02	95.46	32.56
1936	179.41	110.44	154.85	103.21	51.63
1937	193.49	124.49	186.07	129.57	56.50

Table A.12. Cuba: Price Variables (1913 = 100)

	Export Price Px	Import Price Pm	Terms of Trade P_T
1902	81.839	90.001	90.930
1903	85.977	79.667	107.920
1904	95.852	83.432	114.886
1905	118.314	83.286	142.058
1906	102.719	87.847	116.930
1907	105.702	91.894	115.027
1908	100.831	92.873	108.568
1909	90.352	92.574	97.599
1910	115.451	93.518	123.454
1911	107.678	95.306	112.981
1912	118.042	100.270	117.725
1913	100.000	100.000	100.000
1914	105.609	101.848	103.693
1915	141.875	102.855	137.937
1916	171.068	117.084	146.106
1917	193.702	157.217	123.206
1918	201.710	196.664	102.566
1919	240.243	220.487	108.960
1920	429.539	249.660	172.049
1921	162.954	209.063	77.945
1922	112.623	137.773	81.746
1923	206.002	137.998	149.279
1924	187.555	137.033	136.868
1925	121.250	148.664	81.560
1926	105.567	146.885	71.871
1927	125.195	135.890	92.129
1928	107.030	121.449	88.127
1929	87.004	120.916	71.954
1930	69.858	118.267	59.068
1931	60.265	87.115	69.179
1932	42.108	70.027	60.131
1933	50.698	66.987	75.683
1934	65.994	83.361	79.167
1935	75.058	88.806	84.519
1936	86.311	93.456	92.354
1937	96.164	104.086	92.389

Table A.13. Cuba: Government Variables (Millions of pesos)

	Current prices		1913 prices	
	Government revenues R (1)	Government expenditures G (2)	Real govt. expenditures G^R (3)	Acc. real govt. exp. $\sum_{i=1}^{\infty} G^R_{t-i}$ (4)
1902	20.06	18.36	20.40	239.07
1903	29.00	32.20	40.41	279.49
1904	35.82	37.03	44.38	323.86
1905	41.29	43.84	52.64	376.50
1906	38.99	38.86	44.23	420.73
1907	38.73	37.88	41.22	461.95
1908	35.29	34.57	37.22	499.17
1909	42.95	46.03	49.72	548.89
1910	45.01	47.93	51.25	600.14
1911	47.01	47.71	50.06	650.20
1912	48.81	50.73	50.59	700.80
1913	49.20	53.34	53.34	754.14
1914	68.29	68.24	67.01	821.14
1915	51.61	54.75	53.23	874.38
1916	63.76	63.54	54.27	928.65
1917	75.63	74.51	47.39	976.04
1918	83.64	83.67	42.54	1018.58
1919	108.18	108.59	49.25	1067.83
1920	123.73	124.14	49.72	1117.56
1921	73.91	81.54	39.00	1156.56
1922	89.54	90.81	65.91	1222.47
1923	108.66	99.79	72.31	1294.79
1924	112.11	108.20	78.96	1373.75
1925	119.30	118.65	79.81	1453.56
1926	115.34	123.86	84.32	1537.88
1927	117.93	119.35	87.83	1625.71
1928	109.30	117.22	96.51	1722.22
1929	112.05	123.22	101.90	1824.12
1930	92.14	111.93	94.64	1918.77
1931	73.07	89.01	102.18	2020.95
1932	63.11	72.60	103.68	2124.63
1933	60.28	58.01	86.60	2211.22
1934	73.76	66.22	79.44	2290.66
1935	71.63	72.79	81.97	2372.63
1936	87.87	84.96	90.91	2463.54
1937	87.62	81.64	78.44	2541.98

Table A.14. Cuba: Price Index Components

Commodity	*Years Included in Index*
Export Price Index Components (16 Commodities)	
Asphalt	1902 to 1914
Hides	1902 to 1937
Honey	1902 to 1937
Iron ore	1902 to 1937
Rum	1902 to 1923
Raw sugar	1902 to 1937
Refined sugar	1926 to 1937
Molasses	1902 to 1937
Tobacco leaf	1902 to 1923
Cigars	1902 to 1923
Cigarettes	1902 to 1923
Cedar	1903 to 1923
Mahogany	1902 to 1923
Spirits	1923 to 1937
Raw tobacco	1923 to 1937
Copper ore	1929 to 1937
Import Price Index Components (53 Commodities)	
Jerked beef	1902 to 1929
Salt pork	1902 to 1937
Lard	1902 to 1937
Condensed milk	1902 to 1929
Maize	1902 to 1929
Rice	1902 to 1937
Wheat flour	1902 to 1937
Vegetables	1925 to 1937
Coffee	1902 to 1929
Wine	1925 to 1937
Manure	1925 to 1937
Crude petroleum	1902 to 1925
Refined petroleum I	1902 to 1925
Petroleum fuel oil	1925 to 1937
Coal and coke	1925 to 1937
Drugs	1925 to 1937
Cotton: raw and yarn	1925 to 1937
Cotton piece goods	1925 to 1937
Other cotton manufactures	1925 to 1937
Linen fabric	1925 to 1937
Sacks for sugar	1902 to 1937

(Continued)

Table A.14–*Continued*

Commodity	Years Included in Index
Import Price Index Components (Continued)	
Paper and cardboard	1925 to 1937
Iron, steel, and manufactures	1925 to 1937
Other metals and manufactures	1925 to 1937
Cement	1902 to 1925
Wood pulp	1903 to 1925
Pinewood	1902 to 1925
Iron and steel bars	1902 to 1925
Laminated iron and steel	1902 to 1925
Other iron and steel	1902 to 1925
Chemical fertilizer	1909 to 1925
Other pharmaceuticals	1902 to 1925
Cotton fabric	1902 to 1925
Twilled fabric	1902 to 1925
Other fabrics	1902 to 1925
Linen fabric	1902 to 1925
Wool fabric	1902 to 1925
Wood furniture	1902 to 1925
Shoes and boots for men	1903 to 1925
Shoes and boots for ladies	1903 to 1925
Parts for machines	1902 to 1925
Other machinery	1902 to 1925
Cars for railways	1909 to 1925
Beans	1902 to 1925
Paper	1902 to 1925
Wine in barrels	1902 to 1925
Eggs	1902 to 1925
Anthracite	1902 to 1925
Bituminous coal	1902 to 1925
Coke	1902 to 1925
Machines	1902 to 1925
Other utilities	1909 to 1925
Refined petroleum II	1925 to 1937

Table A.15. Cuba: Price Indexes (1913 = 100)

	Export price index				Import price index			
	Laspeyres	Paasche	Fisher Ideal	Paasche as a percentage of Laspeyres	Laspeyres	Paasche	Fisher Ideal	Paasche as a percentage of Laspeyres
1902	73.784	81.839	77.707	110.9	78.182	90.001	83.884	115.1
1903	77.428	85.977	81.591	110.4	72.189	79.666	75.836	110.4
1904	87.151	95.852	91.398	110.0	78.163	83.432	80.754	106.7
1905	105.845	118.315	111.906	111.8	79.753	83.285	81.500	104.4
1906	96.667	102.719	99.647	106.3	83.919	87.847	85.861	104.7
1907	106.004	105.703	105.853	99.7	87.684	91.893	89.764	104.8
1908	111.742	100.831	106.147	90.2	89.702	92.873	91.274	103.5
1909	104.905	90.353	97.357	86.1	87.495	92.574	89.999	105.8
1910	118.354	115.451	116.894	97.5	89.200	93.518	91.333	104.8
1911	109.711	107.679	108.690	98.1	92.319	95.305	93.800	103.2
1912	121.067	118.042	119.545	97.5	97.703	100.269	98.978	102.6
1913	100.000	100.000	100.000	100.0	100.000	100.000	100.000	100.0
1914	106.081	105.610	105.845	99.6	101.656	101.847	101.752	100.2
1915	142.189	141.876	142.032	99.8	104.969	102.854	103.906	98.0
1916	169.234	171.068	170.149	101.1	120.350	117.084	118.706	97.3
1917	194.372	193.702	194.037	99.7	162.836	157.217	160.002	96.5
1918	200.648	201.710	201.178	100.5	206.966	196.664	201.749	95.0
1919	235.356	240.244	237.787	102.1	224.875	220.486	222.670	98.0
1920	416.427	429.541	422.933	103.1	258.195	249.658	253.891	96.7
1921	165.277	162.954	164.112	98.6	218.439	209.062	213.699	95.7
1922	117.152	112.623	114.866	96.1	153.169	137.773	145.267	89.9
1923	203.817	206.003	204.907	101.1	150.631	137.998	144.176	91.6
1924	186.107	187.556	186.830	100.8	147.189	137.032	142.020	93.1
1925	121.810	121.250	121.530	99.5	156.764	148.663	152.660	94.8
1926	105.001	105.568	105.284	100.5	156.463	146.884	151.598	93.9
1927	124.976	125.195	125.085	100.2	144.326	135.890	140.044	94.2
1928	107.055	107.031	107.043	100.0	133.057	121.449	127.121	91.3
1929	87.075	87.005	87.040	99.9	133.745	120.916	127.169	90.4
1930	70.132	69.859	69.995	99.6	134.829	118.267	126.277	87.7
1931	59.731	60.265	59.998	100.9	103.252	87.115	94.841	84.4
1932	40.807	42.108	41.452	103.2	85.848	70.027	77.535	81.6
1933	50.148	50.698	50.422	101.1	81.292	66.988	73.794	82.4
1934	65.523	65.994	65.758	100.7	97.073	83.360	89.956	85.9
1935	75.330	75.058	75.194	99.6	105.480	88.806	96.785	84.2
1936	85.268	86.311	85.788	101.2	111.196	93.456	101.941	84.0
1937	96.198	96.165	96.181	100.0	121.484	104.085	112.448	85.7

Table A.16. Egypt: Trade Variables (Millions of Egyptian pounds)

	1913 prices		Current prices		
	Real Exports X^R	Real Imports M^R	Exports X	Imports M	Trade Balance X - M
1889	14.86	9.36	13.39	6.82	6.58
1890	16.29	10.18	13.32	7.88	5.45
1891	23.09	11.98	15.56	9.04	6.52
1892	25.77	12.28	14.99	8.91	6.07
1893	22.66	12.78	14.37	8.56	5.81
1894	26.65	14.96	13.40	9.12	4.27
1895	25.80	14.33	14.22	8.26	5.96
1896	25.45	16.25	14.91	9.63	5.28
1897	28.20	17.74	13.92	10.39	3.53
1898	29.04	17.87	13.38	10.79	2.60
1899	31.30	18.10	17.36	11.21	6.15
1900	25.97	19.73	18.99	13.88	5.10
1901	29.22	21.49	17.90	15.00	2.90
1902	30.86	22.43	20.00	14.55	5.45
1903	26.11	25.05	21.66	16.48	5.18
1904	27.70	29.90	23.07	20.28	2.79
1905	30.94	30.84	22.56	21.25	1.31
1906	30.44	33.16	27.59	23.57	4.02
1907	30.75	32.99	31.08	25.68	5.41
1908	28.94	30.63	23.64	24.72	-1.08
1909	30.91	28.33	28.93	21.81	7.12
1910	26.85	27.04	32.12	23.10	9.01
1911	30.26	29.63	30.41	26.84	3.56
1912	38.15	25.85	34.57	25.46	9.12
1913	31.66	27.29	31.66	27.29	4.38
1914	27.51	21.92	24.09	21.23	2.86
1915	34.53	13.42	27.05	18.84	8.21
1916	25.15	12.39	37.46	30.57	6.89
1917	19.11	9.64	41.06	32.65	8.41
1918	23.13	10.92	45.37	49.78	-4.41
1919	29.15	13.62	75.89	43.10	32.79
1920	17.87	24.64	85.47	99.33	-13.86
1921	22.56	19.85	36.36	49.38	-13.02
1922	29.41	28.26	48.72	40.67	8.04
1923	32.75	32.68	58.39	43.81	14.58
1924	31.40	36.53	65.73	49.27	16.47
1925	27.60	43.54	59.20	56.95	2.24
1926	30.44	39.07	41.76	51.03	-9.27
1927	33.63	39.17	48.34	47.32	1.02
1928	34.19	43.15	56.16	50.65	5.52
1929	35.28	49.92	51.75	54.49	-2.74
1930	29.04	47.97	31.94	46.22	-14.28
1931	35.95	36.55	27.27	30.62	-3.34
1932	34.43	33.77	26.98	26.55	0.43
1933	37.57	34.72	28.85	26.06	2.79
1934	39.16	37.33	31.07	28.65	2.42
1935	39.81	40.07	34.32	31.22	3.10
1936	36.76	39.82	32.97	30.49	2.48
1937	42.82	38.86	38.66	37.10	1.57

Table A.17. Egypt: Price Variables (1913 = 100)

	Export Price Px	Import Price Pm	Terms of Trade P_T
1889	90.138	72.866	123.704
1890	81.781	77.372	105.698
1891	67.390	75.489	89.271
1892	58.146	72.579	80.114
1893	63.439	67.010	94.671
1894	50.273	61.002	82.412
1895	55.109	57.636	95.616
1896	58.602	59.283	98.851
1897	49.371	58.605	84.244
1898	46.080	60.374	76.324
1899	55.483	61.919	89.606
1900	73.112	70.375	103.889
1901	61.262	69.781	87.792
1902	64.824	64.859	99.946
1903	82.962	65.791	126.099
1904	83.264	67.845	122.727
1905	72.911	68.899	105.823
1906	90.624	71.088	127.481
1907	101.083	77.826	129.883
1908	81.694	80.721	101.205
1909	93.603	77.001	121.561
1910	119.604	85.435	139.994
1911	100.484	90.587	110.925
1912	90.630	98.472	92.036
1913	100.000	100.000	100.000
1914	87.581	96.838	90.441
1915	78.337	140.333	55.822
1916	148.974	246.658	60.397
1917	214.886	338.543	63.474
1918	196.155	456.037	43.013
1919	260.355	316.469	82.269
1920	478.183	403.180	118.603
1921	161.187	248.811	64.783
1922	165.649	143.930	115.090
1923	178.279	134.053	132.991
1924	209.317	134.872	155.197
1925	214.502	130.801	163.991
1926	137.186	130.598	105.044
1927	143.760	120.799	119.008
1928	164.252	117.368	139.946
1929	146.666	109.146	134.376
1930	110.007	96.358	114.165
1931	75.873	83.771	90.572
1932	78.363	78.636	99.653
1933	76.779	75.043	102.313
1934	79.352	76.739	103.405
1935	86.218	77.933	110.631
1936	89.699	76.558	117.165
1937	90.297	95.452	94.599

Table A.18. Egypt: Government Variables (Millions of Egyptian pounds)

	Current prices		1913 prices	
	Government revenues R (1)	Government expenditures G (2)	Real govt. expenditures G^R (3)	Acc. real govt. exp. $\sum_{i=1}^{\infty} G_{t-i}^R$ (4)
1889	10.36	9.97	13.68	333.57
1890	11.89	11.25	14.54	348.11
1891	11.22	10.08	13.35	361.46
1892	10.63	9.88	13.62	375.08
1893	10.60	10.56	15.75	390.83
1894	10.53	9.90	16.24	407.06
1895	10.72	9.73	16.88	423.95
1896	11.05	10.60	17.88	441.83
1897	11.48	10.70	18.27	460.09
1898	12.48	11.12	18.41	478.50
1899	11.67	11.41	18.42	496.93
1900	11.87	10.84	15.40	512.33
1901	11.51	12.20	17.49	529.81
1902	12.78	12.67	19.53	549.35
1903	13.38	12.50	19.00	568.35
1904	14.48	12.95	19.09	587.44
1905	17.10	15.00	21.77	609.21
1906	16.81	17.84	25.10	634.31
1907	16.83	18.93	24.32	658.63
1908	16.42	18.01	22.31	680.94
1909	15.89	16.90	21.95	702.88
1910	16.34	16.95	19.84	722.72
1911	17.18	17.08	18.85	741.57
1912	17.85	17.57	17.84	759.41
1913	17.71	17.66	17.66	777.07
1914	15.30	17.06	17.62	794.70
1915	17.76	16.59	11.83	806.52
1916	19.93	17.24	6.99	813.51
1917	23.17	22.50	6.65	820.16
1918	27.63	23.38	5.13	825.28
1919	33.68	28.99	9.16	834.45
1920	46.45	62.05	15.39	849.84
1921	41.81	37.75	15.17	865.01
1922	35.77	28.25	19.63	884.63
1923	36.26	31.47	23.47	908.11
1924	37.70	29.98	22.23	930.33
1925	39.59	34.20	26.15	956.48
1926	41.94	38.97	29.84	986.32
1927	38.57	35.39	29.30	1015.62
1928	40.37	37.23	31.72	1047.34
1929	41.89	41.13	37.68	1085.02
1930	38.59	41.22	42.78	1127.80
1931	37.77	36.99	44.16	1171.96
1932	37.14	35.95	45.71	1217.67
1933	32.63	30.55	40.71	1258.38
1934	33.72	31.60	41.18	1299.56
1935	34.96	33.65	43.18	1342.74
1936	35.18	35.15	45.91	1388.65
1937	37.15	36.33	38.06	1426.72

Table A.19. Egypt: Price Index Components

Commodity	Years Included in Index
Export Price Index Components (12 Commodities)	
Beans	1889 to 1914
Maize	1889 to 1914
Cotton	1889 to 1937
Cotton seed	1889 to 1937
Oil cake	1889 to 1914
Onions I	1889 to 1914
Onions II	1924 to 1937
Rice II	1924 to 1937
Sugar	1889 to 1902
Tobacco	1914 to 1937
Raw wool	1889 to 1914
Eggs	1902 to 1937
Import Price Index Components (22 Commodities)	
Butter	1889 to 1914
Cheese	1889 to 1914
Coal	1889 to 1937
Coffee	1889 to 1937
Cotton: yarn	1889 to 1914
Cotton piece goods	1889 to 1911
Flour	1889 to 1929
Rice	1889 to 1914
Empty sacks	1889 to 1914
Silk	1889 to 1914
Soap	1889 to 1914
Tobacco	1894 to 1937
Sugar	1902 to 1929
Chemical manufactures	1902 to 1925
Oil fuel, mazout	1925 to 1937
Tea	1925 to 1937
Nitrate of soda	1925 to 1937
Other oils	1925 to 1929
Cement	1925 to 1937
Jute sacks	1925 to 1937
Iron bars	1925 to 1937
Chemical manufactures	1902 to 1925

Table A.20. Egypt: Price Indexes (1913 = 100)

	Export price index			
	Laspeyres	*Paasche*	*Fisher Ideal*	*Paasche as a percentage of Laspeyres*
1889	89.491	90.138	89.814	100.7
1890	81.312	81.781	81.546	100.6
1891	66.301	67.390	66.843	101.6
1892	57.792	58.146	57.969	100.6
1893	62.837	63.439	63.137	101.0
1894	50.294	50.273	50.284	100.0
1895	54.673	55.109	54.891	100.8
1896	58.125	58.602	58.363	100.8
1897	49.090	49.371	49.230	100.6
1898	46.491	46.080	46.285	99.1
1899	55.655	55.483	55.569	99.7
1900	72.792	73.112	72.952	100.4
1901	61.459	61.262	61.360	99.7
1902	64.608	64.824	64.716	100.3
1903	82.902	82.962	82.932	100.1
1904	83.224	83.264	83.244	100.0
1905	72.513	72.911	72.712	100.5
1906	90.719	90.624	90.672	99.9
1907	101.165	101.083	101.124	99.9
1908	81.741	81.694	81.717	99.9
1909	93.351	93.603	93.477	100.3
1910	118.910	119.604	119.256	100.6
1911	100.322	100.484	100.403	100.2
1912	90.509	90.630	90.570	100.1
1913	100.000	100.000	100.000	100.0
1914	87.338	87.581	87.459	100.3
1915	78.059	78.337	78.198	100.4
1916	147.292	148.974	148.131	101.1
1917	213.551	214.886	214.218	100.6
1918	197.568	196.155	196.860	99.3
1919	255.855	260.355	258.095	101.8
1920	477.729	478.183	477.956	100.1
1921	160.436	161.187	160.811	100.5
1922	164.603	165.649	165.125	100.6
1923	177.225	178.279	177.751	100.6
1924	207.248	209.317	208.280	101.0
1925	212.190	214.502	213.343	101.1
1926	136.095	137.186	136.639	100.8
1927	142.053	143.760	142.904	101.2
1928	162.201	164.252	163.223	101.3
1929	144.991	146.666	145.826	101.2
1930	109.129	110.007	109.567	100.8
1931	76.334	75.873	76.103	99.4
1932	77.240	78.363	77.800	101.5
1933	76.003	76.779	76.390	101.0
1934	79.202	79.352	79.277	100.2
1935	85.918	86.218	86.068	100.3
1936	89.018	89.699	89.358	100.8
1937	89.757	90.297	90.027	100.6

Import price index			
Laspeyres	Paasche	Fisher Ideal	Paasche as a percentage of Laspeyres
68.756	72.866	70.781	106.0
73.141	77.372	75.227	105.8
71.438	75.489	73.436	105.7
68.589	72.579	70.556	105.8
63.652	67.010	65.309	105.3
58.273	61.002	59.622	104.7
55.233	57.637	56.422	104.4
57.063	59.283	58.163	103.9
55.681	58.605	57.124	105.3
57.005	60.374	58.665	105.9
58.911	61.920	60.397	105.1
67.063	70.375	68.699	104.9
66.489	69.781	68.115	105.0
62.622	64.859	63.731	103.6
63.592	65.792	64.682	103.5
65.596	67.845	66.711	103.4
66.043	68.899	67.456	104.3
69.221	71.088	70.149	102.7
76.404	77.826	77.111	101.9
78.830	80.721	79.769	102.4
73.373	77.001	75.165	104.9
83.574	85.435	84.499	102.2
91.104	90.587	90.846	99.4
98.939	98.472	98.705	99.5
100.000	100.000	100.000	100.0
96.814	96.838	96.826	100.0
151.514	140.333	145.816	92.6
250.059	246.658	248.353	98.6
370.509	338.543	354.166	91.4
489.034	456.037	472.247	93.3
340.571	316.469	328.299	92.9
450.563	403.179	426.213	89.5
247.785	248.811	248.298	100.4
151.644	143.930	147.736	94.9
140.801	134.053	137.385	95.2
140.307	134.872	137.563	96.1
137.350	130.801	134.036	95.2
138.094	130.598	134.294	94.6
127.118	120.799	123.918	95.0
122.348	117.368	119.832	95.9
114.900	109.146	111.986	95.0
101.952	96.358	99.116	94.5
89.052	83.771	86.371	94.1
86.010	78.636	82.240	91.4
79.808	75.043	77.389	94.0
80.172	76.739	78.437	95.7
81.291	77.933	79.594	95.9
81.146	76.558	78.819	94.3
100.984	95.452	98.179	94.5

Table A.21. India: Trade Variables (Millions of rupees)

	1913 prices		Current prices		
	Real Exports X^R	Real Imports M^R	Exports X	Imports M	Trade Balance X - M
1888	1542.11	699.53	988.34	694.40	293.93
1889	1563.08	723.26	1053.67	691.97	361.69
1890	1618.81	758.77	1023.50	719.75	303.75
1891	1711.96	771.93	1114.60	694.32	420.28
1892	1621.79	711.29	1135.54	662.65	472.89
1893	1575.71	847.06	1106.03	770.21	335.82
1894	1657.90	819.89	1171.40	735.29	436.11
1895	1691.02	790.79	1185.94	729.37	456.58
1896	1559.12	812.08	1089.22	761.17	328.04
1897	1590.81	819.02	1047.81	736.47	311.34
1898	1874.79	823.34	1202.11	721.01	481.10
1899	1801.72	821.37	1170.40	753.04	417.35
1900	1737.06	816.01	1219.46	808.95	410.51
1901	1865.50	978.38	1363.66	887.81	475.86
1902	2028.82	992.24	1390.54	858.19	532.35
1903	2342.41	1063.62	1684.59	925.92	758.67
1904	2454.95	1191.43	1742.63	1044.13	698.50
1905	2314.67	1291.25	1773.06	1121.14	651.92
1906	2241.03	1337.19	1827.48	1172.42	655.06
1907	2144.27	1457.54	1829.34	1366.48	462.86
1908	1956.14	1389.55	1594.63	1287.87	306.77
1909	2344.31	1346.89	1943.67	1226.51	717.16
1910	2395.93	1397.43	2170.88	1337.06	833.83
1911	2522.04	1442.26	2383.79	1440.55	943.23
1912	2636.81	1661.37	2568.50	1666.30	902.20
1913	2560.90	1913.08	2560.90	1913.08	647.82
1914	2097.36	1412.35	1874.65	1449.31	425.35
1915	2304.16	1206.87	2077.88	1381.69	696.19
1916	2457.06	1099.66	2537.95	1602.49	935.46
1917	2294.96	908.28	2524.48	1643.55	880.93
1918	1947.09	829.79	2643.20	1885.62	757.57
1919	2168.38	966.15	3497.01	2217.02	1279.99
1920	2063.59	1292.28	2939.39	3475.74	-536.35
1921	2127.83	1409.65	2677.25	2825.97	-148.73
1922	2242.67	1363.87	3187.93	2461.92	726.01
1923	2523.45	1313.73	3668.48	2371.83	1296.65
1924	2610.79	1455.87	4002.43	2533.64	1468.79
1925	2524.74	1517.63	3868.12	2360.01	1508.11
1926	2303.13	1691.46	3110.50	2408.18	702.32
1927	2478.33	1983.39	3302.64	2615.24	687.40
1928	2594.07	2004.74	3391.51	2633.98	757.53
1929	2649.13	1980.30	3189.90	2497.07	692.82
1930	2401.89	1606.08	2265.02	1730.91	534.11
1931	2072.10	1379.85	1612.03	1306.44	305.59
1932	1853.09	1596.28	1360.67	1350.17	10.49
1933	2159.28	1383.21	1502.36	1172.76	329.60
1934	2181.70	1585.28	1554.97	1345.83	209.15
1935	2231.32	1672.98	1645.97	1367.63	278.35
1936	2722.35	1521.52	2024.89	1277.21	747.68

Table A.22. India: Price Variables

	1913 = 100			Exchange rate (rupees per Pound) π
	Export price Px	Import price Pm	Terms of trade P_T	
1888	64.090	99.267	64.563	14.694
1889	67.409	95.675	70.457	14.545
1890	63.226	94.858	66.653	13.333
1891	65.107	89.946	72.384	14.328
1892	70.018	93.162	75.157	16.000
1893	70.193	90.927	77.197	16.552
1894	70.655	89.682	78.785	18.461
1895	70.132	92.232	76.038	17.778
1896	69.861	93.732	74.533	16.552
1897	65.867	89.921	73.249	15.652
1898	64.120	87.572	73.219	15.000
1899	64.960	91.681	70.854	15.000
1900	70.202	99.134	70.816	15.000
1901	73.099	90.742	80.557	15.000
1902	68.539	86.490	79.245	15.000
1903	71.917	87.054	82.612	15.000
1904	70.984	87.636	80.999	15.000
1905	76.601	86.825	88.224	15.000
1906	81.546	87.678	93.007	15.000
1907	85.313	93.752	90.998	15.000
1908	81.519	92.683	87.955	15.000
1909	82.910	91.062	91.048	15.000
1910	90.607	95.680	94.698	15.000
1911	94.518	99.881	94.630	15.000
1912	97.409	100.296	97.122	15.000
1913	100.000	100.000	100.000	15.000
1914	89.381	102.616	87.102	15.000
1915	90.180	114.486	78.769	15.000
1916	103.292	145.726	70.881	15.000
1917	110.001	180.952	60.790	15.000
1918	135.751	227.242	59.739	15.000
1919	161.273	229.470	70.281	10.000
1920	142.441	268.961	52.960	10.000
1921	125.820	200.474	62.761	15.000
1922	142.149	180.511	78.748	15.000
1923	145.376	180.542	80.522	15.000
1924	153.303	174.029	88.090	13.333
1925	153.209	155.506	98.523	13.333
1926	135.055	142.373	94.860	13.333
1927	133.261	131.857	101.065	13.333
1928	130.741	131.388	99.508	13.333
1929	120.413	126.095	95.493	13.333
1930	94.302	107.772	87.501	13.333
1931	77.797	94.680	82.168	13.333
1932	73.427	84.582	86.811	13.333
1933	69.577	84.785	82.062	13.333
1934	71.273	84.895	83.955	13.333
1935	73.767	81.748	90.237	13.333
1936	74.380	83.943	88.608	13.333

Table A.23. India: Government Variables (Millions of rupees)

	Current prices		1913 prices	
	Government revenues R *(1)*	*Government expenditures* G *(2)*	*Real govt. expenditures* G^R *(3)*	*Acc. real govt. exp.* $\Sigma_{i=1}^{\infty} G_{t-i}^R$ *(4)*
1888	816.97	813.66	819.66	35684.18
1889	850.85	824.73	862.01	36551.31
1890	857.42	820.53	865.01	37421.46
1891	891.43	886.76	985.87	38413.18
1892	901.72	910.06	976.86	39395.84
1893	905.65	921.12	1013.03	40414.88
1894	951.87	944.94	1053.66	41474.80
1895	983.70	968.36	1049.91	42530.95
1896	941.30	958.35	1022.44	43559.45
1897	964.42	1018.01	1132.12	44698.28
1898	1014.27	974.65	1112.97	45817.86
1899	1029.56	987.94	1077.58	46901.83
1900	1129.08	1104.03	1113.68	48022.12
1901	1145.17	1070.91	1180.17	49209.30
1902	1161.52	1115.48	1289.72	50506.68
1903	1256.34	1211.40	1391.55	51906.48
1904	1272.19	1220.35	1392.52	53307.27
1905	1274.96	1243.59	1432.28	54748.05
1906	1097.17	1073.33	1224.17	55979.49
1907	1065.05	1060.46	1131.13	57117.33
1908	1046.42	1102.49	1189.53	58313.92
1909	1118.90	1109.80	1218.73	59539.88
1910	1210.24	1151.19	1203.17	60750.20
1911	1242.54	1183.43	1184.83	61942.06
1912	1302.94	1256.32	1252.61	63202.11
1913	1278.11	1243.42	1243.42	64452.91
1914	1217.36	1244.14	1212.42	65672.50
1915	1266.20	1284.03	1121.56	66800.69
1916	1470.76	1358.58	932.29	67738.56
1917	1689.93	1568.63	866.87	68610.56
1918	1848.87	1906.17	838.83	69454.37
1919	1956.11	2083.68	908.04	70367.75
1920	2061.58	2321.66	863.19	71236.06
1921	1855.94	2215.79	1105.28	72347.94
1922	1971.10	2129.80	1179.88	73534.75
1923	2118.70	2080.37	1152.29	74693.94
1924	2187.13	2090.45	1201.20	75902.25
1925	2207.18	2159.28	1388.55	77299.06
1926	2180.57	2216.18	1556.60	78864.87
1927	2205.09	2185.59	1657.55	80532.25
1928	2204.54	2221.48	1690.78	82233.06
1929	2272.24	2258.92	1791.43	84035.19
1930	2076.29	2298.96	2133.16	86181.00
1931	2048.00	2198.67	2322.21	88517.00
1932	2097.33	2097.33	2479.64	91011.31
1933	2022.67	2053.33	2421.80	93447.50
1934	2084.00	2072.00	2440.66	95902.69
1935	2101.33	2097.33	2565.62	98483.50
1936	2101.76	2111.77	2515.72	101014.19

Table A.24. India: Price Index Components

Commodity	Years Included in Index
Export Price Index Components (48 Commodities)	
Coffee	1880 to 1937
Raw cotton	1880 to 1937
Raw jute	1880 to 1936
Opium	1880 to 1934
Rice	1880 to 1909
Saltpeter	1880 to 1929
Seeds	1880 to 1909
Raw silk I	1880 to 1909
Raw silk II	1909 to 1929
Spices	1880 to 1937
Sugar	1880 to 1909
Raw wool	1880 to 1936
Tea	1880 to 1937
Coir, and manufactures of	1880 to 1929
Wheat	1880 to 1937
Hides and skins	1880 to 1901
Coal and coke	1881 to 1937
Raw hides and skins	1901 to 1909
Tanned hides and skins	1901 to 1937
Barley	1901 to 1937
Grain: gram	1901 to 1929
Grain: pulse	1901 to 1937
Raw hemp	1901 to 1937
Pig iron	1901 to 1937
Manganese ore	1901 to 1937
Manure and animal bones	1901 to 1937
Raw mica	1901 to 1937
Raw rubber	1901 to 1937
Cotton: twist and yarn	1909 to 1937
Cotton: grey and white	1909 to 1929
Cotton: colored, printed, or dyed	1909 to 1929
Rice in the husk	1909 to 1929
Rice not in the husk	1909 to 1937
Ground nuts	1909 to 1937
Bran and pollard	1909 to 1937
Raw hides	1909 to 1937
Raw skins	1909 to 1937
Gunny bags	1909 to 1937
Gunny cloth	1909 to 1937
Lac	1909 to 1937

(Continued)

Table A.24—*Continued*

Commodity	Years Included in Index
Export Price Index Components **(48 Commodities)**	
Oil cakes	1909 to 1937
Oils	1909 to 1929
Castor oilseed	1909 to 1937
Cotton oilseed	1909 to 1937
Linseed oilseed	1909 to 1937
Rape oilseed	1909 to 1937
Sesamum oilseed	1909 to 1937
Cotton piece goods	1929 to 1937
Import Price Index Components **(50 Commodities)**	
Copper	1880 to 1929
Iron	1880 to 1907
Spelter or zinc	1880 to 1929
Steel	1880 to 1907
Salt	1880 to 1937
Spices	1880 to 1937
Spirits	1880 to 1927
Coal I	1880 to 1881
Malt liquors	1880 to 1888
Tin	1880 to 1937
Raw silk	1880 to 1937
Sugar and molasses	1880 to 1901
Tea	1880 to 1937
Lead	1880 to 1929
Coal II	1881 to 1937
Coke	1881 to 1909
Ivory	1881 to 1929
Horses	1881 to 1929
Coffee	1888 to 1909
Kerosene	1881 to 1929
Paints and colors	1881 to 1929
Umbrellas	1881 to 1923
Liquors	1888 to 1923
Unmanufactured tobacco	1888 to 1937
Manufactured tobacco	1900 to 1937
Wines II	1888 to 1929
Beer and ale	1888 to 1937
Raw cotton	1901 to 1937
Iron and steel	1907 to 1937
Raw cotton: twist and yarn	1909 to 1937

Table A.24–*Continued*

Commodity	Years Included in Index

Import Price Index Components (Continued)

Grey cotton manufactures	1909 to 1937
White cotton manufactures	1909 to 1937
Colored, printed or dyed cotton manufactures	1909 to 1937
Fish	1909 to 1929
Fruits	1909 to 1929
Soap	1901 to 1937
Sugar	1901 to 1937
Molasses sugar	1901 to 1929
Confectionery sugar	1901 to 1923
Motor cars	1924 to 1929
Trucks	1924 to 1929
Other spirits	1929 to 1937
Wheat	1929 to 1937
Whiskey	1929 to 1937
Copper	1929 to 1937
Brass 192	1929 to 1937
Aluminum	1929 to 1937
Silk piece goods	1929 to 1937
Total motor vehicles	1929 to 1937
Total oils	1929 to 1937

Table A.25. India: Price Indexes (1913 = 100)

	Export price index			
	Laspeyres	Paasche	Fisher Ideal	Paasche as a percentage of Laspeyres
1880	64.800	67.290	66.033	103.8
1881	61.389	63.689	62.528	103.7
1882	57.973	59.972	58.964	103.4
1883	58.897	61.142	60.009	103.8
1884	59.206	61.226	60.208	103.4
1885	57.797	59.893	58.836	103.6
1886	57.642	59.627	58.626	103.4
1887	59.613	61.548	60.573	103.2
1888	62.534	64.090	63.307	102.5
1889	65.595	67.409	66.496	102.8
1890	61.671	63.225	62.443	102.5
1891	63.097	65.106	64.094	103.2
1892	68.319	70.018	69.163	102.5
1893	68.112	70.192	69.144	103.1
1894	66.127	70.655	68.354	106.8
1895	67.319	70.132	68.711	104.2
1896	67.872	69.861	68.859	102.9
1897	65.478	65.867	65.672	100.6
1898	61.803	64.120	62.951	103.7
1899	62.301	64.960	63.617	104.3
1900	72.039	70.202	71.115	97.4
1901	71.133	73.098	72.109	102.8
1902	67.127	68.539	67.829	102.1
1903	70.082	71.917	70.994	102.6
1904	70.212	70.984	70.597	101.1
1905	74.629	76.600	75.608	102.6
1906	80.766	81.546	81.155	101.0
1907	85.312	85.313	85.313	100.0
1908	79.827	81.519	80.669	102.1
1909	80.319	82.910	81.604	103.2
1910	88.611	90.607	89.603	102.3
1911	93.385	94.518	93.950	101.2
1912	97.371	97.409	97.390	100.0
1913	100.000	100.000	100.000	100.0
1914	87.303	89.381	88.336	102.4
1915	86.705	90.180	88.426	104.0
1916	101.277	103.292	102.280	102.0
1917	110.161	110.001	110.081	99.9
1918	142.232	135.751	138.954	95.4
1919	163.283	161.273	162.275	98.8
1920	144.584	142.440	143.508	98.5
1921	129.295	125.820	127.546	97.3
1922	141.827	142.149	141.988	100.2
1923	144.817	145.375	145.096	100.4
1924	155.814	153.303	154.554	98.4
1925	154.420	153.208	153.813	99.2
1926	135.256	135.055	135.156	99.9
1927	136.452	133.260	134.847	97.7
1928	134.715	130.740	132.713	97.0
1929	127.315	120.412	123.815	94.6
1930	99.810	94.301	97.016	94.5
1931	81.898	77.796	79.821	95.0
1932	77.923	73.427	75.642	94.2
1933	74.686	69.577	72.086	93.2
1934	75.634	71.273	73.421	94.2
1935	78.673	73.766	76.182	93.8
1936	80.072	74.380	77.174	92.9

	Import price index		
Laspeyres	Paasche	Fisher Ideal	Paasche as a percentage of Laspeyres
88.705	101.874	95.062	114.8
85.598	97.007	91.124	113.3
85.980	96.607	91.139	112.4
85.630	96.290	90.804	112.4
81.487	89.942	85.610	110.4
78.467	86.543	82.406	110.3
81.570	87.941	84.696	107.8
86.117	93.148	89.564	108.2
94.255	99.267	96.729	105.3
95.264	95.674	95.469	100.4
92.224	94.857	93.531	102.9
87.386	89.946	88.657	102.9
90.405	93.160	91.772	103.0
89.916	90.928	90.421	101.1
87.628	89.681	88.649	102.3
89.492	92.232	90.852	103.1
90.552	93.731	92.128	103.5
87.768	89.921	88.838	102.5
85.178	87.570	86.366	102.8
89.905	91.681	90.789	102.0
97.038	99.133	98.080	102.2
89.506	90.741	90.121	101.4
85.575	86.490	86.031	101.1
86.977	87.053	87.015	100.1
86.941	87.637	87.288	100.8
85.612	86.824	86.216	101.4
87.768	87.677	87.723	99.9
92.797	93.752	93.273	101.0
92.057	92.681	92.369	100.7
90.297	91.062	90.679	100.8
95.900	95.679	95.789	99.8
99.672	99.882	99.777	100.2
99.752	100.295	100.023	100.5
100.000	100.000	100.000	100.0
102.541	102.617	102.579	100.1
115.208	114.486	114.847	99.4
149.766	145.724	147.731	97.3
193.978	180.950	187.351	93.3
244.932	227.240	235.920	92.8
245.833	229.468	237.510	93.3
276.940	268.958	272.920	97.1
210.499	200.473	205.425	95.2
187.060	180.510	183.756	96.5
186.786	180.541	183.637	96.7
181.547	174.029	177.748	95.9
162.615	155.504	159.020	95.6
150.468	142.372	146.364	94.6
139.499	131.856	135.624	94.5
137.282	131.387	134.302	95.7
132.794	126.095	129.401	95.0
114.775	107.772	111.218	93.9
102.896	94.679	98.702	92.0
96.348	84.582	90.274	87.8
91.798	84.785	88.222	92.4
92.823	84.894	88.770	91.5
90.164	81.747	85.852	90.7
94.706	83.943	89.162	88.6

Table A.26. Jamaica: Trade Variables (Millions of pounds)

	1913 prices		Current prices		
	Real Exports X^R	Real Imports M^R	Exports X	Imports M	Trade Balance X - M
1884	1.46	1.51	1.38	1.53	-0.15
1885	1.41	1.50	1.21	1.48	-0.27
1886	1.19	1.44	1.10	1.29	-0.20
1887	1.38	1.48	1.35	1.27	0.09
1888	1.69	1.80	1.68	1.55	0.13
1889	1.47	1.78	1.52	1.54	-0.02
1890	1.71	2.48	1.82	2.13	-0.30
1891	1.56	2.00	1.66	1.75	-0.09
1892	1.66	2.19	1.71	1.93	-0.22
1893	1.72	2.42	2.00	2.12	-0.12
1894	1.70	2.66	1.86	2.16	-0.30
1895	1.77	2.80	1.79	2.27	-0.48
1896	1.58	2.41	1.40	1.83	-0.43
1897	1.72	2.09	1.39	1.64	-0.25
1898	2.05	2.26	1.57	1.80	-0.23
1899	1.99	2.26	1.82	1.77	0.05
1900	1.92	2.13	1.76	1.69	0.07
1901	2.21	2.16	1.86	1.73	0.14
1902	2.68	2.38	2.24	1.99	0.25
1903	1.88	2.34	1.50	2.00	-0.51
1904	1.80	2.06	1.35	1.68	-0.33
1905	2.39	2.20	1.79	1.92	-0.13
1906	2.52	2.37	1.91	2.17	-0.26
1907	2.39	3.00	2.25	2.86	-0.61
1908	2.41	2.47	2.12	2.41	-0.29
1909	2.56	2.59	2.55	2.55	-0.00
1910	2.59	2.63	2.45	2.61	-0.16
1911	2.78	2.93	2.81	2.79	0.02
1912	2.43	3.07	2.61	3.02	-0.41
1913	2.25	2.84	2.25	2.84	-0.59
1914	2.77	2.53	2.83	2.55	0.28
1915	2.09	2.10	2.23	2.33	-0.10
1916	1.96	2.24	2.80	3.03	-0.23
1917	1.70	1.60	2.48	3.30	-0.82
1918	1.72	1.40	2.69	3.38	-0.69
1919	2.64	1.94	5.63	4.87	0.75
1920	2.03	3.21	6.83	10.31	-3.48
1921	1.94	2.68	3.05	5.46	-2.41
1922	2.88	3.14	4.17	4.83	-0.66
1923	2.35	3.48	4.22	5.56	-1.34
1924	2.38	2.97	3.13	5.08	-1.95
1925	3.00	3.36	3.93	5.63	-1.70
1926	3.39	3.52	4.25	5.63	-1.38
1927	3.72	4.10	4.86	6.00	-1.14
1928	3.26	4.46	4.18	6.37	-2.19
1929	2.73	4.83	4.66	7.02	-2.37
1930	3.18	5.48	4.08	6.10	-2.02
1931	2.99	5.42	3.33	4.94	-1.61
1932	3.40	5.44	3.24	4.75	-1.51
1933	2.46	5.61	2.50	4.36	-1.87
1934	3.02	6.39	3.17	4.76	-1.59
1935	3.50	6.62	3.81	5.01	-1.20
1936	3.45	6.75	3.80	5.07	-1.27
1937	4.42	7.44	4.96	6.13	-1.17
1938	4.10	8.04	5.03	6.42	-1.39

Table A.27. Jamaica: Price Variables (1913 = 100)

	Export Price Px	Import Price Pm	Terms of Trade P_T
1884	94.282	101.653	92.749
1885	85.253	98.706	86.371
1886	91.977	89.567	102.691
1887	97.905	85.370	114.683
1888	99.471	85.914	115.780
1889	103.111	86.261	119.533
1890	106.790	85.855	124.384
1891	106.149	87.504	121.307
1892	103.079	88.163	116.918
1893	116.513	87.446	133.240
1894	109.893	81.451	134.919
1895	100.789	81.161	124.185
1896	88.663	75.891	116.829
1897	80.771	78.576	102.793
1898	76.593	79.571	96.257
1899	91.478	78.290	116.844
1900	91.657	79.439	115.380
1901	84.099	79.753	105.450
1902	83.639	83.453	100.223
1903	79.757	85.517	93.264
1904	75.316	81.332	92.603
1905	74.937	87.501	85.642
1906	75.846	91.653	82.753
1907	94.186	95.488	98.637
1908	88.122	97.588	90.300
1909	99.442	98.489	100.968
1910	94.621	99.160	95.423
1911	101.296	95.181	106.424
1912	107.232	98.374	109.004
1913	100.000	100.000	100.000
1914	102.054	101.000	101.044
1915	106.485	110.808	96.098
1916	143.354	135.575	105.737
1917	145.850	206.048	70.784
1918	155.775	241.875	64.403
1919	213.330	251.095	84.960
1920	335.852	320.726	104.716
1921	157.395	203.442	77.366
1922	144.774	154.016	93.999
1923	179.273	159.606	112.322
1924	131.672	171.458	76.796
1925	131.128	167.358	78.352
1926	125.315	160.095	78.275
1927	130.665	146.222	89.360
1928	128.249	142.890	89.754
1929	170.488	145.400	117.254
1930	128.423	111.269	115.416
1931	111.424	91.252	122.106
1932	95.397	87.406	109.143
1933	101.650	77.800	130.656
1934	105.004	74.589	140.777
1935	109.070	75.609	144.255
1936	110.302	75.106	146.862
1937	112.198	82.493	136.009
1938	122.756	79.886	153.664

Table A.28. Jamaica: Government Variables (Millions of pounds)

| | Current prices | | 1913 prices | |
	Government revenues R (1)	Government expenditures G (2)	Real govt. expenditures G^R (3)	Acc. real govt. exp. $\Sigma_{i=1}^{\infty} G_{t-i}^{R}$ (4)
1884	0.58	0.56	0.55	12.64
1885	0.61	0.58	0.59	13.43
1886	0.58	0.59	0.66	14.12
1887	0.61	0.62	0.73	14.88
1888	0.69	0.62	0.72	15.62
1889	0.70	0.65	0.75	16.41
1890	0.79	0.67	0.78	17.24
1891	0.78	0.74	0.84	18.27
1892	0.71	0.74	0.83	19.18
1893	0.76	0.76	0.87	20.10
1894	0.79	0.77	0.94	21.11
1895	0.82	0.78	0.96	22.16
1896	0.75	0.81	1.06	23.29
1897	0.70	0.76	0.97	24.33
1898	0.75	0.73	0.92	25.28
1899	0.79	0.72	0.92	26.32
1900	0.88	0.91	1.14	27.59
1901	0.92	0.88	1.10	28.75
1902	1.01	0.89	1.07	29.87
1903	1.08	0.94	1.10	30.98
1904	0.89	0.93	1.15	32.14
1905	1.00	0.91	1.04	33.19
1906	1.04	0.92	1.00	34.19
1907	1.16	1.05	1.10	35.29
1908	1.08	1.02	1.05	36.35
1909	1.16	1.17	1.19	37.55
1910	1.17	1.14	1.14	38.69
1911	1.35	1.26	1.32	40.02
1912	1.38	1.46	1.48	41.50
1913	1.24	1.28	1.28	42.79
1914	1.16	1.23	1.22	44.01
1915	1.15	1.28	1.16	45.16
1916	1.34	1.27	0.94	46.10
1917	1.23	1.29	0.63	46.73
1918	1.35	1.45	0.60	47.33
1919	2.03	1.67	0.67	48.05
1920	2.35	2.33	0.73	48.82
1921	1.93	2.25	1.11	49.97
1922	2.06	1.95	1.27	51.23
1923	2.06	2.07	1.30	52.84
1924	1.92	2.02	1.18	54.09
1925	2.02	2.01	1.20	55.36
1926	2.15	2.05	1.28	56.71
1927	2.28	1.98	1.35	58.15
1928	2.21	2.32	1.62	59.87
1929	2.29	2.31	1.59	61.70
1930	2.20	2.32	2.09	63.90
1931	2.09	2.14	2.34	66.44
1932	2.17	2.08	2.38	69.29
1933	2.04	2.19	2.81	72.26
1934	2.26	2.26	3.02	75.48
1935	2.12	2.18	2.88	78.53
1936	2.21	2.21	2.94	81.60
1937	2.48	2.27	2.75	84.55
1938	2.84	2.87	3.60	88.15

Table A.29. Jamaica: Price Index Components

Commodity	Years Included in Index
Export Price Index Components	
(15 Commodities)	
Coffee	1884 to 1938
Ginger	1884 to 1938
Pimento	1884 to 1938
Rum	1884 to 1938
Sugar	1884 to 1938
Wood: logwood	1884 to 1938
Oranges	1884 to 1938
Coconuts	1884 to 1938
Cocoa	1885 to 1938
Hides	1885 to 1921
Cigars	1885 to 1938
Wood: fustic	1885 to 1914
Wood: spars, lancewood	1885 to 1914
Bananas	1888 to 1938
Honey	1888 to 1929
Import Price Index Components	
(32 Commodities)	
Bread	1884 to 1919
Butter	1884 to 1931
Cornmeal	1884 to 1931
Dried fish	1884 to 1929
Wet fish	1884 to 1929
Flour and wheat	1884 to 1938
Ale and beer	1884 to 1938
Coals	1884 to 1938
Wet pork salted	1884 to 1925
Rice	1884 to 1938
Soap	1884 to 1938
Lumber	1884 to 1929
Bacon and hams	1885 to 1929
Fish	1929 to 1938
Indian corn	1885 to 1931
Wet beef	1885 to 1925
Petroleum	1885 to 1925
Tobacco	1885 to 1938
Cement	1900 to 1938
Cheese	1900 to 1925
Cottonseed oil	1900 to 1925
Spirits, whiskey	1900 to 1925

(Continued)

Table A.29—*Continued*

Commodity	Years Included in Index
Import Price Index Components (Continued)	
Meat of all kinds	1925 to 1938
Edible oils	1925 to 1931
Fuel	1925 to 1938
Kerosene	1925 to 1938
Lubricating oil	1925 to 1938
Motor spirit	1925 to 1938
Potable spirits	1925 to 1931
Sugar	1925 to 1931
Cotton piece goods	1925 to 1938
Motor cars	1925 to 1938

Table A.30. Jamaica: Price Indexes (1913 = 100)

	Export price index				Import price index			
	Laspeyres	Paasche	Fisher Ideal	Paasche as a percentage of Laspeyres	Laspeyres	Paasche	Fisher Ideal	Paasche as a percentage of Laspeyres
1884	97.543	94.283	95.899	96.7	101.044	101.654	101.349	100.6
1885	87.949	85.253	86.590	96.9	96.491	98.706	97.592	102.3
1886	94.898	91.977	93.426	96.9	87.574	89.567	88.565	102.3
1887	103.464	97.905	100.646	94.6	83.299	85.370	84.328	102.5
1888	99.739	99.472	99.605	99.7	84.103	85.914	85.004	102.2
1889	105.322	103.111	104.211	97.9	84.659	86.262	85.457	101.9
1890	107.739	106.791	107.264	99.1	84.270	85.856	85.059	101.9
1891	106.710	106.149	106.429	99.5	86.183	87.505	86.842	101.5
1892	104.430	103.079	103.752	98.7	87.361	88.164	87.762	100.9
1893	117.824	116.513	117.167	98.9	85.706	87.446	86.572	102.0
1894	111.333	109.893	110.611	98.7	79.897	81.451	80.671	101.9
1895	100.355	100.790	100.573	100.4	79.555	81.161	80.354	102.0
1896	88.832	88.663	88.747	99.8	75.660	75.892	75.775	100.3
1897	80.288	80.771	80.529	100.6	78.596	78.577	78.587	100.0
1898	76.022	76.593	76.307	100.8	78.428	79.571	78.998	101.5
1899	84.713	91.477	88.030	108.0	77.322	78.290	77.805	101.3
1900	87.890	91.656	89.753	104.3	79.250	79.440	79.344	100.2
1901	77.764	84.099	80.869	108.1	79.571	79.753	79.662	100.2
1902	73.070	83.639	78.176	114.5	83.633	83.453	83.543	99.8
1903	75.034	79.756	77.359	106.3	84.555	85.518	85.035	101.1
1904	72.475	75.317	73.882	103.9	81.110	81.333	81.221	100.3
1905	73.276	74.938	74.102	102.3	87.994	87.501	87.747	99.4
1906	74.001	75.846	74.918	102.5	91.368	91.654	91.511	100.3
1907	91.788	94.187	92.980	102.6	94.826	95.488	95.156	100.7
1908	87.559	88.122	87.840	100.6	95.623	97.588	96.601	102.1
1909	95.227	99.442	97.312	104.4	98.166	98.489	98.327	100.3
1910	93.343	94.622	93.981	101.4	99.055	99.160	99.107	100.1
1911	99.957	101.295	100.624	101.3	94.843	95.182	95.012	100.4

298   *Appendix*

Table A.30. Jamaica: Price Indexes (1913 = 100)

	Export price index				Import price index			
	Laspeyres	Paasche	Fisher Ideal	Paasche as a percentage of Laspeyres	Laspeyres	Paasche	Fisher Ideal	Paasche as a percentage of Laspeyres
1912	105.946	107.232	106.587	101.2	99.036	98.374	98.705	99.3
1913	100.000	100.000	100.000	100.0	100.000	100.000	100.000	100.0
1914	100.539	102.055	101.294	101.5	105.474	101.000	103.213	95.8
1915	97.777	106.485	102.038	108.9	115.045	110.809	112.907	96.3
1916	104.321	143.354	122.290	137.4	139.807	135.576	137.675	97.0
1917	120.689	145.849	132.674	120.8	203.745	206.049	204.894	101.1
1918	131.430	155.774	143.086	118.5	250.697	241.876	246.247	96.5
1919	177.665	213.329	194.682	120.1	270.902	251.096	260.811	92.7
1920	259.515	335.852	295.227	129.4	341.750	320.726	331.071	93.8
1921	164.493	157.394	160.904	95.7	237.427	203.441	219.778	85.7
1922	151.799	144.774	148.245	95.4	171.624	154.015	162.581	89.7
1923	185.847	179.272	182.530	96.5	172.729	159.605	166.038	92.4
1924	145.266	131.672	138.302	90.6	187.528	171.458	179.313	91.4
1925	139.104	131.128	135.057	94.3	185.378	167.358	176.138	90.3
1926	140.824	125.315	132.843	89.0	177.356	160.094	168.504	90.3
1927	147.701	130.664	138.922	88.5	162.037	146.222	153.927	90.2
1928	146.595	128.249	137.116	87.5	158.010	142.889	150.259	90.4
1929	184.928	170.487	177.561	92.2	152.603	145.399	148.958	95.3
1930	138.980	128.422	133.596	92.4	126.072	111.269	118.439	88.3
1931	123.748	111.424	117.425	90.0	107.310	91.251	98.956	85.0
1932	108.774	95.397	101.866	87.7	102.639	87.405	94.716	85.2
1933	111.031	101.651	106.238	91.6	91.858	77.799	84.537	84.7
1934	119.774	105.004	112.146	87.7	88.090	74.588	81.058	84.7
1935	121.413	109.069	115.076	89.8	88.675	75.609	81.882	85.3
1936	122.016	110.301	116.011	90.4	87.583	75.106	81.105	85.8
1937	125.701	112.199	118.758	89.3	95.939	82.493	88.962	86.0
1938	132.356	122.755	127.465	92.7	93.320	79.885	86.573	85.1

Table A.31. Nigeria: Trade Variables (Millions of pounds)

	1913 prices		Current prices		
	Real Exports X^R	Real Imports M^R	Exports X	Imports M	Trade Balance X - M
1900	3.24	2.18	2.02	1.95	0.07
1901	3.46	2.44	2.24	2.24	-0.01
1902	3.60	2.71	2.66	2.42	0.25
1903	4.02	3.03	2.68	2.64	0.04
1904	4.40	3.39	3.08	3.07	0.01
1905	4.08	3.24	3.00	2.98	0.02
1906	4.50	3.22	3.15	3.15	0.00
1907	5.20	4.21	4.20	4.44	-0.24
1908	4.89	3.87	3.41	4.28	-0.88
1909	5.78	4.81	4.17	4.96	-0.79
1910	5.85	5.78	5.30	5.86	-0.55
1911	6.16	5.97	5.39	5.68	-0.29
1912	6.92	6.44	6.09	6.43	-0.34
1913	7.35	7.20	7.35	7.20	0.15
1914	7.23	6.77	6.61	6.90	-0.29
1915	7.40	3.82	5.66	5.02	0.64
1916	7.56	3.71	6.10	5.75	0.35
1917	9.00	4.04	8.72	7.54	1.18
1918	9.16	3.19	9.56	8.30	1.27
1919	11.06	3.78	14.73	11.64	3.08
1920	9.25	4.79	16.96	22.44	-5.48
1921	8.92	2.58	9.69	10.74	-1.05
1922	11.29	3.60	10.45	10.90	-0.46
1923	12.15	4.18	11.70	11.74	-0.04
1924	13.12	4.31	14.38	12.91	1.48
1925	14.94	5.37	16.90	16.19	0.71
1926	14.53	4.67	16.54	13.48	3.06
1927	13.61	5.85	15.47	15.09	0.38
1928	14.76	6.29	16.93	16.10	0.82
1929	16.57	5.29	17.58	13.39	4.19
1930	16.35	5.76	14.78	12.69	2.08
1931	15.28	3.59	8.55	6.51	2.04
1932	16.30	4.28	9.27	7.19	2.07
1933	16.28	3.97	8.46	6.34	2.12
1934	18.48	3.75	8.50	5.36	3.14
1935	20.11	5.17	11.20	7.80	3.39
1936	22.56	7.08	14.69	10.83	3.86
1937	24.41	8.44	19.06	14.62	4.43

Table A.32. Nigeria: Price Variables (1913 = 100)

	Export Price Px	Import Price Pm	Terms of Trade P_T
1900	62.369	89.297	69.845
1901	64.631	92.050	70.213
1902	73.960	89.036	83.068
1903	66.640	87.093	76.516
1904	70.036	90.596	77.305
1905	73.446	91.760	80.041
1906	70.107	97.917	71.598
1907	80.785	105.480	76.588
1908	69.756	110.752	62.984
1909	72.112	103.093	69.949
1910	90.704	101.350	89.496
1911	87.558	95.119	92.051
1912	88.035	99.840	88.176
1913	100.000	100.000	100.000
1914	91.377	101.875	89.695
1915	76.446	131.161	58.284
1916	80.694	154.941	52.080
1917	96.959	186.821	51.899
1918	104.385	259.917	40.161
1919	133.088	307.912	43.223
1920	183.390	468.006	39.185
1921	108.647	416.406	26.092
1922	92.538	302.833	30.557
1923	96.328	280.978	34.283
1924	109.655	299.451	36.619
1925	113.156	301.251	37.562
1926	113.802	288.955	39.384
1927	113.636	257.901	44.062
1928	114.701	256.082	44.791
1929	106.086	253.107	41.913
1930	90.383	220.276	41.032
1931	55.976	181.112	30.907
1932	56.838	167.978	33.836
1933	51.964	159.508	32.577
1934	46.007	143.001	32.173
1935	55.687	150.914	36.900
1936	65.110	152.933	42.574
1937	78.089	173.243	45.075

Table A.33. Nigeria: Government Variables (Millions of pounds)

	Current prices		1913 prices	
	Government revenues R (1)	Government expenditures G (2)	Real govt. expenditures G^R (3)	Acc. real govt. exp. $\sum_{i=1}^{\infty} G^R_{t-i}$ (4)
1900	0.64	0.74	0.82	11.35
1901	0.68	0.87	0.94	12.31
1902	0.87	1.10	1.23	13.73
1903	0.91	1.28	1.47	15.07
1904	1.05	1.39	1.54	17.56
1905	1.04	1.38	1.51	19.06
1906	1.28	1.56	1.59	20.65
1907	1.67	1.72	1.63	25.12
1908	1.64	1.90	1.71	26.84
1909	1.65	2.22	2.15	28.99
1910	2.28	2.16	2.13	34.34
1911	2.57	2.55	2.68	37.02
1912	2.76	2.82	2.83	39.84
1913	3.33	2.92	2.92	42.76
1914	2.95	3.60	3.53	46.29
1915	2.60	3.43	2.62	49.06
1916	2.84	3.61	2.33	51.39
1917	3.42	3.22	1.72	53.12
1918	3.96	3.46	1.33	55.80
1919	4.96	4.53	1.47	56.71
1920	6.82	6.49	1.39	58.81
1921	4.88	7.17	1.72	60.53
1922	5.56	6.57	2.17	64.58
1923	6.26	5.50	1.96	66.54
1924	6.94	5.77	1.93	68.47
1925	8.27	6.58	2.19	72.06
1926	7.73	7.58	2.62	74.69
1927	6.30	6.72	2.61	77.30
1928	6.03	6.86	2.68	79.98
1929	6.05	6.29	2.49	84.35
1930	5.62	6.33	2.87	87.23
1931	4.78	6.05	3.34	90.27
1932	4.98	4.98	2.97	93.24
1933	4.89	5.04	3.16	96.49
1934	4.96	4.84	3.38	99.87
1935	6.00	5.76	3.81	101.56
1936	6.26	6.06	3.96	105.53
1937	7.34	7.38	4.26	109.79

Table A.34. Nigeria: Price Index Components

Commodity	*Years Included in Index*
Export Price Index Components (13 Commodities)	
Cocoa	1900 to 1938
Cotton	1900 to 1938
Palm kernels	1900 to 1938
Palm oil	1900 to 1938
Rubber	1900 to 1938
Shea nuts	1908 to 1929
Tin ore	1908 to 1938
Ground nuts	1908 to 1938
Tanned hides I	1908 to 1924
Tanned hides II	1924 to 1929
Untanned hides I	1908 to 1924
Untanned hides II	1924 to 1938
Cottonseed	1924 to 1938
Import Price Index Components (27 Commodities)	
Coal	1900 to 1938
Rice	1900 to 1938
Kola nuts	1900 to 1938
Kerosene	1900 to 1938
Tobacco	1900 to 1938
Gin	1900 to 1924
Rum	1900 to 1911
Whiskey	1900 to 1924
Fish	1911 to 1924
Flour	1911 to 1938
Soap	1911 to 1938
Steel bars	1911 to 1915
Steel sheets	1911 to 1938
Unbleached piece goods I	1915 to 1924
Unbleached piece goods II	1924 to 1938
Bleached piece goods I	1915 to 1924
Bleached piece goods II	1924 to 1938
Printed piece goods I	1915 to 1924
Printed piece goods II	1924 to 1930
Dyed piece goods I	1915 to 1924
Dyed piece goods II	1924 to 1930
Colored piece goods I	1915 to 1924
Colored piece goods II	1924 to 1930
Printed, dyed, and colored piece goods	1930 to 1938
Bags and sacks	1924 to 1938
Cement	1924 to 1938
Petrol	1924 to 1938

Table A.35. Nigeria: Price Indexes (1913 = 100)

	Export price index				Import price index			
	Laspeyres	Paasche	Fisher Ideal	Paasche as a percentage of Laspeyres	Laspeyres	Paasche	Fisher Ideal	Paasche as a percentage of Laspeyres
1900	58.417	62.370	60.361	106.8	88.312	89.297	88.803	101.1
1901	60.935	64.631	62.756	106.1	91.280	92.050	91.664	100.8
1902	70.056	73.960	71.982	105.6	88.242	89.037	88.639	100.9
1903	63.174	66.640	64.884	105.5	87.444	87.094	87.269	99.6
1904	66.749	70.036	68.373	104.9	90.827	90.597	90.712	99.7
1905	70.458	73.446	71.936	104.2	100.200	91.761	95.888	91.6
1906	68.501	70.107	69.299	102.3	97.512	97.918	97.715	100.4
1907	79.933	80.785	80.358	101.1	103.268	105.480	104.368	102.1
1908	68.030	69.757	68.888	102.5	111.492	110.753	111.122	99.3
1909	70.691	72.113	71.398	102.0	105.821	103.094	104.448	97.4
1910	88.555	90.704	89.623	102.4	101.495	101.350	101.422	99.9
1911	87.148	87.558	87.353	100.5	94.336	95.119	94.727	100.8
1912	88.312	88.036	88.174	99.7	99.476	99.840	99.658	100.4
1913	100.000	100.000	100.000	100.0	100.000	100.000	100.000	100.0
1914	92.345	91.377	91.860	99.0	100.396	101.875	101.133	101.5
1915	77.054	76.446	76.749	99.2	135.476	131.161	133.301	96.8
1916	79.971	80.694	80.331	100.9	157.990	154.941	156.458	98.1
1917	99.119	96.959	98.033	97.8	187.366	186.821	187.094	99.7
1918	111.407	104.385	107.839	93.7	255.696	259.919	257.799	101.7
1919	142.816	133.088	137.867	93.2	324.771	307.913	316.229	94.8
1920	187.572	183.390	185.469	97.8	462.761	468.007	465.377	101.1
1921	114.962	108.647	111.760	94.5	405.391	416.408	410.863	102.7
1922	103.682	92.537	97.951	89.3	287.728	302.834	295.185	105.3
1923	107.729	96.328	101.869	89.4	257.732	280.980	269.105	109.0
1924	117.452	109.655	113.487	93.4	270.850	299.454	284.793	110.6
1925	121.783	113.156	117.390	92.9	275.033	301.252	287.844	109.5
1926	122.872	113.802	118.250	92.6	264.011	288.957	276.202	109.4

Table A.35. Nigeria: Price Indexes (1913 = 100)

	Export price index				Import price index			
	Laspeyres	*Paasche*	*Fisher Ideal*	*Paasche as a percentage of Laspeyres*	*Laspeyres*	*Paasche*	*Fisher Ideal*	*Paasche as a percentage of Laspeyres*
1927	120.923	113.636	117.223	94.0	238.047	257.903	247.776	108.3
1928	120.582	114.701	117.605	95.1	236.256	256.083	245.970	108.4
1929	113.190	106.086	109.581	93.7	231.581	253.109	242.106	109.3
1930	96.637	90.382	93.457	93.5	196.776	220.276	208.195	111.9
1931	59.791	55.976	57.852	93.6	163.935	181.113	172.310	110.5
1932	61.527	56.837	59.136	92.4	157.704	167.979	162.761	106.5
1933	58.222	51.964	55.004	89.3	157.794	159.509	155.090	105.8
1934	54.044	46.007	49.864	85.1	132.221	143.001	137.506	108.2
1935	64.029	55.687	59.712	87.0	138.250	150.915	144.443	109.2
1936	71.679	65.110	68.316	90.8	139.666	152.934	146.150	109.5
1937	83.754	78.089	80.872	93.2	156.756	173.244	164.794	110.5
1938	52.912	47.177	49.962	89.2	155.042	164.632	159.765	106.2
1939	51.875	46.786	49.265	90.2	153.205	161.940	157.512	105.7
1940	58.920	53.798	56.301	91.3	197.903	213.111	205.366	107.7
1941	58.619	52.970	55.723	90.4	215.508	227.178	221.266	105.4
1942	61.892	57.405	59.606	92.8	256.692	273.947	265.179	106.7
1943	70.682	64.601	67.573	91.4	324.646	351.542	337.826	108.3
1944	82.771	75.816	79.217	91.6	352.999	387.985	370.079	109.9
1945	92.582	83.597	87.975	90.3	345.104	371.569	358.092	107.7
1946	115.124	104.125	109.487	90.4	388.847	404.788	396.737	104.1
1947	211.180	182.982	196.576	86.6	480.908	475.790	478.342	98.9
1948	321.257	273.091	296.197	85.0	494.622	479.856	487.183	97.0

Table A.36. Philippines: Trade Variables (Millions of pesos)

	1913 prices		Current prices		
	Real Exports X^R	Real Imports M^R	Exports X	Imports M	Trade Balance X - M
1902	70.29	70.30	57.34	66.68	-9.34
1903	82.20	68.53	64.79	67.62	-2.83
1904	69.66	61.19	58.30	59.16	-0.86
1905	76.34	64.60	66.91	60.10	6.81
1906	69.90	56.92	65.29	52.81	12.48
1907	75.86	62.09	66.20	60.91	5.29
1908	87.96	60.48	65.20	58.37	6.83
1909	102.67	60.51	69.85	62.17	7.68
1910	104.66	94.05	81.26	99.44	-18.18
1911	116.92	95.02	89.67	96.05	-6.37
1912	127.98	106.54	109.85	123.34	-13.49
1913	95.55	106.63	95.55	106.63	-11.08
1914	108.37	98.90	97.38	97.18	0.20
1915	125.16	105.08	107.63	93.62	9.00
1916	135.15	87.65	139.87	90.99	48.88
1917	151.36	108.91	191.21	131.59	59.61
1918	193.33	128.10	270.39	197.20	73.19
1919	173.69	134.55	226.24	237.73	-11.49
1920	153.26	151.45	302.25	298.88	3.37
1921	178.70	148.02	176.23	231.68	-55.45
1922	233.55	126.90	191.17	160.40	30.77
1923	229.75	148.82	241.51	175.00	66.51
1924	235.12	186.07	270.69	216.02	54.67
1925	261.33	204.07	297.75	239.47	58.29
1926	249.83	214.40	273.77	238.60	35.17
1927	289.79	218.13	311.15	231.70	79.44
1928	318.07	250.21	310.11	269.31	40.80
1929	359.85	287.17	328.89	294.32	34.57
1930	336.05	250.55	266.33	246.19	20.15
1931	317.73	244.65	207.94	198.36	9.59
1932	325.89	224.05	190.68	158.79	31.89
1933	380.77	207.86	211.54	134.72	76.82
1934	444.58	230.01	220.81	167.21	53.59
1935	347.84	235.83	188.49	171.05	17.44
1936	397.73	270.19	272.90	202.25	70.64
1937	394.23	278.34	302.53	218.05	84.48
1938	431.45	319.58	231.59	265.21	-33.62

Table A.37. Philippines: Price Variables (1913 = 100)

	Export Price Px	Import Price Pm	Terms of Trade P_T
1902	81.587	94.855	86.012
1903	78.825	98.672	79.885
1904	83.692	96.680	86.565
1905	87.641	93.029	94.208
1906	93.403	92.780	100.671
1907	87.260	98.091	88.958
1908	74.125	96.514	76.802
1909	68.034	102.739	66.221
1910	77.642	105.726	73.437
1911	76.699	101.079	75.880
1912	85.828	115.768	74.138
1913	100.000	100.000	100.000
1914	89.860	98.257	91.454
1915	85.989	93.859	91.616
1916	103.498	103.817	99.692
1917	126.329	120.830	104.551
1918	139.858	153.942	90.851
1919	130.251	176.680	73.721
1920	197.210	197.344	99.932
1921	98.618	156.514	63.009
1922	81.853	126.390	64.762
1923	105.115	117.593	89.388
1924	115.127	116.100	99.163
1925	113.938	117.344	97.097
1926	109.584	111.286	98.470
1927	107.370	106.224	101.079
1928	97.498	107.635	90.583
1929	91.398	102.490	89.178
1930	79.253	98.257	80.659
1931	65.447	81.079	80.720
1932	58.510	70.871	82.558
1933	55.556	64.813	85.716
1934	49.666	72.697	68.319
1935	54.189	72.531	74.712
1936	68.614	74.855	91.663
1937	76.741	78.340	97.958
1938	53.677	82.988	64.681

Table A.38. Philippines: Government Variables (Millions of pesos)

	Current prices		1913 prices	
	Government revenues R *(1)*	*Government expenditures* G *(2)*	*Real govt. expenditures* G^R *(3)*	*Acc. real govt. exp.* $\Sigma_{i=1}^{\infty} G^R_{t-i}$ *(4)*
1902	21.32	26.27	27.69	360.14
1903	27.37	30.31	30.71	390.85
1904	30.70	26.26	27.16	418.01
1905	33.26	34.94	37.55	455.57
1906	36.27	32.58	35.11	490.68
1907	35.40	33.18	33.83	524.51
1908	38.93	36.17	37.48	561.99
1909	42.42	43.75	42.58	604.57
1910	48.35	47.00	44.45	649.02
1911	56.25	53.37	52.80	701.82
1912	61.17	58.87	50.86	752.67
1913	58.96	61.87	61.87	814.55
1914	53.25	55.78	56.77	871.32
1915	72.88	70.47	75.08	946.40
1916	78.17	73.65	70.94	1017.33
1917	83.01	70.07	57.99	1075.33
1918	98.39	91.83	59.65	1134.98
1919	110.32	120.24	68.06	1203.04
1920	134.49	120.31	60.96	1264.00
1921	158.96	158.43	101.22	1365.22
1922	111.80	113.68	89.94	1455.17
1923	110.62	132.86	112.98	1568.15
1924	122.14	131.60	113.35	1681.51
1925	131.49	124.38	105.99	1787.50
1926	129.84	139.72	125.55	1913.05
1927	132.77	129.40	121.82	2034.87
1928	147.67	140.28	130.33	2165.20
1929	149.28	141.76	138.31	2303.51
1930	148.47	157.26	160.05	2463.56
1931	126.96	139.47	172.01	2635.58
1932	120.11	124.84	176.16	2811.73
1933	113.07	115.20	177.75	2989.48
1934	119.86	112.19	154.33	3143.81
1935	130.31	118.53	163.43	3307.24
1936	154.82	136.50	182.35	3489.59
1937	170.80	156.65	199.97	3689.55
1938	163.63	173.67	209.28	3898.83

Table A.39. Philippines: Price Index Components

Export Price Index Components
(6 Commodities)

Leaf tobacco	1902 to 1938
Copra	1902 to 1938
Sugar	1902 to 1938
Cigars	1902 to 1938
Abaca	1902 to 1938
Coconut oil	1914 to 1938

Table A.40. Philippines: Export Price Index (1913 = 100)

	Export price index			
	Laspeyres	*Paasche*	*Fisher Ideal*	*Paasche as a percentage of Laspeyres*
1902	79.402	81.587	80.487	102.8
1903	76.161	78.825	77.481	103.5
1904	81.241	83.692	82.458	103.0
1905	84.719	87.641	86.168	103.4
1906	92.389	93.403	92.894	101.1
1907	86.645	87.260	86.952	100.7
1908	69.766	74.126	71.913	106.2
1909	64.604	68.034	66.297	105.3
1910	73.484	77.642	75.535	105.7
1911	71.049	76.699	73.820	108.0
1912	81.777	85.828	83.778	105.0
1913	100.000	100.000	100.000	100.0
1914	91.220	89.860	90.538	98.5
1915	89.025	85.990	87.494	96.6
1916	104.638	103.498	104.067	98.9
1917	130.190	126.330	128.246	97.0
1918	145.135	139.859	142.472	96.4
1919	158.644	130.251	143.748	82.1
1920	243.264	197.211	219.030	81.1
1921	104.903	98.618	101.712	94.0
1922	88.844	81.853	85.277	92.1
1923	118.070	105.115	111.404	89.0
1924	124.841	115.128	119.886	92.2
1925	128.083	113.939	120.804	89.0
1926	120.772	109.585	115.042	90.7
1927	119.297	107.371	113.177	90.0
1928	106.399	97.499	101.852	91.6
1929	100.541	91.399	95.861	90.9
1930	86.857	79.253	82.968	91.2
1931	69.614	65.447	67.498	94.0
1932	56.796	58.510	57.646	103.0
1933	55.633	55.556	55.594	99.9
1934	50.914	49.666	50.286	97.6
1935	62.283	54.190	58.096	87.0
1936	74.675	68.614	71.580	91.9
1937	84.865	76.741	80.701	90.4
1938	59.139	53.677	56.342	90.8

Table A.41. Taiwan: Trade Variables (Millions of yen)

	1913 prices		Current prices		
	Real Exports X^R	Real Imports M^R	Exports X	Imports M	Trade Balance X - M
1900	26.84	25.90	14.93	22.01	-7.08
1901	29.53	26.92	15.58	21.59	-6.01
1902	35.48	27.22	21.13	19.34	1.80
1903	34.43	28.24	20.72	22.20	-1.49
1904	36.70	24.64	22.72	22.75	-0.03
1905	38.62	24.33	24.29	24.45	-0.16
1906	44.93	25.01	28.04	28.37	-0.33
1907	40.97	26.27	27.38	30.97	-3.60
1908	49.67	33.43	33.72	38.00	-4.28
1909	66.22	33.99	48.00	36.60	11.40
1910	75.44	46.58	59.96	48.92	11.04
1911	90.26	57.22	64.82	53.29	11.52
1912	74.12	64.91	62.79	62.63	0.16
1913	53.39	60.86	53.39	60.86	-7.47
1914	68.87	55.02	58.72	52.91	5.81
1915	99.18	56.94	75.62	53.41	22.21
1916	134.13	56.88	112.35	65.92	46.43
1917	162.04	60.53	145.80	88.89	56.92
1918	137.82	55.50	139.36	104.22	35.14
1919	131.63	72.89	177.83	154.70	23.13
1920	90.13	77.57	216.20	172.44	43.77
1921	105.75	84.00	152.44	133.95	18.49
1922	138.48	76.91	157.86	119.09	38.77
1923	149.47	72.63	198.59	110.13	88.47
1924	184.16	82.60	253.67	133.03	120.65
1925	195.22	107.20	263.21	186.39	76.82
1926	208.42	117.22	251.42	183.41	68.01
1927	207.24	132.23	246.68	186.95	59.73
1928	230.27	137.40	248.42	190.65	57.76
1929	266.12	147.65	271.89	204.91	66.98
1930	250.50	146.69	241.44	168.26	73.18
1931	288.93	161.26	220.67	145.62	75.05
1932	316.73	157.87	240.73	164.50	76.23
1933	274.67	138.12	248.41	165.39	83.02
1934	329.90	179.69	305.93	215.02	90.91
1935	372.71	190.16	350.74	263.11	87.64
1936	364.40	210.54	387.95	292.69	95.26

Table A.42. Taiwan: Price Variables (1913 = 100)

	Export Price Px	Import Price Pm	Terms of Trade P_T
1900	55.649	84.994	65.474
1901	52.768	80.216	65.783
1902	59.565	71.042	83.844
1903	60.164	78.639	76.506
1904	61.906	92.327	67.051
1905	62.897	100.497	62.586
1906	62.401	113.463	54.997
1907	66.821	117.902	56.675
1908	67.892	113.677	59.724
1909	72.480	107.676	67.313
1910	79.486	105.022	75.685
1911	71.815	93.148	77.097
1912	84.722	96.485	87.809
1913	100.000	100.000	100.000
1914	85.262	96.174	88.654
1915	76.249	93.795	81.293
1916	83.758	115.893	72.272
1917	89.982	146.845	61.277
1918	101.118	187.793	53.845
1919	135.101	212.232	63.657
1920	239.884	222.303	107.908
1921	144.145	159.467	90.392
1922	113.998	154.847	73.620
1923	132.867	151.634	87.623
1924	137.747	161.046	85.533
1925	134.833	173.876	77.545
1926	120.632	156.462	77.100
1927	119.029	141.377	84.193
1928	107.882	138.757	77.749
1929	102.169	138.779	73.620
1930	96.384	114.705	84.028
1931	76.377	90.303	84.578
1932	76.004	104.195	72.944
1933	90.441	119.741	75.530
1934	92.735	119.659	77.499
1935	94.107	138.363	68.015
1936	106.461	139.015	76.582

Table A.43. Taiwan: Government Variables

	Current prices		1913 prices	
	Government revenues R (1)	Government expenditures G (2)	Real govt. expenditures G^R (3)	Acc. real govt. exp. $\Sigma_{i=1}^{\infty} G_{t-i}^R$ (4)
1900	14.40	14.80	17.41	220.49
1901	12.90	13.40	16.70	237.19
1902	13.90	13.30	18.72	255.91
1903	12.50	12.70	16.15	272.06
1904	14.10	11.60	12.56	284.63
1905	12.30	10.70	10.65	295.27
1906	13.70	13.30	11.72	307.00
1907	17.20	15.10	12.81	319.80
1908	17.40	18.50	16.27	336.08
1909	22.60	18.60	17.27	353.35
1910	30.60	26.60	25.33	378.68
1911	29.40	29.30	31.46	410.13
1912	30.00	31.20	32.34	442.47
1913	25.10	28.40	28.40	470.87
1914	27.70	31.80	33.07	503.94
1915	23.10	21.20	22.60	526.54
1916	27.90	22.20	19.16	545.69
1917	30.70	24.40	16.62	562.31
1918	35.60	29.70	15.82	578.13
1919	40.90	38.30	18.05	596.17
1920	47.50	51.50	23.17	619.34
1921	50.80	58.20	36.50	655.83
1922	52.70	53.10	34.29	690.13
1923	50.70	44.30	29.22	719.34
1924	45.60	42.30	26.27	745.61
1925	46.90	41.80	24.04	769.65
1926	56.70	48.70	31.13	800.77
1927	55.00	57.70	40.81	841.59
1928	63.00	61.70	44.47	886.05
1929	61.50	71.90	51.81	937.86
1930	55.30	63.40	55.27	993.13
1931	53.10	55.70	61.68	1054.81
1932	62.50	56.30	54.03	1108.85
1933	62.40	56.80	47.44	1156.28
1934	60.30	59.40	49.64	1205.92
1935	68.20	65.10	47.05	1252.97
1936	80.02	71.02	51.09	1304.06

Table A.44. Taiwan: Price Index Components

Commodity	Years Included in Index
Export Price Index Components (9 Commodities)	
Rice and paddy	1900 to 1938
Fresh bananas	1907 to 1938
Oolong tea	1900 to 1938
Poochang tea	1900 to 1938
Sugar	1900 to 1938
Salt	1900 to 1938
Canned pineapples	1907 to 1938
Camphor	1900 to 1938
Camphor oil	1900 to 1938
Import Price Index Components (21 Commodities)	
Swine	1906 to 1938
Soya beans	1911 to 1938
Wheat flour	1906 to 1938
Soy sauce	1906 to 1938
Fish	1907 to 1938
Beer	1906 to 1938
Cigarettes and cigars	1907 to 1938
Kerosene oil	1906 to 1936
Matches	1906 to 1938
Gunny, hemp, and jute	1906 to 1938
Cement	1906 to 1938
Iron bars and rods	1907 to 1936
Iron rails	1906 to 1936
Iron pipes and tubes	1911 to 1936
Other iron products	1907 to 1936
Copper	1907 to 1936
Timber	1906 to 1938
Railroad sleepers	1906 to 1938
Soy bean oil cakes	1906 to 1938
Crude ammonium sulphate	1922 to 1936
Fertilizer	1922 to 1936

Table A.45. Taiwan: Price Indexes (1913 = 100)

	Export price index				Import price index			
	Laspeyres	Paasche	Fisher Ideal	Paasche as a percentage of Laspeyres	Laspeyres	Paasche	Fisher Ideal	Paasche as a percentage of Laspeyres
1900	61.272	55.649	58.393	90.8				
1901	58.590	52.768	55.603	90.1				
1902	67.025	59.565	63.185	88.9				
1903	65.592	60.164	62.820	91.7				
1904	67.651	61.906	64.715	91.5				
1905	68.779	62.897	65.772	91.4				
1906	67.124	62.401	64.719	93.0	97.349	113.464	105.098	116.6
1907	72.052	66.821	69.387	92.7	99.834	117.904	108.493	118.1
1908	74.092	67.892	70.924	91.6	98.293	113.677	105.706	115.7
1909	75.923	72.480	74.182	95.5	95.141	107.676	101.215	113.2
1910	78.450	79.486	78.966	101.3	94.497	105.023	99.621	111.1
1911	72.632	71.815	72.223	98.9	86.692	93.148	89.862	107.4
1912	83.869	84.722	84.295	101.0	95.083	96.485	95.782	101.5
1913	100.000	100.000	100.000	100.0	100.000	100.000	100.000	100.0
1914	84.674	85.262	84.968	100.7	97.192	96.174	96.682	99.0
1915	75.418	76.249	75.832	101.1	95.522	93.795	94.654	98.2
1916	82.295	83.758	83.023	101.8	120.057	115.894	117.957	96.5
1917	90.585	89.982	90.283	99.3	157.238	146.846	151.953	93.4
1918	101.782	101.118	101.449	99.3	200.434	187.794	194.011	93.7
1919	133.132	135.101	134.113	101.5	215.689	212.232	213.954	98.4
1920	227.449	239.884	233.584	105.5	229.752	222.304	225.997	96.8
1921	142.632	144.146	143.387	101.1	169.404	159.468	164.361	94.1
1922	117.261	113.999	115.618	97.2	161.139	154.847	157.961	96.1
1923	132.467	132.867	132.666	100.3	158.186	151.635	154.876	95.9
1924	136.696	137.747	137.221	100.8	166.077	161.046	163.542	97.0
1925	132.143	134.834	133.481	102.0	178.354	173.876	176.101	97.5
1926	118.822	120.632	119.724	101.5	160.745	156.462	158.589	97.3
1927	117.293	119.029	118.158	101.5	150.306	141.377	145.773	94.1
1928	108.065	107.882	107.974	99.8	149.792	138.758	144.169	92.6
1929	104.053	102.170	103.107	98.2	149.336	138.779	143.961	92.9
1930	98.184	96.384	97.280	98.2	124.109	114.705	119.314	92.4
1931	78.843	76.378	77.601	96.9	99.673	90.304	94.873	90.6
1932	77.622	76.004	76.809	97.9	114.528	104.196	109.240	91.0
1933	96.160	90.441	93.257	94.1	129.845	119.741	124.691	92.2
1934	96.416	92.736	94.558	96.2	128.630	119.660	124.064	93.0
1935	101.121	94.107	97.551	93.1	151.590	138.363	144.826	91.3
1936	113.866	106.462	110.101	93.5	155.033	139.016	146.806	89.7

Table A.46. Thailand: Trade Variables (Millions of baht)

	1913 prices		Current prices		
	Real Exports X^R	Real Imports M^R	Exports X	Imports M	Trade Balance X – M
1900	50.13	33.11	51.70	37.71	13.99
1901	75.47	39.97	74.76	43.48	31.28
1902	85.92	45.96	86.14	47.65	38.49
1903	65.42	48.91	73.34	51.33	22.01
1904	90.69	63.06	99.88	66.99	32.89
1905	95.71	56.67	106.57	61.05	45.52
1906	95.62	67.56	105.56	66.78	38.78
1907	94.64	70.86	105.81	66.51	39.30
1908	105.20	75.25	107.57	66.82	40.75
1909	108.24	68.65	109.59	62.61	46.98
1910	119.27	65.37	119.03	61.92	57.11
1911	82.92	69.20	98.30	68.21	30.09
1912	77.93	70.50	99.78	72.39	27.39
1913	131.87	83.62	131.87	83.62	48.25
1914	124.09	77.85	117.02	71.76	45.26
1915	134.38	76.14	125.53	71.75	53.78
1916	140.82	73.28	141.16	84.36	56.80
1917	137.49	66.65	151.48	93.39	58.09
1918	109.46	54.95	194.30	93.56	95.74
1919	79.85	67.26	198.26	123.28	74.98
1920	70.74	85.49	89.79	152.44	-62.65
1921	150.24	104.24	183.47	134.20	49.27
1922	149.02	112.43	169.86	133.30	36.56
1923	161.47	116.18	200.29	142.02	58.27
1924	147.63	125.05	202.48	158.97	43.51
1925	169.59	138.50	244.09	168.79	75.30
1926	161.70	157.76	238.56	179.18	59.38
1927	201.42	170.62	276.06	188.68	87.38
1928	188.18	164.52	252.43	180.86	71.57
1929	164.27	180.18	219.59	198.45	21.14
1930	148.93	158.77	159.88	149.46	10.42
1931	173.85	122.57	116.91	97.18	19.73
1932	198.18	127.25	129.23	87.69	41.54
1933	204.80	132.64	129.79	92.42	37.37
1934	245.82	148.80	161.04	101.35	59.69
1935	194.10	171.05	149.31	108.55	40.76
1936	221.66	179.72	179.38	109.08	70.30
1937	189.66	156.64	165.93	111.12	54.81
1938	222.79	188.70	176.76	127.22	49.54

Table A.47. Thailand: Price Variables

	1913 = 100			Exchange rate (baht per Pound) π
	Export price Px	*Import price* Pm	*Terms of trade* P_T	
1900	103.137	113.908	90.544	16.750
1901	99.056	108.788	91.054	17.300
1902	100.260	103.669	96.711	19.300
1903	112.098	104.949	106.812	19.000
1904	110.134	106.229	103.676	17.800
1905	111.344	107.729	103.356	17.150
1906	110.394	98.844	111.685	15.600
1907	111.807	93.859	119.122	13.700
1908	102.250	88.799	115.147	13.000
1909	101.248	91.207	111.009	13.000
1910	99.797	94.720	105.360	13.000
1911	118.544	98.564	120.271	13.000
1912	128.037	102.679	124.697	13.000
1913	100.000	100.000	100.000	13.000
1914	94.303	92.173	102.310	13.000
1915	93.415	94.235	99.130	13.000
1916	100.241	115.120	87.075	13.000
1917	110.172	140.122	78.626	13.000
1918	177.514	179.348	98.978	13.000
1919	248.298	183.292	135.466	9.540
1920	126.934	178.323	71.182	9.540
1921	122.118	128.743	94.854	9.540
1922	113.987	118.566	96.138	11.000
1923	124.038	122.242	101.469	11.000
1924	137.157	127.126	107.891	11.000
1925	143.932	121.867	118.106	11.000
1926	147.531	113.578	129.894	11.000
1927	137.056	110.587	123.935	11.000
1928	134.140	109.934	122.019	11.000
1929	133.678	110.137	121.374	11.000
1930	107.351	94.139	114.035	11.000
1931	67.248	79.285	84.818	10.130
1932	65.207	68.913	94.622	9.950
1933	63.375	69.675	90.959	11.000
1934	65.511	68.110	96.184	11.000
1935	76.925	63.460	121.218	11.000
1936	80.924	60.694	133.331	11.000
1937	87.490	70.939	123.331	11.000
1938	79.340	67.420	117.680	11.000

316   *Appendix*

Table A.48. Thailand: Government Variables (Millions of baht)

| | Current prices | | 1913 prices | |
	Government revenues R (1)	Government expenditures G (2)	Real govt. expenditures G^R (3)	Acc. real govt. exp. $\Sigma_{i=1}^{\infty} G^R_{t-i}$ (4)
1900	35.61	19.54	17.15	128.74
1901	36.16	24.49	22.51	151.25
1902	39.15	26.79	25.84	177.09
1903	43.46	30.83	29.38	206.47
1904	46.05	38.47	36.21	242.68
1905	50.46	39.49	36.66	279.34
1906	55.52	38.92	39.38	318.72
1907	54.28	44.58	47.50	366.22
1908	58.92	44.11	49.67	415.89
1909	60.69	43.48	47.67	463.56
1910	61.36	42.14	44.49	508.05
1911	59.46	43.95	44.59	552.64
1912	64.78	53.07	51.69	604.33
1913	72.09	54.72	54.72	659.05
1914	71.15	56.79	61.61	720.66
1915	74.36	58.55	62.13	782.79
1916	79.50	57.63	50.06	832.85
1917	82.46	58.53	41.77	874.62
1918	87.81	75.01	41.82	916.44
1919	90.68	72.74	39.69	956.13
1920	80.34	75.47	42.32	998.45
1921	79.63	71.49	55.53	1053.98
1922	78.08	68.12	57.45	1111.43
1923	81.60	68.19	55.78	1167.21
1924	85.18	75.76	59.59	1226.80
1925	92.71	82.08	67.35	1294.15
1926	100.59	92.39	81.34	1375.49
1927	117.44	103.97	94.02	1469.51
1928	106.96	92.70	84.32	1553.83
1929	108.12	93.10	84.53	1638.36
1930	96.32	85.75	91.09	1729.45
1931	78.95	77.24	97.42	1826.87
1932	79.65	66.12	95.95	1922.82
1933	83.73	70.71	101.49	2024.31
1934	94.00	74.26	109.03	2133.34
1935	94.66	89.56	141.13	2274.47
1936	119.49	108.69	179.08	2453.55
1937	109.41	123.58	174.21	2627.76
1938	118.23	130.53	193.61	2821.37

Table A.49. Thailand: Price Index Components

Commodity	Years Included in Index
Export Price Index Components (5 Commodities)	
Rice	1896 to 1938
Rubber	1906 to 1938
Teak	1899 to 1938
Sticklac	1896 to 1938
Tin	1907 to 1938
Import Price Index Components (28 Commodities)	
Yarn	1905 to 1938
Sugar	1905 to 1938
Tea	1907 to 1938
Fish	1914 to 1938
Dried vegetables	1914 to 1938
Fruits	1914 to 1938
Spices	1914 to 1926
Matting	1914 to 1938
Medicines	1914 to 1938
Cigarettes	1914 to 1938
Gold leaf	1905 to 1929
Gunny bags	1905 to 1938
Petroleum oil	1905 to 1914
Opium	1905 to 1929
Unprinted paper	1914 to 1938
China and earthenware	1914 to 1938
Iron and steel bars	1924 to 1938
Motor cars	1914 to 1926
Fireworks	1914 to 1938
Matches	1914 to 1929
Spirits	1905 to 1938
Mineral oil	1924 to 1938
Oil, kerosene, etc.	1914 to 1924
Wood	1914 to 1924
Tobacco and cigars	1914 to 1924
Canned milk	1914 to 1938
Cotton manufactures	1905 to 1938
Coal and charcoal	1926 to 1938

Table A.50. Thailand: Price Indexes (1913 = 100)

	Export price index			
	Laspeyres	*Paasche*	*Fisher Ideal*	*Paasche as a percentage of Laspeyres*
1896	86.421	85.350	85.883	98.8
1897	77.164	76.232	76.696	98.8
1898	97.637	96.444	97.039	98.8
1899	98.668	97.459	98.062	98.8
1900	104.423	103.135	103.777	98.8
1901	99.913	99.054	99.483	99.1
1902	101.572	100.262	100.915	98.7
1903	113.288	112.099	112.692	99.0
1904	111.705	110.133	110.916	98.6
1905	112.402	111.345	111.872	99.1
1906	111.674	110.393	111.032	98.9
1907	113.153	111.809	112.479	98.8
1908	103.757	102.253	103.002	98.5
1909	101.341	101.247	101.294	99.9
1910	99.995	99.801	99.898	99.8
1911	118.412	118.544	118.478	100.1
1912	126.485	128.040	127.260	101.2
1913	100.000	100.000	100.000	100.0
1914	94.279	94.305	94.292	100.0
1915	93.402	93.418	93.410	100.0
1916	100.538	100.241	100.389	99.7
1917	109.006	110.171	109.587	101.1
1918	180.068	177.520	178.789	98.6
1919	296.041	248.300	271.121	83.9
1920	124.348	126.936	125.635	102.1
1921	120.926	122.122	121.522	101.0
1922	113.774	113.988	113.881	100.2
1923	124.285	124.041	124.163	99.8
1924	138.182	137.156	137.668	99.3
1925	144.575	143.933	144.253	99.6
1926	148.502	147.531	148.015	99.3
1927	138.592	137.059	137.823	98.9
1928	135.003	134.144	134.573	99.4
1929	136.930	133.681	135.296	97.6
1930	110.383	107.350	108.856	97.3
1931	68.018	67.247	67.631	98.9
1932	65.503	65.208	65.355	99.5
1933	66.115	63.376	64.731	95.9
1934	67.424	65.511	66.460	97.2
1935	78.165	76.925	77.542	98.4
1936	80.185	80.923	80.553	100.9
1937	88.256	87.488	87.871	99.1
1938	79.400	79.341	79.370	99.9

Import price index			
Laspeyres	Paasche	Fisher Ideal	Paasche as a percentage of Laspeyres
107.955	107.729	107.842	99.8
99.160	98.844	99.002	99.7
94.258	93.859	94.058	99.6
89.317	88.799	89.058	99.4
91.254	91.207	91.230	99.9
95.372	94.720	95.045	99.3
95.844	98.564	97.195	102.8
100.167	102.679	101.415	102.5
100.000	100.000	100.000	100.0
91.834	92.173	92.003	100.4
94.293	94.235	94.264	99.9
116.093	115.120	115.605	99.2
141.319	140.122	140.719	99.2
190.152	179.348	184.671	94.3
211.764	183.292	197.015	86.6
197.328	178.323	187.585	90.4
138.856	128.742	133.704	92.7
127.331	118.566	122.870	93.1
135.158	122.241	128.538	90.4
142.140	127.126	134.423	89.4
136.657	121.867	129.050	89.2
128.385	113.578	120.755	88.5
125.536	110.587	117.825	88.1
124.875	109.934	117.167	88.0
124.788	110.137	117.233	88.3
107.162	94.139	100.440	87.8
89.130	79.285	84.063	89.0
79.844	68.913	74.177	86.3
80.675	69.675	74.974	86.4
79.597	68.110	73.629	85.6
76.403	63.460	69.632	83.1
73.217	60.694	66.662	82.9
83.881	70.939	77.139	84.6
84.437	67.420	75.450	79.8

Table A.51. United Kingdom: Variables

	Real net national income (millions of 1913-14 pounds) Y_{UK}^R	Real net national income deflator (1913-14 = 1.0) P_{UK}	Index of industrial production excluding building (1913 = 100) Q_{UK}	Price index of raw Materials (1913 = 100) P_{UK}^R
1884	1202	0.950	58.5	80.2
1885	1235	0.910	56.7	76.9
1886	1281	0.890	55.5	73.6
1887	1314	0.890	58.2	73.6
1888	1390	0.900	62.5	75.8
1889	1456	0.920	66.6	76.9
1890	1544	0.910	66.2	78.0
1891	1513	0.920	66.5	74.7
1892	1536	0.890	63.5	71.4
1893	1501	0.890	61.9	71.4
1894	1646	0.840	65.8	65.9
1895	1746	0.830	68.0	65.9
1896	1780	0.830	71.5	65.9
1897	1841	0.830	72.0	64.8
1898	1894	0.850	74.6	67.0
1899	1912	0.880	78.1	76.9
1900	1881	0.940	77.9	87.9
1901	1949	0.890	76.6	79.1
1902	1967	0.890	78.0	78.0
1903	1929	0.900	78.0	79.1
1904	1949	0.900	77.6	79.1
1905	2013	0.910	82.8	82.4
1906	2076	0.940	86.0	91.2
1907	2113	0.970	87.7	94.5
1908	2109	0.920	85.1	81.3
1909	2176	0.913	85.6	82.4
1910	2165	0.960	87.8	89.0
1911	2221	0.970	91.6	91.2
1912	2166	1.010	93.3	96.7
1913	2371	1.010	100.0	100.0
1914	2317	0.990	93.9	96.7
1915	2153	1.218	97.1	118.7
1916	2140	1.455	92.4	153.8
1917	2113	1.752	87.2	196.7
1918	2223	2.010	84.4	226.4
1919	2445	2.284	92.3	244.0
1920	2234	2.590	99.8	290.1
1921	1921	2.380	77.8	168.1
1922	1952	2.030	92.6	145.1
1923	1934	2.042	99.9	147.3
1924	2120	1.900	108.0	160.4
1925	2153	1.900	109.8	157.1
1926	2121	1.900	101.4	144.0
1927	2320	1.840	117.6	141.8
1928	2324	1.840	116.9	136.3
1929	2350	1.830	122.3	130.8
1930	2290	1.780	117.7	106.6
1931	2236	1.690	110.0	90.1
1932	2218	1.660	110.1	89.0
1933	2374	1.620	116.3	91.2
1934	2471	1.620	127.4	93.4
1935	2616	1.620	138.1	98.9
1936	2759	1.640	150.2	103.3
1937	2816	1.690	159.5	120.9
1938	2759	1.746	155.6	105.5

Table A.52. United States: Variables

	Real GNP (millions of 1929 dollars) Y_{US}^R	GNP price deflator (1929 = 1.0) P_{US}	Index of manu- facturing output (1929 = 100) Q_{US}	Import price index (1913 = 100) P_{US}^{mm}	Crude materials import price index (1913 = 100) P_{US}^m	Motor vehicle factory sales CAR
1889	24391	0.5119	18.3	83.0	86.0	24250
1890	26196	0.5012	19.7	82.2	85.0	24250
1891	27365	0.4944	20.2	77.6	87.9	24250
1892	30010	0.4756	21.9	74.9	81.9	24250
1893	28569	0.4848	19.4	75.6	80.2	24250
1894	27756	0.4546	18.8	68.5	70.5	24250
1895	31082	0.4481	22.4	70.0	71.8	24250
1896	30444	0.4367	20.4	71.0	71.0	24250
1897	33327	0.4386	22.0	71.4	69.1	24250
1898	34068	0.4517.	25.1	76.2	68.4	24250
1899	37172	0.4669	27.5	83.2	72.3	24250
1900	38197	0.4891	27.7	87.7	81.0	24250
1901	42587	0.4853	30.9	82.0	79.4	24250
1902	43004	0.5012	35.5	83.0	81.4	24250
1903	45123	0.5067	35.4	88.5	86.6	24250
1904	44559	0.5128	34.2	89.2	86.9	24250
1905	47870	0.5247	39.0	93.5	83.7	24250
1906	53420	0.5376	41.6	100.7	89.9	33200
1907	54277	0.5602	42.1	106.2	95.2	43000
1908	49790	0.5563	33.7	89.7	90.1	63500
1909	55893	0.5755	43.4	95.3	94.3	123900
1910	56499	0.5905	45.1	104.8	102.1	187000
1911	58312	0.5877	42.7	99.9	93.5	210000
1912	61058	0.6111	51.3	100.4	95.5	378000
1913	63475	0.6155	53.8	100.0	100.0	485000
1914	58636	0.6212	51.1	92.8	97.7	573039
1915	60424	0.6411	59.9	89.7	105.1	969930
1916	68870	0.7226	71.2	115.1	135.5	1617708
1917	67264	0.8912	70.6	139.8	177.0	1873949
1918	73361	1.0384	69.8	147.3	206.1	1170686
1919	74158	1.0640	61.0	161.6	215.7	1876356
1920	73313	1.2120	66.0	179.1	232.5	2227349
1921	71583	1.0329	53.5	99.8	157.5	1616119
1922	75788	0.9763	68.1	106.2	143.8	2544176
1923	85819	1.0034	76.9	123.2	154.2	4034012
1924	88361	0.9909	73.4	119.3	151.1	3602540
1925	90529	1.0086	81.9	147.1	153.2	4265830
1926	96405	1.0134	86.2	145.1	140.8	4300934
1927	97337	0.9891	87.1	121.9	131.6	3401326
1928	98503	0.9966	90.1	110.9	134.7	4358759
1929	104436	1.0000	100.0	103.2	133.6	5337087
1930	95130	0.9576	85.6	81.9	119.2	3362820
1931	89454	0.8496	72.0	55.5	91.5	2380426
1932	76403	0.7657	53.8	39.3	79.2	1331860
1933	74178	0.7549	62.8	40.6	82.2	1889817
1934	80781	0.8046	69.1	48.4	96.6	2737070
1935	91435	0.7929	82.8	51.6	98.7	3971241
1936	100907	0.8196	96.8	60.6	100.7	4461462
1937	109112	0.8322	103.3	72.2	106.9	4820219
1938	103232	0.8234	80.9	60.6	99.7	2508407

Table A.53. Japan: Variables

	Real GNP (millions of 1934–36 yen) Y_{JP}^R	GNP price deflator (1934–36 = 100) P_{JP}
1902	6983.8	42.04
1903	7289.3	44.08
1904	7190.0	44.62
1905	7030.7	47.41
1906	6732.1	61.81
1907	6725.9	68.29
1908	7429.2	62.56
1909	7592.4	58.32
1910	8094.4	56.10
1911	8167.4	63.55
1912	8181.0	70.31
1913	8221.6	71.80
1914	8323.7	63.64
1915	8842.9	63.88
1916	9574.9	72.43
1917	10345.7	90.58
1918	11067.6	115.21
1919	11799.6	146.95
1920	11840.9	135.61
1921	12641.0	120.39
1922	12491.0	120.73
1923	11833.0	129.38
1924	13193.1	120.64
1925	12918.6	125.93
1926	13087.0	123.32
1927	13505.8	123.10
1928	14345.9	117.73
1929	14361.8	115.19
1930	14478.8	99.09
1931	14663.9	90.90
1932	15416.1	94.02
1933	16721.2	95.85
1934	18465.0	94.70
1935	19432.4	96.01
1936	19870.2	102.05

Sources

ARTICLES

1. Adelman, Irma, and Adelman, Frank L. "The Dynamic Properties of the Klein-Goldberger Model." *Econometrica* 27 (October 1959): 597–625.

2. Bateman, Muriel I. "Aggregate and Regional Supply Functions for Ghanian Cocoa, 1946–1962." *Journal of Farm Economics* 47 (May 1965): 348–401.

3. Birnberg, Thomas, and Resnick, Stephen. "A Model of the Trade and Government Sectors in Colonial Economies." *American Economic Review* 63 (September 1973): 572–87.

4. Bower, Penelope. "The Mining Industry." In *The Economics of a Tropical Dependency*, vol. 2, edited by Margery Perham. London: Faber and Faber, 1948.

5. Chow, Gregory C. "Tests of Equality Between Sets of Coefficients in Two Linear Regressions." *Econometrica* 28 (July 1960): 591–605.

6. Crouchley, A. E. "The Visible Balance of Trade Since 1884." *Egypt Contemporaine* 26 (1935): 491–512.

7. Dhrymes, Phoebus J. "Full Information Estimation of Dynamic Simultaneous Equations Models with Autoregressive Errors." Discussion Paper no. 203, Department of Economics, University of Pennsylvania, March 1971.

8. Fair, Ray C. "The Estimation of Simultaneous Equation Models with Lagged Endogenous Variables and First Order Serially Correlated Errors." *Econometrica* 37 (May 1970): 507–16.

9. Fisher, Franklin M. "Dynamic Structure and Estimation in Economy-Wide Econometric Models." In *The Brookings Quarterly Econometric Model of the United States*, edited by James S. Duesenberry, et al., ch. 15. Chicago: Rand McNally, 1965.

10. ———. "On the Cost of Approximate Specification in Simultaneous Equation Estimation." *Econometrica* 29 (April 1961): 139–70.

11. ———. "Tests of Equality between Sets of Coefficients in Two Linear Regressions: An Expository Note." *Econometrica* 38 (March 1970): 361–66.

12. Fisher, Walter D. "Simplification of Economic Models." *Econometrica* 34 (July 1966): 563–84.

13. Flint, John E. "Nigeria: The Colonial Experience from 1880 to

1914." In *Colonialism in Africa, 1870–1960,* vol. 1, edited by Lewis H. Gann and Peter Duignan. Cambridge: Cambridge University Press, 1969, pp. 220–60.

14. Griliches, Zvi. "Distributed Lags: A Survey." *Econometrica* 35 (January 1967): 16–49.

15. Hymer, Stephen. "The Multinational Corporation and the Law of Uneven Development." In *Economics and World Order,* edited by Jagdish N. Bhagwati. New York: World Law Force, 1970.

16. Hymer, Stephen, and Resnick, Stephen. "International Trade and Uneven Development." In *Trade, Balance of Payments and Growth,* edited by Jagdish N. Bhagwati, et al. Amsterdam: North Holland, 1970.

17. ———. "A Model of an Agrarian Economy with Nonagricultural Activities." *American Economic Review* 59 (September 1969): 493–506.

18. ———. "Interaction Between the Government and the Private Sector: An Analysis of Government Expenditure Policy and the Reflection Ratio." In *Economic Development and Structural Change,* edited by Ian G. Stewart. Edinburgh: Edinburgh University Press, 1969.

19. Ingram, James. "Thailand's Rice Trade and Allocation of Resources." In *The Economic Development of Southeast Asia,* edited by C. D. Cowan. New York: Praeger, 1964.

20. Kibuka, Robin. "British Expansion in West Africa (1870–1914): Some of its Effects and Consequences." Unpublished, 1973.

21. Lamb, Helen B. "The 'State' and Economic Development in India." In *Economic Growth: Brazil, India, and Japan,* edited by Simon Kuznets, Wilbert E. Moore, and Joseph J. Spengler. Durham, N.C.: Duke University Press, 1955.

22. Leubuscher, Charlotte. "The Policy Governing External Trade." In *The Economics of a Tropical Dependency,* vol. 2, edited by Margery Perham, pp. 137–75. London: Faber and Faber, 1948.

23. Mars, J. "Extra-Territorial Enterprises." In *The Economics of a Tropical Dependency,* vol. 2, edited by Margery Perham, pp. 43–136. London: Faber and Faber, 1948.

24. Mitchell, Bridger M., and Fisher, Franklin M. "The Choice of Instrumental Variables in the Estimation of Economy-Wide Econometric Models: Some Further Thoughts." *International Economic Review* 11 (June 1970): 226–33.

25. Pim, Sir Alan. "Public Finance." In *The Economics of a Tropical Dependency,* vol. 2, edited by Margery Perham, pp. 225–326. London: Faber and Faber, 1946.

26. Rajaratnam, S. "The Ceylon Tea Industry, 1886–1931." *Ceylon Journal of Historical and Social Studies* 4 (July–December 1961): 169–202.

27. ———. "The Growth of Plantation Agriculture in Ceylon, 1886–1931." *Ceylon Journal of Historical and Social Studies* 4 (January–June): 1–20.

28. Resnick, Stephen A. "The Decline of Rural Industry Under Export Expansion: A Comparison Among Burma, Philippines, and Thailand,

1870–1938." *Journal of Economic History* 30 (March 1970): 51–73.

29. Rippy, J. Fred. "Trinidad and Ceylon: Two Profitable British Crown Colonies." In *Underdeveloped Areas,* edited by Lyle W. Shannon, pp. 247–52. New York: Harper and Brothers, 1957.

30. Rowe, John W. F. "Studies in the Artificial Control of Raw Materials Supplies: No. 2, Rubber." In *Special Memorandum of the London and Cambridge Economic Service,* no. 34 (March 1931).

31. Sargan, J. D. "The Maximum Likelihood Estimation of Economic Relationships with Autoregressive Errors." *Econometrica* 29 (July 1961): 414–26.

32. Scott, Richenda. "Production for Trade." In *The Economics of a Tropical Dependency,* vol. 1, edited by Margery Perham, pp. 217–91. London: Faber and Faber, 1946.

33. Thomas, P. J. "India in the World Depression." *Economic Journal* 45 (1935): 469–83.

34. Vanden Driesen, I. H. "Some Trends in the Economic History of Ceylon in the 'Modern' Period." *Ceylon Journal of Historical and Social Studies* 3 (January–June 1969): 1–17.

BOOKS

35. Anstey, Vera. *The Economic Development of India.* New York: Longmans, Green and Co., 1952.

36. Barclay, George W. *Colonial Development and Population in Taiwan.* Princeton: Princeton University Press, 1954.

37. Bauer, Peter T. *The Rubber Industry.* Cambridge: Harvard University Press, 1948.

38. Bhattacharyya, Dhires. *A Concise History of the Indian Economy.* Calcutta: Progressive Publishers, 1972.

39. Bruce, Sir Charles. *The Broad Stone of Empire.* London: Macmillan & Co., 1910.

40. Chang, Kowie, ed. *Economic Development in Taiwan.* Taipei: Cheng Chung Book Company, 1968.

41. Commission on Cuban Affairs (abbreviated CCA). *Problems of the New Cuba.* New York: Foreign Policy Association, 1935.

42. Corpuz, Onofre D. *The Philippines.* Englewood Cliffs, N.J.: Prentice-Hall, 1965.

43. ———. *The Bureaucracy in the Philippines.* Manila: University of the Philippines, 1957.

44. Crouchley, Arthur E. *The Economic Development of Modern Egypt.* London: Longmans, Green and Co., 1938.

45. Cuban Economic Research Project (abbreviated CERP). *A Study on Cuba.* Coral Gables: University of Miami Press, 1965.

46. Davidson, James W. *The Island of Formosa. Historical View from 1430 to 1900.* New York: Paragon, 1903.

47. Deane, Phyllis, and Cole, W. A. *British Economic Growth, 1688–1959.* Cambridge: Cambridge University Press, 1967.

48. Dike, Kenneth O. *Trade and Politics in the Niger Delta*. Oxford: Oxford University Press, 1956.

49. Eisner, Gisela. *Jamaica 1830–1930: A Study in Economic Growth*. Manchester: Manchester University Press, 1961.

50. Ellsworth, Paul T. *Chile: An Economy in Transition*. New York: Macmillan Co., 1945.

51. Feis, Herbert. *Europe, The World's Banker, 1870–1914*. New Haven: Yale University Press, 1931.

52. Fisher, Walter D. *Clustering and Aggregation in Economics*. Baltimore: The Johns Hopkins University Press, 1969.

53. Frank, Andre Gunder. *Capitalism and Underdevelopment in Latin America: Historical Studies of Chile and Brazil*. New York: Monthly Review Press, 1967.

54. Frankel, Sally Herbert. *Capital Investment in Africa*. London: Oxford University Press, 1938.

55. Fromm, Gary, and Taubman, Paul. *Policy Simulations with an Econometric Model*. Washington, D.C.: Brookings Institution, 1968.

56. Galdames, Luis. *A History of Chile*. Translated by Isaac Joslin Cox. Chapel Hill: The University of North Carolina Press, 1941.

57. Geary, Sir William Nevill M., bart. *Nigeria Under British Rule*. London: Methuen and Company, 1927.

58. Goldberger, Arthur S. *Econometric Theory*. New York: John Wiley & Sons, 1964.

59. ———. *Impact Multipliers and Dynamic Properties of the Klein-Goldberger Model*. Amsterdam: North Holland, 1959.

60. Hancock, William K. *Problems of Economic Policy, 1918–1939*. Vol. 2 of *Survey of British Commonwealth Affairs*. London: Oxford University Press, 1964.

61. Helleiner, Gerald K. *Peasant Agriculture, Government, and Economic Growth in Nigeria*. Homewood, Ill.: Richard D. Irwin, 1966.

62. Ho, Samuel. "Statistical Appendix to Taiwan." Unpublished.

63. ———. Unpublished study on Taiwan.

64. Ingram, James S. *Economic Change in Thailand, 1850–1970*. Stanford, Ca.: Stanford University Press, 1971.

65. Issawi, Charles. *Egypt: An Economic and Social Analysis*. London: Oxford University Press, 1947.

66. Issawi, Charles. *Egypt in Mid Century*. Oxford: Oxford University Press, 1954.

67. ———. *Egypt in Revolution: An Economic Analysis*. London: Oxford University Press, 1963.

68. Jenks, Leland Hamilton. *Our Cuban Colony: A Study in Sugar*. New York: Vanguard, 1928.

69. Johnston, J. *Econometric Methods*. 2d ed. New York: McGraw-Hill, 1972.

70. Kmenta, Jan. *Elements of Econometrics*. New York: Macmillan Co., 1971.

71. Lee, Teng-hui. *Intersectoral Capital Flows in the Economic Development of Taiwan, 1895–1960*. Ithaca: Cornell University Press, 1971.

72. Levin, Jonathan V. *The Export Economies.* Cambridge: Harvard University Press, 1960.

73. Lewis, W. Arthur. *Aspects of Tropical Trade, 1883–1965.* Stockholm: Almqvist and Wiksells, 1969.

74. Lipsey, Robert E. *Price and Quantity Trends in the Foreign Trade of the United States.* Princeton: Princeton University Press, 1963.

75. Luxemburg, Rosa. *The Accumulation of Capital.* New York: Monthly Review Press, 1968.

76. Marlowe, John. *A History of Modern Egypt and Anglo-Egyptian Relations.* Hamden, Conn.: Archon Books, 1965.

77. Mead, Donald C. *Growth and Structural Change in the Egyptian Economy.* Homewood, Ill.: Richard D. Irwin, 1967.

78. Mitchell, Brian R. *Abstract of British Historical Statistics.* Cambridge: Cambridge University Press, 1962.

79. ———, and Jones, H. G. *Second Abstract of British Historical Statistics.* Cambridge: Cambridge University Press, 1971.

80. Myint, Hla. *The Economics of the Developing Countries.* New York: Praeger, 1965.

81. Ohkawa, Kazushi, ed. *Estimates of Long-Term Economic Statistics of Japan since 1868.* Toyo Keizai Shinposha: 1967.

82. Pike, Fredrick B. *Chile and the United States, 1880–1962.* Notre Dame, Ind.: University of Notre Dame Press, 1963.

83. Pina, Rogelio, and de Abad, L. V. *Los Presupuestos del Estado.* Havana: Cultural, 1936.

84. Pinto Santa Cruz, Anibal. *Chile: Un Caso de Desarrollo Frustrado.* Santiago: Editorial Universitaria, 1962.

85. Power, John H., and Sicat, Gerardo P. *The Philippines: Industrialization and Trade Policies.* London: Oxford University Press, 1971.

86. Ray, Parimal. *India's Foreign Trade Since 1870.* London: George Routledge and Sons, 1934.

87. Resnick, Stephen. Unpublished study on the Philippines.

88. ———. "Statistical Appendix to the Philippines." Unpublished.

89. Reynolds, Clark Winton. "Development Problems of an Export Economy: The Case of Chile and Copper." In Markos Mamalakis and Clark Winton Reynolds, *Essays on the Chilean Economy.* Homewood, Ill.: Richard D. Irwin, 1965.

90. Rowe, John W. F. *Markets and Men.* London: Cambridge University Press, 1936.

91. Salamanca, Bonifacio S. *The Filipino Reaction to American Rule, 1901–1913.* Hamden, Ct.: The Shoe String Press, 1968.

92. Sicat, Gerardo P., et al. *Economics and Development, an Introduction.* Quezon City, Philippines: University of the Philippines Press, 1965.

93. Singh, V. B., ed. *Economic History of India, 1857–1956.* Bombay: Allied Publishers, 1965.

94. Snodgrass, Donald R. *Ceylon: An Export Economy in Transition.* Homewood, Ill.: Richard D. Irwin, 1966.

95. Spear, Percival. *India: A Modern History.* 2d ed. Ann Arbor: University of Michigan Press, 1971.

96. Stocking, George W., and Watkins, Myron W. *Cartels in Action: Case Studies in International Business Diplomacy.* New York: The Twentieth Century Fund, 1946.

97. Theil, Henri. *Economic Forecasts and Policies.* Amsterdam: North Holland, 1958.

98. ———. *Principles of Econometrics.* New York: John Wiley & Sons, 1971.

99. Thomas, Hugh. *Cuba; or, The Pursuit of Freedom.* London: Eyre and Spottiswoode, 1971.

100. Wickizer, V. D. *Coffee, Tea and Cocoa: An Economic and Political Analysis.* Stanford, Ca.: Stanford University Press, 1951.

101. Wright, Philip G. *The Cuban Situation and our Treaty Relations.* Washington, D.C.: Brookings Institution, 1931.

102. Zaide, Gregario F. *Philippine Political and Cultural History.* Manila: Philippine Education Company, 1957.

OFFICIAL DOCUMENTS

103. Chile, Oficina Central de Estadistica. *Anuario Estadistico.* Santiago, 1900–38.

104. Chile, Oficina Central de Estadistica. *Sinopsis Estadistica de la Republica de Chile.* Santiago, 1893–1939.

105. Cuba, Secretaria de Hacienda, Seccion de Estadistica. *Commercio Exterior.* Havana, 1903–38.

106. Cuba, Secretaria de Hacienda, Seccion de Estadistica. *Anuario Estadistica de la Republica de Cuba, 1.* Havana, 1915.

107. Great Britain, Board of Trade. *Statistical Abstract for the British Empire,* for the years 1913–29, . . . , 1929–38. Vols. 60–68. London: His Majesty's Stationery Office, 1931–39.

———. *Statistical Abstract for the Several Colonial and Other Possessions of the United Kingdom,* for the years 1850–63, . . . , 1888–1902. Vols. 1–40. London: His Majesty's Stationery Office, 1865–1903.

———. *Statistical Abstract for the Several British Self-Governing Dominions, Colonies, Possessions and Protectorates,* for the years 1889–1903, . . . , 1901–15. Vols. 41–53. London: His Majesty's Stationery Office, 1904–18.

———. *Statistical Abstract for the Several British Overseas Dominions and Protectorates,* for the years 1903–17, . . . , 1913–27. Vols. 54–59. London: His Majesty's Stationery Office, 1920–30.

———. *Statistical Abstract for the British Commonwealth,* for the years 1931–39 and 1945–47. Vol. 70. London: His Majesty's Stationery Office, 1930.

108. ———. *Statistical Abstract for the Principal and Other Foreign Countries,* vols. 15–39. London, 1889–1914.

109. League of Nations. *International Trade Statistics.* Geneva, 1932–39.

110. ———. *Memorandum on Balance of Payments and Foreign Trade Balances.* Geneva, 1924–27.

111. ———. *Memorandum on International Trade and Balance of Payments.* Geneva, 1928–31.

112. ———. *Memorandum on Public Finance, 1922–1926*. Geneva, 1927.

113. ———. *Public Finance, 1928–1935*. Geneva, 1936.

114. Siam, Ministry of Finance, Department of General Statistics. *Statistical Yearbook of the Kingdom of Siam*, vols. 1–21. Bangkok, 1914–44.

115. *The Statesman's Year-book*. London, 1902–38.

116. Taiwan, Provincial Government, Bureau of Accounting and Statistics. *Taiwan Trade Statistics for the Last Fifty-three Years, 1896–1948*. Taipei, 1949.

117. United Nations Secretariat, Department of Economic Affairs. *Instability in Export Markets of Under-Developed Countries*. New York: 1952.

118. United States, Bureau of the Census. *Historical Statistics of the U.S.: Colonial Times to 1957*. Washington, D.C.: Government Printing Office, 1960.

119. United States Tariff Commission (abbreviated USTC). *Chemical Nitrogen*. Report no. 114, Second Series. Washington, D.C.: Government Printing Office, 1937.

120. ———. *Colonial Tariff Policies*. Washington, D.C.: Government Printing Office, 1922.

121. ———. *Reciprocity and Commercial Treaties*. Washington, D.C.: Government Printing Office, 1919.

Index

Abaca (Philippines), 12, 87, 220
Accounting dummy variables, 94–95. *See also* NET; RAIL; WORKS
Accumulated real government expenditures. *See also* Government expenditures; Government reflection ratio; Real government expenditures
  bloc multipliers, 162–63
  calculation of, 51–52
  data: Ceylon, 262; Chile, 268; Cuba, 274; Egypt, 280; India, 286; Jamaica, 294; Nigeria, 301; Philippines, 307; Taiwan, 311; Thailand, 316
  development implications, 40–41, 89, 169–71, 250–54
  domestic price effect on, 197, 203, 211
  dynamic multipliers, 153–71
  dynamic simulation, 133, 146–47
  effect on both trade and government sectors, 251. *See also* Circular process; Government expenditures, infrastructure
  endogenously determined, 253–54
  equation, 51
  export price multipliers, 155, 162, 163–65
  export supply equation: covariance analysis, 103–05; estimated coefficients, 84–85, 88–89; variable in, 37, 40–42
  government expenditure multipliers, 160, 162, 166, 168
  government reflection ratio effect, 166–68
  government revenue multipliers, 159, 166
  Great Depression effects, 232
  impact upon itself, 166–68
  import price effect on, 184, 185, 188
  initial stock calculation, 51–52

  multipliers, own, 161, 165–67
  nominal export multipliers, 156, 165
  nominal import multipliers, 157, 165
  not depreciated, 51–52
  not time proxy, 41–42, 51–52, 251
  price elasticity effect, 165
  productivity effect, 165
  real export multipliers, 154, 163–65
  real government expenditure multipliers, 161
  real import multipliers, 157, 163, 165
  real income effect on, 197, 198, 201
  short-run multipliers, 123–32
  tax effort effects, 246, 248
  terms of trade multipliers, 155
  trade balance multipliers, 158
  U.S. trade restriction effects, 237, 238–39
  World War I effects, 219, 223, 224
Aggregation loss, 107
American controls. *See* U.S. controls
Application of model
  to development since World War II, 2, 252–53, 255–57
  to history, 2, 5–6
  to other countries, 5–6
Autoregressive process
  influence on multipliers, 131, 133, 148–49, 150
  model specification, 98–100
  parameters, 83
  simultaneous equation model, 82–83

Balance of trade. *See* Trade balance
Bananas (Jamaica), 19, 221, 238
Behavioral equations. *See* Econometric model; Estimated coefficients; Export demand, equation; Export supply, equation; Government revenues, equation; Government expenditures,

331

productivity bloc classification, 162, 163, 168

real income multiplier classification, 199, 200, 201

revenue derived from trade sector, 63–64

short run multipliers, 128

sugar. *See* Sugar, Philippines

trade dependence, 62–64

U.S. control, 12, 31–32, 62–64, 255

U.S. trade restriction effects, 234–39

Platt Amendment *(1902)*, 12, 28–31, 59

Political control. *See also* Colonial controls

overall economic development impact, 251, 252, 254–55

Pooled regression, 117–18

Preventive policy, Cuba, 28–29

Price elasticity. *See* Elasticity

Price expectations, 42–43, 42n21

Price index components: Ceylon, 263; Chile, 269; Cuba, 275–76; Egypt, 281; India, 287–89; Jamaica, 295–96; Nigeria, 302; Philippines, 308; Taiwan, 213; Thailand, 317

Price variables

data: Ceylon, 261, 264–65; Chile, 267, 270–71; Cuba, 273, 277; Egypt, 279, 282–83; Japan, 327; India, 285, 290–91; Jamaica, 293, 297–98; Nigeria, 300, 303–04; Philippines, 306, 308; Taiwan, 310, 313; Thailand, 314, 318–19; United Kingdom, 320; United States, 321

Prices. *See* Domestic prices, developed country; Export price; Import price

Private investment

Chile, 26–28, 61

Cuba, 28–31, 59, 85

related to government expenditures, 41

Taiwan, 34, 65

United Kingdom, 15–16, 26–27

United States, 26–28, 28–31, 85

Process of export development. *See* Colonial development process

Productivity blocs. *See also* Low productivity bloc; High productivity bloc

comparisons, 89

definition, 111

differences between, 112–13

effect on multipliers, 165

Progressive merger procedure, 107, 119–20. *See also* Cluster analysis

QUOTA (Dummy variable for Cuba and the Philippines), 57, 84, 86, 90, 234

RAIL (Dummy variable for Jamaica), 57, 94, 95

Real exports. *See also* Export demand; Export supply

accumulated real government expenditures effect on, 154, 165, 169

data: Ceylon, 260; Chile, 266; Cuba, 272; Egypt, 278; India, 284; Jamaica, 292; Nigeria, 299; Philippines, 305; Taiwan, 309; Thailand, 314

domestic price effect on, 203, 204

dynamic simulation, 133, 145

government revenues equation: estimated coefficients, 93–94; variable in, 48–49

Great Depression effects, 226–28, 232

import price effect on, 174, 185, 186, 187, 188

lagged: demand equation, 43, 83, 86–87, 88–90, 110–11; short-run multipliers, 123–32; supply equation, 37, 42–43, 83–85, 88, 89, 110–11

real import equation: covariance analysis, 104–05; estimated coefficients, 91–92; variable in, 47–48

real income effect on, 188, 190, 198, 199, 201

rubber regulation scheme effects, Ceylon, 239–41

short-run multipliers, 123–31

simulation of, 133–43, 145

tax effort effects, 246–47

U.S. trade restrictions effects, 235–36, 238–39

World War I effects, 215–16, 220–23, 224–26

Real government expenditures. *See also* Accumulated real government expenditures

accumulated real government expenditures effect on, 160

data: Ceylon, 262; Chile, 268; Cuba, 274; Egypt, 280; India, 286; Jamaica, 294; Nigeria, 301; Philippines, 307; Taiwan, 311; Thailand, 316

domestic price effect on, 210

equation for, 50–51

import price effect on, 183, 185, 187, 188

real income effect on, 196

short-run multipliers, 124–30

Economic Growth Center Book Publications

Werner Baer, *Industrialization and Economic Development in Brazil* (1965).

Werner Baer and Isaac Kerstenetzky, eds., *Inflation and Growth in Latin America* (1964).

Bela A. Balassa, *Trade Prospects for Developing Countries* (1964). Out of print.

Thomas B. Birnberg and Stephen A. Resnick, *Colonial Development: An Econometric Study* (1975).

Benjamin I. Cohen, *Multinational Firms and Asian Exports* (1975).

Carlos F. Díaz Alejandro, *Essays on the Economic History of the Argentine Republic* (1970).

Robert Evenson and Yoav Kislev, *Agricultural Research and Productivity* (1975).

John C. H. Fei and Gustav Ranis, *Development of Labor Surplus Economy: Theory and Policy* (1964).

Gerald K. Helleiner, *Peasant Agriculture, Government, and Economic Growth in Nigeria* (1966).

Lawrence R. Klein and Kazushi Ohkawa, eds., *Economic Growth: The Japanese Experience since the Meiji Era* (1968).

A. Lamfalussy, *The United Kingdom and the Six* (1963). Out of print.

Markos J. Mamalakis and Clark W. Reynolds, *Essays on the Chilean Economy* (1965).

Donald C. Mead, *Growth and Structural Change in the Egyptian Economy* (1967).

Richard Moorsteen and Raymond P. Powell, *The Soviet Capital Stock* (1966).

Douglas S. Paauw and John C. H. Fei, *The Transition in Open Dualistic Economies: Theory and Southeast Asian Experience* (1973).

Howard Pack, *Structural Change and Economic Policy in Israel* (1971).

Frederick L. Pryor, *Public Expenditures in Communist and Capitalist Nations* (1968).

Gustav Ranis, ed., *Government and Economic Development* (1971).

Clark W. Reynolds, *The Mexican Economy: Twentieth-Century Structure and Growth* (1970).

Lloyd G. Reynolds and Peter Gregory, *Wages, Productivity, and Industrialization in Puerto Rico* (1965).

Donald R. Snodgrass, *Ceylon: An Export Economy in Transition* (1966).